Worthy is the Lamb!

A WALK THROUGH REVELATION

*There's one storyline in this ultimate
action thriller ... Jesus!*

Sam Gordon

AMBASSADOR

Belfast Northern Ireland Greenville South Carolina

Worthy is the Lamb!
© 2000 Trans World Radio

ISBN 1 84030 087 6

Ambassador Publications
a division of
Ambassador Productions Ltd.
Providence House
Ardenlee Street
Belfast
BT6 8QJ
Northern Ireland
www.ambassador-productions.com

Emerald House
427 Wade Hampton Blvd.
Greenville
SC 29609, USA
www.emeraldhouse.com

Trans World Radio
11 St James Gardens
Swansea
SA1 6DY
United Kingdom

01792 483050

Trans World Radio
P O Box 8700
Cary
NC 27512, USA

1 800 456 7TWR

www.twr.org

DEDICATION

to
David

*your godly life and servant leadership are
a constant challenge and inspiration to me*

thank you ... and ... keep on dreamin'

Truth for Today

~ Mission Statement ~

*'To teach the entire Bible in a warm expository
style so that people's lives are influenced to such
a degree that they impact their world for Christ.'*

First Word

This year, Queen Elizabeth, the Queen Mother, celebrated her one hundredth birthday. She is greatly loved by the people because of her graciousness and serenity. Many queued for hours on her birthday just to catch a glimpse of her kindly smile and gentle wave of the hand. The people of Britain well remember her visits to devastated areas in the midst of the bombing of London sixty years ago.

The penman of Revelation, the Apostle John, is a model for all of us. He is a very old man who is captivated by his past experiences of Jesus of Nazareth, his Lord and Master. While suffering the rigours of hardship and persecution, he was given an awesome revelation of Jesus Christ ... he is the one who wrote the words that have been translated from the original language for us to read today!

Sam Gordon is a Bible teacher and colleague in Trans World Radio. He crafts words to paint pictures which are based on an accurate portrayal of the text of Scripture. It would be relatively easy to quickly divert from the central theme of the book of Revelation; Sam, however, stays with the glorious subject – the revelation of Jesus Christ. All else is secondary and peripheral. Jesus is supreme and he alone is worthy to receive an accolade of praise.

This book will greatly assist you in your own life ... it will enable you to keep Jesus as your focus of worship and witness. The years of our lives are not within our control. I am content, however, when I realise that everything comes under the sovereignty of the 'ruler of the kings of the earth!' He who has the power must receive all the glory. Hallelujah!

As Sam guides you through the complexities of the book of Revelation, may the Lord inspire your heart to adoration and worship and may that trigger a compelling desire that leads to a life of dedicated service which is empowered by a continual vision of Jesus!

David Tucker

Executive Vice President and Chief Operating Officer
Trans World Radio International

September 2000

Second Thoughts

One Sunday morning, some years ago, a preacher was travelling by train to a ministry engagement. With him in the compartment were a number of men. All were deeply engrossed in the national tabloid, the *News of the World*. The old preacher brought his Bible out and started to read. Not many minutes passed before he realised he was the focus of interest and attention. Conscious that all eyes were looking at him, he quietly set the word of God to the side and chatted to his fellow commuters. He said to them: 'Gentlemen, I see that you are keenly interested in the content of your newspapers and, no doubt, you find them highly informative. I have something that is a million times better. You have the 'news of the world' but I have 'news of the world to come!'

That is what the book of Revelation is all about. It shows us God's programme for the ages, it projects us into the future and gives us some breathtaking insights into the eternal purpose of God. It is a fast moving, upbeat account of God's agenda for today's world, it pulls no punches when it shows us God's unmistakable intention regarding modern man and his hot pursuit of all things earthly. It reminds us of the utter folly of doing a tango in the dark with the devil as it thinks the unthinkable in relation to life without a personal knowledge of God.   It draws back the curtain and gives us a fascinating glimpse into heaven itself; in actual fact, dear old John had a wonderful taster and he was forever spoiled for life on planet earth! Yes, when you read the book through at a single sitting, there is so much to excite us, there is so much for us to anticipate, there is so much to look forward to, it is the kind of book which leaves you sitting on the edge of your seat!

I can let you into a secret ... you may not understand all that you read in the Apocalypse, do not worry, join the club! Read on ... it will do your heart good, it will encourage you in the Lord, it will stimulate your faith, it will motivate you to engage in acts of service - and, the good news is, you are guaranteed a blessing if you read the book through from cover to cover, that is the best kept secret of Revelation 1:3. It is more than a secret, it is a firm promise!

Sam Gordon

Contents

1	Jesus ... the man with a personal touch	13
2	The good, the very good, and the not so good	61
3	Four down, three to go	85
4	Touching the throne	107
5	Worthy is the Lamb!	127
6	Four horsemen on the horizon	145
7	A divine interlude	169
8	When heaven holds its breath	187
9	A tale of two armies	203
10	When God explains the reason why	221
11	The best of times, the worst of times	231
12	War in heaven!	257
13	The devil's deadly duo	279
14	Something special	299
15	A sign ~ a song ~ a scene	313
16	Armageddon ... the coming world conflict	323
17	The last world empire	339
18	The two Babylon's	361
19	The King is coming	379
20	The great judgment morning	405
21	All things new!	419
22	No loose ends in God's plan	439

1

Jesus ... the man with a personal touch

A dream or a nightmare?

It's a dream! It's a nightmare! Those are just two comments I heard recently from people who have been studying the book of Revelation. You see, it all depends on where you are coming from. It also depends on where you are going to. It is hardly a book of fantasies; it is certainly not the kind of thing you want to read late at night before hopping into bed! What we have here is a book that scratches where modern man is itching. It answers the questions men are asking: *Why are we here? What on earth is happening in today's world? Where is this out-of-control world heading?* All these, and many more!

You see, things are not as they seem and things are not the way they should be! The bottom line is, God rules and reigns on high. That truth remains untarnished in a world badly bruised by one crippling crisis after another; it holds as true today in the third millennium as it did in the closing years of the first century. That is why the book of Revelation is right up to date; it has never been more relevant than it is today.

But, it is one thing reading it ... how are we to make sense of it? When you leaf through its chapters you quickly discover it is all about terrible multi-headed beasts and cosmic upheaval; there are spectral battles and sky-splitting displays of supernatural power. At times, the scene is awesome and glorious; other times, it is baffling and frightening. It is almost paradoxical!

Winston Churchill once described the former Soviet Union as 'a riddle wrapped in a mystery inside an enigma.' The plain fact is, many well-meaning evangelical Christians view the book of Revelation in much the same way. Richard Bewes makes a valid comment when he writes, 'Ordinary Christians have left it unread; turned off by the bizarre flights of fancy, by the mathematical labyrinths in which some of its readers appear to have become enmeshed.' To me, that is a pity, for they are the ones who are really missing out, in so many ways.

The big question is, how can we best understand what John is saying to us?

There is no doubt about it, the picturesque images, the mysterious symbols, the apocalyptic language, combine to make Revelation one of the most challenging books in the entire Bible to interpret. In one sense, that is probably an understatement, nevertheless it is true. It seems to me, there are four main interpretative approaches to unlocking the mysteries of the book.

Idealists

The idealist approach tends to view the images in a strictly non-literal manner. They see them as a collection of spiritualised symbols that represent timeless truths. From their perspective, the book of Revelation is a profound illustration of the ultimate victory of good over evil, it is a message of triumph in the face of adversity. Apart from anything else, the downside here is that this view relegates Revelation to a place where it is neither a historical record nor a predictive prophecy.

Preterists

The preterist approach is inclined to limit the meaning of the book to its original readers. They say the images represent only first century subjects such as Caesar, Rome and the persecution. They believe that all the events detailed by the apostle John have already taken place and the prophecy is given to encourage the harassed church of that time. Such a view conveniently ignores the book's own claims to be a prophecy (1:3; 22:7). I believe the proponents of this view have buried their head in the sand when it comes to the ripening of God's eternal purpose.

Historicists

The historicist approach sees the book as a timeline from the first century up to this present time. They see it as a history written in advance! For example, the heptad of evangelical churches in chapters 2 and 3 depict seven distinct periods of church history. They often resort to allegorising the text in order to find in it the various events they believe it depicts - that tends to be those events of history familiar to them, usually the history of western Europe; that subjective approach, as you will appreciate, tends to open a Pandora's box of all things wild and weird and wonderful in relation to fanciful interpretation.

Futurists

The futurist approach tends to view the book, and especially chapters 4 to 22, as an open window on the end of time. They say the various images represent the people allied to significant events that will play a key role in the final drama of global history. This approach, in contrast to the other three, does full justice to Revelation's inherent claim to be a prophecy.

That is a quick résumé of the four mainline views regarding the interpretation of the book of Revelation. I imagine, you are probably wondering which approach I am going to adopt and follow! It seems to me, when you compare the book of Revelation with the book of Daniel and other prophetic volumes, the best line of interpretation to take on board is that of the futurist. This view makes a lot of sense when it comes to understanding Bible prophecy, but it also maintains a consistent approach to biblical hermeneutics in relation to the rest of Scripture. I love the way John MacArthur sums it up: 'The futurist approach takes the book's meaning as God gave it.'

Having said that, I want to emphasise the hugely important fact that this manuscript was most relevant to the people living in John's day; it will have given them the impetus they needed to hang in there; it will have given them enormous encouragement to keep on going; it will certainly have provided them with an incentive when they realised that, at the end of the day, the Lord comes out on top!

You see, the living Lord is the central figure of the book. He is the one to whom all the symbols point. To miss seeing Christ in the book of Revelation is like squinting into the sky at twelve noon and not seeing the sun. The presence of Christ is everywhere. Realistically, you cannot miss him!

When you come to Revelation for the first or second time, you may think the whole message is quite intimidating and you could be forgiven for feeling scared but, the more you get into it, the more you realise it is the most worshipful book in the Bible! From start to finish, from beginning to end, it radiates and reflects the glorious splendour of Jesus, our wonderful Lord! This book is a beautiful chronicle of God's mystery, majesty and mercy, as he meticulously plans for the future of planet earth, and beyond!

Outlines are always helpful. They are like signposts on a journey. As far as I am aware, Revelation is the only book in the Bible that contains an inspired outline of its contents! That makes it quite unique! You can locate it in 1:19.

'What you have seen'	**chapter 1**
'What is now'	**chapters 2, 3**
'What will take place later'	**chapters 4-22**

John Phillips has an excellent outline of the book, which is as follows:

Chapter 1	**Visions of God**
Chapters 2, 3	**Visions of grace**
Chapters 4-20	**Visions of government**
Chapters 21, 22	**Visions of glory**

You can see what is happening. The focus of Revelation is on the person and majesty of Jesus Christ. The spotlight is on the Lord of all glory. He is the coming King of kings and centre stage is where he deserves to be.

Having said that, we can look at it from another angle. An old pastor friend of mine, who is now with the Lord, gave me an outline many years ago. It is one that I have never forgotten. He divided the book like this:

Chapters 1-3	**Jesus is the Lord in the midst of the churches**
Chapters 4, 5	**Jesus is the Lamb in the midst of the throne**
Chapters 6-18	**Jesus is the Lion in the midst of the nations**
Chapters 19, 20	**Jesus is the Lover in the midst of the wedding celebrations**
Chapters 21, 22	**Jesus is the Light in the midst of eternal glory**

On a recent visit to the Keswick Convention, I picked up a novel commentary by Anne Graham Lotz on Revelation. Her outline warmed my heart ... it is based on what a vision of the glory of God can do for us. It gives us:

Hope ... when we're depressed	**Chapter 1**
Hope ... when we're deluded	**Chapters 2, 3**
Hope ... when we're discouraged	**Chapters 4, 5**

Hope ... when we're distressed	**Chapters 6-19**
Hope ... when we're defeated	**Chapters 20-22:5**
Hope that ignites our hearts	**Chapter 22:6-21**

1:1-3

'The revelation of Jesus Christ'

Those five words in the opening phrase of verse 1 say all that has to be said for they tell us straightaway what is on the heart and mind of God! He puts all his cards on the table and he leaves us in no doubt as to the thinking behind this particular book. It is not an imaginative piece of spiritual fiction. It is a revelation of his Son, the Lord Jesus Christ! This book is both about him and by him.

An open book

The word *'revelation'* means, an unveiling, a disclosure, an uncovering. Things that would be normally hidden from us are made known in apocalyptic writing. Such writing takes you behind the scenes and reveals the unseen principles that affect history, and the future. It actually comes from the Greek word *apokalupsis* which appears eighteen times in the New Testament, always when used of a person, with the meaning 'to become visible' (Luke 2:32; Romans 8:19; 1 Corinthians 1:7; 1 Peter 1:7). You will probably recognise that one for we get our English word 'apocalypse' from it. That explains why this final chapter in God's story book of redemption is sometimes called, 'The Apocalypse.'

God is turning over the pages of his photograph album and showing us pictures of Christ. We have the Holy Spirit drawing back the curtain and giving us the rare privilege of seeing the glorified Christ in heaven. At the same time and almost in the same breath, he shows us the fulfilment of his sovereign purposes in the world. It is thrilling when we recognise that Revelation is like an open book. It is where God reveals his agenda to his church.

Remember Daniel, when he finished writing his monumental prophecy, he was told in 12:4 to 'close up and seal the words of the scroll.' John is told exactly the opposite! We read in 22:10, *'Do not seal up the words of the prophecy of this book, for the time is near.'*

The question is, why the gaping difference between the two? It is because Calvary has come ... the resurrection has happened ... the Holy Spirit has descended ... the church has been born ... a new age has been ushered in called the Last Days (Hebrews 1:1,2). In other words, when it comes to the maturing of the purposes of God, God is not on a go-slow, he is not dilly-dallying, he is not dragging his heels, he is fast fulfilling his word.

The key phrase is one you find in 22:10 and again in 1:3, *'the time is near.'* The implication is that his advent is soon, it is imminent, the Lord is at hand! Each day is one day nearer and, with every passing hour, we are rapidly approaching the climax of the ages; we are looking forward with bated breath to the magic moment when the King will come.

A unique book

Because of the way it was given

How did it all come about? The answer is found in verses 1 and 2 where we read, *'The revelation of Jesus Christ, which God gave him to show his servants what must soon take place. He made it known by sending his angel to his servant John, who testifies to everything he saw.'*

What apparently happened was this: God the Father gave the revelation to the Son as a reward for his faithfulness during his humiliation at Calvary - the book describes with a remarkable eye for detail his exaltation; then the Son shared it with the apostle John by means of a third party, an angel, whom he used as an intermediary, a kind of go-between; when the angel had given it to John, he then gave it to the church. (As an aside, it is worth noting that the words 'angel' or 'angels' are used seventy-one times in the book of Revelation, more than in any other book in the Bible. In fact, one out of every four uses in Scripture of those words is in the book of Revelation.)

Sometimes the Lord himself gave the vital information to John, as in the second half of chapter 1. At other times the message was conveyed to him by an elder, as in 7:13. There were occasions when it was communicated directly to him by an angel, as in 17:1 and again in 19:9,10. From time to time there was 'a voice from heaven' which told John what to say and what to do, as alluded to in 10:4. The lesson is simply this: whatever the channel of communication, it was all inspired by the Holy Spirit and, for what it is worth, John was often taken into another realm in the Spirit.

It seems to me, no matter what angle you view it from, this book has the stamp of God written all over it. His thumb print is on every page! The golden thread of eternity is woven right through it. You find that impression echoed and substantiated in verse 2 where we read that he *'testifies to everything he saw, that is, the word of God and the testimony of Jesus Christ.'*

Because of the worth of its message

Simple question: do you want to be blessed?

Simple answer: read the book of Revelation!

You may not fully understand it ... join the club! You may not be able to unravel all its mysteries; the symbols may seem seriously irrelevant in today's hi-tech consumer oriented environment. You may not be able to crack the code to adequately decipher what John is saying ... do not worry! Just keep on reading! You may be tempted to ask, 'why persevere when the odds are stacked against me?' ... well, the answer is immediate, it is right there in verse 3 where we read, *'Blessed is the one who reads the words of this prophecy, and blessed are those who hear it and take to heart what is written in it, because the time is near.'*

Did you see that ... if you read it, if you hear it read, you are guaranteed a blessing! Now, as far as I know, this is the only book in the entire Bible which promises a blessing like this. That makes it a little bit special, it is truly unique! It is a one-off! It is equally true to say, if someone comes along and tampers with the message, he is the loser for he will be cursed. You find that warning label in 22:18,19. The message is crystal clear: read it, hear it, take it to heart, obey it, then trust God for the blessing which is sure to follow! You know, I cannot think of a better way to get a blessing.

Why study the book?

Some people feel it is best to leave it alone; they feel more at home with the soothing poetry of the Psalms and the simple promises of the Beatitudes. They much prefer to leave a tome like this to the theological heavyweights or the professional pundits! Their attitude is to avoid it because it is too difficult to understand, it is too controversial to discuss, it is too meaningless to be personally relevant. To put it mildly, that is a rather negative approach!

We do not study it because we have a one-track-mind fascination with the future; it is definitely not because we are in the risky business of setting dates. As Warren Wiersbe says: 'We do it not because we are on the planning committee for the second advent, we do it because we are on the welcoming committee!' We study it because we passionately love the Lord and we are numbered among those who genuinely love his appearing. We approach a book like this with the adrenaline flowing through our veins, with our heart beating faster, and with our mind filled with the twin components of wonder and worship. We can do no better than come like John and fall down in humility before the feet of Jesus.

You see, a moment with majesty leaves us overwhelmed and gasping for breath! As the song says, 'We stand in awe of him.' We come because we want to get to know Jesus better. That has to be the supreme goal, the aspiration and the longing in each of our hearts.

Because the time is near

Why? What is the big deal? What is the panic? Because John tells us at the end of verse 3, *'the time is near.'* The six million dollar question is, how near is near? 2000 years have come and gone; a lot of water has gone under the bridge; we are certainly a lot closer now than we were then. When John put quill to parchment, he was a relatively old man, he was in the sunset years, he was in the eventide of life. He wrote the book about the year 95 AD. At that time he was living in exile on an island in the Greek Aegean Sea. Patmos is one of a cluster of small islands off the coast of modern-day Turkey. They were ceded to Greece after the second World War.

It goes without saying, a lot has happened in the intervening years and so the thought encapsulated here is one of extreme suddenness. It has the strategically important element of surprise in it. The phrase conveys the idea, not of immediacy, but of imminence. It is soon and it could happen at any minute! That is why, when we talk about the advent of Jesus, we need to be ready; we should be watching and waiting. We should be living with a rising sense of expectancy in our hearts, with a keen sense of anticipation, for it may be today when Jesus will break through the clouds! You see, the panoply of events which are prophesied in this book can happen at any time ... and let us never forget, they will happen without any advance warning.

It is not clutching at straws to say, we are standing on the threshold of a whole new era, we are teetering on the brink of something big happening in the world in which we live, we are hovering on the edge of God doing something spectacularly special in relation to Israel and the nations of the world. The more you stop and think about it, the more you realise, it is as close as that! I really believe it is! We have long since passed the eleventh hour; in fact, it has never been so late before.

And that is the paramount message John wants to get across to each of us at this precise moment in time: Jesus is coming again! And when he does, a lot of what we have in the book of Revelation will come to pass. Then, what is now 'his' story will rapidly become history! So this book is not only focusing attention on the coming King, it also informs us of the purpose of his kingdom.

Depending on where you live, you probably have national elections every four or five years; in the run-up to the polls the politicians tell us why we should elect them and what their programme will be if they win office. The truth of the matter is, the book of Revelation is the gripping account of Jesus' campaign to rule planet earth. We are clearly told, without any ambiguity, of his relationship to the church, his appointment by the Father to the throne, his crusade against the satanic forces of evil, and his final victory. Hey folks, there is no need to even count the votes for he knows the result already!

Because he made it known

Let us backtrack for a moment to verse 1 where we read the words, *'He made it known.'* This is a most interesting turn of phrase. Some Bible translations use the word 'signified' in this context and it literally means, 'to give a sign or signal.' I have already hinted that this is a book comprised of many signs and symbols. What we need to remember is this, at least half of them are explained in the book itself. Let me show you what I mean:

Lamps, for example, represent assemblies of God's people; stars represent angels; incense odours represent the prayers of saints (1:20; 8:3,4).

Where we need to exercise spiritual caution and resist the temptation to get carried away is when we try to define those symbols which are not explained. When that is the case, we need to look at other parts of the Bible in an attempt to unravel the mystery. You see, biblical symbols are consistent with the whole of biblical revelation. God does not say one thing in one place and then say something different somewhere else. It is a fundamental principle of hermeneutics that God is his own interpreter. When we deviate from that axiom, we run into all kinds of problems. We are at serious risk of coming up with all sorts of fanciful ideas. Oh, they may sound really good, they may look good on paper, they may be bright ideas, they may add a touch more gloss to what is there ... after all, what is 20% more hype to something which is quite sensational already!

Well, just because it tickles your fancy, does not necessarily mean to say it is right! If we opt to go down that road, sure, we will come up with a smattering of mouth-watering ideas; the downside is, we will end up missing the message because we cannot see the wood for the trees. It seems to me, we must anchor our interpretation to what God has already revealed.

Why did John use symbols?

Why did he not just write in plain language and tell it like it is? Good questions!

Because they are understood only by those who know Jesus Christ personally

It is a kind of spiritual code. Look at it like this: if any Roman officers had tried to use the book of Revelation as evidence against Christians, the book would have been a puzzle and an enigma to them. More about that in a minute. There is another reason, however, and it is even more important.

Symbols are not weakened by time

With the passing of time, words frequently change their meaning but symbols remain constant. John was able to draw on the great images in God's revelation and write them into an exciting and exhilarating drama. That just proves the point that symbols can stand the test of time without relating to one particular culture or era.

Symbols can impart values and arouse emotions

How much more graphic it is to speak of 'beasts' instead of chattering on about 'dictators!' There is a lot more colour in referring to 'Babylon the Great' than there is in talking about 'the world system.' I cannot help but think, if our emotions are not stirred by some of the words used as symbols, we have a huge problem on our hands and the chances are we need to have our red blood count taken!

Symbols can be used as a secret code

It is a well-known fact in the tight-lipped world of business and commerce that top-secret projects are given specific code names because these guys are afraid of industrial espionage; John had something similar up his sleeve, the prisoner of Patmos had a spiritual code which was circulated to the churches. Now, hold on! Relax, I am not getting carried away! There is nothing airy-fairy about what I am saying.

The political climate of the period in which John was living was not unlike that of the 1940s. A diabolically wicked leader, believing in his own powers, realised that these people who called themselves Christians had an allegiance to another God. He was not impressed! He certainly was not amused! But then, neither was Hitler when he brutally annihilated the Jews; he did it his way in the unthinkable horrors of the holocaust. The Emperor Domitian did it his way when he set out to abolish the influence of the followers of a man called Jesus. Some Christians were killed; others, like John, were imprisoned for their faith.

When you go back to the first century, it is obvious that the Christians were looking eagerly for the return of Jesus Christ but, sixty years after his death at Calvary, this hope was still unfulfilled. John desperately wanted to encourage those believers ... that is the principal reason why he wrote the book of Revelation. That is why he had to disguise his message in such a way that the Roman authorities would not understand it. The Christians could decipher this secret code but Domitian and his henchmen would be puzzled by it. It would be similar to POWs in our century tapping out codes on cell walls to encourage their fellow prisoners.

Back in the first century, in the early church, they knew what John was talking about. As someone has rightly said, 'We don't need to be Bible scholars to be able to decode the messages.' So there is a lot more to it than meets the eye. We are in for a great study! We are going to have a good time around the word of God ... oh yes, we will put the spotlight on the future, but I can tell you, the main beam will be shining on Jesus as he says to a crazy and confused world, *'Yes, I am coming soon!'*

I just wonder ... are you ready to meet him?

> **Thinking of the giver, the purpose and the blessing spoken of in these verses, what motivation for reading Revelation does this give?**

1:4-6

When we move into verse 4, John introduces himself and tells us the people to whom he is writing; when he has done that, he then offers to them and to us an unbelievable greeting. *'John, to the seven churches in the province of Asia.'* We have no problem identifying these seven churches as they are explicitly detailed for us in verse 11. They are then singled out for further special attention in chapters 2 and 3.

It is interesting to note that the apostle Paul sent a number of different letters to seven churches. He wrote to the believers in Rome, Corinth, Galatia, Ephesus, Philippi, Colossae and Thessalonica. And now we have John sending one book to seven different churches. There is no question about it, it was for them alright! But in the providence of God, it is also for us!

Here is God's last word to man, this is his final message to churches scattered all around the world. What a tremendous way to start a book!

A benediction at the beginning

He offers to everyone *'grace'* and *'peace'*. This is a dual blessing, a double-barrelled blessing. These are the twin towers of the gospel of Christ. We have grace and peace and what we need to underscore is the order in which they are mentioned. This is of mega importance. If we do not get it right here, we will end up putting the cart before the horse.

You can never know peace in your heart without experiencing, first of all, the grace of God. Peace is a wonderful spin-off from the grace of God. Grace is the fountain of which peace is the stream. You could not wish anything better for a person than to extend to him a measure of grace and peace.

Grace is something which comes to us that we do not deserve and which we cannot repay. Grace stoops to where we are and it lifts us to where we ought to be. Peace is something which happens within us; it is a freedom from inner distraction which enables us to enjoy an internal rest. Peace is a tranquillity of soul that frees you from fear. It takes the sharp edges off your anxiety and tension.

Grace and peace do not come from ourselves, no matter how positive our thoughts may be; they do not come from others either, no matter how assuring their counsel and advice may be. They come directly from the open heart and open hand of our loving heavenly Father. God is the dispenser of both and he does it in a lavish manner. How can I say that with such confidence?

> **Spend some time thinking over what it means that 'grace and peace' have come from God to 'you'.**

Meet a God for whom time is of no consequence

John goes on to tell us in verse 4 that the one who has given this priceless blessing to us is someone *'who is, and who was, and who is to come.'* These extraordinary characteristics cannot be ascribed to anyone else but God the Father; quite honestly, no-one else fits the bill. He is described here in anthropomorphic terms because that is the only way we can possibly hope to understand it - he views God through the lens of time dimensions (past, present and future), although he is timeless.

Here is a God who transcends all time;
Here is the Eternal God, one with whom there was no beginning and with whom there is no end;
Here is a God who has always existed, one who cuts across all the ages of time;
Here is a God who reads the past, a God who rides the present and a God who rules the future;
Here is a God who dwells in all tenses of time ... for he is 'I Am.'

And what does he do? He gathers the ages into one hand and he holds the world in his other hand and, even though he is responsible for running the show, he takes quality time out and he whispers a word into each of our hearts. He says, *'Grace and peace to you!'*

Seven in relation to the Spirit

It is interesting that the final phrase of verse 4 makes reference to *'the seven spirits before his throne.'* I think this is a veiled reference which is appropriate to the Holy Spirit. It can be easily translated to read, 'the sevenfold Spirit.' John is talking about one Holy Spirit with a sevenfold ministry and it probably refers back to what is recorded in Isaiah 11:2. There we are told, 'the Spirit of the Lord will rest on him, the spirit of wisdom and of understanding, the spirit of counsel and of power, the spirit of knowledge and of the fear of the Lord.'

The number seven obviously gives the game away for it speaks here of the perfection of his person and of the plenitude of his power. He is perfect and complete in himself because he is God! He is taking up a position before the throne of God. The question is, why? His is a unique role in relation to the Godhead in that he is the executor of the purposes of God. You see, up until now, the Holy Spirit has been the executor of God's purposes in grace; then he will become the executor of God's purposes in government. So the blessing we mentioned earlier comes from God the Father and God the Holy Spirit, but right here in verse 5, it also comes from God the Son, even our Lord Jesus Christ.

A threefold description of the Lord Jesus

The faithful witness

That enables us to see him as a *prophet* and it underlines something of his credibility.

The firstborn from the dead

That enables us to see him as a *priest* and it highlights something of his superiority.

The ruler of the kings of the earth

That enables us to see him as a *king* and it makes much of his sovereignty.

So there he is: we see Jesus Christ as Prophet, Priest, and King! Three splendid titles, three identifiable roles, three impeccable credentials, each of which can be narrowed down to find their focal point in one individual.

A trio of titles that reveal the Lord's relationship to the present age

Faithful witness: an indicator of how the age begins

That is the primary reason Jesus came into the world, a world that is dark and degenerate, a world fast spiralling out of control as it goes from bad to worse. He came to bear witness to the name of God, to the nature of sin, to the need for personal righteousness, and to the nearness of judgment. As a faithful witness, Jesus brought the exceedingly good tidings of a great salvation through faith in his finished work at Calvary.

Firstborn from the dead: an indicator of how the age continues

Here is one who has tasted death for every man. Here is one who has risen in triumph from the tomb! Here is one who has ascended into glory to implement God's programme for the ages.

'Firstborn' actually implies priority and sovereignty for it is suggestive of a title of honour. He is the leader of all who will ultimately rise from the dead, all those who will rise to everlasting life. In that sense, he is pre-eminent, he is the premier one.

Ruler of the kings of the earth: an indicator of how the age ends

You see, here is one who was born in a barn; one who died on a wooden cross; one who was buried in a borrowed tomb in a beautiful floral garden and, yes, he is the same one who is coming back to rule and to reign! He is coming in pomp and in power! Think of the regal nature of such a splendid occasion, it will be a royal visit; the sheer magnificence of the sight and the awesomeness of the moment blows the mind! It is something you will definitely not want to miss!

So what we have here is the Trinity in action. The book begins with a blessing from the triune God and together they offer to you and to me the rich blessing of grace and peace!

From benediction to doxology

It seems to me, when we receive the blessing of grace and peace, the least we can do is offer him a benediction in return. And that is what we have here in the last half of verse 5 and also in verse 6. There we read: *'To him who loves us and has freed us from our sins by his blood, and has made us to be a kingdom and priests to serve his God and Father, to him be glory and power for ever and ever. Amen!'* We have his plan of redemption in the first part and his purpose for the believer in the second part.

A God of love

This glowing doxology is directed initially *'to him who loves us.'*

Here is a God who has loved us from eternity past; here is a God who continues to love us with an unbreakable love; here is a God who will keep on loving us until we come to the end of the road; and even when we reach heaven itself, it will only be to experience the extravagance of his love in a fuller measure.

You see, his is a big expansive heart, a heart overflowing with love; you only have to look at the cross to see how great his love really is. His is a love which has no limits; it is a love that will not let us go; it is a love that keeps on loving, no matter what. The old song says,

> *O the love that sought me,*
> *O the blood that bought me,*
> *O the grace that brought me to the fold!*

A God of grace

This paean of praise also makes much of the wonderful grace of God in our lives, it reinforces the tremendous power of God to change lives for the better.

He has freed us, because sin is a chain that binds us; he has washed us (as one translation has it), because sin is a stain that blots us. But how has he done it? *By his blood!*

You see, as the song tells us, 'there was no other way a God of love could find, but Calvary.' In a different generation, Charles Wesley got it right when he penned the words:

He breaks the power of cancelled sin,
He sets the prisoner free;
His blood can make the foulest clean,
His blood avails for me.

That is not all! There is more! For the God who has loved us, and the God who has loosed us, is the same God who has lifted us!

A God who elevates

We are a kingdom, and that means, we have all the majesty of a prince; we are priests, and that means, we now have a ministry to others and on behalf of others. We have power with men and we have power with God, and when you put them both together, you understand what Peter meant when he called us 'a royal priesthood.'

What we have here is best summed up in the words of a great old hymn:

Wonderful grace of Jesus, greater than all my sin!
How shall my tongue describe it, where shall its praise begin,
Taking away my burden, setting my spirit free,
For the wonderful grace of Jesus, reaches me!

Grace for us ... Glory for him!

And it does, for that is the meaning of the closing few words in the benediction. It is *'to him be glory and power for ever and ever.'*

It is personal for it is directed exclusively to him. His is the glory that outshines the noonday sun; this is the glory he had with the Father before the world began.

It is positional for it is a glory which one day will be acknowledged by all mankind when he returns in splendour from the sky.

It is perpetual for it goes on for ever and ever. There is no stopping it. It just keeps on rolling. And rightly so! For he alone deserves it!

It is no wonder John says a hearty *'Amen'* at the end of it. It is the right word at the right time. A word of affirmation, a word of agreement.

> **In what ways do these verses expand your understanding of what God - Father, Son and Holy Spirit - is like?**

1:7-8

The coming of Christ ... a sneak preview

After the introduction and greetings, verse 7 begins the first great prophetic oracle in the book of Revelation. It sets the tone for the rest of the volume with one prediction hard on the heels of another. This is a powerful reminder that history is not just drifting aimlessly along ... everything is moving purposefully and deliberately to the most momentous event to hit planet earth since its inception. The great juggernaut of history rumbles toward its final consummation.

The 'A' of anticipation

John says, *'Look.'* It is a simple four letter word, it is a word we hear bandied about on a daily basis; nevertheless, it is one which is asking for our rapt attention. You will find it used around twenty-five times· in the book and it means, *look for yourself.* This exclamation is intended to arouse the mind and activate the heart to seriously contemplate what follows, it is an arresting call. It highlights our personal responsibility to be avidly watching for the second advent of Christ.

The 'A' of association

We read, *'he is coming with the clouds.'* Remember Acts 1:9-11; at his ascension from the Mount of Olives he was received into heaven by a cloud. When he returns at the end of time, he is coming back with the clouds of heaven! The cloud is often linked with the visible manifestation of the presence of God; an obvious example of that is the shekinah glory of the tabernacle and temple era. The cloud also symbolises the brilliant light that accompanies the divine presence; actually, it was a light so powerful that no-one could see it and live (Exodus 33:20). It is worth noting, the present tense of the phrase *'is coming'* suggests that Christ is already on the way; that would indicate his coming is certain for nothing and no-one will stand in his way.

The 'A' of attitude

We discover that *'every eye will see him, even those who pierced him, and all the peoples of the earth will mourn because of him.'* This is Philippians 2 coming alive. It is a grand and decisive fulfilment of what Paul writes about in verses 9 and 10. Make no mistake about it! Every eye will see him and with the wonders of modern technology, that is possible right now. Such an event will be witnessed simultaneously by all people in both hemispheres. In a touch of irony, it also includes those who pierced him and, it has to be said, that is not just a passing reference to the Roman soldiers who nailed him to the cross.

You find a similar allusion to this in the Old Testament in the book of the prophet Zechariah. The cross reference there is in 12:10-14 where it applies specifically to the various groups within the house

of Israel. What we have envisaged here is a stunning demonstration
of the power of God; it is the awesome victory of a triumphant Christ!
And to make the occasion so much bigger and better, it will be out in
the public domain for all to see. People will quickly realise, he is
the one they ignored, rejected and spurned. They will realise, he is
the one to whom they gave the cold shoulder. In that moment, on
bended knee, they will cry out, 'Jesus Christ is Lord!'

Again, John follows with a second *'Amen'* but this time he
prefaces it with the words, *'So shall it be!'* It is almost like a double
amen for John's response uses the strongest words of affirmation
both in the Greek and Hebrew languages. It is like someone saying,
'Yes, Lord; yes, Lord!' There is a lot of undiluted passion and steely
conviction in his voice.

The character of Christ

In verse 8, it would appear that the Lord is putting his signature on
the prophecy recorded in the previous verse. It is a guarantee that it
will happen for he is the divine underwriter! The mere mention of
his name is a sufficient warranty in and of itself. In a bold attempt to
eliminate any nagging fears or suspicions that his people may have,
his promise is set against the velvet backdrop of three of his attributes:
he is an all-knowing God, he is an eternal God, and he is an all-
powerful God.

He is the Alpha and the Omega

These are the first and last letters in the Greek alphabet so the Lord
reminds us that he is the beginning and the ending; if you like, he is
God's alphabet. He is the first and final source of knowledge, wisdom
and understanding. He knows everything. That means he has never
had a new thought! Our Lord is everything that can be said. Here is
one who is omniscient.

'The First and the Last' does not only apply to the Lord Jesus,
the Living Word; it can also be applied to the written word. You see,
on one side of the shelf we have book number one which is the book
of Genesis. On the other side, we have book number sixty-six which

is the book of Revelation. If you like, these are the book-ends of the canon of Scripture.

In the book of Revelation, we see the completion and fulfilment of the work God began in the book of Genesis. If Genesis is the seed-bed of all theology, then Revelation offers the fruit of all theology ... it is the golden clasp which binds the volume of the Bible together. The parallels to these two books are many:

GENESIS	REVELATION
The first man, Adam, reigns on planet earth.	The last man reigns in heaven in glory.
The darkness and the seas are created.	There is no more darkness, nor any sea.
A bride, Eve, is presented to her husband.	The church, as a radiant bride, is presented to her husband, the Lord Jesus Christ.
We see the tree of life in the midst of the Garden of Eden.	We see the fruit-bearing tree of life in God's new creation.
The beginning of sin brings death and a curse.	Sin is done away with; there is no more curse and no more dying.
Satan appears to man for the first time.	He appears for the very last time.
Man is driven from the Garden and the presence of God.	Man sees the face of God in glory and he is brought into a place of intimate communion with the Lord.
Men look for a city by faith.	The Holy City, the new Jerusalem, as the eternal home of the redeemed, is seen coming down out of heaven from God.
We see paradise lost.	We see paradise regained.

He is the one who is, and who was, and who is to come, the Almighty

In three words, he is omnipotent. Here is the eternal God who can do anything, the God who can do everything. Here is the God who spans the generations. There is power in his presence! It was Amy Carmichael who wrote, 'When we are facing the impossible, we can count upon the God of the impossible!' Ten times you find this appellation used in the New Testament, but nine of them are right here in the book of Revelation.

What an amazing title! Here is a God who is gloriously able; man will surely fail, the old devil is living on borrowed time, but God is able. He will prevail. He will succeed. He will be victorious at the end of the day. Isn't that fantastic! That has to be very good news for you and me at this point in time! A former Chancellor of Germany, Helmut Kohl, said a while back, 'The wheel of history is turning faster now.' You know, I think he is absolutely right. He hit the nail on the head with that insightful and perceptive comment.

> **God has changed the negatives of Genesis into the positives of Revelation. Use this as a springboard for worshipping him!**

John was an old man on a remote island and he is the one who was given the inspiration and information to write the greatest story of all time. More often than not, that is how God chooses to work. He takes the most unlikely and most unpromising material and he shapes us into the kind of people he wants us to be. He longs that we might find our potential realised in him. I am thrilled when I realise that the God who is willing to take the time and invest so much energy into moulding your life and mine is the same God who is actively working behind the scenes in today's world. He knows what he is doing; he knows where he is going. He can see tomorrow and the day beyond. Like John, we fall down before him and worship!

1:9-11

The recipient of the vision

The recipient of the vision in the book of Revelation is the apostle John. He is the same man who single-handedly wrote the gospel of eternal life; he is the same man who often leaned on the bosom of Jesus and, in later years, skilfully wrote three letters on the theme of love. He is the one who started out in life as a fisherman and then he heard the call of God. He responded positively to the claims of Christ on his life and, eventually, he became a best friend and a trusted confidante to the Lord Jesus; he watched his ministry develop over the years.

John was there on snow-capped Hermon, the Mount of Transfiguration; he was there in the Garden of Gethsemane; he was there at the foot of the cross on Calvary. Some of the last words Christ spoke in this world were given to John when he encouraged him to look after his dear mother, Mary. This is the man who now receives an awesome vision of the shimmering splendour of the glory of God.

John would never be the same again. Here is the man who, on earth, looked into the face of Jesus. Here in Revelation, he sees the lovely face of Jesus in heaven itself. Having sampled heaven, he would be forever spoiled for life on planet earth.

The reason for his exile

It is clear from verse 9 that John had been banished to Patmos. His only crimes were those related to his personal faith and trust in Jesus. He tells us he was there *'because of the word of God and the testimony of Jesus.'* He witnessed bravely to his dynamic relationship with Christ. He unashamedly nailed his colours to the mast. And he paid the price; his faithful, unequivocal, uncompromising preaching of the gospel of Jesus Christ cost him his personal freedom.

The authorities had the option of silencing him by throwing him to the lions; if they had gone down that road, John would have been hailed as a martyr. That was the last thing they needed and it was certainly the last thing they wanted. So they did the next best thing, they shipped him off to the prison island of Patmos.

Tradition has it that before he was deported and sent off into exile, John was first of all plunged into boiling oil. It does not bear thinking about, does it! Life was tough on this barren, rugged, craggy isle, an island where vegetation was scarcely seen. It was an inhospitable place about fifteen miles off the coast from Ephesus. It was a volcanic island about ten miles long and six miles wide. It was the Alcatraz of the day. It was like being transported to Siberia for the winter. John spent his days labouring in the mines and quarries, breaking rocks as a member of a chain gang. He was separated from other believers, he was cut off from his family, he suffered severe persecution, he had meagre rations in terms of decent food, he was improperly dressed, he slept on the bare ground in a dark cave ... as you will appreciate, John experienced considerable deprivation. And remember, he is around ninety years of age! On a human level, this was the last thing he needed!

How true it is, sometimes it is out of the suffering of God's people that we have some of the greatest triumphs. At times, when circumstances look their darkest, it is in moments of such loneliness and despair that God has the opportunity to shine the brightest.

For John, this tiny prison island became the gateway to heaven. The Patmos of persecution enabled John to walk through a wide open door to a further period of service and an extended time of unscheduled ministry.

I imagine John probably thought that his life and long fruitful ministry were all behind him but, in the good providence of God and unknown to him, his most significant ministry was still before him.

It was while John was exiled to the bleak and austere island of Patmos that he received this unique revelation. What, if any, can be the lasting value of your 'barren' experiences? How does knowing God make a difference at these hard times?

His reference to himself

John speaks of himself as *'your brother and companion in the suffering and kingdom and patient endurance that are ours in Christ.'* That means he was no stranger to trial and trouble, and neither were they - each could identify with the other. Sure, we have an apostle here, but he is not in the business of waving titles around, he only sees himself as a *'brother.'* His was a household name in the early church and yet he is happy and privileged to share in their sufferings as well. What a man, a man who knows how to empathise.

When the bad times come, so many of us cry, 'why me?' Perhaps the question would be better rephrased, 'why not me?' After all is said and done, why should we be exempt from life's trials? Why should we be immune from the hassles of daily living?

His reaction to adversity

John had every right to bemoan his fate. He had been a faithful follower of Jesus and now, in spite of his total dedication to Christ and his cause, he is a common prisoner, and on top of that, he is pension material, he is a geriatric! I suppose, he could have buried his wrinkled brow in his callused hands and cried, 'What did I do to deserve all this?' But he didn't! Have you ever wondered, why did John not react that way? Why is he so incredibly different to the rest of us mortals? Why does he have such a sweet spirit? Well, I think we have the answer in verse 10, for we read there that John was *'in the Spirit.'*

His remarkable experience

The real meaning of being *'in the Spirit'*

Let me tell you, first of all, what it does not mean! It does not mean that John was Spirit filled on a Sunday morning. John obviously lived his life in the fulness of the Holy Spirit from Monday to Saturday, and I can assure you, Sunday was no exception.

John was on a remote island and, at the same time, he was in the Spirit. Two places at once! It was a double location: a human and a heavenly environment. He was fettered and shackled by Rome but he was also at the feet of Jesus.

John was not only witnessing for the Lord, he was an adoring worshipper of the Lord; and, it seems to me, he discovered a priceless secret. It is one that Margaret Thatcher frequently referred to when she was Prime Minister of the UK. The baroness, as she is presently titled because of her life peerage, animatedly spoke of number 10 Downing Street as 'living above the shop.' To me, that is the vital lesson John grasped. He worked down here but he lived up there!

The real meaning of *'the Lord's day'*

When we read about the Lord's day in this context, it is not a reference to Sunday. I do not think John is talking about the first day of the week. Generally, when you survey the trend adopted in the epistles, when the Holy Spirit wished to refer to the first day of the week, he called it just that!

This probably refers to the Day of the Lord, that great and terrible day when God will take over the reins and settle accounts with this earth. You can read all about it in the extensive coverage it is given in the Old Testament, courtesy of the major and minor prophets; Peter and Paul also talked about it, Jesus himself spoke of it in his Olivet Discourse in Matthew 24. It is a reference to the period of Tribulation that spans the seven years between the two stages of the second advent of Jesus.

Phase one is when he comes to the air for his church;
phase two is when he comes to the earth with his church.

The time in between these two pivotal points is often called 'the day of the Lord' or, as you have it here, 'the Lord's day.'

For John, to be *'in the Spirit'* means he was projected into the future. He was given a remarkable preview of things to come. And what he saw with his own two eyes is what he has written in this great book; it was all recorded on the scroll as mentioned in verse

11. It was then promptly despatched to the seven churches in Asia Minor (modern-day Turkey). They were specifically selected because they were strategically located in the key cities of the seven postal districts into which Asia was divided. They were, therefore, the central points for disseminating information.

John tells us that he *'heard a loud voice like a trumpet.'* That means it was not only loud, it was clear and concise. And when he turned around in response to the voice, he could not believe his eyes for *'he saw seven golden lampstands.'* These are representative of the seven church fellowships to whom he is writing, which are briefly referred to in verse 11. These are the assemblies in Ephesus, Smyrna, Pergamum, Thyatira, Sardis, Philadelphia and Laodicea.

1:12-16

And there, centre stage among the lampstands, is the one who is the focal point of this breathtaking vision: he saw Jesus! Remember, he had not seen the Lord Jesus for the best part of six decades, until now. John sees him and he is electrified! He collapsed. He froze in time and space. The pieces of the jigsaw all came together and John saw the Lord as we will some day. Think of it! In that day we will see the King in all his beauty!

In verses 12 and 13, he is standing among the lampstands; by the time you come to 2:1, he is walking among the seven golden lampstands. John MacArthur reminds us, 'These were like the common portable oil lamps placed on lampstands that were used to light rooms at night.' From John's perspective, they typify churches as the lights of the world (Philippians 2:15). They are *'golden'* because gold was the most exclusive and precious metal. The implication is that the church is to God the most beautiful and valuable entity on planet earth, so costly that Jesus was willing to purchase it with his own blood (Acts 20:28).

Oh yes, he is there! When two or three are met together in his name, he is among them. No matter how many or how few there may be of us, the Lord is always there. That is his promise and he always honours his precious word. He is seen to be central in authority. He is sovereign in his presence. He indwells his church to lead and empower it. How we need to feel and sense the reality of his presence and power in our churches today! The reality is, we do not matter, other people are not that important, our programmes and activities are not the be-all and end-all either: the living Christ is and he should be at the centre!

John's nine-fold vision of Jesus

I came across a lovely story the other day. It was about a father who was trying to get peace to read his copy of the *Daily Telegraph*. The problem was, every time he settled down and was engrossed with his nose in the paper, his little girl kept asking him questions. And so he came up with the bright idea that he would give her something to do! A diversionary tactic, at least that is what he hoped! He leafed through one of the missionary magazines lying on the coffee table and he found a map of the world. He cut it out in small pieces and said, 'Look, here's a map of the world, see if you can put the jigsaw puzzle together!' Feeling rather chuffed, he settled down for the nth time. In a few minutes she was back! He just could not believe it! He was taken completely by surprise, so he asked her, 'How did you do it so fast?' Like a flash of lightning, she replied, 'Well, Dad, it was easy, I found a picture of Jesus on the other side and I knew when I had him in the right place, the whole world would be all right!'

How simple, yet, how profound!

This portion is a brilliant masterpiece of Christology. Every single stroke of the Spirit's brush on the canvas of Scripture has a special meaning for John sees Jesus as he is! I believe there is wonderful truth in the familiar lines penned by Helen Lemmel:

Turn your eyes upon Jesus,
Look full in his wonderful face;
And the things of earth will grow strangely dim
In the light of his glory and grace.

As the Son of Man ... the Lord is risen!

Here is the one with whom John conversed in his gospel; now, for John, at the end of the journey, this same Jesus is still there. That is reassuring! He has not changed for 'yesterday, today, forever, Jesus is the same.' He became a man for us so that he might know human life by personal experience. He knows what we are like. He knows what makes us tick. He has been touched with the feeling of our weakness and need. He is the one who experienced great problems of pain, persecution, and pressure; and now, John was seeing Jesus in the midst of those who also had great problems!

This was a favourite title with the Lord Jesus, he often used it when speaking about himself. Although it seems to speak of his humanity, in reality it is a pointer to his deity. Perhaps our Lord used the name because it carried no nationalistic associations during his ministry; it implied an identification with man; so, as Richard Bewes points out, 'It had both overtones of divinity and undertones of humanity.' It has special meaning to students of Bible prophecy. Away back in Daniel 7, we see the Son of Man being given a kingdom that shall never be destroyed. He is set before us on that auspicious occasion as the coming Messiah. The Son of Man: God became a man ... that is the heart of the gospel message. The bottom line is:

if he is not God, then he can do nothing to save us from our sin; if he is not man, then he could not have died and paid the price for our sin. At one and the same time, he is both God and man!

There is a lovely thought envisaged here: the fact that Christ retains his humanity following his resurrection is a guarantee to all believers of our bodily resurrection, as well as a blessing that we will have an everlasting revelation of God in human form. That is a tremendous aid to our understanding in the life which is to come.

As the great High Priest ... the Lord is reigning!

We read of him that he is *'dressed in a robe reaching down to his feet and with a golden sash round his chest.'* This is not the garment of the average peasant of Middle Eastern culture; it is not the short tunic. It is a garment of wealth, a garment which denotes high position and one which points in the direction of royalty.

There is something similar alluded to in Isaiah 6 where we read that 'the train of his robe filled the temple.' What a sight for the human eye! It speaks of the greatness of Christ. In some ways, it is not unlike the garment of the high priest which we read about in Exodus 39. The sash or girdle speaks of service. Did you notice, it is not on the loins which is the place of strength, it is on the chest which is the place of compassion! The fact that it is golden suggests that it is something which is everlasting. After all, we read in the book of Hebrews that Jesus is a priest, not after the order of Aaron, but after the order of Melchizedek. His is a priesthood which is unchanging, undertaking and understanding.

It is good to reflect for a moment on the majesty of the priestly ministry of Jesus Christ for the golden sash around the chest also speaks of his authority as King of kings. When Isaiah had his vision of the Lord, he saw the train of his robe filling the temple; it was a scene of unsurpassed royalty and dignity. That thought of our regal Lord is captured in the beautiful song which goes like this:

> *Majesty! Worship his majesty!*
> *Unto Jesus be glory, honour and praise;*
> *Majesty, kingdom authority, flows from his throne unto his own.*
> *His anthem raise!*
> *So exalt, lift up on high the name of Jesus!*
> *Magnify, come glorify Christ Jesus the King!*
> *Majesty, worship his majesty, Jesus who died, now glorified,*
> *King of all Kings!*

As the Ancient of Days ... the Lord is righteous!

In his third thumbnail sketch of Christ, John describes him quite vividly when he says, *'his head and hair were white like wool, as white as snow.'* This is strangely similar to the picture found in Daniel 7:9 of the one who is from everlasting to everlasting.

Here is one who is all-wise; that means there are no accidents with him in control, he makes no mistakes, he knows exactly what he is doing, he never has to second-guess himself, his hindsight is never better than his foresight, his wisdom does not improve with age or experience, he does it exactly right the first time! It also speaks of one who is totally pure, one who is whiter than white as the Redeemer and Saviour of his people. It is not in his nature to be mean or vindictive or sadistic or cruel or petty or selfish. He is just not like that! The fact remains, the sinfulness of man cannot exist in the presence of the blinding holiness of Jesus. A single look at him and we quickly realise, here is one who is unimpeachable!

As the Judge ... the Lord is revealing!

In the fourth vignette, we read that his *'eyes were like blazing fire.'* He is the one who sees all things. He has x-ray vision. He has 20/20 vision. Absolutely nothing is hidden from him. He is the one who can penetrate the depths; he can see beyond the facade; he has eyes which can search the innermost being. Peter discovered that, didn't he? It was Matthew Henry who noted, 'God not only sees men, he sees through them!' You cannot run away from him or hide behind any mask, he sees through it all; he has no hidden agenda for in that day when we see him, all will be brought out into the open. We may cover up down here and we may leave a few skeletons concealed in the cupboard but one day our sin will find us out!

Because his eyes are like fire, it means he is indignant and angry with so much of what he sees. Oh yes, he will judge, for man is both responsible for his actions and accountable for whatever he does. He will do that which is right and he will be seen to do that which is right.

As the Lamb of God ... the Lord is relentless!

In verse 15, we are told that *'his feet were like bronze glowing in a furnace.'* In the Old Testament era, the mention of brass or bronze always indicated judgment. You will remember in the tabernacle, the first piece of furniture inside the gate was the brazen altar, it was there that the lamb was sacrificed as an atonement for the sin of the individual. The lamb was consumed because the bronze could stand the fire. It is quite amazing, it really is, for under the old economy the fire consumed the lamb, but when you linger around Calvary, you find it is the Lamb who consumed the fire. This also looks forward to the day when, as the Lion of the tribe of Judah, he will put all his enemies and every evil power beneath his feet. He will crush his foes!

As the Voice of our Beloved ... the Lord is regal!

We are then reminded that *'his voice was like the sound of rushing waters.'* Think of their incredible power as the waters roar and rush on by; it is what I tend to call, the Niagara syndrome - tens of millions of cascading gallons tumbling irretrievably over the edge. John probably has in mind the mighty ocean waves incessantly crashing against the jagged rocks of Patmos. It is the kind of thing that keeps him awake at night.

The fact is, when Jesus speaks, all men will hear and all men will know that he has spoken. The psalmist David tells us, 'The voice of the Lord is over the waters, the God of glory thunders, the Lord thunders over the mighty waters; the voice of the Lord is powerful, the voice of the Lord is majestic' (Psalm 29:3,4). The ear-splitting sound of his voice will shake the four corners of heaven and earth. I tell you, one deafening word from him and men will jump! A single word from him drowns out all other voices!

As the Lord of the Harvest ... the Lord is the regulator!

'In his right hand are seven stars.' These are the angels directly related to each of the seven churches, they are the messengers or the spiritual leaders who are linked to each congregation and they are in his hand. It seems to me, that is a fairly safe and secure place to be! But it is also a place where he can shape us! You see, if I am not in his hand where he can use me and mould me, basically I am wasting my time. Because of the frailty of our flesh and the foibles of our human nature, we need to place ourselves under his control out of deference to him. After all is said and done, he is the one who is in charge.

It is good to remind ourselves that he is in total control of all the forces in today's world, those seen and unseen. They are in his right hand which is the hand of power. Someone has said: 'The things that overtake us are not overlooked by him, they are overruled by him!' It is not that the Lord is careless, we know he is not, for the hand that holds the stars still bears the scars of Calvary's nails.

As the Captain of our Salvation ... the Lord is resourceful!

Did you notice what it says? *'Out of his mouth came a sharp double-edged sword.'* That is the potent word of God for that is what will guide us along the journey of life and on into heaven itself. The Lord has gone on before us, and by his word, and with his word, and through his word, he will ensure our safe arrival there.

Allied to that truth is the fact that he will defend his church against external threats as in 19:15,21. By the same token, he will exercise a ministry of judgment on those enemies from within the church, he will fell them with his word (2:12,16; Acts 20:30). John MacArthur reminds us, 'Those who attack Christ's church, those who would sow lies, create discord, or otherwise harm his people, will be personally dealt with by the Lord of the church.'

As the Altogether Lovely One ... the Lord is resplendent!

In the closing phrase of verse 16 (which John borrowed from Judges 5:31), we discover that *'his face was like the sun shining in all its brilliance.'* What a radiant countenance! It is so bright, it is so warm, it is dazzling, it is blinding, it is resplendent in all its glory! This is the glow of God! The sun, as we all know, can bless and it can burn. In such light, all else fades before him for he is pre-eminent. He is the incomparable Christ. He is unique! He is the unapproachable one and yet, by his grace and through faith, we can draw near.

> **How does the nine-fold portrait of Jesus inspire and strengthen your relationship with him?**

1:17-20

A vision ... too hot to handle!

Given a sensationally astonishing vision of the glorified Christ, John, bless him, just melted in the Lord's presence. There he was, viewing the majesty of the man he knew in Judea and he got the wobbles. He lost consciousness when his heart missed a beat and his legs turned to jelly. This was an instinctive human reaction, it was one of devastating fear. It paralysed him as he fell enervated to the ground! As Anne Graham Lotz points out, 'John's patience and preoccupation with Christ resulted in his prostration before Christ.'

There are many instances recorded in Scripture where ordinary men have had a similarly frightening encounter with the living God. They have one common denominator. To a man, the reaction of those who genuinely saw the Lord was inevitably one of fear. Those brought face-to-face with the incandescent glory of a thrice holy God are terrified, they are petrified, realising their sinful unworthiness to be in his company.

Many examples spring to mind, but the more obvious ones are: Abraham, he fell flat on his face when God talked with him; Moses, he hid his face for he was afraid; Balaam, he bowed his head and hit the ground; Isaiah, he saw the Lord seated on a throne in the temple and he cried out, 'Woe to me, I am ruined!'; the three disciples on the Mount of Transfiguration, they saw his face shining like the noonday sun and their immediate response was to fall to their knees; Saul of Tarsus, he dropped to the ground and was momentarily blinded.

So it should not surprise us when we read that John fainted. This man, made of exactly the same material as the rest of us, was overwhelmed by the loftiness and nobility of the glorified Son of Man. He shrivelled within; he shrank from such an awesome encounter. It seems from reading between the lines, it was all too much for John, he was out of his depth.

A visit ... how the Lord handled him!

We read in verse 17, *'When I saw him, I fell at his feet as though dead.'* The sequel to this is quite astonishing for the Lord did not leave John lying there. We read in verses 17 and 18, *'Then he placed his right hand on me and said, do not be afraid, I am the First and the Last. I am the Living One; I was dead, and behold I am alive for ever and ever! And I hold the keys of death and Hades.'* Here is Jesus, the man with a personal touch!

What we have here is a tender 'pick-me-up' kind of touch. It is a touch of reassurance, a touch that says, 'all is well.' When Jesus placed his right hand on the trembling shoulder of John, he said to him, in effect, 'Don't be afraid, John! It's me!' I think it is wonderful for us to realise that Jesus was not afraid to touch ordinary people. In fact, when you read through the gospel narrative, you find he touched all sorts of people:

> *when he healed a leper, he touched him;*
> *when he restored sight to the blind, he put his hands upon their eyes;*
> *the touch of his hand brought healing to broken lives;*
> *the touch of his hand brought strength to those who were crushed;*
> *the touch of his hand brought comfort and acceptance to those who were marginalised to the fringes of society.*

How Jesus introduced himself

The express words of comfort and consolation that Jesus gave to John are based on his person - who he is, and on his authority - what he has.

'I am the First and the Last' ... the all-sufficient One!

There were none before Jesus and there will be none after him - nothing came before him and nothing will come after him. There never was a time when he did not exist and there never will be a time when he does not exist. He is from everlasting to everlasting, the eternal word. It is helpful for us to realise that this was a title used of God in the Old Testament (Isaiah 44:6; 48:12). By virtue of the fact that Jesus took it to himself, it means he is asserting his deity.

'I am the Living One' ... the all-victorious One!

John would recall this designation with little or no difficulty. He had heard it many times before and he knew precisely what it meant. Like the previous one, this title is also used interchangeably within the Godhead (Joshua 3:10; Psalm 84:2; Romans 9:16).

'I hold the keys of death and Hades' ... the all-powerful One!

He was more or less saying to John that he was sovereign in all matters relating to time and eternity. Hey! what tremendous encouragement that is for the children of God!

> *We need not fear life for he is the Living One.*
> *We need not fear death because he died and is alive, having conquered death!*
> *We need not fear eternity for he has the keys in his hand.*

Our future is in his hands and it could not be in a safer pair of hands. He has the whole world there and we are there as well! Every time I read these wonderful verses, these luminous words, I cannot help but recall the words of the song:

> *God of glory, we exalt Your name;*
> *You who reign in majesty;*
> *we lift our hearts to You*
> *and we will worship,*
> *praise, and magnify*
> *Your holy name.*
> *In power resplendent*
> *You reign in glory;*
> *Eternal King,*
> *You reign for ever:*

Your word is mighty,
releasing captives,
Your love is gracious -
You are my God!

Jesus' commission to John

When you see what happened to John and read what follows in the rest of the book, you quickly realise that this vision was for real; this man was not suffering from hallucinations, he was not living his life in dream mode. He saw and recorded events that will shape the future of every one of earth's teeming millions. It seems to me, the book of Revelation can knock us out of our complacency, out of our fear of the future, and into confident living.

The commission given to John in verse 19 gets to the heart of the matter when he is told to, *'Write, therefore, what you have seen, what is now and what will take place later.'* Basically, this triple command encompasses the past, the present and the future. You will remember, I pointed out earlier, this is an index to the book, it is a table of contents:

'What you have seen' is appropriate to chapter 1;

'What is now' is relevant to chapters 2 and 3;

'What will take place later' applies to chapters 4-22.

Jesus' explanation of the stars

In the next verse, verse 20, he then unravels the mystery surrounding the seven stars and the seven golden lampstands. He makes the connection between them and the letters to the seven churches in Asia Minor. This is a classic example of Scripture explaining itself! So we have no problem identifying the seven churches. John talks about them further up the chapter in verse 11 and again you find them detailed in chapters 2 and 3 as being specific churches in specific locations. Actually, when you start with Ephesus and finish with Laodicea, you have gone on a circular tour of the region; it is a round trip of about 300 miles.

The problem is not with the churches, it is with the angels or the stars! There are many people who have genuine queries at this point.

They ask, why seven? That is the number of perfection, the number of completeness, the number of fulness. It is as if the Lord is saying, 'Here is a picture of the church in its totality.' They say, can we easily identify the seven stars? Who is John speaking about when he talks about them? You will find that each of the seven letters is prefaced with the phrase: *'To the angel of the church in Ephesus'* or wherever. There are two main avenues of thought:

The 'angel' refers to the pastor or leader of a church

This idea is based on the fact that the broad meaning of the word 'angel' is that of a messenger. According to this view, John was addressing the pastor or presiding elder of each church in order to impress upon them the message that Jesus Christ would have them deliver to their congregation.

The 'angel' refers to a supernatural being

We read in Hebrews 1:14 that angels are 'ministering spirits sent to serve those who will inherit salvation.' Basically, the role of an angel is to ensure that God's desires and plans are always accomplished. They operate under his direction and control.

The choice is yours! You can take your pick as to which one you feel is the better interpretation. On a personal level, I prefer the first one as I think it makes a lot more sense. It seems to me, when the Lord has a special message for his people in a given church, the best way to impart it is to go directly to the leadership of that church and share it with those whom the church has set apart for that specific role. When that happens, they then have the solemn responsibility of passing it on to the members of the congregation over which they have been given spiritual oversight.

No mileage would be gained if our Lord was to bypass the recognised leadership of a local assembly and appeal over their heads to the ordinary people sitting in the cushioned oak pews on a Sunday morning. You only get people's backs up if you go down that particular road; and, in the final analysis, you do not achieve very much with such a heavy-handed approach.

It seems to me, some folk today are living their lives on a different wavelength to the Lord ... they do not think churches are important. God does not look at it like that. He believes they are very important! So much so that he shared a vision with John, not of one church, but of seven churches, and in chapters 2 and 3, we see them through his looking glass.

I suppose most people have an opinion about their local church and they are not behind the door when it comes to telling you what they think! 'It's dead, it's too old fashioned, it's over the top, they've gone charismatic, they're far too liberal, it's too right wing, walk in there and you get caught in a time warp, they're up to date in that place, they're relevant!' Comments, you have heard them! Criticisms, you have maybe made them! You ask three people about their church and you will walk away with four or five different impressions!

When you look at the churches which John is talking about, people who were living near the end of the first century, you sit back and fold your arms and say to yourself, 'Well, well. Time has not changed anything ... people are still people ... problems are still problems ... they are just like some of our modern churches two millennia down the road!'

They were real churches; people attended them, people sang in them, people worshipped in them, people prayed in them, people found the Lord in them, people listened to the word preached in them. Two thousand years later we come back and pay them a visit. We take a fresh look at these churches in the first century because there is a lot we can learn from them.

Three attributes of the seven churches

They are real

We need to realise that Christ had a direct message to seven actual churches at that particular time. There were many more which he could have chosen but he opted for these. So we have seven letters to seven real churches. They were contemporary. Each one was different, no two were the same. You cannot really compare churches and expect to do them justice. When we view them from a practical perspective, we note that each one gives a special promise to the overcomer!

They are relevant

The message to each church was relevant then and, I can tell you better than that, it is relevant today! These letters are meant to be applied by all churches in all ages. When you see them as a composite, you soon realise that somewhere on that list, you will find a church that resembles yours and mine. These letters are as current as today's calendar. They are of perennial value!

They are representative

When you take them all together, they give us a preview, an overview, of church history from Pentecost to the advent of Jesus. That means each church depicts a particular period of church history. In that sense, we can view them from a prophetic standpoint. They give us a panorama, a sweep, a vista, of church history. The implication is, there are seven great periods of the Christian era, and when you look back into history, you can see that picture unfolding and evolving before your eyes. So we have here a chronological account of church history.

A potted history of the church from day one

Period 1   **The church at Ephesus: the primitive church from Pentecost to the end of the 1st century**

The challenging comment for this era is found in 2:5 where we read: *'Remember the height from which you have fallen.'* You see, even in the halcyon days of the apostles, there was a gradual cooling of their love for the Lord Jesus. The drive, the dynamic, that characterised the early years was replaced by a more staid and settled-down form of Christianity. The church rested on her oars and started to drift from her moorings. She began to tolerate trends and teachings that brought a razor sharp response from the likes of Paul and Peter, John and Jude, in their letters.

Period 2   The church at Smyrna: the persecuted church from 100 AD to around 313 AD

'You will suffer persecution for ten days' (2:10). When you go back in the annals of church history, you will find there were ten major outbreaks of persecution against the church of Jesus Christ.

The last one, under Diocletian, was so concentrated it lasted for the best part of a decade; it was cruel in the extreme as Rome vented her spleen against the Lord's own people. Their only crime was that they were deeply devoted to Jesus, they worshipped and revered him as Lord. Whether to the lion or before a sword, so many of God's dear people faced death with a song of praise and a word of prayer and thanksgiving on their lips. These folk proved that the blood of the martyr was indeed the seed of the church.

Period 3   The church at Pergamum: the pampered church from 314 AD to 590 AD

The telling phrase found in 2:14 that speaks of *'the teaching of Balaam'* underlines the serious problems which characterised this day and generation. It was riddled with compromise and this was never more the case than in the days of Constantine when he popularised Christianity. This was, undoubtedly, a sea change for the worse.

The church became prosperous and worldly; it was chic to be a Christian at this point in time. It was during this time that there was a marriage of sorts, a kind of merger between church and state. We live even today with the legacy of that momentous and historic decision. What we have here is a church whose character is seriously blurred and a church whose testimony is radically diminished.

When you compare the second and third periods of church history, I think Campbell Morgan offers a rather perceptive comment when he says, 'It's a very remarkable thing that the church of Christ patronised has always been the church of Christ impure.'

Period 4   **The church at Thyatira: the papal church**
                        from 590 AD to 1517

The period represented here is that of the Dark Ages and it is highlighted best by the emergence and strategic influence of the papal church. Here is a millennium when the light was almost extinguished. It has often been called the devil's millennium for the ordinary people were kept in a place of ignorance as regards spiritual truth.

The clue to this era is probably found in 2:20 where we read, *'You tolerate that woman Jezebel.'* She was a pagan woman married to one of Israel's worst and weakest kings. She became the secret power behind the throne and she made a priest-ridden paganism the national religion.

The question is, what happened after the days of Constantine? Rome became the effective centre of ecclesiastical affairs. History confirms that days of corruption followed, days of evil and rampant wickedness were soon the norm again ... so much so, that the church became the home of heathenism.

We can trace many developments during those dark days such as the acceptance of pagan feast days as Christian festivals, pagan gods became Christian saints, pagan rituals received new life as Christian rites, pagan priests became the ordained servants of the church. These were dark days, there is no question about that.

Period 5   **The church at Sardis: the prophetic church**
                        from 1517 to 1700

This period reveals a prophetic glimpse of the Protestant church. I suppose the very essence of Protestant religion is summed up in the words of 3:1, *'You have a reputation of being alive, but you are dead.'* Yes, we sincerely thank the Lord for those who escaped from the clutches of pagan organised religion and ushered in a brand new era.

The Reformation was brought in by godly and gifted men of the calibre and ilk of Wycliffe, Hus, Luther, Melancthon, Zwingli, Knox, and Calvin, all household names to those within evangelical circles. The sad fact is, it was not very long before its impetus died out. It is true, according to 3:2, that there are things that remain but what is left does not look good; it is on the way out, it is about to breathe its last!

Period 6 **The church at Philadelphia: the partitioned church from 1700 to 1900**

Most evangelical scholars are agreed on the fact that the Reformation did not go quite far enough. The downside of that fateful movement is that you have various groupings or denominations emerging with each one espousing its own pet doctrines. Having said that, it was also a time when the phrase found in 3:8 is most relevant, there we read of *'an open door.'* For many believers, there was a welcome return to a simplicity of faith and a genuine return to the plain teaching of the word of God. It also suggests a season of great revival when God moved in powerful ways in the lives of individuals and communities.

Many missionary societies were born in this era because men had a burden to reach others with the life changing message of the gospel. They had a vision which reached beyond these shores to the regions beyond. We are talking of such men as the Wesley brothers, Charles and John; D L Moody and Ira Sankey; Finney, William Carey, David Livingstone, Hudson Taylor and Adoniram Judson, who mark this period as quite distinctive, and so many more!

.God brought the church back from the brink. He drew her close to himself and then sent her forth with renewed passion and zeal to reach a lost world.

Period 7 **The church at Laodicea: the present-day church from 1900 to ...**

The character of our day and generation is best summed up in the descriptive word used in 3:16 where it talks about people being *'lukewarm.'* They are neither cold nor hot; they are neither one thing nor the other; they are sitting on the proverbial fence; they want the best of both worlds - it is one foot in the world and the other foot in the church. It is a nauseating pot pourri of anything and everything. It is an incredible mish-mash of you-name-it-you-have-it! Not very encouraging, is it?

There you see the history of the church of Christ. We have leapt across the centuries. We have spanned these seven great periods of time from day one up to the present. It seems to me, our only hope is to get back to the Bible, back to God, back to Calvary, back to an empty tomb, back to a throne occupied in heaven itself! You see, there is a great need for each of us to examine our own lives!

Are we like the Christians in the church at Ephesus, an evangelical centre of witness?

Are we like the believers in Smyrna, a suffering church?

Are we like the folk down in Pergamum who make up an inner-city church?

Perhaps we are found among those in Thyatira who are pretty much an urban fellowship?

What about those in Sardis ... are we part of a liberal community?

Are some of us like the folk in Philadelphia, part of an active missionary-minded church?

Are we up to our necks in a church like the one at Laodicea where Christianity is weak and tepid?

If we are like Ephesus, a formal church, a church with neglected priorities, we need to be reminded of the presence of the Lord as in 2:1, where we read, *'He walks among the seven golden lampstands.'*

If we are like Smyrna, a fearful church, a church facing satanic opposition, we need to reflect on the position of the Lord as in 2:8, where we read, *'He is the First and the Last, the one who died and came to life again.'*

If we are like Pergamum, a faltering church, a church engaged in religious compromise, we need to look at the possession of the

Lord as in 2:12, where we read, *'He has the sharp, double-edged sword.'*

If we are like Thyatira, a false church, a church indulging in immoral practices, we need to think about the perception of the Lord as in 2:18, where we read, *'He has eyes like blazing fire and feet like burnished bronze.'*

If we are like Sardis, a fruitless church, a church known for spiritual apathy, we need to focus on the power of the Lord as in 3:1, where we read, *'He holds the seven spirits of God and the seven stars.'*

If we are like Philadelphia, a feeble church, a church of lost opportunities, we need to consider the prerogative of the Lord as in 3:7, where we read, *'What he opens no-one can shut, and what he shuts no-one can open.'*

If we are like Laodicea, a fashionable church, a church famed for material prosperity, we need to gaze upon the person of the Lord as in 3:14, where we read, *'He is the Amen, the faithful and true witness, the ruler of God's creation.'*

That is, I believe, an enormous challenge to every one of us. You see, the church is at the crossroads. We are, at this precise moment, in the era portrayed by the lukewarm church; it is the time of the last church on planet earth prior to the second coming of Christ!

It reminds me of this scenario: the hour hand on God's time clock is wound up and spinning. We are being swept along the path of history by a swift wind at our backs. Our individual ability to weather the storm will come from our understanding of the word of God. We need only to give heed to an age-old message that has reverberated down through the centuries in the final verse in chapter 3 (remember, he fires the same parting shot to every church) where he says, *'He who has an ear, let him hear what the Spirit says to the churches.'*

> **In what ways does your church hear what the Spirit is saying?**

It is true, each of these seven letters to seven ancient churches was written with history in mind. Their history. Future history. Your history. My history. I believe, we are links in that unbroken chain of church history! Our response to these studies in the book of Revelation will determine the impact we make today! Let us never forget, we are history makers!

2

The good, the very good and the not so good

'Do you love me?'

That was the simple, straightforward question a Russian peasant named Tevye asked his wife in the musical, *Fiddler on the Roof.*

Love him? The problem was Golde had never even met Tevye until the day of their arranged wedding! Now, after twenty-five years of marriage, he wants to talk of love? It just sounds so ridiculous, so alien to her that she thinks he has indigestion and should lie down.

Tevye repeats the question, in earnest.

Golde wonders at his thinking, is there a hidden agenda? Then she explains how hard she has worked as his wife - cooking his meals, washing his clothes, having his children, and so on, and so forth.

Still, it doesn't satisfy the inquisitive Tevye. So he asks the same question, one more time.

This time, with more than a hint of exasperation, Golde falls back on the obvious: she is his wife, after all!

Still not content with the answer, Tevye persists ... does she love him?

It took a wee while for the response to come, but come, it certainly did. Golde answers in the affirmative, she does indeed love him, realising that her life has not just been an endless cycle of meaningless chores. In all honesty, she has worked so hard *because* of her commitment and love for Tevye.

It is possible, though, as Tevye recognised and almost dreaded, for activity to replace love!

Therein lies the danger ...

2:1-7

Ephesus ... the city

Ephesus was the chief city of the province of Asia. It was known as the vanity fair of Asia and it was also widely acclaimed as one of the top three cities of the eastern Mediterranean. It was a thriving centre for trade, business and commerce, with its own harbour and a population approaching a quarter of a million inhabitants. It was a pagan city with all sorts of weird things taking place. You name it, they had it!

Ephesus could boast with considerable pride that within its boundary there stood one of the seven wonders of the world, the famous temple of Diana or the temple of Artemis, as it was sometimes called. It featured a gross multi-breasted colossal statue-cum-monstrosity to the goddess of sex and fertility. This shrine actually served as the bank of Asia; it doubled as an art gallery and played host as a safe sanctuary for the criminal fraternity. The temple grounds were a chaotic cacophony of priests, prostitutes, bankers, criminals, musicians, dancers, and frenzied, hysterical worshippers. The city was also known for its great library which rivalled those of Rome, Athens and Alexandria. It was a cultural centre and a place where you could find people from all over the world representing every occupation, every language and every belief.

Ephesus ... the church

What is so incredibly special about the church at Ephesus? It is the only church in the New Testament which has letters addressed to it by two apostles, Paul and John. When Paul wrote his letter, the church was in its heyday, it was at its peak, it was at its very best. Paul revealed many wonderful truths to many different churches but none excel that which he shared with the folk in Ephesus. It is the Everest of his epistles. He prays for them twice: in chapter one, it is a request for more light; in chapter three, it is a request for more love.

But, when John picked up his quill a few years later and wrote, it was the crisis church of the day! The tide was going out, they had lost their way, they had left their first love. The furnace was still there but the fire was almost extinct. There was still a measure of warmth but the coals had lost their glow. It was the dying embers syndrome. A coolness had crept into their relationship with the Lord. It is to this community of believers that the Lord now speaks.

We have here a company of people who were members of an evangelical fellowship. When Paul made Ephesus a centre for evangelism during the three years he spent there, the church apparently flourished. It seems, from reading between the lines, that after Paul's release from prison, he probably visited the church another time and established his young protégé, Timothy, as pastor. It is well within the bounds of possibility to assume that John may have succeeded Timothy ... we cannot say for definite, we cannot be dogmatic, we are only going on early tradition which has been handed down ... but, it seems reasonable to think that he did. That is a fairly impressive group of ministers for any congregation, don't you think? These were the big guns in the early church. It was stellar leadership, if you want to see them as 'stars' as Jesus does in verse 1.

The all-important question is, what is in the letter which has been delivered to the leadership of the church at Ephesus?

The Master's revelation

The Lord writes to *'the angel of the church.'* This reminds us that he has his own messenger, his servant, in every church. This is the person responsible for the spiritual welfare and pastoral care of the people of God.

Where is the messenger? He is held as a star in the right hand of Jesus. That is the place of power and authority. That is the only place where his servants can be strengthened and sustained. When we are there, we will be under his control, for he is the manager of every messenger. As John MacArthur says, 'It indicates that they are his ministers, under his power, as he mediates his sovereign rule in the church through its human leaders.'

> **What are the gains for church leaders to be in the right hand of Jesus?**

Where is the Master? He is walking among the seven golden lampstands. He is surveying the churches under his control. He is walking up and down every aisle reminding us that the members are ruled by the divine overseer. He is the master of the members. They are reminded of a beautiful truth that he is in their midst. It seems to me, so long as he is in the central place, they can enjoy a real sense of his presence.

The Master's remarks

This was a very good church to belong to. They are extremely active and there is so much to readily commend it. It was a dynamic fellowship and a lot of dedicated people went along to it. It was a church where discipline was exercised and where the leadership had the rare gift of spiritual discernment. When you stand back and look inside, you cannot help but be very impressed.

They are serving for the Lord talks about their *'deeds.'* The place was really buzzing, things were happening in Ephesus. They were not content to sit with their arms folded up in the terraces watching it all happen down below, they are down there where the action is, they are on the field of play!

They are sacrificing for mention is made of their *'hard work.'* A number of the members were obviously extremely busy and probably a few of them were reaching the point of exhaustion. The word describes an all-out effort demanding all that a person has to give - physically, mentally and emotionally. It was gutsy stuff!

They are stedfast for Jesus highlights their *'perseverance'* as a rich quality. They kept on going even when the going was getting tougher. It was not a grit-your-teeth-and-bear-it mentality; it is more a case of triumphant fortitude. This was no fatalistic resignation but a courageous acceptance of hardship.

They are separated as they did not let any Tom, Dick or Harry into the pulpit. Prospective preachers were vetted and they had to be seen to be genuine. Here we have men in key positions who were alert to false teaching and doctrinal error. They had their finger on the pulse and their ear to the ground. They could smell a heretic a mile off. These believers separated themselves from anything that smacked of false doctrine and they would have nothing to do with those who peddled their pseudo spiritual wares.

This little church was a citadel of orthodoxy. It was a bastion to biblical truth. Now, this is of mega importance, for the church that stands for nothing will generally fall for anything! The bottom line is, any ministry can be only as strong as its doctrinal purity.

They are a suffering fellowship for they bore massively heavy burdens. In spite of the cross they were carrying, they never called it quits. They did not give up, they did not give in. These folk were bearing up under a stressful load but the thought of throwing the towel into the ring never entered their minds.

Looks like a good church, doesn't it! They are standing up to the task in hand, they are standing for the truth of Scripture, they are standing firm in the hour of trial; sure, we take our hats off to them. We salute them for their faithful and solid biblical ministry. I can assure you, this was no exclusive spiritual country club; they did not look like saints on Sunday and act like aint's on Monday!

'Yet' ... a little word which packs a powerful punch ... *the Lord sensed, and he knew, something was not quite right! Something significant was missing!*

The Master's rebuke

When I read verse 4, I discover what the penetrating laser eyes of the Lord detected, there is a fatal weakness in the fellowship. There was a potentially serious flaw in their church. He has a bone to pick with them!

'You have forsaken your first love'

Our greatest strengths can often become our greatest weaknesses. As Charles Swindoll says, 'The Ephesians were the pit bulls of orthodoxy - guarding truth, chasing away false teachers. But in their zeal, they substituted knowledge for knowing, hating for loving.' Someone has written, 'These believers had not only become professional and perfunctory in the expression of their faith, they had become deluded by the importance of service, placing it above their love for Jesus Christ.' That is the solemn verdict of the Lord who was looking behind the brick exterior. The passion was gone, the fire was almost out, there were only the smouldering remains left. They were going through the motions but it was all so mechanical. The days were full, the diary was crammed, the numbers attending were encouraging, but first love had evaporated, it had gone with the wind. There is the real tragedy of what was happening in the church at Ephesus. (A quick glance at Jeremiah 2:2-13 and Ezekiel 16:8-15 illustrates what happens when the honeymoon ends for the people of God.)

What is 'first love'?

Can we define it? I think we can! To me, it is the love we had for Jesus when we first knew him. It is the kind of love which stops the heart or, if it does not stop the heart, it certainly makes it beat faster. It is the brand of love that will do anything for the person who is loved. It is a love with no strings attached! But, over the years, the thrill goes, we begin to take him for granted, we go off the boil spiritually. The wonder of it all has more or less gone from our daily experience. We do not feel excited about him any more. We become comfortable in our lifestyle, we become cushioned with all the trappings of faith, we become complicated in our outlook. We become sophisticated saints when, all of the time, he is looking only for our love. He wants a people who will be taken up with him and a people who will be taken in with him. But, you see, even though all was not well, all was not lost!

The Master's request

His impassioned appeal is found in the final paragraph of the letter and it entails a threefold strategy, three Rs ...

Remember what it was like!
Repent and turn your life around!
Repeat and do the things you used to do!

They had to remember back to when they first came to personal faith in Christ;
they had to refocus on those times when they really loved the Saviour;
they had to replay that initial excitement.

Remember! It was a time to *'remember'* the freshness and the fervency of their first love. To remember, when it was springtime in their souls. To remember, how they yearned to learn more of the word. To remember, how their hearts were overflowing with a love for Christ and his people. To remember, when they had hearts filled with holy passion for the souls of sinful men. It is apparent from what the Lord says here that memory is the handmaid of revival.

Repent! They were also to *'repent'* and get back to where they once were in their relationship with the Lord. He told them quite bluntly if they did not get their act together, he would come and the light would be extinguished. They needed to sort out their personal priorities; they needed to look again at the agenda of their lives. Failure on their part spelt removal and the Lord was deadly serious when he said it.

How do we know? Well, today, you can walk around the ancient city of Ephesus as I have often done and what do you see? It is all ruins! It is just so sad, for search as you might, you will not find a vibrant fellowship of God's people there. You can travel for miles and you probably will not find a single believer in Jesus. Oh, the grave danger of losing our first love for Jesus! Here is a church that was missing out. Here are a people who were missing out. I wonder, can you say without blushing: 'I love Jesus!' 'It is not virtue that can save the world or anyone in it, but love,' wrote Archbishop Temple.

The promise is given in verse 7, if they do what he wants them to do, he will *'give them the right to eat from the tree of life which is in the paradise of God.'* What a tremendous promise that is to claim! What does it mean?

The tree of life was a symbol of eternal life originally found in the Garden of Eden. Adam and Eve forfeited this blessing when they sinned against the Lord, but for you and for me who are forgiven by the grace of God, the promise holds true. He offers us the assurance of eternal life; he offers us the prospect of being with the Lord forever in the paradise of God. You see, the Garden of Eden was merely a shadow of what our future holds as the people of God!

Repeat! It makes a lot of sense to me to put God first in our lives. After all, this exciting promise is as relevant today as it was when it was first given so many years ago. Let us pull out all the stops! Let us get back to a life of walking with the Lord! What is the point of having a saved soul and, at the same time, having a lost life? Let us put him first!

> **From the way Jesus deals with the church at Ephesus, is there an encouragement and a challenge you can apply to your own church situation?**

2:8-11

Smyrna ... where life was tough as a believer

I am sure you will be familiar with the saying, 'the blood of the martyr is the seed of the church.' That is exactly what happened to the good folk in Smyrna. Polycarp was a former bishop of the church in Smyrna. His name is etched on the granite of history. He was a student and disciple of the apostle John, the man who wrote the book of Revelation.

In the year 155 AD, Polycarp was in the eventide of life; the sun was setting on his long and fruitful life and the shadows were lengthening. He was 86 years of age when one day the unthinkable happened: there was the dreaded knock on the front door! When he answered, he was met by the Roman authorities who promptly took him away. He was hauled before the courts and told to renounce Jesus Christ. He flatly refused. He never flinched. He never wavered. This is what he said, '86 years I have served the Lord Jesus. He never did me any harm. How can I blaspheme my King, my Lord, and my Saviour?' You know the outcome? He was burned alive. He died rejoicing in the Lord Jesus. That is what happened at Smyrna.

Smyrna ... where life was a soft touch for the locals

Back in the days of John, the city was a thriving and bustling seaport. It was renowned as a centre of commerce and was known as the gateway from the east into Europe. It was famous for its fabulous wealth; it was a beautiful city because of its architecture. It housed the largest public theatre in Asia as well as a famous stadium and library. Some historians say it was the most exquisite city the Greeks ever built and they called it, a designer's dream. The local Chamber of Commerce hailed it as the pride of Asia. Its one claim to international fame was that it was the birthplace of the Greek epic poet, Homer.

Today, it is the third largest city in Turkey and is home to the prestigious Aegean University. It is a major international trade centre and base for the headquarters of NATOs southern command. A city of prominence has emerged from the ancient ruins of Smyrna. Today, it has a different name, it is called Izmir.

It is hard to believe, in these idyllic surroundings there was a church under tremendous pressure, a church under fire, a church in the crucible of suffering. It was tough! It was a long uphill struggle. It is into this situation that our Lord comes when he pays them a surprise visit.

Here is something quite intriguing. Smyrna actually means 'myrrh' which is a fragrant spice, it is a resinous substance used as a perfume for the living (Matthew 2:11) and the dead (John 19:39). It was obtained when the flowering myrrh tree was pierced or crushed. In an amazing way, the church lives up to that name. There was a rare scent, a beautiful aroma, emitted from the suffering saints within her walls.

Words of introduction

In his initial comment, the risen Lord revealed himself as the one *'who is the First and the Last, who died and came to life again.'* Basically, he wants to remind them of his uniquely held position for he is the exalted and enthroned Lord. Charles Swindoll says, 'In the opening line of his letter to the Smyrnaean believers, Jesus immediately taps into the universal language of suffering and extends hope to a church near dead for thirst of encouragement.'

He talks about himself

As the one who is the *'First,'* it means he is the director of his people; he is the one who goes before us. He is up front. He is ahead of us. As the one who is the *'Last,'* he is seen as the protector of his people; he follows behind us. He is at the rear. As the one *who 'died and now lives,'* he is the victor of his people; we are on the winning team. We will not miss out, we will not lose out. We are on the victory side. Ours is the team that will ultimately triumph.

Here is a church made up of ordinary people who were living their lives on the ragged edge. There were two completely opposite extremes: there was the loving fellowship of the family of God and there was the hostile and cruel society in which they lived.

Jesus sees himself as the one who can effectively bridge the gap. He can encompass such extremes. He can span the divide. He was present at the beginning of creation; he was there at its dawn. He will be there when it all grinds to a halt. As it were, he is the top line, the bottom line and every line in between.

Words of identification

The Lord then proceeds to identify what is happening in the church at Smyrna. This he does in verse 9, where he says, *'I know.'* Two words that communicated volumes to pained hearts. That says it all! That was all they needed to know. There is nothing he does not know, right down to the minutest detail. He is familiar with all the facts, he is aware of all their fears, he sees and knows all their faces, he is up-to-date with all that is happening in their families, and he is au fait with all the comings and goings in the fellowship.

Yes, God knows! He could sit where they were sitting, that was no problem to him; he could stand alongside them and give them a shoulder to lean on. He could offer loads of sympathy to them and, by the same token, he could empathise with them, for Jesus knows all about our struggles. He knows every pinpoint of pain and every little flicker of feeling we experience as his children.

And what a titanic struggle it was! There were *'afflictions and poverty.'* In classical Greek, the term for tribulation paints a picture of a huge rock crushing whatever lies beneath it. This was symptomatic of their experience for the pressure they were under was so intense, they felt as though they were caught in a vice and were being slowly squeezed. This was adversity in capital letters. There was nothing glamorous about their lifestyle as they had been reduced to beggars. They were destitute, they lost everything. They were, so to speak, out on the street.

The lovely thing is that the Lord Jesus can identify with them. He left the splendour of heaven and came down to earth. He who was rich became poor. He knows, sure he does! He has been there,

he has done that! He could put his arm around them and say, *'I know!'*
That would have meant everything to them. It was Corrie ten Boom
who said, 'There is no pit so deep that Christ is not deeper still.'

Words of insight

It really is quite remarkable because, in the next breath, Jesus says
to them, in spite of what you do not have, *'you are rich.'* They had
something money could not buy. What they had in him was worth
more than acres of diamonds. They had a priceless treasure in the
presence of Jesus. They were rich in faith, love and grace. There
was a depth to their fellowship that is only born in the hour of great
trial. There was nothing shallow or superficial about them. There
was an added dimension to their walk with the Lord. They lived, as
it were, on the edge of eternity. Heaven was in their hearts.

Words of intrigue

He also informs them in verse 9 that he knows *'the slander of those
who say they are Jews and are not, but are a synagogue of Satan.'*
These folk were being slandered by many people in town. They
were the victims of a scurrilous campaign to discredit them. They
were the objects of a smear campaign in the local community. Their
reputation was being ruined as they were grossly misrepresented.
Talk about character assassination and protracted intimidation, they
knew all about it!

It beggars the question, who was doing it? Jesus points the finger
and lays the blame fairly and squarely at the door of those who are
paid-up members on the devil's payroll. Those responsible were
Satan's undercover agents. And, yet again, the Lord says to them, *'I
know.'*

Words of information

The Lord drops a bombshell into their lap. The chances are, it was
something they did not want to hear. He told them, *'Do not be afraid
of what you are about to suffer. I tell you, the devil will put some of*

you in prison to test you, and you will suffer persecution for ten days.' He breaks the news to them that there would be more trials and troubles for them to pass through. There would be more ups and downs for them to face on the journey of life. Suffering as a saint is still very much on the cards for them. What they needed to realise was this: *God was allowing it to happen.* He permitted it. He knows how much they can take and so he sets a time limit. And he never moves the goal posts. It would have a starting point, it would have a finishing point. After all, had he not introduced himself to them as the one who is the First and the Last.

Words of incentive

The penny would eventually drop and they would realise that this is all that really matters in this life. He says to them and he repeats it to each of us, *'Be faithful, even to the point of death, and I will give you the crown of life.'* In other words, do not buckle under! Be loyal. Be strong. Be courageous. Do not shrink from the trials of this life and my grace will see you through. He guarantees the future with the promise of a crown of life. At the end of the day,

> *It will be worth it all when we see Jesus;*
> *Life's trials will seem so small, when we see Christ.*
> *One glimpse of his dear face, all sorrow will erase,*
> *So bravely run the race, till we see Christ!*

Oh yes, he knows all about our circumstances. If things stay the same, the Lord will be our fortress. If things get worse, the Lord will see us through.

Here were a handful of people on the verge of cracking up under the tremendous strain they were facing. The stress was sometimes unbearable but the glorified Lord says to them, *'take heart ... the cross is not greater than my grace!'*

> **Why is it often true that those who suffer most are also those Jesus calls 'rich'? In what ways could you increase your personal wealth?**

2:12-17

Pergamum ... the culture capital of Asia

Can you imagine a capital city bristling with civil servants and military personnel? Add to that, a university full of bookish, half-rim-spectacled intellectuals. Make sure it houses an eminent teaching hospital and quite a few rather strange alternative religions. When you put all of that together and more, you could well be thinking about this place.

Pergamum was touted as the Washington of Asia. The sheer beauty of the city would leave even the most cynical traveller breathless. It was renowned as a centre of culture. It boasted one of the finest libraries in the world with over 200,000 handwritten volumes; it was second only to the world famous library in Alexandria in Egypt. Actually, it was the place where parchment was first used. Such a city attracted the best brains and boffins in academia.

It was also a focus of religion. You name it, they were sure to have it. It was a city infested with idolatry, it was a notorious place where religious groups mushroomed. Anybody with anything to say could find a soap box and begin to pontificate. Every corner was a veritable Speaker's Corner as in London's Hyde Park. As far back as 29 BC, it became the first city of Asia to receive permission from Rome to build a temple dedicated to the worship of a living human ruler. That was only the thin edge of the wedge, for within a relatively brief period, Pergamum had three temples in which Roman emperors were worshipped as gods.

Sadly, the church in Pergamum was faltering; she had almost lost her way. We could describe it as an inner-city church, a church surrounded by tower blocks. Here is a church guilty of compromise. These folk wanted the best of both worlds. They wanted to run with the foxes and, at the same time, they wanted to hunt with the hounds. She was flirting with the world and, by so doing, was two-timing the Lord Jesus.

There are four chillingly accurate statements we can make about the church as we read her profile in 2:12-17.

There were Christians in the church

This letter is not penned to professors sitting in ivory towers. It is addressed to believers who were living on the edge of hell. These were everyday people who were struggling to keep their faith in what has been called, Satan's city. Verse 13 also reminds us that Jesus knows they live in a highly dangerous environment. He says, *'I know where you live, where Satan has his throne.'*

They were behind enemy lines; it is the devil's territory, it is the enemy's backyard. It is where Satan has his throne. He is seen as the prince of this world and, for a time, it would appear that his global activities were centred on Pergamum. What a terrible place to live! I cannot think of anywhere worse ... living next door to Satan's bunker!

Many of the Christians were devoting their time to the cause of Christ. Much energy was expended in the service of God. He is most appreciative of all they were doing for him and in his name. He knows about their loyalty as they were true to his name. There was nothing wishy-washy about them.

The battle fought here was over the deity of Jesus Christ. His is a name above all other names and in Pergamum that did not go down very well. It was a war between Caesar and Christ. Who is Lord? Here were a group of people who were willing to stand up and be counted. Because of their intense sense of loyalty, some of them paid the supreme sacrifice. They died because they would not deny the Lord Jesus. When pressed, they did not flinch; when threatened, they did not flee; when tested, they stayed true.

Antipas is singled out for special mention in verse 13 for he is reputed to have been roasted slowly in a brass kettle during the persecution instigated by Emperor Domitian. Under enormous pressure, thank God, these folk did not bend or break. They were brave and bold.

There is confusion in the church

Verses 14 and 15 say as much. The Lord says, *'I have a few things against you. You have people there who hold to the teaching of*

Balaam, who taught Balak to entice the Israelites to sin by eating food sacrificed to idols and by committing sexual immorality. Likewise you also have those who hold to the teaching of the Nicolaitans.' You see, there were some choice people there, some fine young people, some key personnel, but there was something there that should not have been there. If the truth be told, he has a couple of things against them. Two doctrines: one was the teaching of Balaam and the other was the teaching of the Nicolaitans.

These twin doctrines had infiltrated their fellowship. People had swallowed them hook, line and sinker. As a result, their testimony was being ruined and their effectiveness for God was being eroded. They lost the razor sharp edge in their witness for Jesus. They were blunt! Sadly, the false teaching was openly tolerated rather than being confronted and removed. They were content to put up with it because the leaders did not want to rock the boat. It was the 'anything for a quiet life' syndrome. They were happy to sweep it under the carpet and hope it would go away.

The doctrine of Balaam would say, let us be more relaxed in our loyalties. You can read all about the well-documented exploits of Balaam in Numbers 22-25. In a nutshell, he went softly, softly on sin and he encouraged the people of God to compromise. He had one plank in his theology: if you can't beat them, join them. It is fitting in with the prevailing mindset, it is the 'accommodation' principle being put into practice; if you like, it is the 'all things to all men' philosophy!

The doctrine of the Nicolaitans would declare, let us be more restricted in our leadership. These guys were akin to the heavy shepherding movement seen in some of our evangelical churches today. Here we have the emergence of a form of clericalism in which leaders would lord it over their people. It is a kind of dictatorship that crept in through the back door when people were not fully aware of all the implications. It put a massive wedge between the clergy and the ordinary man sitting in the back seat.

> **What is revealed here about how much Jesus values true teaching?**

There is a crisis in the church

They certainly had their problems in Pergamum! There was confusion and a sense of total bewilderment. The people sitting in the pew were feeling uncertain and were not sure what they believed. There was a crisis in the church. Jesus pulled no punches as he lays it on the line to them in a few carefully chosen, ca ʰing words found in verse 16, where he says, *'Repent, therefore; otl ⸱rwise I will soon come to you and will fight against them with the sword of my mouth.'* Phew, rather them than me hearing words like that!

To put it bluntly, the Lord says, either you sort out the problem among yourselves or I will come and do it for you. At the end of the day, it is a clarion call to repentance, it is a rousing call for them to get right with God. His intention is transparently clear as he has placed all his cards on the table. They know precisely where he stands ... now, the ball is fairly and squarely back in their court.

When he introduced himself to them in his opening comments, he referred to the fact that he has a sharp double-edged sword at his disposal. Now you can see the reason why: they have a double error in their assembly. *He is the Living Word and with the sword of the word, he would cut their feet from under them.* Surely this is a powerful reminder to us that it is the word that does the work. He calls his believing people to a life of separation, he invites us to walk a path of holiness, he longs for each of them to come to a point where they are sold out exclusively to him.

There is a challenge to the church

In verse 17, in modern speak, Jesus more or less says to them: you have two ears, do not only listen to what I am saying to you, be sure to hear what I am saying! If they did that, if they bit the bullet, if they lived a life of overcoming, then two things would be given to them.

They would receive a portion of *'hidden manna'* which means that Christ would nourish and sustain them. He would be to them as the bread of life. They could enjoy spiritual fellowship with him, even in their darkest hour. They could, by faith, feast upon him.

Anne Graham Lotz writes, 'Jesus promises hidden manna to those who not only overcome doubt, denial, distortion, and dilution of his word but who also repent of tolerating those who do.'

He would also give them *'a white stone with a new name written on it.'* This probably refers back to the Urim and Thummim that we read about in the Old Testament. It means they could enjoy the intimacy of friendship with him. They would be justified and acquitted. They could sit freely at his table in his banqueting house.

> **What pressures do you face which tempt you to compromise your beliefs and how can the promise of verse 17 help?**

This is an age when anything goes, it is an age when anything is acceptable, it is an age when standards are falling by the hour. This is an age of compromise, it is an age of tolerance, it is an age of political correctness! It seems to me, the old devil is having a field day for modern man has virtually abandoned God. Today's world has ditched God's laws and openly spurned his values. All around us the waters are muddied!

Satan is a past master in the craft of seduction. It is the mix-and-match syndrome in religion. What we learn from the church in Pergamum is that God wants us to be different; he wants us to be distinctive. And because of that, we need to be determined and daring. We need a fresh dose of Acts 4:12 which tells us that, 'salvation is found in no-one else, for there is no other name under heaven given to men by which we must be saved.'

I believe we need to come to a point where we start to share with a watching world that Jesus Christ is unique, and because he is unique, it necessarily follows that Christianity is unique. There is always the danger of compromise in a situation of religious pluralism and Christ can never be merely one of many viable alternatives. Could it be that the Lord is saying to your church and mine, to the global church of the 21st century, 'Look, now is the time to get your act together; it is high time to come clean; this is a defining moment, it is time to stand clear. I want your undivided attention and your total allegiance.'

2:18-29

Thyatira ... where one woman was a liability, not an asset

You will remember the thrilling story of Lydia in Acts 16. She was the seller of purple who was gloriously converted when Paul was preaching in Philippi; but home for her was not Philippi, she was originally from Thyatira. The chances are, and I am only surmising at this point, that she was instrumental in starting a church in her home city. She may have played a vital role in such a venture and she could well have been one of the foundation members.

It is ironic, but another woman had a major part to play in the downfall of the church at Thyatira. This fellowship was in grave danger of being swept out to sea on a tidal wave of heresy. It had broken anchor and was drifting from its moorings. Can we identify her? Oh yes, we certainly can! Her name is Jezebel. Even the mention of that name sends the shivers down the spine as you recall her namesake in the Old Testament. A thumbnail sketch reveals her as a battle axe who happened to be the wife of a weak-kneed Ahab. She spent all morning putting on her war paint and then spent the rest of the day on the warpath! Mind you, this woman in Thyatira is not much better. You see, for a woman to be called Jezebel is every bit as bad as calling a man Judas.

This letter, the longest of the seven letters, was sent to the church in the smallest city; it was delivered to a group of people in what amounted to a hill-billy place. That speaks for itself!

The bottom line for Thyatira and for us is, *who do I worship?* As A W Tozer observed, worship is the missing jewel in many of our lives.

The act of worship

Worship is when we praise God from redeemed hearts.
Worship is when we engage our souls in prayer and meditation on the word.
Worship is when we give our tithes and offerings as the Lord has prospered us.

Worship is when we yield ourselves to him and place our all on the altar.
Worship is when we ascribe to him the love and adoration of our hearts.

The attitude of worship

We come into his presence with clean hands and a pure heart.
We draw near to the throne of grace in spirit and in truth.
We fall at his feet in humility, having seen something of the beauty of his holiness.
We are overwhelmed with a sense of the greatness and glory of God.
We can only cleave and cling to the Lord Jesus.

Real worship, heart worship, spiritual worship, is something he deserves and desires. But the acid test of our Christian experience comes when we ask ourselves the question, who do I worship? That is the base line in our relationship with God. We can worship a man, we can worship a church, but when we opt to go down that road, God is dethroned. That was the root problem in the church at Thyatira.

We can talk about the examination

Their hour of assessment has come. Their day of accountability has dawned. This is the moment when their ministry, and their methods, and their message, will be evaluated.

He is the Son of God. This is the only time this title is used in the book of Revelation and yet John used it so often in the gospel which bears his name. It is a title which speaks of the deity of the Lord; it underscores his supremacy and his authority. This title is in stark contrast to his portrayal as the Son of Man in the vision of chapter 1; there the emphasis was on his humiliation, here it is focused primarily on his status as one who is equal with the Father.

He is the Sovereign of the church. His *'eyes are like blazing fire.'* In other words, the Lord misses absolutely nothing (if you have any doubts on that score, ask Hagar in Genesis 16:13). His penetrating gaze enables him to see everything that goes on, both in public and in private. He sees through the disguises and pretensions of his people. He sees behind closed doors, he is conscious of all that happens in a closed mind, he is aware of what makes sinful man tick in a closed heart. Nothing can be hidden from the searching laser-like eye of God.

He is the Saviour of men because his *'feet are like burnished bronze.'* It reminds us of his severity when he moves in judgment against sin. He has an ability to trample sin and injustice underfoot. The brilliant glow from his feet depicts his purity and holiness as he stamps out impurity.

We can look at the evidence

Their deeds. The Lord, in a wonderful piece of investigative journalism, says about them, *'I know your deeds, your love and faith, your service and perseverance, and that you are now doing more than you did at first.'* What we have here is a church which is growing and yet, at the same time, she is dabbling in sin. It is frighteningly possible! It is scary! The simple fact is, their rapid growth has nothing to do with them; it can all be attributed to the grace of God. You see, God works in spite of us, not because of us!

I suppose we could say, it is an attractive church, at least on the outside. Let us give credit where it is due. They had a proper motivation because their love is blossoming. They had a hugely effective ministry with a very full programme of activities for all ages and, apparently, meeting all types of need. They had the right message as they were orthodox in their basic beliefs. They had a tough mentality as they were bearing up well under an unbearably heavy load. This is the church at Thyatira ... well, not quite, there is more!

Their development. They were not standing still nor were they resting on their laurels. We read, they are now doing more than they did at first. The fellowship was moving forward, they are pulling out all the stops, it was a never-say-die spirit which they adopted. Things were happening. Really happening! Impressed? Better believe it! You've gotta be! These folk had so much going for them. But, and I hate to have to say it, there was a big dark blotch on the landscape.

We can see the example

Sadly, their example is an appallingly bad one! This church had become a hotbed of heresy. The permissive society had gained an inroads into the church family. A spirit of sensual indulgence permeated the atmosphere. They were extremely tolerant and were willing to put up with anything and everything. What they conveniently turned a blind eye to, the Lord saw with two open eyes. What they brushed under the carpet, the Lord brought out into the open. What they did behind closed doors, the Lord made centre stage. There was a cancer eating away at the life blood of the church and, even though the fellowship was haemorrhaging rather badly, they persistently refused to face up to the problem. It needed censorship, it needed surgery, but they failed miserably when it came to dealing with the root cause. What was the issue? They tolerated a woman by the name of Jezebel. In today's speak, we call it, naming and shaming!

They are **wrong in principle** because they gave her an inch and she took a mile. They gave her a place of prominence in assembly affairs and, to all intents and purposes, she ended up putting the men in the shade for she was not willing to work under their guidance. She had her own agenda. She rode roughshod over the leadership and usurped their authority.

They are **wrong in precept** because she led them astray and the thought here is one of deception.

They are **wrong in practice** because the sins we are talking about are those involving gross immorality and idolatry. It was a downward spiral. To add fuel to the fire, the Lord had given her ample opportunity to repent, to change her ways, but all to no avail. That is what we find in verse 21, where it says, *'I have given her time to repent of her immorality, but she is unwilling.'* It is a tragic situation that has snowballed. It has gone far beyond the point of no return and is seen to be totally out of hand. The chances are, no-one in their right mind ever thought it would end up like this!

> Tolerance is one of society's cardinal virtues. But what does this passage tell us about when it is right to be intolerant?

We can hear the explanation

It is into this 'don't say anything that would hurt their feelings' situation that the Lord comes with a message based on a trio of *I wills,* for here is one who is unbelievably patient, even in the hour of judgment. He says in these verses, *'So I will cast her on a bed of suffering, and I will make those who commit adultery with her suffer intensely unless they repent of her ways. I will strike her children dead.'*

It is truly amazing but, even after she has said a defiant 'no,' the Lord still leaves the door wide open. He still talks about the possibility of repentance. Should she continue to flout his laws and do her own thing, then he will act in a way which will not only be a salutary lesson to her but it will also serve as an example to others. That is what he means when he says, *'Then all the churches will know that I am he who searches hearts and minds, and I will repay each of you according to your deeds.'* I think that reinforces the idea that judgment is not only intended to be something which is, first and foremost, disciplinary; it is also exemplary.

The one who is perfect in judgment is more than capable of getting the message across. He will drive home the inescapable truth that salvation is always according to faith but judgment is ever according to works. It does not matter what the sin is, it has a payday, someday. As they say, every kick has a kickback! So far as a holy God is concerned, sin can never and sin will never go unchecked.

We can listen to the exhortation

My heart is stirred when I realise that even in a church like Thyatira, there are a handful of believers who have stayed loyal and true to the Lord Jesus. There may not be very many of them but the few that there are, are worth their weight in gold. Jesus assures them of his unfailing love and constant care. On a purely human level, they have plenty to worry about, they have more than they can handle and the upbeat news is, he knows all about it. He knows they have enough on their plate as it is so he commits himself to them by saying, he will not add to their load any more.

That is what is meant by the compact little phrase tucked away in verse 24, '*I will not impose any other burden on you.*' We need to remind ourselves that the Lord does not ask the impossible of his children. He does not want them to bend or buckle under the weight of excess baggage. He just reminds them that it will not be long until they see him face to face. And, between now and then, he wants them to stand firm, to hold their heads high, to keep their light shining bright.

> How does overcoming and persevering equip us to exercise authority as implied in verse 26?

We can share in the encouragement

In verse 28, the Lord gives them a promise of '*the morning star,*' the star that appears just before the breaking of a new day. Astronomers identify the morning star as the planet Venus. It is the second planet from the sun and it is the brightest object in the night sky. Depending on where it is in its orbital path, the morning star can be seen to rise as much as three hours before the sun. How wonderful it is to know, it is always darkest before the dawn! He says to them and, consequently, he says to you and to me, '*I'm coming back, I'm coming soon!*' You see, hope is always present in the midst of the worst circumstances imaginable.

That is why, like the few good folk remaining in Thyatira, we should not be taken by surprise and caught on the back foot when big problems occur in little, out-of-the-way, obscure places. And that is why, we worship him, the glorified Lord, for our future is as bright and as rosy as the promises of God!

3

Four down, three to go

The story is told of a certain minister who had a reputation for being eccentric. One Sunday morning, he told his congregation that he believed his church was dead. You can imagine the murmurous rumble from the oak pews when he said, 'Come back tonight, I'm going to preach the funeral service of the church.' The members were shocked, they were horrified, they were speechless, they couldn't believe their ears; needless to say, the attendance for the evening service was larger than it had been in years.

In front of the pews was a casket and as the people sat in stunned silence, the pastor delivered the message. After the benediction, the pastor said, 'Some of you may not agree with me that this church is dead. So that you may be convinced, I'm going to ask you to view the remains. I want you to file by the casket, one by one, and see who is dead.'

In preparation for this unorthodox presentation, the minister had placed a mirror in the bottom of the casket. It is obvious who everyone saw when he came to view the deceased!

It is not a technique that I would be too enthusiastic to recommend or endorse; the fact is, he made a perfectly valid point and it was incredibly effective, the people would never forget it!

When you read the opening half-dozen verses in chapter 3, you could be forgiven for feeling like the minister in the story! This portion reads more like the last rites than a letter. As Charles Swindoll says, 'What begins as a deathbed scene, however, suddenly shifts to an emergency room drama. Rather than officiating over a funeral, Christ makes a last-ditch attempt to revive the hearts of the saints in Sardis.'

3:1-6

Sardis ... a church in a coffin

This church is found in a city which has been described as one of the most famous cities in the world. It was built on the summit of one of the hills making it almost impregnable. It was, therefore, a relatively secure place to live. Economically, it was a boom town. It was fabulously wealthy and it quickly became the playground for the rich and famous. If the city was not exactly paved with gold, it was the nearest thing to it. You could actually pan for gold in the streams within the city limits. Apparently, gold and silver coins were first minted here.

Sardinians were not afraid of hard manual work; over the years they built up a flourishing carpet manufacturing base. It was also recognised as an important centre for wool production and the garment industry; in fact, Sardis claims to have discovered and developed the art of dyeing wool. Aesop, the famous writer of fables, may have been from Sardis. You could say, all things considered, it was a picture postcard setting, quite ideal and most idyllic. The climate was excellent. The palaces and architecture were stunningly out of this world. Yes, it had so much going for it! It had a name!

It was in this environment that the Lord met with his people. A church had been planted in the city. We are not told when it came into being. We have no idea who was used of the Lord to bring it to birth. What matters is this, the church was there. And just like the city, it had a name to live up to. Sure, it had a good name! It had a glowing reputation for miles around. It was the place to be seen to go to. It had a long line of worthies who exercised a ministry in its pulpit. The most prominent person from the church at Sardis known to history is Melito. He was an apologist who served as bishop of the area in the late second century. It had a good heritage and a background to be proud of. It had a grand reputation, in the opinion of many, of being a live and vibrant church, a church with vitality ... but, from the Lord's perspective, and his is the only opinion that matters, it was dead. It was a fruitless church! She was past her sell-by date, she was a has-been church. As someone has said, 'Theirs was a name without life, a form without power, a façade without reality.' They talked the talk, they walked the walk, but it was all a hollow sham!

The lasting impression you get when you read this letter is that the church was dying through apathy and indifference. It has given up the struggle against the world around it. It has given up the fight and is not reaching its world for Jesus. Believe it or not, it is a perennial problem! So many fine churches in our day are going down the same road. They talk about their glorious and illustrious past, they savour the immortal memory of great men who have laboured among them, they have all the ingredients of former days. Sadly, and it breaks my heart to have to say it, they have misplaced their zeal and lost their enthusiasm for souls and for the Lord.

If that alarming trend continues, the church will soon be a relic of the past. Surely that is a timely reminder to all of us of what can happen when apathy sets in. As Warren Wiersbe says, 'The church that does not reach out will eventually pass out!'

His assessment

The all-important question is, who is the one who surveys the dismal and depressing scene in Sardis? Who is the coroner who carries out a spiritual autopsy on the body of believers? Can we identify the person conducting a post-mortem on the church in Sardis? We certainly can! He is introduced in verse 1 as the one *'who holds the seven spirits of God and the seven stars.'*

Seven spirits in one hand

The seven spirits of God do not mean there are seven Holy Spirit's operating at large in the world. It does mean there is one Holy Spirit with a sevenfold ministry. The phrase is probably an allusion to the comments found in Isaiah 11:2. Whatever, his is a ministry which is powerful, it is a ministry which is perfect, and it is a ministry which is plentiful in the hearts of men.

Seven stars in the other hand

The seven stars are the messengers in each of the churches. This is a reference to those responsible for pastoral leadership in the local church. They are in the grip of the hand of God! They are controlled by him; they are held by him; they are directed and motivated by him. Christ is the one who is over all but he delights to do his work through men.

These twin components are two sides of the same coin. We can look at it like this: the Spirit of God is actively working in the church and that automatically begs the question: does the church match his holy character? Alongside his ministry and with his empowerment, the servants of God are working in the church and that poses another inevitable question: does she measure up to her heavenly calling?

> **What encouragement is there from knowing Jesus holds church leaders in one hand and the 'powerful, perfect and plentiful' Spirit in the other?**

Your deeds

Over the years a great work has been done for the Lord in Sardis. Many people have been brought out of darkness into light; many evangelistic missions and special outreach events have been held; many missionaries have gone out from her to the regions beyond. There was something geared to all the family. These believers made a great show of being spiritual. As someone has said, 'They were

Bible-toters and Bible-quoters!' You name it, they certainly did it. In the not-too-dim-and-distant past she had been the city's conscience. What a resounding reputation they have! They are alive! That is what we would be tempted to say; Jesus takes a look and says the exact opposite.

You are dead!

To all intents and purposes, this church was a well-kept mausoleum. It was beautiful and dignified but inside were the bones of dead men. They were smug in their complacency. They were living down memory lane. The catchwords of their earlier better days were still remembered! They thought they had arrived, they were content. They had a superb sanctuary, a beautiful multi-purpose building. They enjoyed each other's company. They were going through the motions. All was well outwardly: plenty of activity, packed to the doors, loads of money in the bank, progressive.

Yet, Jesus says, they are dead. They lacked reality. They were artificial. The church was a shrine to the good old days, to better times. There was nothing jubilant or buoyant about it; it was anaemic. It was a corpse wrapped in grave clothes. It was a church in a coffin. What started off as a movement had, over the years, become a monument. Here was the church of the walking dead, they were spiritual zombies. John MacArthur describes it as '... a museum in which stuffed animals are exhibited in their natural habitats. Everything appears to be normal, but nothing is alive.'

She died because she relied on past success.
She died because she allowed sin to creep into the membership.
She died because she was insensitive to her own spiritual condition.

The Lord of the church now bares his heart. How it aches! How it pines! How it beats and bleeds!

Are there areas of your life where you are in danger of living on past successes without a present reality?

His appeal

Wake up!

The Lord says the obvious to them; when he opens his mouth, every word comes with a sharp, staccato ring to it, it is like a rat-a-tat-tat from a machine gun: *'Wake up! Strengthen what remains and is about to die, for I have not found your deeds complete in the sight of my God. Remember, therefore, what you have received and heard; obey it, and repent.'*

If it does anything, this tersely worded command pictures an individual shaking someone who is going into shock, possibly a coma from which there is no return. In that sense, these words are like a slap in the face. They are like a splash of icy cold water thrown around you. They are like a sniff of ammonia! The problem is, the people are sound asleep. Jesus says, 'Be alert! Open your eyes! Be vigilant! Come on, people, don't you see what's happening!'

Basically, the Lord wants them to take the first steps towards spiritual renewal and honestly admit there is something wrong. They needed to pull themselves together and shake themselves out of their padded pew mentality, their brick-walled lethargy, and their stained-glass complacency.

Wise up!

It appears as though they were not fully aware of the dreadful seriousness of their condition, for what little remained, and that was nothing much to write home about, was about to die off. The candle light was flickering in the wind. To change the pun, they desperately needed to fan the flames. The dying embers can be brought together. Prayer can fan the smallest flame into a mighty blaze.

Work up!

The congregation at Sardis had no other alternative but to repent before the Lord and get back into top gear for God. If Jeremiah had been around in the first century, he would have called the people back to 'the old paths.' That is a proven formula for revival and renewal. Oh yes, it is good to guard our spiritual heritage and we sincerely thank God for it, but it is fatal to embalm it! Faith must produce life and works in the here and now! Thank God, there is always a road to recovery. For the genuine believer, failure is never final!

His action

He reminds them at the end of verse 3 of his return, when he would come as a thief in the night. This was no idle threat he was making in an attempt to gee them up. Far from it! His comments are earthed to reality and they are etched in the granite of history. William Ramsay in his commentary explains that the people had twice been conquered by stealth, because they were overconfident of their security and unaware of their vulnerability. The first time they were taken had been seven hundred years earlier when Cyrus was eminently successful in his attempt to take the city. His victorious men entered through a cavity in the battlements of the fortress like city. The second time this happened, 320 years later, Sardis fell to Antiochus the Great. History has an uncanny way of repeating itself and that was true on this occasion! It was same again, third time around! Some people never learn!

The Lord speaks here of the hope of his second coming. The problem was the folk in Sardis had lost that keen sense of anticipation. The thought of expectancy had gone from their hearts. They had to learn again to live their lives in the light of the soon return of Jesus Christ. They did not know when he would come, but come, he most certainly would. They would need to be ready lest they were caught napping and unawares! They had to be sure there were no chinks in their armour!

> How do you think the fact that Jesus 'will come like a thief' should affect your lifestyle?

His assurance

A handful of them were untainted. Jesus said, *'You have a few people ... who have not soiled their clothes.'* They were spiritually alive and seen as a godly remnant. Isn't it wonderful to realise that there is never a day so dark that God does not have his stars to shine! In the days before the flood, God had righteous Noah and godly Enoch. In the time of universal idolatry, there was saintly Abraham. Even in Sodom, there was Lot! He never leaves himself without a witness to his praise and glory. They were virtuous but, under God, they would also be victorious.

Jesus said, *'They will walk with me, dressed in white, for they are worthy.'*

What a marvellous promise he gives them! They would enjoy the best of company as they shared sweet fellowship with their Lord. They have been cleansed and brought into a near place with their God. They will be clothed with his purity and stand justified in the sight of God. He says, they are worthy but that is only because of the grace of God. At the end of the day, it is all because of him.

Like them, what a standing is ours! What security is ours for our names will remain in the book of life! We should be rejoicing; we should be the happiest people on planet earth: we are on the winning side! I think the lesson is absolutely clear ... dead bones can live, but that only happens when the wind of God's Spirit breathes upon them.

3:7-13

Philadelphia ... more than cheese! It is a church!

The people in this church were a lovely people and a loving people. I can assure you, they were definitely not cheesed off!

The name Philadelphia actually means, 'brotherly love.' That is what they had, that is what they showed. It was a delightful fellowship, it was the ideal church. There were not very many of them, they were only a handful or two; it was a relatively small gathering as numbers go. Yet, they were both super and superb in their attitude to each other and to the work of the Lord. It may have been a weak church but, I tell you, it was truly wonderful. There is not the slightest hint of rebuke from the Lord. There is nothing but fulsome praise and warm commendation given to it. In his eyes, they scored 10 marks out of a possible 10. Their entire life, inside and out, backward and forward, up and deep down, is pleasing to him. What a testimony this beautiful body of believers had!

It was, according to John Phillips, a revival church: they experienced an *evangelical* revival because they caught a world vision. They experienced an *ecclesiastical* revival because they dealt with those who would have brought a deadening and disruptive influence into the church. They had overcome those who tried to snare them with all sorts of tradition. They also experienced an *eschatological* revival because the truth of the second coming of Jesus was its beacon light.

And so, the Lord stands before the congregation at Philadelphia, not to offer blame, but blessing. He offers them, not the threat of fearful vengeance, but the prospect of a fresh vision. Here is the gripping story of the little church which tried; it is a classic illustration of the 'small is beautiful' concept, for here is the small church with a big God!

The power of Christ

The Lord is in total charge. He is in command! He is in the driving seat. He is on the throne. He is ruling and reigning. It is his authority that is behind the open door.

The righteousness of the King

We see him as one *'who is holy and true.'* He is holy in his character, in his words, in his actions, and in his purposes. He is utterly separate from sin, his character is absolutely unblemished and flawless. In this, Jesus Christ is staggeringly unique. In thought, word and deed, he is holy. He is also true and that is his intrinsic nature. In a world riddled with error and falsehood, in a society where men fabricate evidence, he is truth personified; he is totally reliable and completely dependable. He is original; he is not a copy. He is authentic; he is not manufactured. Jesus Christ is the real McCoy.

Because he is holy, he is right in his character.
Because he is true, he is right in his conduct.

He could not be different in his actions from what he is in his attributes. In other words, he does what he does because he is who he is!

The resources of the King

He also *'holds the key of David.'* You can read about this in Isaiah 22:22: 'I will place on his shoulder the key to the house of David.' The mention of David's name in the equation is an attempt to focus attention on the messianic office as it relates to one who is great David's, greater Son. The one who has the key is the one who has authority, he is the one who has immediate access to the treasures of the king. Oh, what unsearchable riches are there! The riches of his goodness! The riches of his grace! The riches of his glory!

The regality of the King

'...what he opens no-one can shut, and what he shuts no-one can open.' The one who has the key opens and shuts doors. It is tremendous! When he opens, no man can shut; and when he shuts, no man can open! He is the invincible sovereign. He is all-powerful, he is omnipotent. He is the one who opens the door of salvation. He is the one who opens up the door for a life of fruitful service. He is the one who opens the door of Scripture as we come to him with expectant hearts. If he opens the door, then we must work; if he shuts the door, then we must wait. *Thank God for open doors!*

How stupid we are when we try to knock down barriers he has deliberately set up! How foolish we are when we fail to walk down paths which he has painstakingly cleared! The open door is ever the symbol of a golden opportunity ... we should grasp it with open hearts and seize the moment with open hands. A Christian leader used to make this his regular prayer: 'Lord, give me eyes to see, and grace to seize, every opportunity for thee!' That is what the believers did in Philadelphia.

The Lord was aware of their weakness but, bless him, he also knew their willingness! They are reaching out into the regions beyond, they are rising to the challenge of spreading the gospel. They are located in a most strategic area for they were a gateway to many areas of the ancient world. They are at the crossroads. Now, he says to them, 'There's the open door; there may not be very many of you, but go through it, go on, go forward.'

> What assurance or comfort can we gain from remembering it
> is the Lord who opens and shuts the doors, or opportunities,
> of our lives?

The Lord knows all about them that there is to know. They are not the strongest, they are hardly the most influential, they did not have any great numbers, they had very few outstanding leaders, there were no unusual talents, they were not in the premier league, they did not have much to offer; but God took them the way they were, he accepted them and he used them. Strugglers, yes ... stragglers, no!

The lesson is one we all need to learn: *You can be too big for God to use but you can never be too small!*

They may have been little in power but they were big in potential. Their commitment to the things that really mattered is a challenge to all. They were so dedicated that they guarded the gospel by adhering to the word of God. They were known for their biblical fidelity; they were small, but faithful! In many ways, the church at Philadelphia succeeded where the church at Sardis failed. No compromise, no departure, no apostasy.

Their faith was valid, it was real, it was genuine. Their devotion was quite special too because here was a group of people with backbone. They were rock solid; men of iron, men of steel, men of conviction. Nothing had moved them. They had not been blown off course with every wind of doctrine. No, they were very much in love with their Saviour, the Lord Jesus Christ.

Charles Swindoll makes the valid comment, 'In a beautiful reflection, the Philadelphian believers mirrored the character of the one who wrote to them. When Jesus looked at them, he saw himself. The church could receive no greater compliment, project no greater image.'

The protection of Christ

He deals principally here with two great issues, two issues of major importance.

The hostility of a pagan secular world

He says in verse 9, *'I will make those who are of the synagogue of Satan, who claim to be Jews though they are not, but are liars – I will make them come and fall down at your feet and acknowledge that I have loved you.'* The Christians in Philadelphia were getting a rough ride from some of the local Jews. Because of their rejection of Jesus as Messiah, they are branded as those whose allegiance is to the other side, namely, to Satan. Though they claimed they were Jews, that claim was a downright lie. They were economical with the pure truth. Racially, culturally, and ceremonially, they were Jews; but spiritually, definitely not! They did not fit in with Paul's definition of a true Jew, as outlined in Romans 2:28,29.

The Lord reminds them that, no matter what is happening around them, and no matter what lies before them, he will still be with them. They could count upon him to stay by their side and go through each harrowing experience with them. He would not, he could not, leave them alone. They have been loyal to him, in return, he will not turn his back on them.

The coming hour of global trial

'Since you have kept my command to endure patiently, I will also keep you from the hour of trial that is going to come upon the whole world to test those who live on the earth.' This is truly wonderful for it indicates to us that the Lord has a special plan that will keep

them (and us) from the worldwide Tribulation which is sure to come! The *'hour of trial'* is a reference to the Great Tribulation which I will describe in detail in later chapters. Notice, he does not say, 'I will keep you *through* the hour of trial' but *'from* the hour of trial.' I believe this refers to the moment when millions will be missing, it is the event we know as the rapture of the saints of God, it is the believer's ultimate trip when Jesus will catch away his redeemed people for himself (1 Thessalonians 4:13-18). We clearly see therefore, in this promise, that the church will not go through the Tribulation.

These words, in verse 10, are a powerful encouragement and a motivational incentive to us, especially in such decadent times as we are living at present. They clearly show to us that all saints, all sinners, and all situations, are under his sovereign control. God is still on the throne! Our God reigns! As someone has said, 'If we take care of God's work, he will take care of our battles.'

An old country preacher from the southern states of the USA expressed it like this: 'It's time for our church to wake up and sing up, preach up and pray up and never give up or let up or back up or shut up, until the church is filled up or we go up. Amen!'

The purpose of Christ

'I am coming soon.' According to verse 11, one day the clouds will part and Christ will return. The thought here is of imminency. What a day, what a glorious day, that will be! He could come back at any moment, it could happen at any time. Nothing else needs to happen. No signs need to be fulfilled. He is coming ... soon! And it may be today!

'Hold on to what you have, so that no-one will take your crown.' So, with the prospect of a better day just around the corner, the Lord encourages them to hold on. Do not be tempted to surrender! It is not worth it! For when we see him, there will be a crown given to us, that is our reward. We do not want to miss out, we do not want to lose out, we do not want to be empty handed. One of those great crowns is the crown of life, it is the symbol of final victory.

The promise of Christ

'*Him who overcomes I will make a pillar in the temple of my God.*'
We shall overcome, some day, and when we do, he says, he will
make us a pillar in the temple of the Lord! The thought here is of
that which is strong and stable. It also incorporates the twin ideas of
permanence and immovability. Pillars can also represent honour; in
pagan temples they were often carved in such a way as to honour a
particular deity. The marvellous promise afforded to us is that we
will have an eternal place of honour in the house of God. We will be
secure in glory. We will be there forever. Think of it, he will take a
piece of clay and he will make it into a pillar!

He will also mark us. We will be identified in three ways. Here
we see something of the Lord's infinite greatness in that we bear his
name. It depicts ownership, signifying that all true believers belong
to God. It suggests something of the intimate, personal relationship
we enjoy with him, and that, forever. The Lord's invincible
government is reflected in the phrase, '*the name of the city of my
God.*' It means we will be recognised as a member of the aristocracy
of heaven. We belong to no mean city, even the new Jerusalem. We
have eternal citizenship in heaven's capital city.

> **Three times the Lord says 'I will' in verse 12. Think through
> the meaning of each of these for yourself personally.**

He will also write on us his '*new name.*' Here is an echo of his
inherent glory. When you think about him, he is truly incomparable!
The half has not been told. Then, his name was Jehovah ... today,
his name is Jesus ... tomorrow, in God's future, his name is something
'no eye has seen, no ear has heard, no mind has conceived what God
has prepared for those who love him.' We must be content with
that! Charles Swindoll offers the following upbeat encouraging
words: 'A new name - not just a face-lift or a cosmetic alteration but
a whole new identity. And Jesus promises that this one will last
forever.'

What a church!   What a Christ!

3:14-22

Laodicea ... a church that makes God sick

We have eavesdropped on our Lord's assessment of each of the six other churches. Some of them were good, some were bad, some were quite indifferent. There was praise for some and rebuke for others. There was a mixture of commendation and constructive criticism. You see, churches are not bricks and mortar, they are people; and where you have people, you have problems. Now, problems should not be seen as a threat but they should be viewed as an opportunity for us to exercise our faith, to flex our spiritual muscle, and for us to discover a new dimension in God.

To react like that, we need to have hearts in tune with his great purpose and plan. We need to have ears open to hear what he says to us. That is the prime reason why the supreme challenge is there as a postscript to every letter. It is not just tagged on at the end for the purposes of effect, it is not just there because he was unsure of what to say. He says, *'He who has an ear, let him hear what the Spirit says to the churches.'* The message, 2000 years ago, was personal to that church in that generation, but surely, it is relevant to today's church in today's world!

That means the church at Laodicea speaks loud and clear with a stirring challenge to each of us in the third millennium. It is epitomised as a lukewarm fellowship. In a city better known for its high finance, high fashion, and high life, the church in Laodicea was at an all-time low. She was on a real downer. She was a fashionable church, an elitist church, a rich man's church, yet something significant was tragically missing.

The church, then and now, is called to live in a highly secular society. We are in a world where materialism is a god, this is a consumer oriented age. Here is a church which needed to get its act together. It needed to sort out its agenda. It needed to fix clear goals. It needed to establish some priorities. In short, here was a church that needed a profound sense of God.

How does the Lord handle this particularly errant fellowship? Well, he does what he has done so often before! He introduces himself in verse 14 to the lackadaisical church of Laodicea in a variety of ways; the contrast is patently obvious as he identifies himself using three divine titles.

He is 'the Amen'

That is a phrase we use every time we pray, it is a Hebrew term of assent. It is a phrase Jesus used frequently to introduce some important statements. The AV would say, 'verily, verily,' or the NIV would say, 'I tell you the truth.' He could just as easily have said, 'amen, amen.' We say 'amen' at the end of our prayers, or we say 'amen' when someone else is praying. It means we agree with what has been prayed. Jesus is God's affirmation. He is God's 'amen!' He is God's yes man. Because Christ is *the Amen* it implies that he will always have the last word.

He is 'the faithful and true witness'

This would indicate that he sees through the sham of the Laodicean church. He sees through their show, he sees through their shallowness. He tells it like it really is. Why? Because of who he is. He will not dilute the truth because he is the faithful one. He will not distort the truth because he is the one who is true. He communicates the truth, the whole truth, and nothing but the truth. He is not a spin doctor, he is not someone who puts a gloss or a shine on a particular story; what he sees, he says!

As the faithful one, he is faithful to the purposes of God and the
people of God.
As the true one, he is true to the Lord's own children.

In our hour of need, he is always there, he is true to his word, for his word is his bond.

He is 'the ruler of God's creation'

This could be translated to read that all creation has its origin in him. Paul was on a similar wavelength when he said in Colossians 1:16, 'For by him were all things created.' In other words, he is the source, he is the origin of creation. Michael Wilcock explains the significance of this title when he writes, 'For the sake of this disastrous church, he presents himself as the beginning, or (less misleadingly) the origin, of God's creation, the one who is able to go right down into the chaotic abyss of Laodicea's failure and make her anew, as he once made the world.'

As the 'Amen' he is the all-conquering one.
As the 'faithful and true witness' he is the all-convicting one.
As the 'ruler of the new creation' he is the all-controlling one.

He analyses their problem

Having introduced himself to the congregation at Laodicea, he now focuses his attention on the many areas of concern which he perceives to be at the root of their diverse problems. He is not impressed, he is not well pleased, he is not enamoured with what he sees!

No vitality!

When he looks behind the facade of a healthy exterior, he puts his finger on the problem straightaway. He is aware of all that is happening. He knows all about their appalling compromise and their abject complacency. They did not care! They did not take Christ seriously, they did not take the Bible seriously, they did not take the cross seriously, they did not take sin seriously, they did not take the lost world seriously. As one writer says, 'Being a Christian was like a holy hobby to them!'

He tells them the truth about their spiritual state with remarkable precision. His diagnosis is spot on. They are sitting on the fence; they lost their vigour because they were neither hot nor cold, they were lukewarm and tepid. He says, they are just like the local drinking water, and that was nothing to write home about; it was flat, the sparkle had disappeared, the fizz was gone! Jesus is not 'over the moon' with them at all. Theirs is a nominal experience, they are sitting in a lukewarm bath of religion, their Christianity is flabby and anaemic. He takes one look at them and, quite honestly, he feels sick. They give him a terrible feeling of nausea. He wants to vomit, he wants to throw up!

> *When God looks at apostasy, he gets angry ...*
> *when he looks at indifference, he becomes ill!*

No values!

They said they were rich, but he thought differently. They were full of spiritual pride. They had up-to-date statistics to prove the point, the church's annual report was a good read! They reckoned they were streets ahead of the church at the bottom of the next road. The trouble was, they measured what they had by human standards, not by God's rule of thumb. As John MacArthur notes, 'They were rich in spiritual pride but bankrupt in saving grace. Believing they were to be envied, they were in fact to be pitied.'

No vision!

There was a blur in their perception of their true condition. They could not see reality. They could not see the wood for the trees. They were living in a fool's false paradise. They were living in cloud-cuckoo land. They were oozing with seriously inflated egos about a church that was about to be rejected and they did not seem to see it! They did not see themselves as they really were, they could not see the Lord standing outside the front door, they failed to see the open doors of opportunity to spread the word. Basically, they were empire builders, they were immersed in a world of their own making, they were building their own kingdom.

No vesture!

In the eyes of God, they were naked, wretched and pitiful. Someone has said about them, 'they sat, they soaked and they soured!' Jesus saw them in their true colours; he saw them as they really were. What a church! Grim, isn't it! They had their problems, alright!

Let us not jump the gun too quickly though. It is easy to write them off, but what about our zeal for Jesus? What about our personal sense of values? Where is our treasure? What about our degree of commitment? What about our vision, our goals?

> **If you did a stock take of your life, what would be the lukewarm areas?**

I do not know about you but I find that to be an enormous personal challenge. Yes, they had their seemingly insurmountable problems, and lots of them; how wonderful to realise though, that our God is a God oozing with grace! He wants the very best for each of us. The chances are, they would be stung by his criticisms, they would probably be angered. When we feel hurt or angry, we want to settle the score. Thank God, though, that Jesus' nature is to offer grace.

He advocates a prescription

He pleads with them in verses 18 and 19 to get their lives sorted out before it is too late. They needed a reality to their faith which would come about only when the gold is tried in the fire. It would take trials to bring them into a deeper appreciation of the glories of Christ. He longs for them to be clothed in white garments which are suggestive of a life of holiness. The lukewarm lifestyle of the Laodicean church needed to be transformed into a lifestyle of red-hot zeal for the Lord. They needed the cataracts removed from their eyes so that their vision of Christ could be unblurred and undimmed.

It is interesting that in the city of Laodicea there was a renowned medical school. One of the medicinal products, manufactured and exported from that medical centre, was a tablet that was sold all over the Roman empire. This tablet was used to heal a wide range of eye ailments; the instructions said to crush the tablet, mix it with a small amount of water, rub it on the eyes, and wait for the healing.

Jesus took a piece of local knowledge and reminded the blind Laodiceans that they needed more than their precious eye salve to see: they needed the truth of God which only Christ could bring to them. They needed a new perspective on life and a new perception of those things which are of eternal worth and value. We are left in no doubt that the blessings of God are not for sale, neither are they up for grabs; if they want the rich blessings of God, there is a price to pay to have them.

> **How can the Lord love someone by rebuking and disciplining them as indicated in verse 19?**

He asserts a priority

This verse, verse 20, is a text we have all known from childhood and it is one that is often used as the basis for a good evangelistic sermon, but in this context, it is definitely not a text for evangelism. It is a stirring appeal to the child of God to realise the possibilities open to him when Christ is at the centre of his life. It is an open letter to the congregation and in it the Lord distinctly says, 'Look, I'm here, the problem is, I'm standing outside the door, and I desperately want to come in!'

Jesus said to them, *'Here I am! I stand at the door and knock. If anyone hears my voice and opens the door, I will come in and eat with him, and he with me.'* The thought here is not one of union with Christ, it is one of communion with Christ. This is the best remedy for backsliding I know. It is to be fully occupied with the Lord Jesus. He is thinking here about fellowship with a capital 'F'.

He starts knocking on the door of our lives through changing circumstances; he starts calling for a positive response through his word. He will not force his way into our lives; he will not kick down the door into our hearts; he will not come in with all guns blazing; he will never use a sledgehammer to crack a nut. No, he is not like that. He will wait until he is invited. The reality is, he just wanted to spend time sharing with them. He wanted them to get to know him a little better and, when that happened, both would reap handsome dividends.

He adds a promise

Supper room to throne room! He adds a promise in his final comments by showing us how we can move from one room to another one that is bigger and better! You see, it is through communion with Christ that we find victory and live a life of overcoming. What a noble incentive! One day, we will rule and reign with him! To enjoy rich fellowship with Christ in the kingdom, and throughout the countless aeons of eternity, is sufficient blessing beyond all comprehension. And when we arrive over there, it will surpass all our wildest dreams. I cannot think of a better way to end my life and I cannot think of a more challenging way to end a letter.

We have looked at all seven churches. They are God's x-rays! They are as different as chalk and cheese. They are as different as day and night. No two of them are the same. But, the bottom line is this ... what about me? What about you? What about our church? I think it goes without saying, these are the last days; in fact, I would go so far as to say, these are the last of the last days. The countdown to the coming of Christ is getting lower every day.

With that in mind, the paramount message from the seven letters to the seven churches in chapters 2 and 3 is:

let us get back to God,

let us get back to his word,

let us get back to enjoying happy fellowship with him.

4

Touching the throne

We are moving into one of the most exciting portions you will come across anywhere in the word of God. There are many high points in Scripture, many significant peaks in terms of Christian teaching, many key passages which embrace the great doctrines of the faith, I think none can surpass what we have here in this duo of chapters, Revelation 4 and 5. Here we are touching the throne! And, you know, you cannot get much closer to the Lord than that!

The tremendous theme of exultation woven into the fabric of chapter 4 is: 'Let's worship the Lord ... he is the Creator ... he is the giver of life!' On a similar vein, the keynote of chapter 5 is also one of spontaneous worship but this time the difference is one of distinction for the inspired composition is: 'Let's worship the Lord ... he is our Redeemer ... he is the giver of new life!' I believe the lyrics of the old gospel song say it succinctly when they capture the wonder of that special moment when 'the great Creator became my Saviour.'

4:1

The incredible experience of John on the Isle of Patmos was that he was given a triple vision of the grace of God, the government of God, and the glory of God. The prophet Micaiah had a similar encounter when he saw the Lord sitting on his glorious throne 'and all the host of heaven standing by him on his right and on his left' (1 Kings 22:19). 'God reigns over the nations,' declared the Psalmist, 'God sits on his holy throne' (Psalm 47:8). The thrilling experience given to Isaiah after the death of King Uzziah when he saw an earthly throne vacant, he also saw a heavenly throne occupied (Isaiah 6:1). The unbelievable experience of Daniel was that he quickly realised that the God of heaven was the one in total control of events on planet earth and it suddenly dawned on him that God rules and God reigns (Daniel 7:9,10).

This illustrious quintet have one factor in common: in one way or another, all of them touched the throne! But John's experience was quite unique: he was summoned into heaven itself.

'*After this I looked,*' John writes, '*and there before me was a door standing open in heaven. And the voice I had first heard speaking to me like a trumpet said, "Come up here, and I will show you what must take place after this"*'

Even though John was still a prisoner on Patmos, a man well into his golden years, he is given a preview of coming attractions, he is given a pre-launch disclosure of things to come. He saw a sweeping panorama of God's prophetic programme in advance. It was a vista of God's agenda for the nations of the world. What a breathtaking moment that must have been! What we read in the remaining chapters of the book of Revelation is a record of what John saw with his own two eyes.

The hinge of the book

I think it is helpful to note that verse 1 begins and ends with the same two words: '*after this.*' These words actually form the hinge of Revelation. What we have here is a transition, we are progressing from point number two on to point number three in the index of the book as detailed for us in 1:19.

Now you see it, now you don't

We discovered in the previous chapter that the Lord has finished his engaging correspondence with the church at Laodicea which was the last of the seven letters to the seven churches in Asia Minor.

It is interesting to note that after this the church is never mentioned again in the book of Revelation. There is a full stop, a period, so far as the church as the body of Christ is concerned at the end of chapter 3. Seven times in chapters 2 and 3 we read, *'He who has an ear, let him hear what the Spirit says to the churches.'* Then in 13:9, we read, *'He who has an ear, let him hear.'* Did you detect the double difference there?

Number one, the Spirit is missing.

Number two, the church is missing!

Why is that the case? Well, it seems to me, the people of God who comprise the church are in heaven while those people who are left behind on planet earth are suffering in the Tribulation (that is the technical term given to the period of seven years between the two phases of the advent of Christ).

What's in a name?

Another intriguing fact is this, the church's favourite name for God is Father, but from chapter 4 until the end of chapter 19, he is not addressed as Father at all, not once; in actual fact, he is called God, the Lord, the Almighty, and a few other names by which he was commonly known in the Old Testament era.

A heartbeat from heaven

The inclusion of the word *'trumpet'* in verse 1 is highly suggestive. It bears comparison with what we have in 1 Thessalonians 4:13-18 and 1 Corinthians 15:52. You see, when Jesus returns to the air for his redeemed people, the world will not hear the dulcet tones of his voice, nor will they hear the trumpet sound. The ears of the sinner will be deaf, his eyes will be blind. If the truth be told, the rapture of the church will take place so fast that, literally, millions from all around the world will be missing in a fleeting moment. Those who love the Lord will be here on earth one minute and, before you have finished saying their name, they will be with Christ in the glory before the minute is up! In the 'twinkling of an eye' we will be in eternity ... it is as near as that, it is only a heartbeat away! In many ways, what we have here in verse 1 is a beautiful illustration of what will happen to God's people when the church age has run its course.

Heaven's open door policy

It is also worthwhile noting that in chapter 3 we saw a door closed and Christ was seeking entrance into a local fellowship of believers; now, in chapter 4, a door is wide open and we behold the regal splendour of our God for the open door leads us through into a throne room where the King is sitting! I like to think of it like this: it is John being ushered into the oval office of heaven. It is the place where decisions are made; it is the place where the Father, Son and Holy Spirit sit and confer with one another over important matters of state. Jeremiah was on the ball when he wrote of it in 17:12 as, 'a glorious throne, exalted from the beginning.'

Two times in the Apocalypse do we read of an open door. The first one is here in 4:1 and the second one is further on in 19:11. The first time, someone is going up in response to an invitation to come and see; the second occasion dictates that somebody comes down for there we see the coming King returning to planet earth on a white stallion!

4:2-3a

The mystery of the throne

For John to get from earth to heaven, something miraculous had to happen. There is no way he could get there under his own steam, that was a stark impossibility, it was a total non-starter; he had to be transported there, courtesy of another. His trip into the heavenly world is best explained by the choice of phrase in verse 2, where it informs us that he *'was in the Spirit.'* In other words, God would take him there. John was not transported into some mystical fantasy land nor was he taken into a daydream world of make-believe, this was no mind expanding hallucinatory vision; for John, this was real, he was taken where he had never been before, he was transported spiritually into the reality of heaven.

When he arrived, when he made it, John could not believe his eyes! It was sensational! It was spectacular! It was utterly amazing! It defied description for human language fails to convey what is seen; it is awesome, it is strange, it is unexpected. Like dear old John, we feel out of our depth for what we have here is something outside the realm of normal human experience. Most modern-day people who claim to have visions of heaven tend to emphasise the trivial and the bizarre. But John's vision focused on the glorious throne of God and the ineffable majesty of the one who sits on it.

The Bible records, *'and there before me was a throne in heaven with someone sitting on it.'* It is interesting to note that in verses 5, 6 and 9, there are four prepositions or phrases which all specifically relate to the throne. They are: *on* the throne, *around* the throne, *from* the throne, and *before* the throne. The mere mention of a throne in heaven is enough to convince us that the Lord is sovereign, he is in charge of global affairs; and his throne is immovable and permanent - when all else has come and gone, the throne will still be there! John MacArthur reminds us, 'That is a comforting realisation in light of the horror and trauma of the endtime events about to be revealed in chapters 6-19.'

On the throne

So John sees someone sitting on the throne. That is the posture of someone who is ruling and reigning! The thought is not one of resting because the work of redemption has been accomplished, but reigning because judgment is about to take place. Do you see how he describes him in verse 3? He says, *'And the one who sat there had the appearance of jasper and carnelian.'* That, in itself, is quite arresting. The one who occupies the throne is described as a stone. It is hard to imagine, isn't it. The bottom line is, how can any man even begin to describe God? But, the more you stop and think about it, the more you realise how wonderful a description it really is. We need to remember that, like Moses before him, John did not see the actual face of God. No man can do that and live to tell the rest of the story. John simply records that God revealed himself in a dazzling nimbus of coloured lights. It was a scintillating display of colour brilliantly refracting all the colours of the spectrum.

A jasper is a clear gem, as clear as crystal (21:11); it is a bit like our diamond. It is true to say that the glory of God is more perfect than any gem displayed in an up-market jewellers on the High Street. The carnelian is a stone comparable to the ruby.

The jasper speaks of the hardness connected with the government of God. His laws are fixed, they are firm, they are unyielding and unrelenting. That is what today's world badly needs - a firm hand. The jasper is, therefore, symbolic of his government and the way he runs it.

On the other hand, the carnelian is suggestive of the holiness connected with the government of God. It is a deep fiery, flashing, blood-red stone, and it powerfully reminds us that our God is a consuming fire. You will remember that the fire on Israel's altars was to burn on and on; it was never to go out. You see, so long as sin exists, God's attitude toward sin is one of burning holiness, it is one of blazing wrath. His anger against sin burns and flashes like the radiant glow of the carnelian.

When you put them both together, the jasper and the carnelian, they underline the humanity connected with the government of our God. You will recall the high priest in Israel wore on his multi-coloured outer garment, the ephod, a breastplate of twelve precious stones; on each stone was engraved a name of one of the twelve tribes of Israel. The thought is, they were always on his heart when he went into the presence of God on their behalf, and we all know the heart is the place of love and affection. The first stone (representing Reuben) and the last stone (representing Benjamin) of the twelve sons of Jacob was a jasper and a carnelian. As an aside, it is also possible that the names of Reuben ('behold, a son') and Benjamin ('son of my right hand') pictures God the Son, the Lord Jesus Christ, sitting at his Father's right hand in glory.

Whatever angle you choose to view it from, there was a hardness and a holiness associated with the throne; having said that, both characteristics are indissolubly linked to his humanity. You see, the one to whom all judgment is given, is himself, both God and man!

> **How does knowing that God's government is hard, holy and human, make you feel?**

4:3b-6

The majesty of the throne

When we look at the second part of verse 3, we discover there is *'a rainbow, resembling an emerald'* which *'encircled the throne.'* The information we have here is of the utmost significance and importance:

His judgment is independent

To mention that the rainbow went around the throne like a circle underlines the truth that perfection is symbolised. It also represents eternity for a circle has no beginning and no end. Because it was not merely an arc, but a complete circle, it indicates that in heaven all things are completed. The fact it was emerald in colour intimates that the judgment which is anticipated is directly related to planet earth.

His judgment has integrity

The whole scenario is a reminder that, in the final analysis, judgment when it comes will be in keeping with the covenant of God. It speaks of a God who keeps his promises. It speaks of a God who honours every commitment he has made. That is detailed for us as far back as Genesis 9:12-17 when God entered into a covenant with Noah which, he said, would continue 'for all generations to come.'

Even though the judgment anticipated here in the book of Revelation is imminent, the presence of the rainbow is a tangible token that God will be merciful when he strikes the earth. A similar truth is echoed in the impassioned prayer of Habakkuk where he pleads with the Lord, 'In wrath remember mercy' (Habakkuk 3:2). As John MacArthur has said, 'God's attributes always operate in perfect harmony. His wrath never operates at the expense of his faithfulness; his judgments never abrogate his promises. God's power and holiness would cause us to live in abject terror were it not for his faithfulness and mercy.'

Now, you will know as well as I do, a rainbow generally appears after the storm has passed. It normally appears in the sky when the storm has subsided, when the storm has abated. But here in chapter 4, we see the rainbow before the storm! We infer from this that, so far as the Christian is concerned, the storm is something we do not have to worry about. It will not affect the church at all for the emerald can also be taken to signify the colour of life. If that is the case, then the rainbow is a cameo of eternal life which guarantees that the future of the people of God is something to look forward to with bated breath, rather than a feeling of dread and apprehension.

The royal court

The next major item is found in verse 4, where we read that, *'Surrounding the throne were twenty-four other thrones, and seated on them were twenty-four elders. They were dressed in white and had crowns of gold on their heads.'*

This is the first time we come across these noble individuals where their relationship to the throne is of more than passing interest. They are around the throne of God in heaven and that is what needs to be emphasised. It is apparent that the rainbow was around the throne vertically while these persons are sitting around the throne horizontally. They are, as it were, the king's court. They function as a kind of jury and they underline the formal nature of the proceedings which John is privileged to watch. Their role is not to determine whether man is guilty or innocent, their primary role is to approve the righteous acts of the judge of all the earth.

The royal courtiers

One of the questions probably going through your mind at the moment is, can we identify these twenty-four elders? Who are they?

Are they angels? For what it is worth, I do not think they are angels for a couple of reasons. Number one, angels are not numbered and you find that alluded to in Hebrews 12:22 where the writer is talking about the 'heavenly Jerusalem, the city of the living God.' He goes on to tell us, 'You have come to thousands upon thousands of angels in joyful assembly.' We have here a great gathering of celebrating angels whom we join in praising God.

The second reason is that angels are not crowned or enthroned. When you look at 7:11 and compare it with 5:8-11, you find that the elders are clearly distinguished from the angels and the crown which they wear is the victor's crown (the Greek word *stephanos*) and we have no evidence in Scripture that angels receive rewards.

Are they the redeemed? It seems to me, the elders here probably represent the people of God in heaven, a people enthroned and a people rewarded. There were twenty-four courses of priests who came from the line of Aaron in the Old Testament temple system (1 Chronicles 24:3-5,18). When Daniel saw the thrones set up in 7:9 they were empty but, when John saw them, they had been filled. Could it be, since there were twelve tribes of Israel and twelve apostles that the number twenty-four symbolises the completion of the people of God? If you like, these elders comprise the leaders of our heavenly delegation.

'The entire picture,' one writers notes, 'is one of dignified seriousness, instant availability, and deep, genuine sincerity in service. There was no confusion, no casualness, no resistance, and no procrastination in the Lord's court.'

> The twenty-four elders represent believers in heaven who are both enthroned and rewarded. What does this tell us about God's grace towards us?

The golden crown

It is worth noting that the crowns they wear are available to each of us. There are five crowns mentioned in Scripture which are given as rewards to the Lord's own people.

The crown of incorruption (1 Corinthians 9:25) is given specially to those who live a disciplined life. It is for all those who run the race of life with a clear goal in view and with a definite sense of purpose.

The crown of life (James 1:12) is for those who, with patience, endure the hardest of trials. It is for those who hang in there when the going is incredibly tough.

The crown of rejoicing (1 Thessalonians 2:19,20) is designed for those who joyously express their faith. It is for those who are happy to share their faith with others; it is for those who take seriously the great commission in that they pull out all the stops as they seek to win men and women to Jesus Christ.

The crown of glory (1 Peter 5:1-4) is given particularly to those who show faithfulness to the truth of Scripture in all their ministry of the word of God.

The crown of righteousness (2 Timothy 4:8) is designated for those who love his appearing. It is for those keen believers who scan the horizon as they eagerly wait for the return of Jesus Christ.

You see, there is the potential for us to win something in that final day when we cross the finishing line in a blaze of glory! That is good news! Having said that, the downside is the New Testament also makes it very clear that there will be those in heaven who have nothing to show for it. Men and women who have nothing but leaves for the Master; they are there by the skin of their teeth. Because of the amazing grace of God, 'they are,' as Paul advises us in 1 Corinthians 3:15, 'saved, but only as one escaping through the flames.' They are the ones who have wasted their lives on God's second best and who, as John says in his epistle, have lost their reward. The possibility of securing a crown has been taken away from them.

> How does the prospect of receiving a crown spur you on in your Christian walk?

The white robes

The group of elders who we read about in verse 4 are said to be clothed in white robes and have crowns of gold on their heads. That, in itself, is most instructive for we read in the letters to the seven churches that these are the promises given to those who overcome (2:10; 3:5,21). Again, the white garments symbolise Christ's righteousness imputed to believers at salvation. It seems to me, that is another pointer in favour of these men being identified with the church of Jesus Christ.

Their awesome environment

I was captivated when I read the words of Psalm 89:7 to find that, no matter how wonderful and glorious it is for these men to be in the immediate presence of the Lord, to be so near to him, to be within a hair's breadth of him, their elevation to such unthinkable heights fades into oblivion when we realise that, 'He is more awesome than all who surround him.'

In other words, it does not matter one iota who you are, it does not even matter how close you are, the eternal God is still centre stage. The spotlight is shining on him!

He is transcendent.
He is unequalled.
He is unrivalled.
Our God is truly magnificent!

'Worthy, O worthy are You, Lord!
Worthy to be thanked and praised and worshipped and adored!'

A sound and light show

We discover from verse 5 that *'from the throne came flashes of lightning, rumblings and peals of thunder.'* It was not only what John saw with his eyes which was of considerable magnitude, it was also what he heard with his ears. John was treated to a sound and light show which was out of this world in terms of its impact on him as a spectator. The fast moving proceedings which are going on before him are accompanied by terrifying sights and sounds: thunder and lightning! The atmosphere was electric, highly charged with activity and energy. It is more than enough to make any grown man quake in his boots; it is a vivid reminder to all of us that it is 'a fearful thing to fall into the hands of the living God.'

The simplest way to explain it is that this sensational display announces a coming storm which will manifest God's presence, God's power and God's wrath in a mighty way. The combined forces of nature are harnessed and used by him to illustrate the power which he has at his disposal. This is not a one-off. It is something which is repeated several times in the book as a kind of reference point. On every occasion they are mentioned, they are indicative of the judgment of God against rampant evil. You find these audio-visual symbols spoken of in 8:5; 11:19; 16:18.

These phenomena are closely associated with the monumental moment when God gave the Law on Mount Sinai. Moses records in Exodus 19:16 that the mountain was covered by dark clouds, it was lit by flashes of lightning, and the earth shook constantly with great thundering rumbles. In fact, the sight was so awesome and impressive that the people of Israel were stunned with fear, they were numb. So, I think we can safely assume, these symbols represent the comprehensive judgment of God.

Seven lamps

The same verse informs us that *'before the throne, seven lamps were blazing. These are the seven spirits of God.'* The reference here is to the presence of the Holy Spirit on the morning of judgment. He is there in all his fulness and he is seen to be acting in the role of prosecutor of the human race.

We all know what his work is today in relation to the sinner: it is to reprove the world of sin, of righteousness, and of judgment to come (John 16:8-11). In that final day, when the age of grace has come to an end, as the omniscient one, he will have all the available facts at his disposal. No stone will be left unturned. All documentation will be laid bare before him and he will be seen to do what is right before God as the judge of all the earth. In that sense, the Holy Spirit is compared to a divine war torch as in Judges 7:16,20 and Nahum 2:3,4. The implication is that the comforter of those who love Christ will be the consumer of those who wilfully reject him!

It is fascinating to compare the seven lamps which we read about here with the seven-branched lampstand or *menorah* which was located in the holy place of the tabernacle and temple. Its main function was to cast light on the ark of the covenant and the mercy seat in the holy of holies. On a similar vein, the chief ministry of the Holy Spirit is to throw light on Jesus Christ in our lives so that we can see him and understand him better.

A sea of glass

Verse 6 provides us with a most unusual piece of data for we read, *'Also before the throne there was what looked like a sea of glass, clear as crystal.'* Something similar is mentioned in 15:2, where we read, *'And I saw what looked like a sea of glass mixed with fire.'* While the latter one is mingled with fire, this one is definitely not.

When you backtrack to Exodus 24:10, you find that Moses and a number of eminent leaders among the people received a similar manifestation of the presence of the Lord. We read, 'Under his feet was something like a pavement made of sapphire, clear as the sky itself.'

It is a well-established fact that ancient monarchs created something similar in front of their thrones. Such a no-go, don't-come-too-near area, indicated the separation between the king and his subjects. It emphasised their sense of royalty, it gave them a seriously inflated ego, it made them feel distinctly superior. They were aloof and they much preferred it that way; to all intents and purposes, they were unapproachable!

Perhaps the primary point of the sea of glass before the throne of God is to picture the unsullied holiness, the transcendent majesty, and the purity of God himself. This simply underscores the fact that he is wholly separate from his creation; it underlines the fact that he is God. The transparency of that sea of glass could reasonably draw attention to God's penetrating gaze into all things that take place on earth. If you like, he misses absolutely nothing! He sees all things!

Cheer leaders in heaven

'In the centre, around the throne, were four living creatures.' These creatures resemble the cherubim that the prophet Ezekiel saw in his visions in the early chapters of his prophecy and they are mentioned no fewer than twelve times in the first ten chapters of his book. When we listen to their praise in verse 8, they remind us of the seraphim of Isaiah 6. It seems, therefore, from reading between the lines, that this group of four angels has a distinctive role to play in the unfolding drama of God's plan.

Their proximity to God. It is apparent from the verse that these angels are closer to God than the other spirit messengers, as well as the elders, in that they have a unique position in relation to the throne.

Their role. I think it is well within the bounds of possibility to describe this quartet of angels as the worship leaders of heaven when you see the response to their actions. They certainly inspire everyone else in heaven to pour out their worship toward the one who sits upon the throne. They celebrate the government of God in their capacity as cheer leaders. They are intimately involved for they are at the heart of divine government.

Their significance. I was intrigued to read that *'they were covered with eyes, in front and behind.'* This statement is highly suggestive of the omniscience of the one who sits on the throne. These angelic beings do his bidding with a deep awareness of his desire and plan. The eyes are often used to represent the wisdom of our God. They enable us to think about his incredible powers of discernment, they focus on the remarkable insight which he has into every event of life, they home in on the fact that he is all-knowing.

Their mystery. We discover in verse 8 that they even had *'eyes under their wings.'* It is obviously difficult for you and me to visualise such a heavenly being in our mind. We have never seen one, we have never met one! At times, it can seem a little bizarre, there is almost an air of mystery surrounding them. It is surreal. It is the kind of scene you expect to see in a Steven Spielberg movie!

Nevertheless, no matter how weird they may appear to be, they are intrinsically wonderful because of the brilliant job which has been assigned to them. What a tremendous privilege is theirs!

4:7

Talking angels

In this verse, we are provided with an identikit picture of the four living creatures: *'The first living creature was like a lion, the second was like an ox, the third had a face like a man, the fourth was like a flying eagle.'* There are a couple of ways in which we can look at these four living creatures:

As symbols of God's creation and covenant. The faces of the living creatures parallel God's definitive statement in Genesis 9:10 where we read of the covenant he made with Noah, 'I now establish my covenant with you and with your descendants after you and with every living creature that was with you - the birds, the livestock and all the wild animals, all those that came out of the ark with you - every living creature on earth.'

Let me show you what I mean: the divine covenant is with Noah and you see that reflected in the face of the man; the birds are depicted by the flying eagle; the livestock are represented by the face of an ox; and all the wild animals correspond with the face of the lion. This view is given a lot of street credibility because of the presence of the emerald rainbow around the throne which, again, is a sign of the creation covenant.

God has a covenant with his creation and he rules his creation from his throne. The implication is that, irrespective of what happens down here on planet earth, his works will continue to praise him and all nature will join hands in worshipping him.

As an illustration of Christ. Matthew is the royal gospel of the King and is well illustrated by the lion. Mark emphasises the servant aspect of the Lord's ministry and is best seen in the ox. Luke presents Christ as the compassionate Son of Man and is obviously portrayed in the face of the man. The last gospel correspondent, John, conveys the idea that Christ is the Son of God, magnifying his deity and is, therefore, best likened to the flying eagle.

No matter which of the two views is your preferred option, two facts are beyond dispute.

Fact one: That each of the four faces reflects one particular aspect of the likeness of the Lord. John Phillips has commented in a rather succinct manner, 'They are so much like him because they are so much with him!'

Fact two: That they appear in this vision to enhance further the significance and glory of the throne of God.

It seems to me that what they are doing is even more important. These living creatures are saturated with a sense of the felt reality of the presence of God all around them. They are strangely aware of the closeness of God to them. The whole atmosphere is permeated with the undiluted wonder of their worship and praise.

> **The vision of the Almighty in this passage is awe-inspiring.**
> **What place does awe have in your worship?**

4:8

Singing angels

The four living creatures cannot contain themselves, they are bursting at the seams! *'Day and night they never stop saying: "Holy, holy, holy, is the Lord God Almighty, who was, and is, and is to come."'*

And so, all day, every day, all night, every night, they joyfully extol the wonders of his holiness, they magnify his power and ability, they declare the truth that our God is eternal. It is a continuous oratorio of praise and worship. It is unstoppable!

It is good to remind ourselves that angels celebrate and recognise the holiness of God. Three times over they acknowledge it. It is a triple affirmation of who he is in person and in nature. The old Puritan preacher, Jonathan Edwards, has written, 'Holiness is more than a mere attribute of God, it is the sum of all his attributes, the outshining of all that God is.'

That they repeat the word *'holy'* three times may be for added emphasis; in other words, they really believe it, they have no doubts as to the veracity of it, they are totally committed to it, they know it is true. On the other hand, it may be a coded reference to the Trinity, God in three persons, and in that sense, each word 'holy' refers to one member of the Godhead.

When they address him as *'Lord God Almighty,'* they appreciate something of his power, they recognise his omnipotence. Here is a God who can do anything but fail! This was how the Lord revealed himself to Abraham so long ago - he identified himself as one who is the strongest most powerful being, one who is utterly devoid of any weakness, one whose conquering power and overpowering strength none can oppose. He is a God who can do it!

It is interesting to note that the name *'Almighty'* is used nine times in the book of Revelation. The only other time you find it mentioned in the New Testament is in 2 Corinthians 6:18. Having said that, it is found at least 31 times in Job and that is a book which puts the spotlight on the power of God in the world of nature.

The picture emerging is fairly clear. Here is a God who acts, a God who moves, a God who performs ... and, every time he does something at a personal level, on a national scale, or even on a global front, it never contradicts his holiness. His attributes and his actions are working in perfect harmony.

The final phrase in the verse which encompasses three tenses is one we came across in the first chapter. It speaks of a God who is everlasting in his nature: he is above time, he is beyond time, he is outside of time. By the same token, he is ever present in current affairs. He is the God of today, the God of the now!

> God is the one 'who was, and is, and is to come'. What more could you do to cultivate this eternal perspective on life?

4:9,10

Praise is contagious!

Did you see what happened when the four living creatures sang their praises to the Lord? Their praise triggers off an immediate impromptu response from the elders; it is contagious, it is infectious! *'Whenever the living creatures give glory, honour and thanks to him who sits on the throne and who lives for ever and ever, the twenty-four elders fall down before him who sits on the throne, and worship him who lives for ever and ever. They lay their crowns before the throne.'*

The net result is that heaven reverberates with generous thanksgiving and praise unto the Lord. The whole place resonates with an unfinished symphony of joyful worship.

When they fall down before the exalted Lord, they give him his proper place, they recognise his sole authority and peerless position, they take the place of abject humility before the throne of God. When they cast their crowns at the feet of the Sovereign Lord, they realise that before him no-one else is worthy to wear a crown. His is the singular right to rule and to reign. He alone deserves the adoration, the adulation, and the acclaim of his people.

The thought behind the word *'worship'* in verse 10 is the telling forth of the worth of God. You see, what you think of God will be reflected in how you worship him, in the worth you ascribe to him. Someone has coined the phrase that worship is a royal acclamation of his worth. Like the elders and the four living creatures, we would do well to follow their example and become active members of the Lord's 'appreciation society!'

> 'What you think of God wll be reflected in how you worship him.' Using this truth, what practical steps could you take to improve and enhance your times of worship?

4:11

Praise is God-centred!

The stanza which the elders sing to him says, *'You are worthy, our Lord and God, to receive glory and honour and power, for you created all things, and by your will they were created and have their being.'* The theme of their song is on God's glory manifested in creation. Basically, they are acknowledging that he has the right both to redeem and to judge his creation. Their song anticipates paradise lost becoming paradise regained!

It tells me what he deserves:	God deserves glory, honour and power.
It tells me why he deserves it:	He is the great creator and the sustainer of all things.
	He is the one who brought something out of nothing.
	He is the one who keeps it all together.

It was John Calvin who said, 'Creation is the theatre of his glory.' The psalmist David says as much in the opening verses of Psalm 19. When that truth grips your heart and mind, you cannot do anything else but praise him.

> Commit John Calvin's comment to memory, and in the coming week, as you see God's creation around you, use it to inspire a number of one-sentence praises to the Lord!

Our response.   The best response is to borrow the words that we have here in verse 11, and make them a personal tribute to the one who is our God of grace, our God of glory. When you sing a song like that down here and when you hear a song like this emanating from over there, you realise there is nothing boring about heaven, there is nothing dull about the home of the redeemed! It is a land of eternal song! It is a place where praise is the norm!

These few words are a stirring melody of pure theology, it is biblical doctrine set to music. God is seen as the centre of everything, he is in the driving seat, he is on the throne. Heaven rules ... it is as simple as that!

Revelation 4 holds far more than just a casual glimpse into the world of heaven and the world of tomorrow. It is a vivid collage of images which focus our eyes on what true worship should be, at all times, and in all places.

5

Worthy is the Lamb!

Unforgettable! That is one way to describe John's experience when he was ushered into the throne room of heaven. It took his breath away ... he is lost for words ... he is spellbound. I think the indescribable thrill for John is to see the Lamb become the centre of everything - he sees him in a place of pre-eminence; and, slowly but surely, John is occupied with the Lamb, he is captivated by the one who is in the midst of the throne.

The Lamb is the theme of their song.
The Lamb is the centre of their thoughts.
The Lamb is the object of their adoration.

Why? Well, over there, 'the Lamb is all the glory in Immanuel's land!'

Now, for John, the Lamb steps from the shadows into the spotlight and every eye is focused on him. His every move is watched. That is what the poet had in mind when he wrote:

Lamb of God, our souls adore thee,
While upon thy face we gaze.

5:1

The scroll

'Then I saw in the right hand of him who sat on the throne a scroll with writing on both sides and sealed with seven seals.'

What is it? The scroll represents God's plan of history from eternity to eternity. It is an official document that determines the outcome of life on planet earth. It contains the secrets of our world's affairs and its history. It unveils the destiny of the nations. It shows the crisis and climax of global history. It could be spoken of as the title deeds of the earth. It represents all that the Father promised to the Son because of his sacrifice at Calvary.

Why was it sealed? Roman law required that a will be sealed seven times. History confirms that the wills of both Caesar Augustus and the Emperor Vespasian were sealed in this way. The book in the hand of God is a binding document which is relevant to the redemption of the world. It belongs to the one who has paid the price, therefore, he has the legal right to open it and reveal what is written on it.

We need to remember that many of the symbols contained in the book of Revelation must be interpreted in the light of the Old Testament. This one goes back to Jeremiah 32, a chapter which explains the thinking behind Jewish law as regards the redemption of a piece of land. Its primary purpose was to help those in Israel who fell behind with the repayment of their debts, who, as a result, automatically lost their land. The land was forfeited, but they were not without hope, because they had the right to buy back the land at some point in the future.

Even if they did not take advantage of this facility, even if they could not, the law made it absolutely clear that, after a prescribed period of time, their heir or next of kin could buy it. In this way, the land remained in the family and could be handed down from generation to generation.

In Jeremiah 32, God told his servant, the prophet, that his cousin Hanamel would ask him to redeem a field at Anathoth in the territory of Benjamin. Jeremiah did all he was meant to do and he bought it for a sum of seventeen shekels of silver. But there is more! When his cousin lost the plot of land, two scrolls or contracts containing the terms of reference for redeeming the land were drafted.

One scroll became a public record and was there for all to see. It was not sealed. The second scroll was rolled up and sealed with seven seals and placed for safe storage in a clay jar in the temple. It was brought out only when someone showed proof of his right to redeem the land. After this happened, the temple priest would retrieve the scroll, unseal it and read it. If everything was in order, the redeemer would receive it and be recognised as the rightful owner of the land.

You can see the analogy ... when God created all things, he gave the earth to man, but Adam sinned and lost it to Satan. Jesus is the Redeemer and he is the one who can buy it back. That is what he accomplished and achieved at Calvary. It is his. It belongs to him. We are told elsewhere that he is the heir of all things!

Why writing on both sides? This is quite amazing for the ancients hardly ever wrote on both sides of a scroll. Generally, only one side was formed smooth for writing, while the reverse side was rough and uneven. A scroll with writing on both sides is symbolic of a full and important message.

Why was it written? The fact that God's plan was written in the form of a scroll rather than simply being revealed by a voice is of huge significance. A written scroll is symbolic of that which is permanent. It is about truth which is indelible. What God has written, no-one can amend! It is truth unchanged, it is truth unchanging!

> **Knowing that the world's destiny is written and sealed; in what ways should that colour your response to global events?**

5:2

The challenge

'And I saw a mighty angel proclaiming in a loud voice, "Who is worthy to break the seals and open the scroll?"'

He is enquiring, who is worthy to rule the world? Who is fit to rule the world? Who can unravel the plot?

Who is the angel? The word *'mighty'* in relation to the angel could emphasise the importance of the angel and his message but it could also be a clue as to which angel is involved. Some Bible teachers hold that it refers to the angel Gabriel whose name means 'strength of God.' You will recall, it was Gabriel who communicated to Daniel about future events (Daniel 8:16).

The Greek word used here for *'proclaiming'* speaks of a herald passing on the precise message which he has been given. That means, he would make no comments on it, he would add no commentary to it, he would not attempt to explain it in any way; he would, simply, tell it like it is!

The fact that he conveyed the message with *'a loud voice'* implies that his message is one of great concern and of greater urgency. It underlines the gravity of the message and it underscores the sheer importance of what is being said. It is God's word and it cannot be taken lightly. God has spoken and that is it!

Who is worthy? The question posed by the angel is a probing one. He asked, *'who is worthy?'* He did not ask, 'who is willing?'

You know history as well as I do, down through the years there have been many who have been willing, they have been keen and enthusiastic to rule the world; it has been the dream of many a world leader, it has been the aspiration of many a dictator. The prospect of world domination has appealed to quite a few across the decades. For many religions, it has been their avowed intention, it has been their goal and ambition to rule the world! There are people today who are devotees of one cult or another who are fanatical in their pursuit of global supremacy, and woe betides anyone who stands in their way!

This has been the driving force behind many individuals over the centuries; it remains the ultimate thing to play for in the hands of some of those who are major players on the stage of world politics. Some of the key movers and shakers in today's generation will tell you as much. They have no inhibitions. This is what fires them. They eat it, they drink it, they sleep it ... it is a passion! Oh yes, they are willing! There is no question about that!

Maybe you are thinking, 'Ah, that's a bit far fetched ... you're pushing it too far, Sam.' Not really! I certainly do not think so. When you look back through the annals of history, it has all happened before and, we all know, history has an uncanny way of repeating itself!

You only have to go as far back as Nebuchadnezzar to see what I mean. He was number one in the pecking order so far as Babylon was concerned, but his empire soon fell. Alexander the Great thought he achieved a Utopian empire. He wept when there were no more worlds to conquer! In the space of a year, he was a dead man, and within a handful of years, his empire disintegrated. Julius Caesar led his legions across the face of Europe to impose the Pax Romana upon the world by force of arms. History tells us that Rome ultimately fell; there was moral corruption on the inside and there were assaults from the outside by northern barbarians. Charlemagne and Napoleon, each in his own way and in his own time, sought to place the world under the banner of France; Adolf Hitler in the last great war envisioned a worldwide Reich that would last for a millennium.

The graveyards of history are littered with fallen conquerors and their shattered dreams. They are yesterday's men. The best of men and the worst of men have all gone down this road. They have one common denominator: *they have all failed because not one of them was worthy!*

5:3

The response

'No-one in heaven or on earth or under the earth could open the scroll or even look inside it.' The question which echoed around the

world has been met with a stony silence! The response is nil. Nothing stirred, not a single person moved.

Heaven is searched in a vain attempt to find someone who can open the scroll, not even the angels who are before the throne of God can do anything about it. Not a single individual on earth has the ability to do anything about it: no man or woman, no politician, no prime minister or president, no world banker or industrialist, no pope or archbishop, no philosopher or leading thinker, no revolutionary here. No-one! And with an incredible stroke of the quill on the papyrus, we are told that no-one under the earth has the power to do anything about it either: no fallen angels, no spirits of departed men, not even the prince of darkness himself!

It is an eerie silence; there is a hush all around; you can feel the tension in the air. You can sense the impotence of man when faced with such a rousing challenge. This is a verse which beyond all others puts creation firmly in its place!

But wait a minute! There is something else to think about while we observe this scene. We have here what a good friend of mine refers to as an Agatha Christie red herring! There is another question to ask: *why could anyone not be found?* We know that the mystery of the missing worthy person is answered in the Lord Jesus Christ ... but, *where was he, if indeed he was not in heaven, on earth, or under the earth?* Where else *could* he be?

5:4

The impact

The fruitless search tears John apart. He is emotionally distraught for we read that he *'wept and wept because no-one was found who was worthy to open the scroll or look inside.'* Poor John! He is broken hearted. He is devastated. He breaks down and floods into tears. He just cannot control his feelings any longer. He is a fully grown man and he cries here like a young child who has passed through some traumatic experience. He knows that this world needs redemption, he knows it needs a leader. He knows the scroll must be opened and the seals broken for the purposes of God to be fulfilled. The fact that there was no-one worthy to do it spelt gloom into the mind of John. Horror gripped his soul, hopelessness gripped his heart, helplessness gripped his mind! Anne Graham Lotz says, 'He must have sobbed and sobbed with shame for the failure of the entire human race to be what God had originally intended it to be!'

If this was the way it was going to be, he felt that his life was in vain; it meant he had been exiled for no apparent reason. His many friends had been martyred for a lost cause. He weeps because he feels the plan of God will not come to pass, it will not come to fruition, it will all grind to a premature halt, the brakes will be applied to the unfolding drama of redemption. This is what really bothers him, this is the big problem, so far as John is concerned. Hence his display of raw emotion.

It is interesting to note that this is the first time any man has ever shed a tear in heaven! The good news is, it will be the last time for, as the old song tells us, 'Tears will never stain the streets of heaven.' Before you and I reach that far better land, we are told at the end of the book that *'he will wipe away all tears from our eyes!'*

> **What made John react with such depth of emotion? How do we respond when confronted with a lost world?**

5:5

The solution

The silence is broken as one of the elders says to John, *'Do not weep! See, the Lion of the tribe of Judah, the Root of David, has triumphed! He is able to open the scroll and its seven seals.'* And John sees the Lord Jesus Christ ... unrivalled and incomparable! It is a moment of high drama. God has solved the problem! The twenty-four elders of the heavenly council who meet in session around the throne know the answer. One of them moves across to where John is standing and divulges the secret to him. He informs him that someone has been found who is worthy and he tells him exactly who that someone is. In a kind of coded language, the elder introduces him as the *'Lion of the tribe of Judah, the root of David.'* John knows exactly who the elder is referring to, he knows well his Old Testament theology: it is the Lord Jesus Christ! It can be no other! He matches the description like no-one else can. We know that to be true. John knew that to be the case. It seems he just needed to be reminded of it another time.

The Messiah: The two names given to Christ in verse 5 are significant Jewish titles. The average Jew would be familiar with them because they are steeped in the ancient traditions of Judaism. They refer to a couple of old prophecies which predict that there would come one from the tribe of Judah and from the family of David who would ultimately rule the world. The first one is mentioned away back in Genesis 49 where we find Jacob on his deathbed. He has his twelve sons standing around him and he has a special word for each of them. In verses 8-12, he pronounces a blessing on his son, Judah. The second reference is mentioned in Isaiah 11:1,2.

These twin titles find their fulfilment when they converge in one person. Like two great rivers, they come together from different angles and form one which then flows on throughout eternity. They merge in the Messiah, the Christ, the Redeemer, the Saviour of the world. He is the focal point of world history, he is the focal point of Bible prophecy.

You see, the references here to the Lion of Judah and the Root of David are clear signs that Israel is coming back to centre stage as the end of human history approaches. As the scroll begins to unroll, God is calling Israel to the ultimate fulfilment of promises that were made to her so long ago. All of earth's history is moving toward a climax and the key to it all is the nation of Israel. The key to understanding history, the only way to make sense of history, is to see where Israel fits into the picture. The earth cannot be blessed until the nation of Israel is blessed!

Even though the Messiah came to Israel and Israel rejected its Messiah, and even though God has chosen the church as his instrument of ministry to the world from the time of Christ until now, the time of Israel's full restoration is just around the corner. It is coming and it is not too far distant!

The Old Testament prophets foretold it, John describes it here in the book of Revelation; the Messiah, the promised Lion of Judah, the Root of David, is coming to tie up the loose ends and bring to a glorious finale the consummation of the purposes of God.

Jesus alone has triumphed!

There is no human solution to the big problems facing the world today, there is no earthly panacea for the evils of the human race, there is no human answer to the important questions man is asking right now. In the words of the gospel song, our Lord is 'the Christ of every crisis.' He is the only one who can undo the tangles of this life. He is the only one who can unravel the mysteries of this world. He is the one the apostle John was told to look at, to fix his eyes on.

His titles: *'The Lion of the tribe of Judah, the Root of David.'* Each word in the title is worth pondering over, each word in the name has something special to say to us. It plugs the gaps in our thinking as to who Jesus really is. Here we are given a marvellous opportunity to dig a little deeper and, when we do that, we unearth some priceless treasures.

> *The lion tells me of his majesty.*
> *The tribe suggests to me his humanity.*
> *The thought of Judah conveys to me his nationality.*
> *The root speaks of his deity.*

We need to understand, so far as his humanity was concerned, he had his roots in David; but, so far as his deity is concerned, he is the Root of David. At one and the same time, he is both David's Lord and great David's, greater Son. He is the Eternal One, the Ancient of Days, the God who is from everlasting to everlasting.

The mention of the name David reminds me of his royalty.

Did you see what he has done? He has triumphed! He has prevailed! And that speaks of his victory. We know this to be absolutely true. It is watertight.

John goes on to advise us, *'He is able to open the scroll and its seven seals.'* Here is one who, in response to the question from the angel, can step forward into the limelight and take the scroll and do what needs to be done in relation to it. Here is one who is worthy! The elder said to John, *'See.'* When John turned around, what do you think he saw? Did he see a lion? That is what you would expect, isn't it!

> **What qualities do you think made Jesus alone 'worthy'?**

5:6

What John saw: a lamb!

'Then I saw a lamb, looking as if it had been slain, standing in the centre of the throne, encircled by the four living creatures and the elders.' What a moment it must have been for John! He was expecting a lion and all he saw was a lamb! I cannot help but wonder what his initial reaction was! Scripture is silent, it does not tell us.

Seems strange, yet the more you stop and think about it, the more it all makes good sense. What we have here are two themes which are right at the heart of the Old Testament. The lion speaks of majesty and power, rule and authority whilst the lamb is a symbol of meekness, innocence and sacrifice.

Lions conquer ... lambs submit. Lions roar ... lambs go to slaughter.

> **Are there situations in your life at present where you need to overcome using the qualities of the Lamb?**

When the elder announces a lion and then introduces John to a lamb, the meaning is clear. Here is one who conquers by submitting;

here is one who is worthy of power and authority by reason of his meekness, innocence and sacrifice. Here, bound together in a powerful overlapping image is the Lion-Lamb, the one who is the fulfilment of God's earthly promises to Israel and his heavenly calling of the church.

Leon Morris makes the observation that most nations, looking for a symbol of strength, choose powerful animals or birds of prey - the Russian bear, the British lion, the American spread eagle and so on. 'It is only the kingdom of heaven that would dare to use as its symbol of might, not the Lion for which John was looking but the helpless Lamb, and at that, a slain Lamb.'

Jesus is spoken of as *'the Lamb'* at least twenty-eight times in the book of Revelation. God's anger is depicted as *'the wrath of the Lamb'* in 6:16; cleansing is *'by the blood of the Lamb'* in 7:14; the church is seen as *'the bride of the Lamb'* in 19:7; the massed choirs of heaven praise him with a song titled, *'Worthy is the Lamb'* in 5:12.

What is even more remarkable is this, the Greek word for *'lamb'* is a most unusual word. It means, 'a little pet lamb.' This is fantastic! Satan is described as a great red dragon, world power is in the hands of a fearful beast, the forces of hell are everywhere, and against all this, God sets a little lamb! At first glance, it seems a disastrous mismatch to pit a lamb against such colossal opposition, but God knows exactly what he is doing. He has the last laugh!

Did you see where the Lamb is? He is in heaven; he is in the midst; he is at the throne! No longer do we see him in a manger in a cattle shed; no more is he found wandering through the streets of the golden city of Jerusalem. You will not see him hanging on a cross of shame nor even buried in a borrowed tomb in a beautiful floral garden. He is in the glory! He is at the Father's right hand! He is exalted far above all! This is tremendous - it means he has defeated every enemy, it means he controls events on earth from his operations room in heaven, it means he knows precisely what is happening anywhere, at any time. He has his finger on the pulse. Here is one whose suffering has been turned into glory! That has to be good news for the people of God for he has promised to do the same for us!

How John saw the Lamb

He saw him as a Lamb *'looking as if it had been slain.'* This is incredible! The Greek verb is in the perfect tense indicating a past event which is effective today! There is the power of the blood of Calvary! There is the wonder-working power of the death of Christ! It was effective then and, two millennia down the road, it is no less effective now!

> Eternity in the past knew no other future than Calvary,
> eternity in the future knows no other past than Calvary.

And here is where my friend believes we find the solution to the mystery of the missing worthy person! She suggests that the real question in verse 3 is not *where* but *when*. If the crucifixion had not yet taken place, then it did not matter where the Lord was! He could be in heaven, he could be on earth, he could be under the earth, but without having made the supreme sacrifice for the redemption of mankind, even he at that point could not have opened the scroll! And yet, suddenly, he is there, *worthy* to do the task! Crucified and resurrected and worthy!

Calvary is the hinge on which the door of redemption turns. The cross makes a difference!

John also saw him ready to proceed with his mission. When you flick back in your Bible to Hebrews 1, you find the Lamb is seated at the Father's right hand, his work of redemption is finished. The job he came to do at Calvary is complete so far as purchasing our salvation is concerned.

But here, in verse 6, we see him *standing*. It seems to suggest that he is just about to pick up the pieces and get on with the work the Father has given him to do. His is an ongoing mission in relation to the world; in that sense, it is one that will be complete only when eternity begins at the end of time.

He is omni ...

He saw him with *'seven horns and seven eyes, which are the seven spirits of God sent out into all the earth.'* The seven horns speak of one who is omnipotent, one who is all-powerful, one who can do anything, one who is all-strong. The seven eyes remind us he is omniscient, for here is one who knows everything, one who is all-seeing, one who is intelligent and discerning. He has total understanding of the events and dynamics of human history. He is a God who is aware! Putting both traits together, we are reminded of the words of the apostle Paul who told us that in Christ we have 'the power of God and the wisdom of God' combined. We are informed that he is omnipresent for he is everywhere; he is the Lamb in all situations. What we have here are the attributes of deity, qualities you will not find in anyone else, apart from our Redeemer.

> *We have perfection in the Lamb without spot or blemish.*
> *We have power in the Lion of the tribe of Judah.*
> *We have perception in the Lord of all knowledge and wisdom.*

This is no ordinary Lamb ... this is God in the person of his Son, the Lord Jesus Christ!

> **The horns and eyes of verse 6 refer to Jesus as all-seeing and all-knowing. In what ways is this a comfort, and in what sense is it a spur, in your daily life?**

5:7

The Lamb takes the scroll

'He came and took the scroll from the right hand of him who sat on the throne.' John is so matter-of-fact and yet it is no less thrilling for that! Here is the one who can do it! Here is the only one who can do it! The big question is, why can Christ step forward and claim the title deeds to planet earth? Because he can honestly say:

> *The world is mine by right of creation, I made it!*
> *The world is mine by right of Calvary, I redeemed it!*

The world is mine by right of conquest, I am coming back again to it!

Jesus Christ is the heir of all things! He is undisputed in his power in the universe. The reins of the government of the world passed into his nail-scarred palm! The motto of the Moravian church is an excellent one in this context; it says, 'The Lamb has conquered!'

5:8

The response of the elders and four living creatures

'When he had taken it, the four living creatures and the twenty-four elders fell down before the Lamb.' They fall down and worship! They could not do anything better than that! They bow their knees before him, they acknowledge his supremacy, they recognise his sovereignty.

'Each one had a harp.' The harp, as you probably realise, was the traditional instrument of worship from the Old Testament. You find it mentioned especially in the Psalms (see Psalms 33, 98, 147). I love to hear the music of the harp. It does something for me, deep inside. It is special. To think, when we get to heaven, we will hear it over there, that for me has to be the icing on the cake. This is reality, not fantasy!

The harp symbolises the music of inanimate creation. Not only will all human beings glorify God but all of creation will give praise and worship to him. You see this in many of the Psalms. Just as the strings of the harp vibrate in harmony, so one day will the whole of creation vibrate in the harmonious worship of God.

'And they were holding golden bowls full of incense, which are the prayers of the saints.' These elders have a priestly role in the presence of the Lord as they present the prayers of the saints to God. We first come across the altar of incense in the tabernacle and later on in the temple. It was located in the holy place along with two other pieces of furniture: the table of shewbread and the seven-branched lampstand. It stood directly in front of the veil which separated the holy place from the holy of holies.

When the priest stood at the golden altar, as it was called, he was representing the people of Israel before the Lord. The incense rising from the altar typifies the people's prayers ascending to the courts of heaven. Prayer is seen here as a fragrant offering to the Lord. It emits a beautiful perfume, an aroma which God breathes in. It is something which brings immense joy to the heart of God when his people spend time in intercession.

There are a couple of interesting thoughts which spring to mind when thinking about prayer in this context. The first, and it is only a possibility, is that the church in heaven will be praying for those who become believers in the dark days of the Tribulation period as well as for the nation of Israel. It would seem that those who are with the Lord will be conscious of what is happening down here on earth. The other suggestion is that these prayers represent the long-standing prayer of God's people which our Lord instructed us in Matthew 6:10 to pray, 'Your kingdom come.'

5:9,10

'And they sang a new song.' Their immediate reaction is one of positive praise for they recognise his so great salvation! They cannot contain themselves any longer so they break forth into song. It is a benediction of praise, it is a great doxology.

It is a brand *new* song! The Greek word used here for *'new'* does not mean 'new' from the standpoint of time, but 'new' in terms of quality. It is fresh, it is unique, it is original, it has never been heard before! (This is fascinating for when we turn back to the Psalms we find they speak often of singing 'a new song' to the Lord. We find it in Psalms 33:3; 40:3; 96:1; 98:1, to name but a few. The prophet Isaiah jumps on the bandwagon and tells us in 42:10 to 'Sing to the Lord a new song, his praise from the ends of the earth.' We read in 14:3 that the 144,000 Jewish believers from the Tribulation do something similar; the only difference is, theirs is a song unique to them for no-one else could learn it!)

The words of this new song are recorded for us in verses 9 and 10: *'You are worthy to take the scroll and to open its seals, because you were slain and, with your blood, you purchased men for God from every tribe and language and people and nation. You have made them to be a kingdom and priests to serve our God, and they will reign on the earth.'*

> **The Lord's redemption is as wide as the world (verse 9). In what circumstances are you in danger of being exclusive when God wants us to be inclusive?**

I think we can learn some wonderful truths from this song which is expressly dedicated to the Lamb:

It is a **worship** song for it tells us, he is worthy! It puts the main beam on Jesus. It is a song with an **evangelistic** thrust for it reminds us that he paid the price for our salvation. Isn't it great to know that heaven sings about the cross and makes much of his precious blood. It is a song with a **missionary** emphasis for it reaches to the ends of the earth; it embraces all men everywhere. God's love is for the world; it does not matter what one's ethnic origin may be, it does not matter what colour one's skin may be, God has a big heart for ordinary people and his compassion reaches to the farthest outposts on planet earth. It is multinational, it is multicultural, it is multiracial. It is a **devotional** song for it reminds us of our unique position in that we are a kingdom of priests. We have power with God and power with men; we have all the majesty of a prince as we exercise the ministry of a priest. And it is a song with a **prophetic** slant for it tells us of a coming day when we will reign with him down here in this old world. The focus is on the coming millennial kingdom, a thousand years of Jesus rule, an era when Jesus will reign and the glory of the Lord will cover the earth as the waters cover the sea.

> **What privileges and power do we possess as 'priests to serve our God'?**

5:11-13

The song of the angels

John is captivated with all that is happening around him. He looked a second time and he *'heard the voice of many angels, numbering thousands upon thousands, and ten thousand times ten thousand. They encircled the throne and the living creatures and the elders. In a loud voice they sang, "Worthy is the Lamb, who was slain, to receive power and wealth and wisdom and strength and honour and glory and praise!"'*

It is a multitude of angels, an innumerable company! There are so many of them, there are too many to count! But that is not the end of the story. There is more!

The song of all creation

John continues, *'Then I heard every creature in heaven and on earth and under the earth and on the sea, and all that is in them, singing, "To him who sits on the throne and to the Lamb be praise and honour and glory and power, for ever and ever, Amen."'*

It is incredible, isn't it? This vast congregation offering praise to the Lord is not confined to heaven, it is universal, it is global, it is everywhere! It is above the earth, it is on the earth, it is under the earth. It is from every conceivable corner. The entire universe rocked in praise, the entire universe roared in acclamation to the Lamb upon the throne. There is tumultuous praise ringing out! It is a massed choir in a celebration of the greatness of God! Ah, the one who is unequalled in position and undisputed in power also receives universal praise.

The praise item contains seven characteristics thereby indicating the fulness of worship that he deserves. Everything you can think of in terms of adoration should be given to him. Four of these seven features are repeated in the final song which is ascribed to the one who sits on the throne as well as to the Lamb. And, you know, it is not just for a year or two, it lasts for eternity, it is for ever and ever!

5:14

The inevitable response

It all comes to a glorious climax when the four living creatures say *'amen'* and we also read in verse 14 that *'the elders fell down and worshipped.'* It seems to me, there is no option, there is no alternative, there is nothing else we can do but follow their noble example and fall down before him and worship! Josiah Conder put it this way,

> *In thee most perfectly expressed,*
> *The Father's glories shine;*
> *Of the full deity possessed,*
> *Eternally divine:*
> *Worthy, O Lamb of God, art thou,*
> *That every knee to thee should bow.*

Well may we say, along with them, 'Amen!'

6

Four riders on the horizon

In the previous two chapters we found ourselves in heaven ... we were close to the throne of God; we were aware of the dazzling majesty of the Lamb upon the throne; we were conscious of the glowing, blazing reflection of God's glory emanating from the throne. Now the picture changes dramatically to a heart-stopping scene on planet earth. Before, there was nothing but spontaneous praise and worship; now, there is one terrifying judgment hard on the heels of another.

When the trumpet sounds ...

> The church will be gone.
> The Holy Spirit will be removed.
> The salt and light will be absent!

Big trouble begins ...

These are days of unprecedented Tribulation, they are Satan's years when he will initiate and implement an orchestrated campaign of terror throughout the world. You can read all about it in Joel and in quite a few of the other Minor Prophets, you can find out more in Matthew 24 in Jesus' Olivet discourse. It makes the hair stand on the back of your neck. It is a period of seven years when man will be under the domination of the devil to such an extent that he has never known before; it will be a time of unparalleled trouble.

It seems to me, the storm clouds are already gathering. There is tension in the air. When you talk to Joe Public on the Main Street or in the shopping mall, he is not exactly oozing with confidence either; there is an air of pessimism, a sense of ominous foreboding hangs over his head like a dark cloud. The average person is uneasy and apprehensive. That is the mood we sense in the affairs of the world in our day and generation.

It is a well documented fact, the globe bristles with all sorts of sophisticated weaponry. There is barely a day goes by when we do not hear some passing reference to nuclear weapons, chemical weapons, the arsenals of a worldwide Armageddon. The world still shudders at the very real possibility of economic, ecological and energy crises. Poverty, hunger, terrorism, AIDS and crime, are just a handful of the problems that tear at the fabric of our society.

I can assure you, I am not paranoid. You do not only find what I am saying in the Christian press, you expect it there; you find it splashed across the front pages of the secular media as well. I am not an alarmist ... but I am sounding an alarm! And there is a big difference between the two. When you turn back to the pages of Scripture, you find the Bible has long predicted such a global crisis and in chapter 6 we begin to see that crisis take shape; it is tomorrow's news today.

The time scale

When is it all going to take place, is the big question! Where do these pieces slot into God's prophetic timeline? I believe if we answer that one, we will make life a lot easier for ourselves when we get into the thick of the book of Revelation. I think one of the easiest ways to satisfactorily explain it is to turn back to Daniel 9:24-27.

That chapter has been variously described but prophetic pundits generally feel it is the backbone of Bible prophecy, the spinal cord of prophetic truth. Daniel describes a great calendar of events spanning not just centuries but millennia. They reach from his own day right on into our own future.

The seventy weeks: 490 years

This unique calendar is marked out as a time span of what Daniel calls 'seventy weeks.' These weeks are not seven day weeks as in Sunday through to Saturday; they make a lot more sense when they are interpreted as weeks of years. This means each week corresponds to a seven year period. From Daniel's perspective, therefore, his vision encompassed a period of 490 years. [for a fuller explanation of this, see my commentary on the book of Daniel entitled *Our God Reigns!*]

445 BC: the start of the prophecy

We are left in no doubt as to the starting point of this operation. It was the year 445 BC when the go-ahead was given for the rebuilding of the walls of Jerusalem in the days of Artaxerxes. It was then, unknown to him, that the prophetic time clock started ticking. You can read all about that exciting building project in the early chapters of Nehemiah.

31 AD: the presentation of the Messiah

The finishing point of this 69 weeks or 483 years is when Messiah was presented as the Prince or the Anointed One. This is surely a reference to his triumphal entry on Palm Sunday into the city of Jerusalem on the back of a donkey. That was when the milling crowds gave him the green carpet treatment and they hailed him with the words, 'Behold your king!' Sir Robert Anderson of Scotland Yard fame, has calculated that from the first day to the last day, there is a total of 173,880 days. We need to realise that figure is derived from the Hebrew calendar which is based on a 360-day lunar year. It is remarkable, but not in the least surprising, that this is equivalent to 483 years, just as the prophet said it would be.

It is amazing, five centuries, 500 years before the event, God drew an 'X' on the exact date Jesus would appear as the long-awaited son of David. What is the big deal, you might be wondering! It means, if the Jews living in the time of Jesus had studied the book of Daniel they would have realised that, before their very eyes, prophecy was being literally fulfilled! In the bright spotlight of Daniel's prophecy, Jesus could hardly be missed. This was Jerusalem's golden day!

So what we can say is this: all of this is water under the bridge. The 483 years have been consigned to the annals of history. You can read all about them in detail in any decent encyclopaedia. They are gathering dust in the mists of antiquity.

The remaining 7 years

So far so good, but we have accounted for only 483 years; we are still left with an instalment of seven years to match the total of 490 years. The key question is, what happened to the missing seven years? Where have they gone? Where do they fit in God's prophetic agenda?

It seems to me, the events Daniel was told about concerning this period of time have not happened, as yet. So far as God's schedule is concerned, they are still in the future and when they do occur they will be closely associated with the nation of Israel.

Jesus himself refers to these occurrences in the final week of Daniel's prophecy in his great prophetic sermon recorded in Matthew 24. Before his death on the cross at Calvary, as he talked with his disciples on the Mount of Olives, he told them what must come to pass by sketching for them a panorama of endtime happenings. He filled them in on all the vital details, he gave them a rundown on his prophetic programme of the ages. You know, when you sift your way through this comprehensive outline, you quickly realise these guys were privy to an enormous amount of information.

Jesus, in the course of his comments, referred several times to what he calls 'the end of the age,' and other times he just spoke about 'the end.' That little phrase is one he borrowed from the book of Daniel for the old prophet used it over and over again. To me, it is as clear as crystal. The final seven year period which we have anticipated in Daniel 9 is exactly the same circumstance Jesus is referring to when he uses phrases like this. The two concepts dovetail together beautifully. They fit perfectly like two pieces made for each other in a jigsaw puzzle. I personally find this quite thrilling. It has nothing to do with coincidence, it has everything to do with inspiration. It is during these significant years that Israel will once again be brought centre stage in relation to world events. At this moment in time she will be back on track and running on the mainline.

This seven year period which Daniel and the Lord Jesus both talk about actually comprises the fascinating and sometimes frightening series of episodes which we read about in the book of Revelation. There is a considerable overlap between what they say and what you have here in chapters 6-19, one throws a lot of light on the other.

Three action-packed sections:

Chapters 6-9	The first three and a half years
Chapters 10-14	The events which transpire in the middle of the Tribulation
Chapters 15-19	The final three and a half years

Three phases of God's judgment:

Phase 1   occurs as each of the seven seals is opened one at a time. This is a time when the Lamb is prominent.

Phase 2   is ushered in with the sounding of the first of seven trumpets and when each one is heard some further catastrophe happens in the world. Angels are hyperactive on the front line. During this period Satan rules the world.

Phase 3   takes place when the seven bowls of God's wrath are systematically poured out on planet earth. It is clear that God himself is directing events.

Under this heptad of severe judgments, the world is ultimately rescued by God at the second coming of Jesus Christ in power and glory. It appears that what we have in chapters 6 and 7 is a preview of what will happen in the early days of this awful term of Tribulation. It is a horrendous era characterised by three R's: the R of retribution, the R of response, and the R of redemption.

6:1,2

The chapter opens with John sitting in the grandstand as a spectator watching all that is happening down on the field of play. It is worth noting that God does not rush into anything, he bides his time for each seal is opened one at a time! There is almost a sense of reluctance on his part. If he wanted, he could judge all at once, he could get it over and done with in a matter of milliseconds. As someone has said, 'He could just blink his eye and send planet earth spinning out of control, flinging the human race off into the oblivion of the universe.'

The Lamb opens the first seal

John *'watched as the Lamb opened the first of the seven seals.'* Obviously the Lord has the scroll in his hand as he opens seal number one. He goes through the same procedure four times and on each occasion it is followed by an invitation from one of the four living creatures.

John informs us, *'Then I heard one of the four living creatures say in a voice like thunder, "Come!"'* The message from them is fairly clear to John. He cannot mistake it. It is a single word, *'come!'* It is interesting to note that the sound of their voice is compared to thunder. It portends coming judgment; it is an omen that a storm is about to break; it is a signal that no matter how bad it is today, there is worse to come. It is the tone of majesty and might!

The first mention of thunder in the Bible is in connection with God's judgment upon Egypt in Exodus 9:23. This voice as a clap of thunder sounds at the beginning of the Tribulation period, the time of 'Jacob's trouble' that we read of in Jeremiah 30:7. It appears that the volume is turned higher as the thunder rolls with increasing crescendo for seven years until the lightning of Christ's second coming to the earth strikes! You find that allusion in Matthew 24:27.

The first scene: a white stallion bearing a dark prince

Then John writes, *'I looked, and there before me was a white horse! Its rider held a bow and he was given a crown, and he rode out as a conqueror bent on conquest.'* This must have been quite a spectacle for the aged John.

We have here a dark rider on a white horse. He enters the world scene with a flashing smile and exuding an air of total confidence. He chooses for his grand entrance a white horse, the symbol of a conqueror in oriental imagery. At the beginning of the Tribulation this shady individual enters as a victorious leader.

(You probably realise there are two riders on white horses in the book of Revelation. The first one is here and the second one is in chapter 19. The first is this fellow with a bow in his hand and a victor's crown on his head; the second is another man with a sword for his weapon and a kingly crown upon his head. These two men are diametrically opposed; they are as different as day and night, as chalk and cheese. There is no way that the rider in chapter 6 could be identified as the Lord Jesus Christ. But, when we come to chapter 19, that is exactly who it is! There is no problem there, at all!)

The person we are dealing with here in verse 2 is none other than the Antichrist, the great counterfeit, the imitation Christ; he is the devil's Messiah, he is Satan's superman.

Oh, he may have a crown on his head but it is only a victor's crown, he has been crowned by Satan! The crown that adorns the brow of our Saviour is a kingly crown, it is a royal diadem. There is no comparison between the two of them.

A bow with no arrows!

Did you see what this rider has in his hand? It is a bow! He has a bow but he does not have any arrows! You see, this future world dictator begins his career as a peacemaker, he lulls people into a false sense of security.

Here is one who will successfully unite the nations of the world; here is one who will effectively solve many of the problems currently being experienced in the Middle East; here is one whose help will not only be welcomed, it will be sought; here is one who leads a bloodless coup in the corridors of power for he promotes peace in the midst of global turmoil; here is one who is the greatest con-man of all time, the cleverest mimic ever to walk on the face of the earth ... he will conquer without war.

The world of today is actively looking for someone who fits the bill; they are looking for a charismatic Mr Fixit. So, when this hero arrives on the stage, his PR team will not have much work to do. The man on the street will welcome him with wide open arms; ordinary, decent people will worship him for they see him as a kind of divine superstar.

Men and women, fellas and girls, your neighbours and mine, will wonder after him for they see him as the greatest thing since sliced bread.

Delusion!

This is the moment which the Apostle Paul talked about in 2 Thessalonians 2:11,12 where he writes about 'a powerful delusion.' He tells us, in that day, men who refused to believe the truth as it is in Jesus Christ will be so blinded that they will believe the lie, they will swallow all that this man tells them. It is strange, but true.

We read in John 5:43 that the nations which turned their back on Jesus Christ will be ready to receive the devil's Christ. I cannot explain it but I am quite prepared to believe it. People will heave an enormous sigh of relief believing their future will be a million times better than they could ever have imagined. This man will breathe hope into their hearts, he will promise prosperity, he will make them feel good about themselves, and he will present himself to them as one who is the answer to their prayers. And that spells delusion, with a capital D!

The worrying reality is, this deceiving horseman is no stranger in today's world. It is fairly obvious to any clear-headed person that we live in an age of runaway deception. In fact, it seems to me, the more outrageous the lie, the more people seem to believe it!

> **What steps can we take to guard ourselves against being deluded?**

6:3,4

The Lamb opens the second seal

The second living creature instructs John to *'Come!'* And, as before, John responds.

The second scene: a red horse bearing a sinister warrior

This time John says, *'Then another horse came out, a fiery red one. Its rider was given power to take peace from the earth and to make men slay each other. To him was given a large sword.'*

A sword in his hand!

First of all, you see him with a bow in his hand; this time around, it is all so different. It is all change. The bow has gone; it is a sword he is wielding now! And he is not afraid to use it! You see, what began as a peace mission ends in hostility and bloodshed. The world's euphoric mood of peace and harmony will be rudely shattered, it will be short-lived as the second horse and rider appear on the scene. When the people say, 'Peace, peace,' the chilling reality is, 'there is no peace.'

Three things happen when this man appears: *world peace is ended, many people are killed, and military power is placed in the hands of one man.*

The red horseman represents not only nation rising against nation and kingdom against kingdom, but man fighting against individual man. This is class war, race war, and even religious war. It is civil unrest and anarchy. It is the kind of thing that takes place when social order breaks down, when mobs of people take to the streets and begin killing with abandon. He ushers in a time of murder, assassination, bloodshed and revolution; he presides over a maelstrom of rebellion and revolt!

The 1989 massacre of Tiananmen Square in China is a microcosm of what will take place when the rider on the red horse brings his war machine into full force; we have all watched the news flashes on our television screens ... live pictures beamed into our homes from around the world of such alarming, blood-curdling events.

The *'large sword'* which the rider has been given was in John's day seen as a weapon of mass destruction. It was a powerful tool in the wrong pair of hands. It is even worse when you realise that this tyrant is empowered and energised by the devil himself.

The question needs to be asked, 'Does the Bible envisage a day when a battle will be fought with the weapons of mass destruction which we now see stockpiled around the world?' I am not looking for an answer but it is something to seriously think about.

Destruction!

Down through history we have become increasingly aware that red is often a colour associated with terror and terrorist organisations. I think it is quite ironic that in the book of Revelation you see the devil described as the great *'red'* dragon and the Antichrist portrayed in chapter 17 as a *'scarlet beast.'*

The message is coming out loud and clear: destruction follows in the wake of delusion.

It is a proven fact of history that when a devil inspired leader comes upon the world stage with big ideas of conquest in his evil mind, there always follows war and havoc and destruction. General Omar Bradley once said about our generation, 'We know more about war than about peace. We know more about killing than about living. We are a world of nuclear giants and ethical infants.' Sober words, indeed.

6:5,6

The Lamb opens the third seal

In the same pattern as before, the third living creature instructs John to *'Come!'* John is startled and shocked by what he sees, it leaves him dismayed and taken aback.

The third scene: a black horse bearing a cunning merchandiser

John describes the scene: *'There before me was a black horse! Its rider was holding a pair of scales in his hand. Then I heard what sounded like a voice among the four living creatures saying, "A quart of wheat for a day's wages, and three quarts of barley for a day's wages, and do not damage the oil and the wine!"'*

No matter where you look in the world, you usually find hard times come to a country when it is caught up in some kind of internal conflict. When war comes, food is often in short supply. It seems to me, the black horse of famine rides behind the red horse of war during the Tribulation bringing worldwide starvation to the citizens of planet earth.

A pair of scales

One of the inevitable outcomes of such a state of affairs will be seen in the market place where prices will change dramatically. The economic balance is going to be altered because the world economy will be bankrupt. With the modern stock markets in New York, Tokyo, Frankfurt, Paris, London, and others now tied together, it is easy to see how the crash of one would lead to the crash of others in a domino effect. Inflation is a foregone conclusion and, in spite of all the efforts of governments and banking moguls, it will spiral out of control.

It is the old story: when the strong men go off to war and the country's resources are poured into armaments, the availability of food drops, while prices soar. John informs us here that a day's pay will not buy very much in the supermarket - a quart of wheat or three quarts of barley. Not much of a choice is there!

The problem is, inflation will cause prices to rise so high that a man will have to work all day to make enough money to buy enough wheat for one meal for his family. That is basic. It is almost as if the breadwinner will take his hard-earned pittance to the central market and be measured out his ration.

The mention of barley adds a new dimension to the whole scenario for barley is the food they fed to their animals. Families will turn to this kind of food in order to survive. It may be a panic measure but when you are faced with crying children who have hunger pangs clawing away at their tummies, what alternative is there? It is the mindset which articulates, 'I can have three meals a day of barley whilst I can have only one meal a day of wheat.'

You are probably familiar with the phrase, 'The rich get richer and the poor get poorer.' That is what is happening right here for we are talking about luxury items like oil and wine. These products will not be affected by the rising level of inflation; the rich and influential will not have a problem, they rarely do. They can always beat the system; whatever they want, they will be able to get their hands on it. The sad fact is, their conscience will not bother them either. While so many around them will be grovelling in deprivation and struggling to barely make ends meet, they will be living it up, wining and dining in the most expensive country clubs.

It is interesting to compare this situation with the one we come across in chapter 13. It seems to me that inflation may well be the justification the Antichrist will use to impose rigid controls over buying and selling. It is no wonder he will be able to control the economy for the ball is at his feet. He will do so by introducing a strict monetary policy and, at the same time, promise to feed the starving masses so long as they are willing to toe the party line! The triple 6, the so-called 'mark of the beast,' comes into vogue here, but more of that later.

Drought!

The scarcity of food will automatically lead to all sorts of health and community problems on a colossal scale. Such a harrowing experience which reduces people to scraping the bottom of a barrel for something to live on inevitably wears them down, it destroys their will, it saps their strength.

An incredibly vivid picture of people who are enveloped in such a tragedy is presented for us in the book of Lamentations. We read in 4:8,9 that, '... they are blacker than soot; they are not recognised in the streets. Their skin has shrivelled on their bones, it has become as dry as a stick. Those killed by the sword are better off than those who die of famine; racked with hunger, they waste away for lack of food from the field.'

That is grim, it really is. It is a recurring scene we have all witnessed far too frequently on our television screens in recent days. It is real, it is devastating, it is alarming, it is human misery at its worst, it is an appallingly senseless and stupid tragedy. It is bad today but at least it is localised. In that day, it will be infinitely worse for it will be global. In all honesty, it does not bear thinking about.

> **What do you think is the right balance between enjoying the good things available to us, and remembering those who go hungry?**

6:7,8

The Lamb opens the fourth seal

And, yet again, the fourth living creature summons John to *'Come!'* And, yet again, John looks at the macabre vision unfolding before his eyes.

The fourth scene: an ashen-coloured horse bearing Death and Hades

The word *'pale'* is actually a root word for 'green.' It means, a sickly green; the thought is one of decay, rottenness and gangrene. It is a ghastly yellow-green, the colour of a corpse that is decomposing. John describes in verse 8 what he saw, *'I looked and there before me was a pale horse! Its rider was named Death, and Hades was following close behind him. They were given power over a fourth of the earth to kill by sword, famine and plague, and by the wild beasts of the earth.'*

This picture is slightly different to the previous three in that this rider is identified for us as *'Death.'* We are also told he has an accomplice following close by, a figure called *'Hades.'* We all know what that means. *Death takes the body and Hades takes the soul!* The statistics here are quite disconcerting for John advises us that 25% of the world's population will die as a direct result of the opening of the fourth seal. No matter how hard you try to paint a rosy picture, you simply cannot! The chilling fact remains: it is 1 in 4 people. If it were to happen today, that would be a minimum of 1.5 billion people!

> **The statistics are staggering, but death is certain for all of us. The old Puritans used to say you cannot live well until you have learnt to die well. How far have you come to terms with this aspect of your life?**

There are four methods by which this mass extermination will occur: **the sword.** This is a reference primarily to murder. It is the deadly assault of one individual human being upon another. Because society will be in such an atrocious mess, people will take the law into their own hands, they will settle old scores, they will mete out instant justice in a manner that suits them. It is internecine conflict. It is bloodletting at its worst!

Famine and widespread starvation. We mentioned that earlier when we looked at the third horseman; this serves to emphasise the seriousness of the prevailing situation. We have all seen distressing pictures of lands and lives that have been ravaged by drought. We have seen the cracked ground, the swollen, distended bellies of little children with spindly legs and hollow eyes. Any relief worker will tell you that the death that accompanies starvation is one of the most horrible deaths imaginable.

Plague.   A plague can be defined as an epidemic, a rapidly spreading disease. When people think of such an occurrence, they often mention AIDS as a distinct possibility. It may be, it may not be; what it does is to bring this passage into sharp focus. We are told that more people died of the epidemics of influenza and typhoid after World War I than died in the war itself. In fourteenth century Europe, one third of the population died because of the bubonic plague spread by rats. When civilisation crumbles, mankind's defences against disease break down as well. When there is no decent sanitation system, no safe drinking water and not enough nutritious food, diseases like cholera, typhoid and dysentery spread like wild fire.

Who knows, but the plague outlined here may even be linked with the modern horror of biological warfare; it could refer to the killing of masses of people by unleashing clouds of deadly viruses.

Wild beasts. Many will fall victim to the ferocious attacks of predatory creatures. The fact is, they are closely linked with the plague. The most harmful and pernicious creature on earth, so far as man is concerned, is not the lion or the bear, it is the rat! It is clever, it is adaptable, it is destructive. I understand that if 95% of the rat population is exterminated in a given area, it will replace itself within one year. I am also told that rats have killed more people than all the wars in history. It makes its home wherever man is found and it carries as many as thirty-five known diseases. Their fleas carry bubonic plague and history verifies the impact that had throughout Europe six hundred years ago. Their fleas also carry typhus; in four centuries that has killed an estimated 200 million people.

It seems that the beasts in verse 8 are not only linked with the plague but they are also intertwined with the future. Rats menace human food supplies; they both devour and contaminate them. That happens especially in the underdeveloped nations which can least afford to suffer such incalculable loss.

Death ... Damnation!

With the opening of each successive seal there is a chain of events that can easily be traced: delusion, destruction, drought, death, damnation. And there is worse to come! It makes me shudder for those who do not know Jesus as Lord and Saviour! I would not want to be standing in their shoes in these early days of the Tribulation!

If I were a curiosity seeker, a prophecy buff without a personal relationship with Jesus Christ, I think I would hit the floor on both knees, right now!

Before we put the spotlight on seal number five, let me backtrack for just a moment. The utter devastation of what is about to happen has gripped my heart. There are rough times ahead for this old world, days of terror, days of chaos, days when man will reel from one crisis to another. The period spoken of here is the same as Jesus talked about in Matthew 24:21, where we read, 'For then there will be great distress, unequalled from the beginning of the world until now and never to be equalled again.' That is what Jesus said about it!

When we turn back to the words of the royal prophet Zephaniah, we have an opportunity to mull over his comments in 1:14-16: 'The great day of the Lord is near - near and coming quickly! Listen! The cry on the day of the Lord will be bitter, the shouting of the warrior there. That day will be a day of wrath, a day of distress and anguish, a day of trouble and ruin, a day of darkness and gloom, a day of clouds and blackness, a day of trumpet and battle cry against the fortified cities and against the corner towers.' The words in chapter 6 are not much better. In verse 17, this time is described as *'the great day of God's wrath.'* A lot of people out there are going to die. One quarter of all humanity perishes during this nightmare era in world history. It is estimated that during the Second World War, one out of forty people lost their lives, that was bad enough; but here, it is one in four who are plunged into the abyss of death.

Every time I think about this I want to tell more people about Jesus, the one who is mighty to save! That is what Bible prophecy is all about; it should motivate us to communicate to others our faith in a living God.

Is there any hope for planet earth? Sure there is! It is found when men and women exercise a personal faith in Jesus Christ as their Lord and Saviour!

6:9-11

The Lamb opens the fifth seal

There is an immediate response on two fronts: in heaven where we read about the martyrs and their cry is a heart-rending one when they say, *'Avenge us!'* Alongside that, there is an instant response on earth for we hear a cry falling from the lips of sinful men, it is an unbelievably solemn one when they say, *'Hide us!'* In one, we become aware of the brutal persecution of the last days; in the other, we are confronted with the blind panic of the last days.

In this section we are brought face to face with the wrath of an angry God. Now we know why Jesus said when he was here on earth for men to 'flee from the wrath to come!' It all fits neatly into place. It all makes a lot of sense when you read chapter 6 and beyond. It is scary, it is hair-raising, it is unnerving. According to Hebrews 10:31, 'It is a dreadful thing to fall into the hands of the living God.'

The cry of the martyr

We read, *'I saw under the altar the souls of those who had been slain because of the word of God and the testimony they had maintained.'* John is writing about those who have been martyred, those who have paid the supreme sacrifice. Their love for the Lord Jesus and their loyalty to God has cost them everything, they have lost their lives.

These are the ones who will die during the dark and dreary days of Satan's rule and reign of terror. These new believers, people who are only days and weeks, or maybe at most a few months old in the faith, will be victimised in ways we cannot begin to imagine.

When the restraint of the Holy Spirit has been removed, when all hell is let loose, the world rulers of that day will vent their hatred upon anyone who does not bow the knee to the Antichrist. These good folk will die because they are men and women of steely conviction and because they are not ashamed to confess the lovely name of their Lord in a word of testimony to their contemporaries.

The wording in verse 9 lends a fair bit of credibility to the thought that the martyrs seen here are also those who have died in past history. These brave folk have a very special place in the heart of God and here they are honoured in a most exceptional way.

The significance of the altar

The martyrs are *'under the altar.'* That is a pointed reference to the brazen altar that was mentioned in the furnishings for the tabernacle in the wilderness. What happened was this: when the Old Testament priest presented an animal sacrifice, the blood was poured out at the base of the altar (Leviticus 4:7,8). From an Old Testament perspective, blood represented life (Leviticus 17:11). These martyrs, through their sacrifice, poured out their lives as a drink offering to the glory of God. The Apostle Paul says something similar when he uses the same figure of speech in Philippians 2:17 and 2 Timothy 4:6.

The anger of the martyrs

In verse 10 we read, *'They called out in a loud voice, "How long, Sovereign Lord, holy and true, until you judge the inhabitants of the earth and avenge our blood?"'* It is a cry for God to act speedily, swiftly and decisively. It is an earnest plea for God to step into the situation and exercise a ministry of judgment. They say, 'Avenge us!'

You may be saying to yourself, 'That's not a very Christian thing to pray!' You say, 'Look at Jesus, he prayed for those who were doing unthinkable things to him; Stephen did the same when he lifted his eyes to heaven and prayed for his murderers on earth.' Yes, you are absolutely right! I am quite sure these folk also prayed for those who butchered them; it is the proper thing to do, according to Matthew 5.

The question here is not *whether* God will act, but *when* he will act! They cry out in a loud voice, *'How long?'* Basically, they are appealing to God's character. They recognise that he is sovereign; he calls the tune, he writes the score. They know he is Lord. They appreciate the fact that the authority is his alone, he has all power at his disposal. It is just a question of when it will happen. For them, as for the rest of us, the waiting is always the hardest!

I want to emphasise again that, if these believing martyrs had been living in our time, their cry for vengeance would be wrong. In this present age, God is showing grace and mercy to the worst of men and we are told to pray for those who treat us like door mats. However, in the dark era of the Tribulation, God will be handing down judgment. It is a different era, it is a different mindset, and so this cry is not only understandable, it is perfectly justified.

> **'How long, Lord?' is a question we all ask at various times. In what ways does the response of verse 11 help us through those times?**

God answers prayer!

In verse 11 we read, *'Then each of them was given a white robe, and they were told to wait a little longer until the number of their fellow-servants and brothers who were to be killed as they had been was completed.'*

What an amazing verse! It gives us a peep behind the scenes. God heard their cry and he responded by pulling back the curtain and sharing with them a little of what happens on the other side. Here we have some incredible insights into the providence of God in his dealings with his children. There are five points which I have found quite helpful in coming to a clearer understanding of this verse:

The dead are conscious. This knocks on the head the erroneous teaching of 'soul sleep.' These martyrs are very much aware of the promises of God. That is the only possible explanation for their cry of 'how long?' in verse 10.

It is possible that those who have died have an intermediate body until they receive their final resurrection body. That is the new body

Paul talked about at the end of Philippians 3 and which he also mentions in 1 Corinthians 15. The other one is only temporary in nature. The white robe indicates their salvation, it speaks about their righteousness before God. 'Clothed in his righteousness alone, Faultless to stand before the throne,' sings out the hymn-writer, Edward Mote. You cannot hang a robe on a spirit! It needs a body.

Dead believers are said to be resting. What a lovely phrase! We read later in the book in 14:13 that the dead are blessed because *'they rest from their labour.'* The struggles, the trials, the heartaches of this life, are over for those who have died in the Lord.

God's plan is right on schedule. It might appear the opposite when you look around you and see all that is happening in a crazy world. It may seem as if things are careering recklessly out of control, they are not! God has a plan, he has an agenda, he has a timetable. The key words here are the words *'until'* and *'completed.'* God is on track! He is not running late!

Many believers will be killed during the Tribulation period. This is something which our God allows to happen. The encouraging truth is that nothing can touch the believer unless it passes through the grid of the will of God. He has a plan for every one of us. He has a special plan for every one of them. He has a purpose that explains each apparent delay in his plan when we view it from a human perspective.

These good folk are referred to as *'fellow servants'* and *'brothers.'* This is a possible reference to both Gentiles and Jews who will lay down their lives during this horrendous time. We have in this verse a preview of things to come.

6:12-17

The Lamb opens the sixth seal

Worldwide convulsions and catastrophes

The language is quite clinical in the terse statement which follows. It says in five matter-of-fact words, *'There was a great earthquake.'*

This is the first of three major earthquakes which will shake the nations; they will rock the world for the consequences are global (you can read about the other two in chapters 11 and 16).

All of nature will be affected to an alarming degree: the sun, the moon, the stars, the heavens, the mountains, and the islands of the sea. This is no endtime hype, this is no hallucination. No! It is real! It is devastating!

A graphic description

In verses 12-14, John records the details of the vision. *'The sun turned black like sackcloth made of goat hair; the whole moon turned blood red, and the stars in the sky fell to earth as late figs drop from a fig tree when shaken by a strong wind. The sky receded like a scroll, rolling up, and every mountain and island was removed from its place.'*

We read of a similar occurrence in the prophecy of Joel. He says in 2:30,31 that God will 'show wonders in the heavens and on the earth, blood and fire and billows of smoke. The sun will be turned to darkness and the moon to blood before the coming of the great and dreadful day of the Lord.' He reaffirms this by adding in 3:15 that 'the sun and the moon will be darkened and the stars no longer shine.'

When you read the insights of the great evangelical prophet Isaiah, you quickly realise that something big is going to happen, soon! He says, in language reminiscent of John, that 'the stars of heaven and their constellations will not show their light ... the rising sun will be darkened and the moon will not give its light' (Isaiah 13:10). He says as much again in 34:4, only this time the idiom is more colourful and vivid: 'All the stars of the heavens will be dissolved and the sky rolled up like a scroll; all the starry host will fall like withered leaves from the vine, like shrivelled figs from the fig tree.' Strong stuff!

Amos, the country cousin prophet, refers to it as well. He says in 8:9 that the Sovereign Lord 'will make the sun go down at noon and darken the earth in broad daylight.'

Its impact on the people

Do you see the impact this will have on the inhabitants of planet earth? There is a lot of chaos out there, there is a lot of confusion as men are plunged into the dark depths of despair. We read in verses 15-17 that, *'The kings of the earth, the princes, the generals, the rich, the mighty, and every slave and every free man hid in caves and among the rocks of the mountains. They called to the mountains and the rocks, "Fall on us and hide us from the face of him who sits on the throne and from the wrath of the Lamb! For the great day of their wrath has come, and who can stand?"'*

Sobering words! Solemn words! It is grim! The shuddering impact of this colossal upheaval in world affairs does not only affect the underclass, it covers every strata of society. The entire population are in a state of blind panic. It does not matter where you find yourself on the social ladder, everybody is running around like a headless chicken. They have been reduced to a veritable heap of rubble in a few seconds. The bottom has fallen out of their tiny world. *God has brought man to his knees!*

When a man gets down on his knees, it is not always to repent! It is not always to pray the sinner's prayer! There are times he can turn the other way and vent his spleen on those around him and on the unseen God above him and that is exactly what happens here. In that day, those who refuse to believe will have reached a stage where they simply cannot believe. They have gone beyond the point of no return.

Their consternation is there for all to see. World leaders have no answers to all that is happening. They are in the same boat as ordinary Joe or Sadie standing at the bar with a pint in their hand in the local working men's club. They are filled with fear; they are gripped in the tentacles of terror. They run and hide for that is their first instinct. It is the natural thing to do. They want to hide; the reality is, it is an attempt to get away from the Lord.

The people mentioned here would rather hide from God in fear than run to him in faith. That is what sin does to any man, it is what sin does to every man!

These are the days we read of in Luke 21 where it talks about men's hearts failing them for fear. These folk are shaking like a leaf, they are stunned, they are crying! It is quite pathetic in one sense, they do not know what has hit them. On the other hand, they are very much aware that God has intervened. They are reeling under the force of the wrath of God. It is severe, it is intense, it is an unusual phenomenon. It is what the insurance brokers call 'an act of God.' That is a fairly accurate appraisal of this world shattering event which has engulfed mankind. In a word, there is pandemonium.

The plea of the people

This is the greatest earthquake in history, the greatest cosmic disturbance in history and, I suppose it is fair comment to say, it is the greatest prayer meeting in history as well! The problem is, they are praying for the wrong thing. They are crying to the mountains, *'hide us!'* and to the rocks, *'fall on us!'* because they see death as an escape route to oblivion. Ah, you see, the day of the double-barrelled wrath of God and the Lamb has come!

> 'Wrath' and 'Lamb' (verse 16) are two words not usually put together. What do you understand by the word 'wrath' and what place does it have in your understanding of the Lord's character?

'...who can stand?'

The scene closes with a rhetorical question which remains unanswered. It is an echo of the stomach-curdling words you find in Nahum 1:6 and Malachi 3:2. Paul says something similar in 1 Thessalonians 5:3. The fact is, you know and I know, *none can stand!*

John MacArthur writes: *'The world is not too enlightened, humane, civilised, educated, or sophisticated to avoid repeating the atrocities of the past. In fact, the atrocities of the Tribulation will far exceed any that have gone before. With God's supernatural restraint on sin removed and the forces of hell running rampant, the slaughter of that time will be without precedent in human history. But, out of those dark and evil days, will come thousands who sealed their testimony for the word of God and the lordship of Jesus Christ with their own blood.'*

7

A divine interlude

Sherlock Holmes ... I can see him there, puffing on his pipe, magnifying glass in hand, examining all the clues. I can hear him say, 'Elementary, my dear Watson!' Our friend Sherlock solved many baffling crimes by, firstly, having a clear mind and, secondly, by deductive reasoning. A lot of people when they come to the book of Revelation wish they were 21st century Sherlock Holmes'. The whole book is shrouded in a cloak of mystery that needs to be unravelled and they think you have to be an expert to crack it.

Just like Mr Holmes, there are times when you have to sit back and review all the facts in a case. There are times when it is best to put on the brakes and stop and think. We need to sift through all the information we have at our disposal and seek to learn important lessons from it. Maybe we need to ask the question right now, what have we seen in our study so far?

Well, the seven sealed scroll has continued to unroll. In chapter 6, we watched as six seals were opened, bringing one judgment after another crashing down on planet earth. The seeds of devastation were spread with increasing and frightening intensity. We looked at a time of unprecedented disaster, unrelieved terror, and unimaginable slaughter that lies ahead for the world.

The white horse gallops on to the world scene carrying the man of deception, the coming world dictator. Then the red horse appears, he claws the air and any semblance of peace on earth is abolished. Then the black horse with its rider causes consternation, creating hunger and economic disaster. Then the pale horse with its deadly duo in the saddle makes life unbearable for the population as he spreads a dangerous life-threatening plague in his path. Seal number five reveals the brave and courageous martyrs of the Tribulation. When the sixth seal is opened, it unleashes one of the most devastating earthquakes the world has ever seen. It will make the Richter scale look tame as it tries to record all the details.

One astronomer has dubbed the whole scenario, 'a nuclear winter.' I am sure you will agree with me when I say, that is bleak, times are bad! Is it any wonder the question is left hanging at the end of chapter 6, *'Who can stand?'* Who can put up with these heart-stopping catastrophes without losing his mind? Who can survive these seismic events?

But, for now, there is a brief respite, a short pause. There is a welcome intermission between the opening of seal six and seal seven. It is the lull, the calm, before the storm continues unabated. There is a stillness in the air. In one sense, it is an ideal opportunity for us to catch our breath and catch up on the story line. And so, John takes us back to what happens after the church is taken to be with her Lord. He goes back to the sequence of events that immediately follows the rapture of the saints of God and, in so doing, he gives us a breathtaking panorama of salvation during a time of extraordinary trouble on earth. This is not a close-up of a single incident, rather, it is a vista of the big picture!

In this beautiful interlude in chapter 7 we are treated to a flashback. We all know what a flashback is, don't we. It is a conventional storytelling device used in books and films to supply an event from a character's past that is significant to the present flow of the story. The flashback we have in chapter 7 supplies a missing piece of the Revelation puzzle and, when we have it, we will see it all fitting neatly into place, like pieces in a jigsaw.

∧

7:1-3

The purpose of the angels

John informs us, *'After this I saw four angels standing at the four corners of the earth, holding back the four winds of the earth to prevent any wind from blowing on the land or on the sea or on any tree.'* God despatches his special messengers in times of trouble and so he sends four angels to hold back the destruction to come on the earth, the sea and the trees. At each point of the compass, north, south, east and west, they are holding back the four winds of the earth. The storm is brewing, the tempest is raging; it is worldwide, it is global, and believe it or not, they actually stop it happening for a while. During this time of cessation, there will be no wind, no mountain breezes, no waves breaking on the shore, no rustling of leaves in the forests, no movement of clouds in the sky; everything will be deathly still. In itself, that is an incredible display of power!

The reason is actually given in verse 2 for there we read, *'Then I saw another angel coming up from the east, having the seal of the living God. He called out in a loud voice to the four angels who had been given power to harm the land and the sea, "Do not harm them!"'*

Angel number five is the one with the seal. Did you see where he comes from? He comes up from the east. The final disaster comes from the east when Armageddon is ripe (16:12-16). The Lord Jesus also comes from the east when he returns in power and glory (Matthew 24:27); this is also an allusion to a prophecy in Malachi 4:1-3. From John's perspective on the Isle of Patmos, the east would be toward the land of Israel, the land where God's promised salvation came through Jesus the Messiah and from where the twelve tribes of Israel came - members of which are about to be sealed.

Then, in an unmistakably loud voice that reaches the four corners of the earth, the angel declares that judgment is on hold until the servants of God are sealed. The scene now shifts from judgment on the ungodly to special protection for the godly. What a treasured moment that promises to be!

If you fast-forward to 8:7-12, you can see what happens when this restraint is removed. One-third of the earth is burned up, one-

third of the trees are burned up, and one-third of the sea turns to blood.

The divine rationale

God has something tremendously important that he wants to do and it shows us in a powerful way that he is a God of grace and a God of tender mercy. God is on the throne! There is a banner floating across the sky which is plain for all to see. It says in bold, capital letters, 'Heaven rules!' God is in control. He reigns on high. He is the one who calls the tune. The cameo John gives us here is one which underlines the truth of the sovereignty of God and the providential care of God for his own people.

He wants to put a seal on a certain group of people. We see that at the end of verse 3, where it says, *'Do not harm the land or the sea or the trees until we put a seal on the foreheads of the servants of our God.'* The picture flashing on our screen is the selection of a special group of people. These good folk will be allocated a specific mission to be carried out when the darkness is deepening in the early part of the Tribulation. (More later about their unique role.)

The divine imprint

When we talk about a seal, what do we really mean? A seal indicates ownership. It speaks of protection. You probably realise this is not the first time God has sealed off some of his people from judgment.

When he sent the flood, he sealed Noah and his family from the rest of the human race. When he destroyed Jericho, he sealed Rahab and her household by means of a scarlet cord. He did the same for Lot and his family when they escaped from Sodom, just before the fire fell. He sealed the firstborn in Egypt when they applied the blood to the lintel and doorposts of their homes. Back in John's day, it was a common custom for masters to seal or brand their slaves. We are sealed today by the Holy Spirit of God. This is God's guarantee to us that we are saved; it is a divine confirmation that we are safe and that one day he will take us home to heaven. This is because we belong to him and he has undertaken to look after us this side of glory.

> In this chapter God restrains the forces of destruction to allow a great multitude to be saved. How does this highlight his sovereignty and grace?

7:4-8

The people sealed

In verse 4, we are told a little more about this specially selected group of people: *'Then I heard the number of those who were sealed: 144,000 from all the tribes of Israel.'* In a day to come, God will seal 144,000 Jews! They are the firstfruits of Israel which as a nation will be redeemed before Christ returns (Romans 11:26). It is good to remind ourselves that in every age God has his faithful remnant. We read in 14:1 that they will receive the Father's name as their seal (this is in marked contrast to the mark of the beast that the Antichrist will give those who follow him).

> During the Great Tribulation the Lord singles out 144,000 from the Jewish nation, the covenant people, and redeems them. What does this say about his ability and determination to keep his promises?

Israelites identified

This impressive number is comprised of 12,000 from each of the twelve tribes of Israel and, when you cast your eye down to verses 5-8, you will notice that a dozen tribes are detailed there for us. I must warn you, however, there are some aspects of this list which pose problems.

There are three questions which immediately spring to mind: *One, why is the tribe of Levi included when it had no inheritance with the other tribes? Two, why is Joseph named but not his son Ephraim who is usually connected with his brother Manasseh? Three, why is the tribe of Dan omitted here and yet it is included in the list in Ezekiel 48 when the land is divided out?* The answers are not as easy as you may think! God knows and that is sufficient for me. In moments like these, I am just so glad that 'the secret things belong to the Lord.'

We are talking about the tribe of Judah, the tribe of Reuben, the tribe of Gad, the tribe of Asher, the tribe of Naphtali, the tribe of Manasseh, the tribe of Simeon, the tribe of Levi, the tribe of Issachar, the tribe of Zebulun, the tribe of Joseph and the tribe of Benjamin. This is priceless information for it means we have no problem identifying these endtime evangelists. From the Jewish people will come the greatest missionary force the world has ever known! They are Jews! They are only Jews! Now that is vitally important and I realise at the same time it can be highly controversial.

There are a number of well-known religious groups who have taken this definitive number on board and have woven it into their doctrinal position; it forms an integral part of their statement of faith as an organisation and we all know from door-step encounters that many of their committed members are enthusiastic exponents of it.

On the other hand, those of whom John is speaking are sons of father Abraham; they are converted Jews. They owe their total allegiance to Jesus Christ. The hand of God has been placed on their lives for an extra-special reason in an extra-special season ... to them has been given the awesome responsibility of sharing the good news of Jesus to a people who are living their lives as if there were no tomorrow.

To the ends of the earth

They have a specific work to do for the Lord. The 144,000 itinerant preachers will be Spirit filled, Spirit led, and Spirit anointed. They will go here and there proclaiming the gospel of the kingdom; they will be bold and fearless in their witness to Jesus Christ. They will go into all the world, to the uttermost ends of the earth.

The power and dynamic of their preaching will inspire others with tremendous courage. They will complete the task of world evangelisation and it is all going to happen during these dark days of terror. Sometimes we are inclined to forget that it was twelve Jews who turned the world upside down in the 1ˢᵗ century! Just imagine what 12,000 times twelve will do in the not-too-distant future!

When you see what happens during this era, you begin to realise it moves rapidly from bad to worse, and beyond. We catch fleeting glimpses of the inbred hatred of the Antichrist. We see the passion and fanatical commitment of his devotees and it is during these terrible times that the hand of God will be on the lives of these courageous witnesses to Jehovah. The Lord will protect them until their ministry is finished. He will look after them until their mission is accomplished. Anne Graham Lotz has written, 'God's sealed protection ensures that armies cannot touch them, floods cannot drown them, fires cannot burn them, famines cannot starve them, torture chambers and concentration camps cannot hold them, and the secret police cannot hinder them!'

The God who protected three young men in a fiery furnace in Daniel's day has not changed. He is just the same and he can do it again! These servants are sealed because of the promise of God. They will enter the kingdom at the end of the seven years Tribulation to reign with Christ and his glorified church. They are kept from harm during the Tribulation so that they might be alive when the millennium begins; God's covenant promises to his people will be honoured.

7:9,10

The people described

We come across a very familiar phrase in verse 9, when John says, *'After this I looked.'* This implies a connection between the two groups mentioned - the Jewish preachers were the instruments God used to bring these people to a personal faith in Jesus Christ. There is a clear link between the 144,000 who can be numbered and the *'great multitude that no-one could count.'*

There is the amazing ability of Christ to save men and women, to rescue them from the grip of the enemy, to pluck them as brands from the burning. There is a mighty display of the grace of God in the lives of ordinary people. It is an innumerable company; it is so great they are uncountable! There is the dynamism of the gospel of God's dear Son.

The day of Pentecost was a wonderful day ... there were 3,000 saved on that day alone! That was a great victory but it is nothing compared to this! Nineveh repented at the preaching of Jonah ... a conservative estimate tells us around one million people were saved but that is nothing compared to this! Some three million people followed Moses out of the land of Egypt because they sheltered under the blood ... that was absolutely great but this surpasses that by a long shot!

Here we have a vast congregation of redeemed people and it is impossible to calculate with any degree of accuracy how many there are. I suppose the way John puts it, it disappoints the statisticians among us. The bottom line is, the number is not that important ... it is the people that count! And there they are, *'standing before the throne and in front of the Lamb.'* What a fantastic locale! They are in the grandstand of glory. They are on the front row of heaven. They see the King in all his exquisite beauty!

Their nationality

John says they are from all around the world. They are from *'every nation, tribe, people and language.'* I believe that means what it says. Not one is missing ... every people group, every ethnic group, none are passed by! In Acts 2, there was a roll call of the nations at Pentecost but it was nothing like this! The more the Antichrist fans the flames of repression during the Tribulation, the more the Holy Spirit fans the flames of revival!

Today we face a task unfinished in terms of global evangelism. The church has not finished the job handed down to her in the great commission. So much has happened in the last few years as missionary organisations have pushed back the barriers. Enormous strides forward have been taken as the darkness in some regions of the world has been penetrated for the very first time. In our lifetime, modern technology is being harnessed as never before as the gospel is beamed into hearts and homes in areas where it is impossible for man to take it.

And yet, in spite of all that is being achieved and accomplished, the stark reality is, there are so many dear people who up to this moment in time have not heard the precious name of Jesus in their own language. The exciting news is, in that day in the Tribulation, saints will bring the whole project to a grand finale! Something similar is echoed in Matthew 24:14 where we read, 'and this gospel of the kingdom will be preached in the whole world as a testimony to the nations, and then the end will come.' It seems to me, in the darkest hour of human history yet to come, the greatest harvest of souls the world has ever seen will take place. Millions who have never heard the gospel will one day be swept into the kingdom of God. I believe that this multitude will consist entirely of those who never heard the gospel before the Lord's return for the church and the beginning of the Day of the Lord.

> **Salvation blessing out of tragedy and adversity ... what light does this throw on why God allows suffering?**

It seems to me, those who already had an opportunity to hear the gospel and who deliberately rejected it, prior to the moment when Christ returns to the air for his people, that such folk will have hardened their hearts against the Lord Jesus. This means, for them, there is no second chance!

One writer puts it like this: 'During those terrible days of judgment, when the witches of war ride their nuclear brooms across the darkening skies of the world's last night, thousands who have never heard before will hear the gospel of the coming kingdom of God, and they will believe.'

Their nature

We discover in verse 9, *'they were wearing white robes and were holding palm branches in their hands.'* In other words, they are both virtuous and victorious! They are overcomers! The white robes clearly point to their righteousness and salvation. The palm branches are a picture of triumph and rejoicing. These folk have every reason to be glad in their God, they have so much to sing about.

It is a celebration of the grace of God for they are the first to recognise that salvation belongs to the Lord. We read in verse 10, *'And they cried out in a loud voice: "salvation belongs to our God who sits on the throne, and to the Lamb.'* Oh yes, they paid the supreme sacrifice (they are the ones we read about in 6:11). It cost them everything yet that does not dampen their desire to thank God for so great a salvation. They are saved even though their exit from the world has been one of horror and pain.

It is a celebration of the government of God for they acknowledge the one who sits on the throne. Their days on earth were dark and dreadful, times were harsh and cruel. No doubt they cried out many times, 'Why, O Lord, why?' and, 'How long, O Lord, how long?' In moments when all was sinking around them and they were in grave danger of going under themselves, they maybe felt as if God was silent, that the heavens were like brass, that evil appeared to triumph on every street corner, that the heathen raged. The thought must have filtered through their minds on more than one occasion, has God abdicated, has God stepped down, has God been toppled from power? But now, they see him on the throne; now they know, he is still in control, he is sovereign, he is active!

It is a celebration of the gift of God. The focus is on the Lamb. They are in heaven not because they were willing to be martyred for their new-found faith in Jesus, not because they gave their bodies to be burned, not because they were counted as sheep for the slaughter, not because they were rendered destitute and subjected to a torrent of vulgar abuse from everyone in the community, not because they endured to the end, not because they came through the Great Tribulation ... no, a thousand times, no! They are there only because of the Lamb and well they know it! It is a humble recognition that they owe everything to the one who is seated on the throne.

Their song is a vocal tribute to a God whose grace is amazing and to a Lamb whose death is atoning.

7:11,12

The stimulus of praise

I think it was A W Tozer who said that worship is the missing jewel in the service of the church. That may be true on earth but there is no shortage of real worship in heaven. Verse 11 is an outburst of spontaneous praise. Heaven is full of people who do not deserve to be there! That is why they get so excited and enthused about the grace and mercy of God; that is why they fall down in loving submission before the king of glory.

It is contagious!

The angels cannot resist joining in.   John informs us, *'All the angels were standing round the throne and around the elders and the four living creatures. They fell down on their faces before the throne and worshipped God.'* It is the ripple-in-the-pool syndrome. When the rest of heaven see these victorious martyrs standing before the throne, when they see them dressed in their magnificent white robes, when they see them waving their green palm branches high above their heads, when they hear them lift up their voices in an anthem of praise, they cannot contain themselves! They cannot stand on the sidelines, they cannot resist the opportunity to join in ... so the numbers are swelled considerably and the volume is turned up so much higher as this great massed choir praises the God of glory! It is natural, it is unrehearsed, it had to happen! And, thank God, it did!

> The example of the great multitude inspires the angels to worship. Think of one or two ways in which you could change your lifestyle to achieve the same response in other people!

It is harmonious!

They are all singing from the same song sheet and the lyrics are recorded for us in verse 12. They go like this: *'Amen! Praise and glory and wisdom and thanks and honour and power and strength be to our God for ever and ever. Amen!'*

To me, that is the kind of song you could imagine them singing at the last night of the Proms! The chances are this kind of rousing worship would make some Christians nervous. As they say, you could hear them for miles around! Most of us have been conditioned not to make any noise in the sanctuary of our churches or, if we do, it tends to be fairly muffled.

What about waving palm branches? Well, that is an activity most folk associate with some kind of religious ritual which takes place in some churches on Palm Sunday. It is not the done thing! And as far as falling on your face goes, well that would happen only if you fell asleep in a prayer meeting!

When you look at what worship is like in heaven, it seems to me that God intended it to be a stimulating and invigorating experience. The fact is, when the fire of God is kindled in your heart and mine, there is no point in chafing at the bit; we cannot help but be animated in the presence of our God.

> Is worship an uplifting experience for you? If not, what help is offered by the example of the angels in verses 11 and 12?

An expression of victory and gratitude

You see, they worship God because out of the fire and fury of the Great Tribulation has come such a multitude of martyrs. His strength has been made perfect in their human weakness. From our limited perspective, it is true to say that we are prone to weep because of our trials and troubles, but on the other side of death, we shall worship God for it.

I think these victorious saints are a tremendous challenge to each of us. We should see to it that we act in such a way that God is praised by those who surround his throne. The words of Fanny Crosby's much-loved song complement it beautifully:

Blessed assurance, Jesus is mine;
O, what a foretaste of glory divine!

Heir of salvation, purchase of God,
Born of his Spirit, washed in his blood.
This is my story, this is my song,
Praising my Saviour, all the day long!

And it goes right back to the words of the psalmist David, 'Let everything that has breath, praise the Lord!' In one gigantic leap into the future, John has given us a glimpse of believers dancing in the aisles of glory. Heaven will reverberate with the sound of music! For them, the misery of earth will be over, they are in a glorious new world! They are home at last! And so far as the angels are concerned, if as we are told in Luke 15 they rejoice over one sinner who is saved, imagine what they will do when all these saints come marching in!

The amen sandwich!

The ascription of praise begins and ends with a hearty *'Amen!'* It is a word of affirmation, it is a word to get you going on the right note. It rounds off their praise and reminds us, 'this is true, we're all agreed.' It is the 'and-so-say-all-of-us' syndrome. It means, it is real, it is right! It sharpens our focus and puts the main beam on Jesus. It is the kind of word they could repeat after every phrase in the song.

When you look at the jam in the 'amen sandwich' you find there are seven characteristics outlined: we have *praise and glory, wisdom and thanks, honour and power and strength.* This indicates the fulness of worship that the Lord deserves and that is where the number seven, the perfect number, comes into the equation. Everything you can think of in terms of adoration should be given freely to him. This is very similar to what we read being ascribed to him in the doxology of chapter 5. It is pure praise directed to a God who is eternal with the inference that this paean of praise will continue throughout the aeons of eternity. There is no stopping it; such worship will never cease through all of an endless eternity.

7:13-17

A conversation about the martyrs

We read in verse 13 that one of the elders comes across to John and pointing a finger at the crowd assembled before the throne asked him a double-barrelled question. He says, *'These in white robes - who are they and where did they come from?'* John's response is a brief one, an honest one, it is a straightforward, *'Sir, you know!'* The implication is, John did not know!

It seems to me, the elder knew all along who they were but God wanted John to know and, in a strange kind of way, he wants us to know as well. He continues in verse 13 to describe them for us by saying, *'These are they who have come out of the Great Tribulation. They have washed their robes and made them white in the blood of the Lamb.'*

The abiding lesson is this: these glorious martyrs have not died as yet; in fact, they may not even have been born yet! But the Lord wants the saints of all the ages to know all about them.

God wants them to be properly recognised, they really do deserve it! He also wants them to be properly rewarded, according to his promises. They will have a special place, complete protection and eternal peace. He wants them to be given the acclaim which is rightfully theirs. He is happy for them to receive the commendation of their peers.

The martyrs are a special group of people, they are unique to the Tribulation period. And yet, their salvation, like yours and mine, is all because of the power of the blood of Jesus to cleanse from sin. Today, and in all our tomorrows, the message of the gospel remains the same ... as Paul himself said, 'We preach Christ crucified.'

Their role in heaven

John tells us, *'They are before the throne of God and serve him day and night in his temple.'* The matchless blessing afforded these martyred believers is that they find themselves in the proximate presence of the Lord. They cannot get much nearer! They are as close as that!

To be before the throne is always seen as a position of prominence and honour. The throne as we have seen earlier is the centre-piece of heaven. It is the focal point and the thought here is that their lives will be lived in relation to it and the one who sits upon it. The preposition *'before'* is extremely significant. It speaks of full and intimate fellowship with no sense for us of being at a distance from God even in that innumerable company.

A life of unwearied service

Another special privilege is extended to them in that they will not only see the Lord, they will also serve him, day and night. You see, heaven is not only a place of rest from earthly labour and struggling with the many hassles and problems of this life; it is also a place where a varied ministry can be effectively carried on. I can assure you, we will not be whiling the hours away twiddling our thumbs in heaven. We will not be sitting all day on fluffy clouds strumming a harp. We are going to be busy!

Some Bible teachers have had problems with the phrase, *'day and night,'* bearing in mind that there is no night in heaven (22:5). That dilemma can be resolved easily when we see it as an expression which means we will continuously serve the Lord; we will not need sleep or restoration as is so essential to life down here on planet earth. It is really nothing more than a figure of speech which underlines the truth that over there these folk are free from every limitation of this life.

Their service is said to occur in the *'temple of God'* and again, it has to be said, this is a clear reference to the immediate presence of the Lord, not to anything else. You find this clarified later in chapter 21.

Is it not thrilling for us to realise that when we get home to heaven we will walk constantly and unbrokenly in the Lord's presence. There will be uninterrupted communion. We will serve him without any signs of weariness, staleness or weakness. We will never before

*have been so deliriously happy in any employment! It will be service
with a smile on our lips and service with a song in our hearts!*

A life of unbounded security

We read at the end of verse 15 that *'he who sits on the throne will
spread his tent over them.'* What a beautiful analogy that is! To be
covered by God's tent! This is God's broadest protection! The words
are quoted from the promise God gave his people in Isaiah 49:10
and Psalm 121. He provides a canopy for them in heaven.

What a stunning picture of the enjoyment of the warmth of God's
love and the sheer delights of his near presence! We are enveloped
in a place which is close to his heart; we are wrapped around with an
overwhelming sense of his presence. That means, there is nothing
to fear, there is nothing to dread.

Down here, in this old world, there is so much tension and stress
and strain, there is so much aggro! When you put it all into the
melting pot it breeds a high level of insecurity in the heart and mind,
but the unassailable fact is that over there, nothing and no-one can
harm the people of God. Thank God, just like them, we are
untouchable! Praise God, we are unreachable, as well!

There is another contrast with life down here. We read in verse
16, *'Never again will they hunger, never again will they thirst.'*
Bearing in mind that these martyrs came through the Tribulation,
these words take on an entirely new meaning. In those awful days
they knew considerable deprivation, they were prevented from
partaking of the essentials of life. They were harassed to such an
extent that even the basics of life were denied them. Many days
they were forced to go without a decent meal; many a night they
went to bed with an empty stomach, all because they were marching
to the beat of a different drum. It was tough. It was not easy.

*But, in heaven, it is all a thing of the past. There is no lack in
God's provision. There will never be a sense of something missing.
We will have everything we desire and desire everything we have.*

At the end of verse 16 we read, *'the sun will not beat upon them,
nor any scorching heat.'* This reminds us that in heaven the forces
of nature will not mitigate against us. The sun is a wonderful bonus

to many of us and it is something we can really enjoy and derive much benefit from; but, you can get too much of a good thing and that is when the problems start!

Down here, these folk were subject to the elements of nature; they had been exposed to the extremes of heat and cold, light and dark. We will not face that complication in heaven for over there the environment is user friendly. We will not need the sun for the glory of the exalted Lord will shine upon us, yet even that will not consume us in its heat or blind us in its dazzling power!

A life of unblemished satisfaction

We come to the climax in verse 17, where we read, *'Then the Lamb at the centre of the throne will be their shepherd.'* We will be shepherded by the Lamb! We have a dual picture here for the Lord Jesus Christ is both the Lamb and the Shepherd!

As the Lamb of God who gave his life for us at Calvary, he bought us with his precious blood. As the Shepherd who supplies our every need, he will look after us in every way imaginable.

Our happiness and our welfare are his major concern. This is highlighted in the next phrase which tells us that *'he will lead them to springs of living water.'* Water in the Bible is often a symbol of salvation and eternal life. That truth is echoed in the words of Jesus when he spoke to the woman at Jacob's well in John 4. But here he leads us to the fountain head; he reminds us that in heaven we will be at the very source and focus of spiritual life and blessing. Here is life in abundant fulness!

The last sentence in chapter 7 is one that God's people have valued and appreciated so much down the years. It is one you often hear read at a funeral or in a situation where people are passing through some kind of devastating and traumatic experience. John rounds off the chapter by saying, *'And God will wipe away every tear from their eyes.'* That is great news! Here on earth our joys are often tempered by our many sorrows, we are no strangers to the vale of tears.

Did you see what he does with our tears? He wipes them away! They are gone! His is a ministry of tenderness and comfort. So far as he is concerned, the past is put behind us and when we arrive in heaven, it is to a brand new future where burdens are no more! The saints in glory will be occupied with the beauty and wonder of heaven and the worship of their Saviour. Because the tears are gone, the vision we have of Christ is unblurred! What an exhilarating prospect awaits those we read about in this amazing chapter. The hymn writer captured the emotion of the moment well when he penned:

Face to face with Christ my Saviour,
Face to face, what will it be?
When with rapture I behold him,
Jesus Christ, who died for me!

> **How do you imagine a life in heaven of service, security and satisfaction, and how does that make you feel?**

8

When heaven holds its breath!

8:1,2

The prelude

We read when the Lamb opened the seventh seal that *'there was silence in heaven for about half an hour.'* This is really difficult for us to imagine, it is incredibly hard for us to visualise. It is such a contrast to all that has been happening; moments before, there was rousing praise, spontaneous worship, wonderful music and bright singing. We have just been participating in a lively celebration where the focus was on the government and grace of God. We have just been to a praise party in heaven and now, all goes strangely quiet. It is a dramatic pause, a hugely effective pause. It is the silence of mystery, intrigue and suspense.

It is probably the longest silence heaven has ever known. It is a time when all heaven holds its breath. As one writer says, 'Heaven will be silent! Awesomely, fearsomely, pregnantly silent!'

Most of us realise that thirty minutes is a fair wee while especially when you are waiting for something big to happen. It may be compared to the silence in a courtroom before the foreman of a jury returns a verdict. It is like waiting at the end of a telephone line for some important news to arrive. It is the kind of silence you can almost feel, it is as though you were able to touch it.

His pause in judgment is like the eye of a hurricane, a lull that gives the world time to reflect on its rebellion, blasphemy, sin, and evil actions. God gives the human race time to think things over. It is the calm prior to the storm; it is the lull before the tempest rages; it is a brief moment of peace in advance of the hour when the turbulence begins. It is the silence of foreboding, of intense expectation, of awe at what God is about to do. John MacArthur says, 'The greatest event since the Fall is about to take place and all heaven is seen waiting in suspenseful expectancy.' Basically, we are waiting for God to take the initiative and make the next move. The plain fact is, number seven seal is so awesome and so terrifying that no-one in heaven dares breathe a word.

We can walk down three paths to discover some rich lessons from this silence for our own lives, it speaks of a sense of:

Awe before the Lord. You find this truth echoed in Habakkuk 2:20 where we read of the divine summons, 'The Lord is in his holy temple, let all the earth be silent before him.' The same challenging outlook is found in Psalm 76:8,9 and again in Zechariah 2:13.

Peace before the Lord. No-one had any grounds for complaint as the Lord has silenced all opposition. It has become clear at last that the judge of all the earth has done right!

Expectation before the Lord. Such a silence prepares us for the awfulness of the judgments that will soon follow. We read all about these in graphic detail in the remaining verses of the chapter. They make the hair stand on the back of your neck!

I often think the period of silence is punctuated at the front end with the opening sentiments of Psalm 46:10 where the Lord is saying, 'Be still and know that I am God!' And as the thirty minutes draws to a close, the silence is broken with the declaration of intent from the same verse where it tells us, 'I will be exalted among the nations, I will be exalted in the earth.'

> **When is it appropriate to be silent before the Lord? And what are the advantages to be gained from such an attitude?**

Seven trumpets!

John informs us in verse 2, *'And I saw the seven angels who stand before God, and to them were given seven trumpets.'* Again we find the number seven is very much to the fore; it is in harmony with the seven seals and the seven bowls which are phases one and three of God's judgment programme. The fact that these angels stand before the living God indicates a place of prominence, such as is given to the angel Gabriel in Luke 1:19.

I came across an interesting piece of information the other day when I discovered there is an ancient apocryphal book that contains a list of the names of the seven high angels. Let me tell you who they are: *Uriel, Raphael, Raguel, Michael, Sarakiel, Gabriel and Phanuel.*

You will notice that all their names end in 'el' which is short for Elohim, one of the names of God! I am not saying that this is what these seven angels in chapter 8 were called. The fact is, we do not know their names and it does not really matter that much anyway.

Trumpets have always had a special place in Jewish national life. When you read Numbers 10, you see that trumpets had a significant and a distinctive role to play. They had at least three important functions:

They were used to call the people together as an entire community, verses 1-8; *they were used to announce the outbreak of war,* verse 9; *they were used to advise the people of special times, such as feasts and festivals,* verse 10.

The trumpets sounded at Mt Sinai when the Law was given to Moses, Exodus 19.

The trumpets were blown when Solomon was anointed and enthroned as king, 1 Kings 1.

The trumpets were heard at the conquest of the city of Jericho, Joshua 6.

When we place these three incidents together, there is a clear picture emerging on the canvas: to sound seven trumpets would certainly announce a declaration of war as well as the fact that God's king was enthroned in glory and was about to judge his enemies, as detailed in Psalm 2. As trumpets declared defeat to Jericho, so they will ultimately bring defeat to Babylon.

Joel says in 2:1, 'Blow the trumpet in Zion, sound the alarm on my holy hill, let all who live in the land tremble for the day of the Lord is coming, it is close at hand.'

8:3-5

The prayers

John writes, *'Another angel, who had a golden censer, came and stood at the altar. He was given much incense to offer, with the prayers of all the saints, on the golden altar before the throne. The smoke of the incense, together with the prayers of the saints, went up before God from the angel's hand.'*

We now see a lovely picture that finds its roots away back in the pages of the Old Testament. It is a profound illustration of what the priests did every day of their lives, every morning and evening they put incense on the golden altar that stood before the veil of the holy place using a golden censer.

On one day of the year, the Day of Atonement, the feast of Yom Kippur, the high priest went behind and beyond the veil. It was then the people remembered the words of God to Moses when he said, 'There I will meet with you.' The role of the priest is to offer the prayers of the people to God. The smoke of the burning incense on the altar represents prayers rising to God and, in this scene, these are the prayers of all the saints!

There are three important lessons we can learn from this about prayer:

God's people are given the great privilege of prayer

That is why I emphasise these are the prayers of all the saints. It is good to remember that saints are not specially selected dead people, they are not people who have been canonised and emblazoned on stained glass windows, far from it! They are very much alive! If you are a Christian, you are a saint!

Prayer should occupy a place at the heart of the Christian life. It is a Calvary bought privilege. We have access into the presence of God through the merits of the death of Jesus. We can come as creatures before the great Creator, we can come as sinners before a holy and just God, we can come as sons before a loving heavenly Father.

God's people are promised great assistance in prayer

That is precisely what is happening in these verses. The prayers of the saints rise up before the Lord, they are made acceptable to God, they are well pleasing in his sight, and they are agreeable to his perfect will.

When you look at the symbol, it is the application of the incense that makes the prayers suitable to God. Go even further back behind the symbol and you will discover we have two great means of assistance promised to every believer so that we may pray aright. Both of them are mentioned in Romans 8: *we have the intercession of the Holy Spirit in verses 26 and 27 and we have the intercession of the Lord Jesus in verse 34.* It is marvellous news that we have such enormous help in prayer!

God's people are guaranteed great answers to prayer

That is what happens in verse 5, where we read, *'Then the angel took the censer, filled it with fire from the altar, and hurled it on the earth.'* You see, their prayers were heard and they made an impact on the heart and mind of God! They asked in 6:10, *'How long?'* Well, here is the answer: *NOW!*

It is maybe not the answer they expected, but it is the one they got! God will always vindicate his name. He will avenge himself against his enemies, he will glorify his people, he will bring in his kingdom and when you pray, 'how long?' such an answer is inevitable. The storm is about to begin; and whether we realise it or not, prayer has played a vital part in that.

There is a direct relationship between prayer and the judgment of God! There is a vital link between the throne and the altar!

The veiled message coming out of these verses is that the throne and the altar are related. The real purpose of prayer is not to get man's will done in heaven, but to get God's will done on earth! And sometimes that spells j-u-d-g-m-e-n-t. True prayer is extremely serious business, so we had better not move the altar too far from the throne!

Following the offering of the prayers of God's people, the silence is abruptly shattered by an electric storm with far-reaching consequences; a divine firestorm bursts upon this planet for we read in verse 5 that *'there came peals of thunder, rumblings, flashes of lightning and an earthquake.'* Prayer which can precipitate such things must truly be potent!

The prayers of God's people have been flung into the scales and have tipped the balance heavily in favour of an immediate resumption of hostilities by heaven. The results are catastrophic as God's judgment falls upon the earth like a massive fireball out of the sky. I think the storm is all the more shocking in its suddenness, contrasted with the silence and stillness that had preceded it. The striking characteristic of these judgments is the precise way in which they are carried out.

> **What is the connection between you being a saint and the privileges and effectiveness of your prayers? On a scale of 1 to 10, how would you rate your conviction that God's will is done through your prayers? What is there in these verses that might move your conviction closer to 10?**

8:6-12

The punishments

'Then the seven angels who had the seven trumpets prepared to sound them.' One by one the angels will sound their trumpets, and as they do, something happens immediately after each blast. It is as though each catastrophe is given a kick-start. What you see taking place here is not unlike the ten plagues in Egypt which we read about in the book of Exodus. There is an uncanny, spine-chilling resemblance between them.

The first four trumpet judgments are natural in that they affect nature to a greater or lesser degree. They are directed towards the land, the salt water, the fresh water and the heavenly bodies. They cause massive environmental damage. They spell desolation in bold capital letters! It is an ecological nightmare.

Trumpets five and six involve the release of hordes of demonic forces. They first torment people and not content with that, they proceed to kill them. You find a harrowing account of the terrible misery they inflict recorded in chapter 9. The caption we write over this particular sequence of events is liberation; however, it is like the proverbial scorpion, there is a sting in the tail.

The seventh and last trumpet is recorded for us in chapter 11 and it involves a serious crisis among all the nations of the world. The reason why is fairly obvious. The stirring message resounding from heaven to earth is summed up in the sentence, *'The kingdom of the world has become the kingdom of our Lord and of his Christ, and he will reign for ever and ever.'*

> These disasters seem to parallel those in Exodus 7-10. What insight does the Exodus experience throw on the ultimate purpose of Revelation's judgments?

The first angel sounds his trumpet

'The first angel sounded his trumpet, and there came hail and fire

*mixed with blood, and it was hurled down upon the earth. A third of
the earth was burned up, a third of the trees were burned up, and all
the green grass was burned up' (8:7).*

This judgment is reminiscent of the seventh plague that befell
Egypt back in the days when Moses was having big problems with
Pharaoh. Then it was restricted to hail and lightning and that was
severe enough. The Bible records in a diary-like entry in Exodus
9:24 that 'it was the worst storm in all the land of Egypt since it had
become a nation.' That is one for the history books. It is a minute
that has been registered for posterity in the meteorological records
of that day. This time, it is hail and lightning, mingled with
blood!

I understand from other sources that this is not a new phenomenon
for scientists and historians have recorded other times when red rain
fell from the sky. *The Atmosphere* is the title of a book published in
the 19th century and it documents a number of such occurrences in
Europe and elsewhere. It refers specifically to the red rain which
fell near Genoa in Italy in 1744. It appears that similar events have
been tabled in the 20th century as well.

We all know that hail storms can do colossal damage, their impact
is terrible but when it is mixed with fire (which may refer to some
kind of severe electrical storm) the possibilities of desolation are
staggering. It is a global legacy of disaster. We need to let the truth
of this sink in. This is not confined to some isolated region populated
by a few nomads in the middle of nowhere, this scene is multiplied
many times over on every continent on the face of the earth.

One-third of the earth is burned up ... it is blackened land, it is
charred, it is smouldering. To all intents and purposes, it will be
rendered unusable for many decades to come.

One-third of the trees are burned up in one huge forest fire. That
puts a new slant on the meaning of the word 'deforestation' and it
also means the door is left wide open for communities to be wiped
out by rising flood water and such like.

One-third of the grass is set on fire. This will affect animal life
which depends upon grass for food. The food supply chain will be
seriously disrupted and that is especially true in relation to meat and
dairy products.

The appearance of the planet will be drastically altered. Life will never be the same again. It seems to me that the earth will experience an immense ecological upheaval that will make our toxic dumps seem like a children's playground. Devastation on this scale undoubtedly affects the delicate balance of nature.

The stark reality is that, even before the dust has settled, this has an immediate impact on the quality of life which can be enjoyed by the inhabitants of the earth. It also spells doom and gloom when you think about the availability of food on the supermarket shelves. 'Earth Day' that year will be a dismal affair; in a scorched and ravaged world there will be little of the environment left to celebrate!

> Seeing how easily ruin could come on the earth, how do we respond to the fact that God has not only preserved but blessed his rebellious world over the centuries (cf. Acts 14:17)?

The second angel sounds his trumpet

John sees *'something like a huge mountain, all ablaze, was thrown into the sea. A third of the sea turned into blood, a third of the living creatures in the sea died, and a third of the ships were destroyed'* (8:8,9).

The first plague of Egypt turned the water of the Nile into blood, that fact is established in Exodus 7. Something similar occurs when the second trumpet sounds. The cause behind this disaster is described by John in symbolic language when he says it was like a huge burning mountain that was tossed into the sea.

Some Bible commentators see all sorts of wild things happening here! Some believe it could be the direct result of a violent volcanic eruption like a Mount Etna Mark 2. Or it could be something akin to a giant meteorite or asteroid surrounded by flaming gases set ablaze by the friction of the earth's atmosphere falling out of space and landing in the sea. John MacArthur makes the point, 'It will hit, striking somewhere in the world's oceans with an explosive power far greater than that of an atomic bomb.' We really do not know!

One-third of the sea is turned into blood. We are inclined to forget that 75% of the earth's surface is ocean and, when we grasp that, we are only scratching the surface. So we can only begin to visualise the extent of this awful judgment.

One-third of the living creatures in the sea died. It is a foregone conclusion that the pollution of the water combined with the death of so much marine life will greatly influence the precarious balance of life in the oceans. That leads to other serious problems that cannot be easily rectified or solved. Think of the long-term impact on the depleted shipping industry; think of the loss of confidence in the mind of Joe Public; think of the tragic and needless loss of human life and so many homes left without a bread-winner.

It is hard to imagine but *one in every three ships will sink* causing untold congestion at sea. Think of the voluminous quantity of cargoes jettisoned; try to envision the utter chaos on the waterways and major shipping lanes of the world. The naval fleets of every major country will be crippled beyond help. And to make matters infinitely worse, seafood will be severely rationed, restaurants will go out of business, people will lose their source of income for their livelihood will be lost and the source of heart healthy food will radically dwindle.

So far as seafaring nations are concerned, this will be an economic disaster from which very few will ever recover. This is a financial collapse of unprecedented proportions. The boom years are a thing of the past; this cataclysmic downturn in their fortunes spells nothing but bust!

The third angel sounds his trumpet

When the third trumpet sounds, John tells us that, *'A great star, blazing like a torch, fell from the sky on a third of the rivers and on the springs of water - the name of the star is Wormwood. A third of the waters turned bitter, and many people died from the waters that had become bitter' (8:10,11).*

A torch-like star falls from the sky, it disintegrates when it enters the atmosphere and scatters itself throughout the earth. The fallout from such a body is what causes the problem. It may be a comet-like object or a meteorite.

One-third of the rivers and springs are irreversibly polluted. Some folk are of the opinion that the type of poisoning we have envisaged here is a form of radiation. Water is basic to human survival. It is fundamental. We just cannot do without it. It is absolutely essential for mankind. This judgment impinges on the world's water supply to such an extent that one-third of the waters are rendered unusable.

The grim statistic is recorded for us when we recognise that any who drink from this so-called bitter water will be signing their own death warrant. People will turn on their taps gasping for a drink of fresh water but, before another day has dawned, they will be just another name on the computer printout of fatal casualties arising from this dreadful epidemic. In our day, we are already grappling with the problem of increased pollution in our drinking water supplies but, in that future day, the fresh water supply will become as putrid as a Calcutta gutter. That is what life will be like during these awful times of Tribulation. This is not an attempt to sensationalise the story; it is simply telling it like it is! The facts are bad enough; they do not need to be embellished in any shape or form.

It is interesting to note that the name of this star is *Wormwood* which is a plant right out of the killing fields. The word translated 'wormwood' gives us our English word 'absinthe' and that is a popular liqueur in some regions of the world. Having said that, because of its high toxicity, its manufacture is also banned in many countries. The Oxford dictionary advises me that it is a green aniseed flavoured potent liqueur based on wormwood which turns milky when water is added. In the Old Testament, it was synonymous with sorrow and great calamity.

Moses warned that idolatry would bring sorrow to Israel like a root producing wormwood (Deuteronomy 29:18); Solomon warned that immorality might seem pleasant at the time but in the end it produces bitterness like wormwood (Proverbs 5:4). It is a phrase that Jeremiah, who was known as the weeping prophet, used on more than one occasion. For example, he says in Lamentations 3:15, 'He has filled me with bitter herbs and sated me with gall.' The word translated 'gall' is wormwood! Amos also uses it in his prophecy where he is talking about those who 'turn justice into bitterness (or wormwood) and cast righteousness to the ground' (Amos 5:7).

I was quite intrigued to discover fairly recently that the National Geographic Society lists about one hundred principal rivers in the world; they range in length from the Amazon which is 4,000 miles long to the Rio de la Plata which is a mere 150 miles long. When you think about it like that, it is only then that the scale of this whole sad affair hits you between the eyes. It is a catastrophe of unbelievable magnitude!

The fourth angel sounds his trumpet

The fourth judgment is in contrast to the previous three for they had to do with the world of nature and it was the earth which was directly influenced. The fourth one is different in that it affects the heavens. Having said that, the inevitable repercussions will be felt on planet earth for many a long day!

We read in verse 12 that when the fourth angel sounded his trumpet, *'A third of the sun was struck, a third of the moon, and a third of the stars so that a third of them turned dark. A third of the day was without light and also a third of the night.'*

The sun, the moon and the stars lose one-third of their light. It is interesting to note that each of these bodies has been worshipped by pagans from all around the world for centuries, but now God touches them to remind us that he alone must be worshipped. This judgment also reminds us of one of the plagues visited on the land of Egypt, as recorded in Exodus 10:21-23. It parallels the ninth plague which lasted for three days.

It is obvious that the earth will become considerably darker. That will affect growth for there will be 33% less energy available to support the life systems required by man and nature. The vast changes in temperature will have a detrimental influence on human health and on food production. It does not only affect nature, it also affects human nature, for the more darkness there is, the more crime there will be, and so it goes on and on!

I have no doubts in my mind that the event outlined here by John is the same one anticipated by Jesus when he said in Luke 21:25,26 that 'there will be signs in the sun, moon and stars. On the earth, nations will be in anguish and perplexity at the roaring and tossing of the sea. Men will faint from terror, apprehensive of what is coming on the world, for the heavenly bodies will be shaken.' In addition to this prophecy, you have several Old Testament prophets saying much the same thing. I am thinking especially of Isaiah 13:10; Jeremiah 4:23; Ezekiel 32:7,8; Joel 2:31; 3:15; and Amos 5:20.

It is quite startling when you analyse each of these four judgments for we quickly realise they all fall on creation. It is as though the Lord is saying, 'You've taken the natural world for granted, you've abused it, you've plundered it. You've depleted and destroyed many of its natural resources. You want a devastated world? Very well then, if that's what you want, that's what you'll have!' The worst judgment God can mete out to sinful man is to give man what he demands.

We are very conscious of the progress man has made in the fields of science, medicine and technology, it is hard to keep abreast of all that is happening around us; at the same time, man is systematically destroying God's earth. After all is said and done, man has no-one else to blame but himself. He has brought it all on himself; in one sense, it was self-inflicted! So far as God is concerned, man always gets his comeuppance. I agree with one writer who concludes: 'The greatest threat to our environment is not fluorocarbons or carbon monoxide or chemical plants or nuclear reactors or bulldozers or arsonists. The greatest threat to our environment is sin!'

> **Confronted with worldwide catastrophe, 'men will faint from terror' (Luke 21:26). What do you think is the right way to use this awful prospect in your evangelistic outreach?**

8:13

The proclamation

Even with all the horrors that man has faced so far in the Tribulation, when will he begin to take God seriously? That is what John is driving home to our hearts in this closing verse of chapter 8.

The triple woe!

John tells us precisely what happened. He says, '*As I watched, I heard an eagle that was flying in mid-air call out in a loud voice, "Woe! Woe! Woe to the inhabitants of the earth because of the trumpet blasts about to be sounded by the other three angels!"'* I have never heard an eagle speak, but John did, and the message he heard was not a particularly cheerful one! It is a treble woe! It is a triple warning that says to the people, 'Look, if you think this is bad, just wait; there is more to come and it is a million times worse!' There is a rising crescendo of judgments!

There are three more judgments to follow before phase two of God's operational strategy in relation to planet earth is completed. And what they do not know is that phase three will be ushered in with even greater intensity, as phase two draws sharply to a close.

The word *'woe'* is one of those unique expressions which is said to be onomatopoeic. It is a word which is formed from a sound which conveys its meaning. It is a bit like the word 'cuckoo' or the word 'sizzle.' You can hear the sound and that gives you a clue to the meaning.

The targets

It should be noted that these judgments are directed to those whom John calls the *'inhabitants of the earth.'* That is a little phrase which pops up no fewer than twelve times in the book of Revelation and it has an interesting application. It is not only referring to those who live 'on' the earth; it is directed primarily to those who live 'for' the earth, those whose lives absorb the things of the earth. They are earth bound in the fullest sense of the word for they are immersed only in the things of time, and that is the root of all their problems. What a contrast to the people of God who are said to be heaven bound!

For the Christian, the best is yet to be. For the unbeliever, the worst is yet to come!

The purposes of judgment

To change our priorities. How do you feel about the judgment of God in your life? Judgment frightens us. It chills our blood. It scares the living daylights out of us. It is supposed to! At the same time, it arrests our attention, it arouses our fear. It should also sober us for it forces us to reassess the way we have been living our lives. As C S Lewis said, 'It can be God's megaphone for reaching a deaf world.'

To correct us. Judgment should also correct us for it forces us to face the unpleasant truth about ourselves. We do not like that, we recoil from it, we shrink away from it. It is like a mirror for it strips away our illusion and restores us to a realistic view of ourselves.

To humble us. Judgment is meant to humble us for it underlines the truth that we are not autonomous, we are not in control of events and circumstances in this life, we are not masters of our own fate, we are not the captains of our own destiny.

To reassure us. And, last of all, judgment should quietly reassure us for it reminds us that God works in our lives in such a way that he wants to bring out the best in us. It is not something that God enjoys for the prophet Isaiah informs us that it is 'his strange work.' Perhaps we can testify with the words of the hymn, *'With mercy and with judgment, my web of time he wove!'*

> We have just examined God's purposes in judgment in your life and mine. Are you going through such a time at present? What changes is God calling you to make as a direct result of this?

9

A tale of two armies

In every sense of the word, Revelation 9 follows on from Revelation 8 ... that was a scary chapter which climaxed with a treble woe. That was God's way of saying to the world, 'Watch out, the worst is yet to come!' And come it did, in chapter 9! Here we have angel number five blowing the trumpet and an army comes from the pit (verses 1-12), then you have angel number six sounding the trumpet and an army comes from the east (verses 13-21). It is a sordidly sensational tale of two armies.

I think it might be helpful to us if we considered verses 1 and 2 and attempted to identify the leader of these locusts. He is spoken of as their king in verse 11, but the question is, who is he? Can we pinpoint him with any reasonable degree of accuracy? I believe we can and I have no doubts in my mind that it is the devil, let me show you why:

9:1,2

His position

He is described as *'a star that had fallen from the sky to the earth.'*
Here is the star that bit the dust! You will also find in verse 2 that
this star is identified by the personal pronoun *he.* That would seem
to indicate we are talking about a real person.

When is a star an angel?

When you backtrack to 1:20, we are told there that stars in the book
of Revelation represent angels. So a star is a symbol for an angel.
That deduction seems fairly reasonable even in this particular setting.
In fact, in 9:11, he is referred to as *'the angel of the Abyss.'*

A fallen star!

It had fallen from heaven to earth and when you read that your
personal antenna begins to receive all kinds of signals. The general
opinion is that this would imply some kind of moral failure on his
part. In Jude 6 and 7, we learn about angels who have experienced
such ruin. The Bible also speaks of 'unclean spirits' and it equates
them with 'demons.'
  When you meet a demon in the gospel narrative, it is clear for
those with eyes to see that they are extremely capable of controlling
a person's mind and actions; human beings can be demon possessed.
The best example which springs to mind is the story in Luke 8
involving the man from Gadara. You will remember the incredible
transformation Jesus brought to this man's life; it is summed up in
verse 36 where we read the man was 'dressed and in his right mind.'
  Think about the devil for a moment. Satan is nothing more than
an angel, and a fallen angel at that! He fell from the sublime heights
of heaven. He was an anointed cherub and was as near to the throne
of God as it was possible to be. He was heaven's worship leader, he
was God's masterpiece, a showpiece of what God could do, but he
blew it and he fell!

He was limited in what he could achieve, he underestimated God and overestimated himself. He was limited in what he could foresee, there was a price to pay but he had no idea what this would be. He was limited in damage control, there was no turning back when he made an irrevocable choice. He was limited in his understanding of God, there was so much he obviously did not know!

It is quite incredible but even in this most ideal of situations, in what was and is a perfect environment, this angel made his choice, he exercised his right and it proved to be one which was seriously flawed. It would appear he miscalculated the consequence of his decision and God's reaction to it.

Pride and arrogance got the better of him! His ambition was to be one up on the Lord of all glory. His passion was to be number one. His aspiration was to be better than God. It was a high risk gamble which backfired very badly. Jesus does not pay him any compliments when he labels him in John 8:44, 'a liar and a murderer from the beginning.' (You can read more about him and the events surrounding his being unceremoniously thrown out of heaven in Isaiah 14 and Ezekiel 28.) The Bible often refers to the 'devil and his angels.' It informs us that these are deceiving spirits. It tells us that Satan is the prince of the power of the air, he is the prince of darkness and he is the prince of this world.

He loses access to heaven

When you read the book of Job you find that Satan has access to God in heaven and when he pops in from time to time, it is with an armful of accusations against the people of God; one day that will all end! Satan will be removed from the heavens during the period of Tribulation. His final destiny is the lake of fire and there he will be tormented day and night for ever and ever (20:10). You see, the devil is always under the feet of Jesus! That is something we must never forget!

> If we have a leadership position, how does verse 1 guide and warn us about what should be the condition of our hearts (cf. 1 Timothy 3:6)?

His power

He has a key!

We read at the end of verse 1 that *'the star was given the key to the shaft of the Abyss.'* It is a key to a subterranean abode. This means, his power and authority are seriously limited. He can go so far and no further. He can do so much and no more. He has his limits imposed by God. He has to operate within certain parameters which God has set down. In 1:18, we are told that *'the keys of Hades and death'* are in the hands of Jesus Christ. Satan is not the king of hell, he is the chief prisoner!

The key that unlocks the chains of those demons in hell was given to Satan; he obviously did not have it in his control. God now allows him to unleash his fury against a world that has rejected Jesus. The day of God's wrath has come and, as always, God will use even the devil to accomplish his divine purposes.

The key which he has in his hand is specifically for the shaft of the Abyss, the bottomless pit. It is described in Luke 16 as a place of torment. It is the place where the demons in pigskin swimsuits in Luke 8 did not want the Lord to send them! 2 Peter 2:4 reminds us that 'God did not spare the angels when they sinned but sent them to hell, putting them into gloomy dungeons, to be held for judgment.' Later in the book, we discover that Satan himself will be penned up here for a thousand years when Jesus is reigning on planet earth.

He is the king!

The picture we have here is of a vast depth approached by a shaft whose top is covered. This is where the plague of locusts comes from; 11:7 also advises us that the beast comes out of the same place. When you put them both together, it appears to suggest that the Antichrist will be a human being who is demon possessed and he will then go on to deceive the world. We also note that he is described as the king of the locusts.

The power of the devil is clearly revealed in the simple statement we have in 9:11 for there we read, *'They had as king over them the angel of the Abyss, whose name in Hebrew is Abaddon and in Greek, Apollyon.'* One of the reasons for believing that this plague is not actual locusts is that it has a king. Proverbs 30:27 informs us that natural locusts do not have a king ruling over them! You see, the devil is the king of demons; he controls a vast empire of evil spirits and through them he can influence the lives of countless millions of people.

We need to understand that the devil is not omnipresent like our God is. That means he cannot be everywhere at the same time. Having said that, through his teeming minions, he can attack many people at any given moment. So he has a fair bit of mobility and a fair bit of clout to go along with it.

His purpose

We note in verse 11 that his name is *'Abaddon'* in the Hebrew and *'Apollyon'* in the Greek. The name means 'the destroyer.' And that sums him up in a nutshell; he is out to wreck people's lives, he is out to ruin ordinary men and women. We see him here as he really is, the mask is removed, the precariously thin veneer of respectability is stripped away, he is no angel of light, he is evil personified.

It is quite intriguing to see that his name is given in both languages, Hebrew and Greek. That gives a fair bit of credibility to the notion that his mission is to all men, irrespective of their religious affiliation. It makes no difference to him whether you are a Jew or a Gentile, if you have not got the treble six on your forehead, he will not rest until he strikes back. He is out to get you on that day if you are a follower of the Lamb!

Having said that, he is on the warpath even today. He is on the prowl right now. He is doing everything in his power to trip up the people of God. He is doing all that he can to frustrate the efforts of those who are seeking to advance the cause of the gospel of Christ to the ends of the earth. It will be true then and, it is certainly true today, that Satan to Jesus must bow. No matter what the devil does, God holds the trump card!

> In verse 11, the devil is described as the destroyer. How does this forewarn us against his schemes, and how does it motivate us to resist his ways and pursue godliness, both for ourselves and others?

9:3-6

The locusts ... their authority

John says in verse 3, *'And out of the smoke locusts came down upon the earth.'* They are demons straight from the caverns of hell itself. Someone has said that '... smoke billows from the prison house of evil unleashing the soot of hell.' John MacArthur suggests that, 'The smoke polluting the sky symbolises the corruption of hell belched forth from the abyss to pollute the world.' A spiritual plague of demonic proportions breaks out upon the whole earth. They are swarming all over the place; in fact, there are so many of them we read that *'the sun and the sky were darkened'* by them. The inevitable outcome where mankind is terrorised is fuelled by the work of millions of these fiendish beings.

John continues by pointing out that they *'were given power like that of scorpions of the earth.'* This statement of intent leaves no doubt in our minds that demons only operate under divine permission. Their power or authority comes ultimately from the Lord. We need to remember this for it means, even in the worst of times, that God is in total control. No matter what happens to any of us, the Lord remains firmly in charge.

The extent of it

We glean from verse 5 that *'they were not given power to kill them, but only to torture them for five months.'* The limit is set by God and it is for five months, not a day more, not a day less. Yes, the Bible is that exact! It is Swiss precision. The boundary is established and it will not, it cannot, be breached.

Mention is made of the targets which are affected by this cutback in their strike capability in verse 4. We read, *'They were told not to harm the grass of the earth or any plant or tree, but only those people who did not have the seal of God on their foreheads.'* In other words, they can cause a lot of pain and they will leave a lot of people writhing in severe agony with all sorts of medical complications. Their attacks on human beings will not be fatal for they are instructed not to kill. The world of nature has its own agenda.

When a plague of locusts hits an area, they will eat everything in sight. Every blade of grass, every leaf on a tree, every flower and stalk of grain will be consumed. They have even been known to strip the bark from the trees. They have a voracious appetite which cannot be satisfied. That is how these demons will be! They have an insatiable lust to wreak havoc in the lives of people. Again this underlines the truth that God is sovereign for even the demons of hell are under divine management!

> **What can we discover about the limitations imposed on fallen angels?**

The effects of it

The raging torment of the unbelievers is graphically described in verse 5 where John compares *'the agony they suffered'* to *'the sting of a scorpion when it strikes a man.'* Here we have the crippling effect of their authority when the entire human race becomes dysfunctional. From what I understand, a scorpion sting is not life threatening except in the case of small children. Apparently the venom attacks the veins and the body's nervous system to such an extent that the intense pain and discomfort will last for several days. When the poison enters the system it sets the nerve centre on fire. That helps explain why the people feel the way they do for their anguish is indescribable.

I read in a medical journal that there is nothing you can take to relieve the pain; in fact, a pain killer would only exacerbate the effect of the venom making the pain infinitely worse! The pain is often accompanied by temporary paralysis and a high fever and there is nothing you can do but grin and bear it. It has to be endured.

John drops a bombshell when he tells us this demonic invasion will persist for five months! *You know, five months is not that long if you are waiting for something exciting to happen in your life, but it is a terribly long time if you are waiting for something awful to end.* Life will become intolerable. In fact, it is so debilitating that people actually want to die; the suffering is so severe that men will be driven to suicide. But God will frustrate all their efforts.

Their attempts to 'run away from it all' will come to nothing. The gun does not fire; the overdose is ineffective; the leap from a tall building is interrupted by some kind of invisible net! Oh yes, they will try alright but they will not be successful. People will seek relief in death only to find that death has taken a holiday! That is what we read in verse 6, *'During those days men will seek death, but will not find it; they will long to die, but death will elude them.'*

9:7-10

The locusts ... their appearance

The next paragraph is unbelievably colourful in its language. The description is so unlike ordinary locusts that we have to recognise John is using them to represent something entirely different; they are symbolic of demons and John is attempting to depict them in this way so that the people of his day will understand what he is talking about. Overall, they are seen in verse 7 as *'horses prepared for battle.'* I am inclined to think John sees a possible tie-up here with the prophecy we have in Joel 2:4,5 where the prophet says, 'They have the appearance of horses; they gallop along like cavalry. With a noise like that of chariots, they leap over the mountaintops like a crackling fire consuming stubble, like a mighty army drawn up for battle.' There is a fascinating consistency between them, it is more than coincidental. They are both addressing the subject of the Day of the Lord.

The apostle then provides us with a specific description of them in the remaining verses in this section. He says, *'On their heads they wore something like crowns of gold, and their faces resembled human faces. Their hair was like women's hair, and their teeth were like lions' teeth. They had breastplates of iron, and the sound of their wings was like the thundering of many horses and chariots rushing into battle. They had tails and stings like scorpions, and in their tails they had power to torment people for five months.'*

You will notice that each comparison is introduced with the word *'like'* for what we have here is a brilliant portrayal of a powerful enemy armed for battle.

With bodies like horses they progress rapidly, they will stop at nothing. They have faces like men which suggests their cunning and craft; like their boss, they are as subtle as they come. Their heads are crowned and that is an allusion to their temporary rule over the world; they feel good when they think they are running the show! That they are covered with long hair is a hint at their tactics for they will entrap both men and women. They appear very alluring and they will use their stunning appearance to seduce unwitting individuals. They have teeth like those of lions for they are ready to shred and tear to pieces those they pounce upon. Their skin is like a coat of mail which implies they are callous and heartless; no matter how people shriek and groan, the demons are pitiless. When they fly, the noise is like an army of chariots rushing by; their victims will not be able to escape the terror of their arrival.

I was interested to discover that the normal lifespan of a locust is about five months from May to September and, when you read verse 11, you find this is the specific length of time the judgment will last. In that day all restraints will be removed, the gloves will be off and man will reel from every blow the enemy inflicts on him. The horror of that day does not bear thinking about. All I can say is this, it will be so much worse than we can possibly imagine! It will be a nightmare for those who experience it.

These demons may be hideous looking creatures but they are powerful, they are invincible, they are indestructible, they are intelligent. It is typical of the old devil though; it does not matter what he does, it is the nature of the beast, he is just like the scorpion, there is always a sting in the tail!

> People are powerless before these demonic forces. In contrast,
> what can we learn from the way Jesus dealt with a legion of
> demons in Luke 8:26-39?

9:12,13

By the time you come down to verse 12, John says all that needs to
be said, *'The first woe is past; two other woes are yet to come.'*

A voice ... its sound and its source

With the sound of the trumpet ringing in his ear, John tells us that he
*'heard a voice coming from the horns of the golden altar that is
before God.'* There is nothing strange or startling about this for John
often informs us that he hears a voice coming from near the throne
of God. It may be the voice of a special angel which John hears, it
may be one of the cherubim who guard the glory of God or it may be
one of the four living creatures who function as the worship leaders
of heaven. All of these are well within the bounds of possibility. On
the other hand, it is not naïve to think, it could be the voice of God
himself. Why not? Why should he not communicate personally
and directly with the sixth angel? The voice is of supreme importance
because of the grave message which is conveyed.

It came from the horns of the altar! That is what we came across
in chapter 8. It is the altar of incense on which was offered before
God the prayers of the saints who were then living on earth. In that
passage, the angel took fire from the altar and threw it down upon
the earth and horrific judgment followed.

It would appear that the impassioned prayers of the saints in
chapter 6 are finally answered in what happens next. Do you
remember their prayer? *'How long, Sovereign Lord, holy and true,
until you judge the inhabitants of the earth and avenge our blood?'*
I think this second woe, the sixth trumpet judgment, is God's specific
answer to their heartfelt cry. It may not be what they had in mind or
even anticipated but their plea is answered nonetheless. That is what
really counts for, if it does nothing else, it underlines the signal truth
that God is sovereign.

9:14,15

The control of this army

The message which filtered through to the sixth angel was clear and concise, there was no mistaking it. We read about it in verse 14 where the eavesdropping John spills the beans: *'It said to the sixth angel who had the trumpet, "Release the four angels who are bound at the great river Euphrates."'* That was some message! God's answer takes the form of releasing four powerful fallen angels who have been bound for centuries at this great river. They are set free in God's time and again this underpins the truth which I have tried to emphasise throughout our study that the Lord rules and reigns; he is in total control!

Four leaders

This quartet of angels are the leaders of a huge army of two hundred million troops which John refers to later in verse 16. He records the mind-boggling statistic by saying, *'The number of the mounted troops was two hundred million. I heard their number.'* This staggering figure made a significant impact on him. In fact, I imagine John was quite taken aback by the massive scale of this entire operation. For him, back in the first century, it must have blown his mind; for you and me living in the third millennium, it is not as far fetched as some punters have made it appear. It is believable!

The cradle of civilisation

Did you notice where these angels were bound? It was at the Euphrates River! That, in itself, is fascinating. It was one of the four rivers which came out of the garden paradise of Eden.

> It was here Satan first alighted on earth and made a successful attack upon the human race!
> It was here all of earth's miseries were introduced!
> It was here the first murder was committed and the first martyr slain!

It was here the Jews dragged out their bitter exile!
It was here Babylon arose!
It was here we have the prototype of the kingdom of the Antichrist!
It is right here where four special emissaries of Satan are chafing
at the bit!

Archaeologists consider the Euphrates as the birthplace of civilisation. It seems to me that God will use it as a graveyard at the end of time; in a mysterious way, he will wrap up the history of the world in this place.

It was with father Abraham that God entered into a covenant regarding his people and the promised land. We read in Genesis 15:18 that the border would extend as far as the 'great river Euphrates.' The river serves as a natural frontier between the lands of the East and the Middle Eastern, European and Western nations. It flows out of the mountains of Armenia, down through the present-day lands of Iraq and Iran and on into the Persian Gulf. It is about 1,700 to 1,800 miles long and, just like the Nile, it floods in the months of March, April and May because of melting snows. In the ancient world, it formed the eastern fringe of the vast Roman Empire. History tells us the Romans lived in constant fear of the warlike Parthians who lived on the other side of the river. The same could be said of Israel for the great warrior nations of Assyria and Babylonia had previously come down from the north across the river and into the Holy Land.

In recent times, the Euphrates River was strategically important during the 1991 Gulf War which liberated Kuwait. 'Stormin' Norman', as they called him, was the top dog, he was the man in charge of Operation Desert Storm. During the one hundred hour ground campaign of that conflict, the US Army's 24th Mechanised and 101st Airborne Divisions trapped the elite Republican Guard of Iraq with its back against the Euphrates River. They were unable to escape, they had nowhere to hide and so they were decimated in one of the most lopsided military victories of all time. And as they say, the rest is history!

The killing fields revisited

It is right here at this location that 9:15 will become a reality. John says, *'And the four angels who had been kept ready for this very hour and day and month and year were released to kill a third of mankind.'*

There is nothing airy-fairy about God's timetable. We are not talking about just the year when this great event will take place; we are not narrowing it down to only a particular month in a particular year; we are not pinpointing only a specific day in a given month in a given year! No! We are a lot more focused than that! We are down to the very hour when it will happen. God has this special moment circled in red on heaven's calendar! The date is set.

When that predetermined hour arrives, all will go according to God's plan. Nothing can happen, nothing will happen, which will cause him to abort his mission. This is quite breathtaking for again it stresses that everything is under his control and that includes all the demons of darkness. Not a speck of dust moves, not a blade of grass stirs, not an army can move, not a shot can be fired, without his knowing all about it.

The unthinkable repercussions of their release is the wholesale slaughter of one-third of mankind. You will remember that earlier in the Tribulation, 25% of the world's population was eliminated; that happened when seal judgment number four transpired. Still others have perished from drinking polluted water as recorded in 8:10,11; and, no doubt, there will have been many other casualties for one reason or another.

But now, what we have our attention focused on, is that a further one-third of the population is to be killed. Death, which had taken a brief holiday under the fifth trumpet, now returns with a vengeance. When you add all the numbers together, it means that a minimum of 50% of the world's peoples have died before the middle of the Tribulation. That sends shivers down my spine! It is an alarming figure which causes me enormous concern. It is the size of the figure which is hard to comprehend; it is so big, it is hard to envisage, I cringe every time I think about it.

That is why we must pull out all the stops in order to share the good news of Jesus Christ with those who are still outside his global family. We owe it to them to warn them to flee from the coming day of God's wrath!

In our often confused and even chaotic world, what encouragement is there in the precise implementation of God's plans as outlined in verse 15?

9:16,17

The characteristics of this army

John moves on in verse 16 to leave us in no doubt as to the incredible size of this army. He informs us that *'the number of the mounted troops was two hundred million.'* And then as if to reinforce his own utter amazement at the staggering size of this military contingent, he says, *'I heard their number.'*

It is almost as if the figure left him speechless, he was dumbfounded, he could not believe what he had just been told! It is a number which is so large, it is difficult to comprehend. In his day there were not even two hundred million people living on the earth! We have seen news footage in recent days of mass demonstrations in a variety of global hot spots and some of these have added up to one million people; but, when you multiply that by two hundred, it blows the mind! I understand from military records that this number is almost twice as many troops as the Allied and Axis powers combined when they were at peak strength in World War II.

It seems to me, it is fairly realistic to assume that the army we are talking about here is one which comes from the lands of the rising sun. It has often been referred to as the 'yellow peril.' I realise it is only speculation but it is well within the bounds of possibility for these vast nations of the Orient are the only ones who are able to fit the bill. China, for example, has a population approaching 1.3 billion people. For them, to muster an army of this size is no big deal. Logistically, there may be all sorts of problems, it would not be that easy. Numerically, they are home and dry.

I think one of the keys to understanding this second phase in God's judgment programme is to compare this portion with a similar event unfolding in phase three. You find it in 16:12-16 where we read about the Euphrates drying up as a curtain raiser to the campaign of Armageddon. In that scenario, the way is opened up for an incursion into the land of Israel from what John describes as *'the kings of the east.'* We will come back to that in more detail later; suffice to say, what we have here in chapter 9 is the world's greatest army causing absolute mayhem among the peoples of the world.

Aggressive and awesome!

John gives a powerful description of the horses and riders he saw in his vision. He says in verse 17 that, *'Their breastplates were fiery red, dark blue, and yellow as sulphur. The heads of the horses resembled the heads of lions, and out of their mouths came fire, smoke and sulphur.'*

Red, blue and yellow ... and when they are combined, they are an effective portrayal of what we can expect from these assailants in the field of battle. No matter how you interpret this verse, these combatants are an aggressive force and, when you see them in full flight, they are an awesome force as well.

It seems clear what John envisions for us is the machinery of modern military capability translated into the terminology of his day. Breastplates of various colours suggest armoured chariots and could refer to tanks, troop carriers, missile launchers, rocket batteries, artillery pieces and aircraft of various countries bearing the identifying colours of their nations of origin.

The lions mouths which spouted fire and smoke suggest cannons, mortars, rocket launchers and even missiles killing great masses of people with fire, radiation, and poison gases. The fact that one-third of the human race is destroyed in this conflict strongly implies that weapons of mass destruction are deployed. Some leaders are trigger happy and even in our day there are those who, it would appear, can hardly wait to flick the switch. In some countries, we have already witnessed the devastating results of germ warfare. The statistics which we are talking about here are frightening and alarming but there is nothing unusual about them when you bear in mind the nature of this particular engagement.

9:18-21

The consequences of this army

This is echoed in verse 18, where it is confirmed that, *'a third of mankind was killed by the three plagues of fire, smoke and sulphur that came out of their mouths.'* And there is another intriguing insight given to us by John in verse 19, where he says, *'The power of the horses was in their mouths and in their tails; for their tails were like snakes, having heads with which they inflict injury.'*

What an amazing picture we have here! I suppose these words could apply to various kinds of modern armaments such as helicopter gunships or even missiles which leave a snake-like trail in their wake and inflict injury with their warheads. They are lethal, they are fatal, they are terminal.

It is hard to say for we cannot be sure, we cannot really be dogmatic. At the end of the day, no matter what way you want to look at it, it paints a picture of untold destruction on an unbelievable scale. It is monstrous slaughter, it is a wipe-out.

> These verses reveal the outworking of God's wrath (cf. Romans 1:18-20). How does knowing this increase our gratitude to Jesus 'who rescues us from the coming wrath' (1 Thessalonians 1:10)? Take a few moments to thank him for rescuing you!

Zero repentance

You would think by this time that men would be driven to their knees. You would imagine that men would be turning to God in their droves. Well, nothing could be further from the truth. That is the last thing on their mind. The truth is spelled out very clearly in the next verse and I think this is one of the most astounding verses in the entire book of Revelation. John concludes in verse 20 that *'the rest of mankind that were not killed by these plagues still did not repent of the work of their hands.'* Man is defiant! He shakes his fist in God's face!

In all honesty, would you not think that by this time the remaining earth survivors would fall down before God and beg for mercy? The 'God-get-me-out-of-this-mess-and-I'll-believe-in-you' form of prayer is not even uttered! There is not even the slightest hint of that happening, there is no record of anyone repenting. The statistics for people trusting in Jesus for the first time remain at zero. The stark reality is summed up in the words of one commentator when he writes, 'Nuclear war, earthquakes, plagues, deadly insects, people dying faster than babies being born, these disasters will not break the pagans.'

It can be summed up in a couple of words which are found many times in the Bible: their hearts are hard! They are like granite. They are like stone. These folk are highly religious; the problem is, the god they worship is the god of materialism.

They are living in a highly secular society which has relegated the true God to the bottom rung of the ladder. They are totally wrapped up in themselves and their own pursuits; they have no time for, nor interest in, the God of the Bible. They are happy to follow the Antichrist and give him their loyal devotion. They fulfil their spiritual aspirations in demon worship and, at the same time, they are enthusiastically committed to all kinds of religious experience which they can find through worshipping Satan. John tells us, *'They did not stop worshipping demons, and idols of gold, silver, bronze, stone and wood.'* And then he adds with a hint of sarcasm in his voice, *'idols that cannot see or hear or walk.'* It is a classic case of dead sinners worshipping dead gods!

The final verse in the chapter catalogues four serious sins which are rampant during these depressingly familiar days of Tribulation. John says in verse 21, *'They did not repent of their murders, their magic arts, their sexual immorality or their thefts.'*

Murder. The first one on the list is murder; it speaks of violent crime and it is the inevitable outcome in a crazed society where life is cheap. Killings will be so common that they will not be reported in the national media. This may even include the killing of the very young through infanticide and abortion and the killing of the elderly through involuntary euthanasia.

Magic arts. This speaks of the occult, spiritualism and witchcraft. It is also a strange fascination with the future and includes horoscopes and astrology. It is linked inextricably with the drug culture. The Greek word is *pharmakeia* and it probably refers, in this instance, to mind-bending and mood-altering drugs. When these are taken and people are addicted to them, they switch between the worlds of fantasy and reality. It means they are immune to the disasters surrounding them.

Sexual immorality. The thought here is one of free love for all. It is the mindset which says, 'everybody's doing it, so why shouldn't I?' In such a libertine environment, people generally tend to revert back to their baser instincts where lust reigns supreme; many of them end up acting like animals.

Theft. This last item on the list highlights the crimes of fraud, burglary and embezzlement. Such things happen when greed is the motivator.

This is what will happen during the Tribulation but, you and I know from experience, we see it happening all around us in today's world. We have lost our moral bearings as a nation and we are drifting aimlessly out to sea. These four sins are part and parcel of our present culture. It is no wonder then that they will be centre stage in the not-too-distant future.

What insight do we glean from verses 20 and 21 into our human nature? How does this deepen your understanding of why we need to be saved by grace and not by works? Repentance is a lifelong process ... are there areas in your life at present where your heart is hard and you need to seek the Lord and apply repentance (cf. Acts 5:31 where Jesus is the giver of repentance)?

10

When God explains the reason why

Sometimes life does not make sense. People often wrestle with the hard questions:

Lord, where were you when my child died?
Lord, where were you when the missionaries were massacred?
Lord, where were you when the guerillas abducted your servants?
Lord, why do the bad guys seem to sail through life so easily?
Lord, where were you when life was so unfair?
Lord, why do bad things happen to good people?

Where is God when heaven seems silent? Revelation 10 shows us there is coming a day when the answers will be given. God does not leave us hanging by our finger tips; he does not keep us in suspense. We read in verse 7 that *'the mystery of God will be accomplished.'* That is a statement of fact. It tells me in a day soon to come, we will see the puzzle of the ages solved. Then all of life's enigma's will be adequately explained. We must await God's time!

With that in mind, I recall a story I heard many years ago about a farmer who worked hard in his field, which was bordered by his neighbour's field. Out of respect and reverence for the Lord's day, the old farmer never worked on a Sunday, while his neighbour always did. Although he worked hard to make up for it, the loss of time cost the farmer. His soil was not ploughed on time, his crops were not planted on time, and in the end, his autumn harvest was not as full and profitable as his neighbour's. When the neighbour pointed out the difference and told the farmer God seemed to have blessed him more even though he had not honoured the Lord's day, the old farmer replied, 'God doesn't settle all of his accounts in October!'

In chapter 10 we have another interlude, a longer intermission than we have had previously; it is a wonderful chance for us to catch our breath. So much has been happening. Events have been moving so fast, we can hardly keep pace. They are accelerating at breakneck speed. It has been so intense. The dark storm clouds have gathered and the anger of God has been felt across the world.

By this time, in the middle of the period of Tribulation, the statistics tell us that 50% of the population has died. The grim reaper has been actively at work. But what we have here is a preview of the triumph of Jesus. We see that the moment will come when Jesus is hailed as the mighty conqueror. The main reason we have it here is to enable us to take heart; at the end of the day, God is the winner, the Lamb wins!

We are right in the middle of the seven year period of Tribulation. The events that take place now can be sorely depressing because the Antichrist shows himself in his true colours. The mask comes off when he breaks his agreement with the nation of Israel and, instead of assuring them of the peace which he initially promised them, he begins to persecute them. Israel as a people and as a nation face the tortuously harrowing prospect of another holocaust experience. Times will be seriously bad but, even in such an awful era of trial and trouble, God is not without a witness to the world.

We discover in chapters 10 and 11 that there are three important testimonies:

The first one comes from a mighty angel (10:1-11)
The second one comes from two special witnesses (11:1-14)
The third one comes from the elders in heaven (11:15-18)

10:1-4

The angel's description

John says in verse 1 that he *'saw another mighty angel coming down from heaven.'* Some of the characteristics that John outlines regarding this angel belong especially to the Lord Jesus Christ. There is every chance that we may have met this angel before: once he held back impending judgments so the 144,000 could be sealed, then he arrived to pour out fire and judgment upon the earth, now he comes as king taking back possession of planet earth. Over the years there has been a lot of speculation as to the identity of this particular angel. It seems to me, at least on this occasion, that it is none other than the Lord himself. There are many instances recorded in Scripture where he is revealed as the Angel of Jehovah.

He was robed!

God is often identified with clouds, that is how deity is often spectacularly depicted. Science can explain the clouds but I like to see them as his special clothing. He is wearing the drapery of the sky over his mighty shoulders. That symbolises his power, majesty, and glory, and the fact that he comes bringing judgment.

> *God led Israel by a glorious cloud as in Exodus 16.*
> *Dark clouds covered Sinai when the Law was given to Moses in Exodus 19.*
> *God appeared again to Moses in a cloud of dazzling glory as in Exodus 24 and 34.*
> *We read in Psalm 104:3 that 'he makes the clouds his chariot.'*
> *In Acts 1, a cloud received Jesus when he ascended up to heaven.*
> *When he returns at the end of the age, it will be with clouds as intimated in 1:7.*

He has a rainbow!

We first came across the rainbow when it encircled the throne of God in chapter 4. Now it sits like a crown upon the head of this mighty angel. The rainbow was God's sign that he would never again destroy the world with a flood (Genesis 9:12-16). Here it reminds us that, even in the day of his wrath, God remembers mercy (Habakkuk 3:2).

You see, God is a God of faithfulness and all his promises will be fulfilled. The English poet William Wordsworth said, 'My heart leaps up when I behold a rainbow in the sky.' I think John must have felt the same way when he saw this special messenger. The book of Revelation takes us on a roller coaster ride of emotions. We go from heartache and depression to scenes of triumph and joyous celebration. It is the seesaw syndrome so far as the ripening of God's eternal purposes are concerned.

His face was like the sun. That is a powerful reminder of his holiness and his glory. It seems to me, this ties in beautifully with what we read of the Lord Jesus in 1:16.

His legs were fiery pillars. This is a stunning symbol of God's strength and the firmness and stability of all his ways and purposes. It is also an echo of 1:15.

His voice is like that of a lion. This is suggestive of the picture we have of him in 5:5 where he is set forth as the Lion of the tribe of Judah.

All in all, when you put each of these features together, it seems to me this could well be our blessed Lord Jesus. He is appearing here to John as a kingly angel. But, that is not all we base our assumption on, there is more! Two more features strike me as being most unusual.

> From the description given of the angel in verse 1, list five or six words, each of which sums up a different aspect of what he is like!

A book in his hand!

In verse 2, we read that, *'He was holding a little scroll, which lay open in his hand. He planted his right foot on the sea and his left foot on the land.'* The book in his hand is a comparatively small scroll and it is open! It contains the rest of the prophetic message that John will deliver. It is a message of supreme importance. It will have a global impact.

The world at his feet!

His posture is most captivating. It is the picture of a conqueror taking possession of his territory! He is claiming the whole world with his right foot on the sea and his left foot on the land, we see him standing there astride the earth like a giant colossus making a declaration that his is the right to rule and reign. The world is his! The earth is the Lord's; he claims dominion over every land, from pole to pole, from sea to sea, from the rivers to the ends of the earth.

He shouts his message. We read in verse 3, *'and he gave a loud shout like the roar of a lion.'* We all know the old devil roars like a lion to frighten his prey (1 Peter 5:8), but the Lion of the tribe of Judah roars to announce victory! This tremendous truth is expanded on in Psalm 95:3-5 and Isaiah 40:12-17.

What a stirring announcement it is! It was so loud that Satan's roar seems like a soft whisper by comparison. It drowns out the devil in a way which he deserves, it muffles all that the enemy says. We read in verse 3, *'When he shouted, the voices of the seven thunders spoke.'* It is just like a seven gun salute in the skies. It is a booming reply; it sounds like something the movie moguls in Hollywood would orchestrate.

Can you recall the words of Job 37:5 where we read, 'God's voice thunders in marvellous ways; he does great things beyond our understanding.' On a similar note, we read in Psalm 29:3 that 'the God of glory thunders!'

What follows next is quite unusual. John was about to write what had been spoken, but he heard another message saying, *'Seal up what the seven thunders have said and do not write it down.'* As far as I am aware, this is the first and only time in the book when John is forbidden to reveal the contents of the message shared with him. What was this message? We just do not know. And there is no point in speculating either; God has chosen to veil the truth in this instance and it is best to leave it that way.

Another way to look at it ...

There is another perspective on this particular episode which I think has a fair bit of credibility. Look at it like this: our Lord has just asserted that he is king of all the earth, he is sovereign. He has claimed this planet as his. And when he did that, the seven thunders spoke. Could it be that this is a backlash from Satan? Could it be that the devil is giving vent to his anger in answer to the Lord's roar?

The nations also give vent to their wrath; if that is the case, the seven thunders would then symbolise the response of the rebels to the Lord's declaration. It is a bit like Pharaoh's response to Moses in Exodus 5:2 when he said, 'I know not the Lord, neither will I let Israel go.'

John is about to record what they said but he is told not to, he is told to disregard what they have been saying. Here is a subtle hint of the majesty of the king for he simply sweeps aside the united thundering of his enemies. What they have to say is not important and John is best to ignore them, he is well advised not to take them under his notice.

So there is more than one way to take notice of it. You can take your pick but the God who makes himself known is the same God who keeps his secrets!

> **In the light of verse 4, how far could the Lord trust you with a secret?**

10:5-7

The angel's declaration

It is based on God's authority

This declaration is one which is carried out under oath. We read, *'Then the angel I had seen standing on the sea and on the land raised his right hand to heaven. And he swore by him who lives for ever and ever, who created all the heavens and all that is in them, the earth and all that is in it, and the sea and all that is in it.'* He swears in the name of one who is eternal and in the name of the one who is the great creator. The words that are employed in this comprehensive statement reveal that the scope of God's creative power is all-encompassing. John MacArthur reminds us that 'His purpose for his creation will be fulfilled through judgment, renovation, destruction and re-creation.'

He begins by raising his right hand to heaven in a gesture familiar to many of us. It is the kind of ritual which witnesses are called to go through when they find themselves in a courtroom. It underlines the seriousness of their commitment to 'tell the truth, the whole truth and nothing but the truth.' The question is, why did he go to such lengths? Well, he did it to confirm that what he was saying was true and it would come to pass. There have been other times in Scripture when deity has taken an oath.

In Hebrews 6, God put himself under oath when he made his covenant with Abraham.
He did the same when he declared his Son to be a high priest in Hebrews 7.
And again, when he promised David that the Christ would come from his family, as mentioned in Acts 2:29,30.

It is rooted in God's timetable

He seems to be saying, 'Look, all the weight of deity is behind it, all heaven is behind it.' *'There will be no more delay!'* is the message given. As sure as night follows day, and Tuesday comes after Monday, it is going to happen. If it does not take place, he would fail to be God! In essence, God is staking his very existence on his message.

The startling implication is that from this day forward, God's foot will be on the accelerator. Every stop is pulled out, all systems are up and running. There is no turning back! That is the message. We always need to remember that God is on time. All is according to his schedule. Everything is going according to his plan. He has it all marked out on his calendar and when the hour comes, that is it! *'There will be no more delay!'*

For decades, for centuries, for all of time, man has been frustrated asking, why the apparent delay? Why doesn't God step into the situation? Why doesn't God do something about it? No matter where we look, Satan is on the rampage. It appears that wrong is on the throne and right is on the scaffold. It appears that sin has run unchecked and evil has been unbridled.

Remember the souls under the altar? They asked about God's timetable in chapter 6. Remember the disciples? They came to Jesus privately and asked him in Matthew 24:3, 'What will be the sign of your coming and of the end of the age?' Oh yes, scoffers have taunted, saints have pleaded, the cry has ascended, *'How long, O Lord, how long?'*

It is grounded in God's promise

Well, the waiting is just about over! It is down the home straight! The end is in sight! We read in verse 7 that *'the mystery of God will be accomplished.'* There is no stopping the Lord now!

> How would you make use of the truth in verse 7 to help someone who was struggling to hold on to their faith, perhaps because of a personal tragedy?

10:8-11

The angel's directions

Up to this point, John has been a virtual spectator in the grandstand of heaven. He is gobsmacked as he has watched each event unfold before his eyes. Now he becomes an actor in the drama of the Apocalypse. He hears a voice from heaven which tells him in verse 8 to *'Go, take the scroll that lies open in the hand of the angel who is standing on the sea and on the land.'* And that is precisely what John does.

Sweet and sour!

No sooner has John done it than he hears the angel's voice a second time saying in verse 9, *'Take it and eat it. It will turn your stomach sour, but in your mouth it will be as sweet as honey.'* Sounds strange, doesn't it! Well, yes and no! You see, tasting and eating in the Bible often refers to hearing and believing. Jeremiah and Ezekiel had a similar experience; both of them had to eat the word before they could pass it on to others.

> The Anglican prayer book advises us to 'read, mark, learn and inwardly digest' the word of God. To what extent have you made God's word a vital part of your inner being?

Absorb and assimilate!

We need to absorb and assimilate the word in our daily lives; it must become an integral part of us for only then can we share it. It is all about digesting the truth of God's word and allowing it to permeate every part of our life. John was to immerse himself in the things of God and saturate himself with Scripture. What an experience this must have been for John! It was sweet to his taste but it was bitter in his belly. It was a bitter-sweet experience! I think many of us can readily identify with John and how he feels at this point. When I study a book like this, I get so excited when I realise the countdown to the coming of Christ is getting nearer every day. It is great news. It is exhilarating. There is a new world waiting for us!

At other times it can be so disturbing and depressing when I think of the awful fate of those who hear the truth and then reject it. They say 'no' to Jesus, even though the clock is ticking away.

You see, the same gospel that makes it possible for me to go to heaven, puts someone else in hell. 'To some,' says Paul, 'it is a savour of life unto life; to others it is a savour of death unto death.' That is what prophetic truth is all about: it is a sweet and sour experience.

John hears the voice a third time in verse 11, when the angel says, *'You must prophesy again about many peoples, nations, languages and kings.'* It is almost as if John is being reminded of his unique task for his mission is not yet complete, his work is not yet finished. There is more for him to do!

Come to think of it, the same is true in your life and mine!

> **Specifically, what work might the Lord be calling you to fulfil (verse 11)? What should you do about it?**

11

The best of times, the worst of times

Charles Dickens was a prolific writer. In his *Tale of Two Cities* he describes in vivid language what life was like immediately prior to the coming of the French revolution. At the very beginning of the story, he tells us with a cluster of pithy and colourful sayings:

It was the best of times, it was the worst of times;
It was the age of wisdom, it was the age of foolishness;
It was the epoch of belief, it was the epoch of incredulity;
It was the season of light, it was the season of darkness;
It was the spring of hope, it was the winter of despair;
We had everything before us, we had nothing before us;
We were all going direct to heaven, we were all going direct the other way.

Each statement is either a paradox or a contradiction. The chilling reality is that people did not know whether they were coming or going. What strikes me is this, when I read through the opening verses of chapter 11, the same superlatives which Dickens used are most appropriate for the age which John is describing.

It is the worst of times, an age of foolishness, an epoch of incredulity, a season of darkness, a winter of despair with nothing except judgment facing those who are conned and deluded by the Antichrist. On the other hand, when you look at it from a different angle, it is the best of times, an age of wisdom, a season of light, the spring of hope with everything before those who are bound for heaven and home! *The bottom line is: for the unbeliever, the worst is yet to come; for the believer, the best is yet to be!*

This is a most fascinating chapter. There are parts of it which are fairly easy to follow and there are other portions which are most difficult to grasp; that does not really matter too much for the golden thread woven into the fabric of this section is that God never leaves himself without a witness. As one Bible commentator has said with remarkable insight, 'The more degenerate the times, the more definite the testimony.' Before the flood, the Lord raised up Enoch and Noah; in the days of Israel's darkest apostasy, he raised up Elijah and Elisha. God will do the same again!

From this chapter forward, we have a slightly different perspective on all that is happening in the world. The total story is presented to us in a brand new format. Instead of pulling back from the events of the last days with a wide-angle lens where we see the big picture, this section of Revelation zooms in for a tight close-up of the personalities caught up in the final drama of the human race. All the major players on the stage of world affairs are in the frame. They are real flesh and blood. The drama intensifies and the temperature rises as we learn how the programme of God is going to be carried out in the end times and through whom it will be performed. When John ate the bitter-sweet scroll, an important change came over the whole narrative. From this point on, John is no longer a mere observer viewing the last days of mankind on earth as if watching a news broadcast on CNN. For the rest of this compelling story, John himself becomes an integral part of the action.

11:1,2

The temple measured

We are told that John *'was given a reed like a measuring rod and was told, "Go and measure the temple of God and the altar and count the worshippers there. But exclude the outer court; do not measure it, because it has been given to the Gentiles. They will trample on the holy city for 42 months."'* You are probably thinking 'that seems a rather strange thing to do!' I am inclined to agree! The reed which John is given is compared to a rod. It is one which is commonly grown in the Jordan Valley and, because of its light weight, it is fairly versatile. They grow to an average height of fifteen to twenty feet. It has a stalk that is hollow, yet it is rigid enough to be used as a walking staff (Ezekiel 29:6), it could even be shaved down into a pen (3 John 13). The stalks, because they were long and lightweight, were excellent as a measuring device.

John is instructed by the divine director to act out the prophecy of the rebuilt temple that the regathered Jews will build in Jerusalem. The Old Testament prophet Ezekiel said the Jews will go back to Jerusalem in unbelief. We read as much in 36:34 and the verses which follow where he tells us, 'For I will take you out of the nations; I will gather you from all the countries and bring you back into your own land.' The result is, the Jews will build a temple in the name of Jehovah God but they will not know him at all. (There is a vast amount of information on this in Ezekiel 40 and 41.)

The measurement is a symbolic action. We have come across it before in the prophecies of Ezekiel and Zechariah and we will come across it one more time in the book of Revelation. These measurements represent God's ownership. He is staking his claim on them! The Lord was saying to John, 'I own this city and this temple and I claim both for myself!' I have been to Jerusalem many times over the past few years and I have spent hours walking all over the place. I have seen many sites of biblical and historical significance but I have never found the temple. The fact is, it is not there! Maybe I should qualify that statement and say, it is not there yet!

The history of the temple

The temple mount

Standing on the temple site today is the Dome of the Rock or the Mosque of Omar, as it is sometimes called. It is the third holiest Muslim shrine. It was built between 685 and 691 by the Arab caliph, Abdel Malik. Its brilliant blue Persian tiles of marble and mosaic and its soaring golden dome dominate one of the most fiercely contested pieces of real estate in the world! You can see it for miles around; it is truly resplendent, it is spectacular especially when the sun is going down.

Islam regards the site of the Dome to be the place where the prophet Mohammed ascended into heaven. Standing alongside it is the famous silver Al-Aqsa mosque. For the better part of two millennia, Jews, Muslims and Christians have been slaughtered in their attempts to control this plot of land.

The first temple

Away back in the halcyon days of King Solomon, in the first millennium BC, it was his stunningly magnificent temple which caught the eye. It rose above the Jerusalem skyline until the invasion by Babylon in 587 BC. It is terribly sad, but Nebuchadnezzar wasted no time in destroying it.

The second temple

It was then lavishly rebuilt by King Herod over a period spanning 46 years. He made it one of the wonders of the world. According to the Jewish historian Josephus, apparently the rabbis often said, 'He who has not seen Herod's temple has never seen a beautiful building.' If you had the time and found yourself in the city of Jerusalem, you could spend a fruitful couple of hours visiting a scale model of this. It is well worth seeing!

A number of key events in the life of Jesus revolve around this particular temple. You find it mentioned many times in the gospel narrative. The day came though when Jesus prophesied to his disciples in the Olivet discourse that not one stone of those great buildings would be left standing.

The destruction of the temple

And that is precisely what happened in AD 70 when Titus tightened his grip on Jerusalem (he was the son of the Roman Emperor Vespasian). He is the one who led the campaign to quell the Jewish uprising which began in AD 66 against Roman rule. It engulfed the entire region of Judea and it ended only after his troops laid siege to the city. In the process, he massacred the population; it is conservatively estimated that over one million Jews died by Roman swords. History confirms that the siege led to such cruel privation and starvation that the people of the city had no option but to eat their own children in order to survive! It was grim! It was the first century equivalent of ethnic cleansing.

When the Romans finally breached the defences of Jerusalem, they levelled the city and razed the temple to the ground. Tradition tells us that the flames were so intense that the gold and silver adorning the temple buildings melted and ran between the cracks. The words of Jesus in Matthew 24 were fulfilled and from that day to this there has been no Jewish temple on that sacred site.

The only remnant of the second temple to be seen today is the western wall or the Wailing Wall, as it is sometimes called. Religious Jews come here day after day and especially on the Sabbath to pour out their hearts in grief and anguish and plead for the Messiah to come. Three times a day, Orthodox Jews recite the words, 'May it be thy will that the temple be speedily rebuilt in our own time.'

There has been a lot of aggro and tension and passion in recent days about rights of access to the temple site. The situation has been inflamed because of the actions of a few fanatical zealots trying to blow the whole site to pieces. Their goal is to clear the site and build the temple we are talking about here in chapter 11, but God has his own way of working and he does not need you or me to speed up the process!

The third temple

When you turn back in your Bible to Daniel 9:24-27, the prophet
foretold that a covenant would be signed between the Antichrist and
the leader of the Jewish people and that after three and a half years
the Antichrist would break the treaty and desecrate the temple.
By then we will have gone full circle. It is almost a repeat
performance of what Antiochus Epiphanes did in 168 BC which is a
prototype of what will happen when Israel rebuilds the temple in the
Tribulation.

We also read in 2 Thessalonians 2:3,4 that the Antichrist will set
himself up as God in that temple. In other words, this temple will
not be defiled by a statue of a pagan deity; it will be polluted by a
man proclaiming himself to be God. This clash would usher in the
second half of the period of Tribulation. This means the temple
must be rebuilt for this to take place! The big question is, where?

In order to answer the question surrounding the rebuilding of the
temple, the exact location of the former two temples must be correctly
identified. One reason for this is that it is argued that the original
site for the temple was divinely appointed (Genesis 22:2; Exodus
15:17; 2 Samuel 24:18; 1 Chronicles 21:18).

Another reason is that there also appears to be a continuity
between the temples. Each one was built with its holy of holies
enclosing the same protrusion of Mount Moriah known as 'the
foundation stone' (*Even ha-Shetiyah*). Because it was upon this stone
that the ark of the covenant had been set and the divine presence in
the shekinah glory had been manifest in 1 Kings 8, it is thought that
no other place can be substituted. The problem, as you will
appreciate, has been in locating this place! Can we pinpoint with a
reasonable degree of accuracy where it is?

Well, we can and we cannot! Ever since the six day war of 1967,
when Jerusalem became a united city under Israeli control, there has
been a tremendous amount of archaeological work done in and around
the temple mount. One man, who stands out among many others, is
Dr Asher Kaufman, a physics professor at the Hebrew University.
He is an orthodox Jewish immigrant from Scotland who has long
been interested in the topography of the temple mount.

After many years of probing and painstaking research, he arrived at a startling conclusion. He said the ancient temple was actually about one hundred yards north of the traditionally held location in relation to the Dome of the Rock. His ideas first appeared in the local broadsheet, *The Jerusalem Post,* in the early 1980s. They then found their way into the pages of the highly acclaimed scholarly journal, *Biblical Archaeology Review,* in Spring 1983. And when you sit down and think them through, they make a lot of sense. They do not solve all the problems but they are certainly worthy of serious consideration. Let me give you a résumé of his main arguments:

The only gate that entered into the temple area from the east is appropriately called the Eastern Gate. This gate has been sealed since the Middle Ages. Most scholars believe it is built over the original eastern gate that led directly into the temple courtyard. I came across an interesting story in the *Mishnah* which illustrates the importance of this. It reveals that during the ceremony of the slaying of the red heifer (Numbers 19) the high priest could look from the top of the Mount of Olives, directly over the eastern gate, into the temple sanctuary. This implies that the temple building was located directly behind the gate. This would not be the case if the temple were situated on the present site of the Dome of the Rock. If you were able to enter the bricked-up Eastern Gate today, you would have to make a left turn going south to reach the Dome of the Rock.

Also if you drew a straight line from the centre of the Eastern Gate, through the temple mount area, what do you think you would encounter? I can tell you, that line would go directly through a small domed structure that covers a round, flat piece of bedrock of Mount Moriah itself. This is known in Arabic by either of two names, the Dome of the Spirits or the Dome of the Tablets. It is intriguing, for when you read Josephus and compare his notes with a number of rabbinic sources, you discover that during the Second Temple period, the holy of holies was actually empty. The ark of the covenant had been removed before the destruction of the temple in 587 BC. In the temples of Zerubbabel and Herod, the only thing in the holy of holies was the flat bare rock of the mountain.

Could it be that this simple Muslim structure preserves an ancient idea that on the rock was the original ark containing the tablets of the Law engraved by the finger of God on Sinai? And could it be that the Dome of the Spirits is the site of the holy of holies where the glory of God dwelt in visible form?

I do not know the answers! It may be, it may not be! Having said that, if Dr Asher Kaufman is correct, if his conclusions are valid, it means a third temple could be built without even disturbing the Dome of the Rock!

From where I stand today, this raises an interesting possibility relative to the task John has been given to measure the earthly temple. The scenario is this: if the new temple is constructed to the north and slightly to the west of the Dome of the Rock, it means the outer court of the temple would encompass the complex we know as the Dome of the Rock. Some Bible commentators see a connecting link between this and the words of 11:2 where John is specifically told to *'exclude the outer court, do not measure it, because it has been given to the Gentiles.'*

At the end of the day, whatever happens, however it all works out, we know with certainty that the temple will be rebuilt and there will be some non-Jewish control of a portion of the temple mount for three and a half years. There is a line of demarcation clearly drawn. Because John is told not to measure the outer court, it implies that God is making a difference between those who know him and those who do not. There is a division between those who truly worship him and those who do not. It is good to remind ourselves that this all transpires during the first half of the period of Tribulation.

If we can believe all that we hear and all that we read, it is fascinating to realise that the preparations for the fulfilment of this prophecy are well underway. They have begun already, in your lifetime and mine! I understand from other sources that detailed blueprints for the third temple have existed since the middle of the 1990s. I was equally amazed to discover that since 1987, a group of rabbinical researchers, designers and craftsmen, under the direction of a prominent rabbi have been creating in the Jewish quarter of Jerusalem what they call a 'temple-in-waiting.' They are known collectively as the Temple Institute and much of their research is well documented in various academic and religious publications. Some Yeshiva students are presently being trained in the order of priestly service. Many of these activists have been buying up Arab properties in the Muslim Quarter, next to the temple mount. So far as they are concerned, the closer they are to the temple, the better!

So many pieces are coming together in God's prophetic jigsaw that we can hardly believe it. Prophecy is being fulfilled before our eyes. I believe the stage is set for so much is already in place; however, when it comes to the nitty-gritty of rebuilding the temple, like everything else, it is down to God's time.

In verse 2, we discover that Jerusalem is overrun by the Gentiles for a period of time that refers to the second half of the period of Tribulation. We read that *'they will trample on the holy city for 42 months.'* At the end of this era, the Lord will return in power and great glory to set up his millennial kingdom and bring to a finale the period known as 'the times of the Gentiles.' Jesus himself said as much in his prophecy of Luke 21:24 which began in 606 BC when Babylon began to devastate Judah and Jerusalem, and it will continue until the second advent of Jesus Christ as King of kings and Lord of lords (Zechariah 14:9).

> **The temple is a place for worshippers. What is worship, why do it, and how do you worship God in the routine of your life?**

11:3-14

The two messengers

This is the story of two men who made their mark for God, two men who impacted the world in the end times, two men who appear on the stage with no fanfare and no advance publicity, two men who have no PR people to boost their ratings and no spin doctors to put a gloss on their message; two men whose importance and influence dare not be underestimated; two men who remain anonymous in Scripture but whose fame is universal; two men whose real identity is concealed in the Bible but who end up as household names; two men in the business of performing miracles; two men who are immortal until their work for God is complete; two men who left people with their mouths gaping as they made a dramatic exit from planet earth; two men who found their niche in the purpose of God and, because of that, made a huge difference!

> **What does being a witness for God mean to you?**
> **In what ways do you see yourself occupying and fulfilling**
> **such a role?**

In an era when Satan has his two men, the Antichrist and the False Prophet, so the Lord has his two men, and what a pair they are! The little phrase *'My two witnesses'* pays eloquent tribute to that fact! It is not hard to tell whose they are and whom they serve! They are automatically linked with the God of heaven as his representatives on earth; they are his emissaries or, if you like, his ambassadors. We have a most remarkable insight concerning them in 11:3, where the Lord says, *'And I will give power to my two witnesses, and they will prophesy for 1,260 days, clothed in sackcloth.'*

This is the first time we have come across the number 1,260 in our studies in Revelation. The previous verse spoke about 42 months and this was particularly relevant to the second half of the seven years of Tribulation. The key question is, what does the figure 1,260 refer to? Well, again it is a time span and again it points to an era which lasts for three and a half years, using the Biblical 360 day calendar as the basis for calculation.

The God who numbers the hairs on our head, the God who knows the name of every star in space, the God who sees a sparrow fall to the ground, he is the God who is much more specific in recording the ministry of his two envoys than he is in mentioning the duration of the Antichrist's ranting. Did you notice that? He describes the vital ministry of his two spokesmen as a day-by-day ministry and counts it up to an exact figure. So far as Satan's superman is concerned, he talks about 42 months, that is all! This is amazing!

> The witnesses worked for a specific number of days as God
> determined ... the same is true in your life and mine. How does
> 'numbering our days' help us 'gain a heart of wisdom' as
> suggested in Psalm 90:12?

Does this refer to the first half or the second half of the Tribulation?
I think there is some mileage to be gained in the fact that the two
three-and-a-half-year periods are described in different ways: as 42
months versus 1,260 days.

A simple explanation of this is that John did it in order to show
that they are not talking about the same three-and-a-half-year time
slot. In other words, they are two different halves of one seven year
epoch. I have no doubts in my mind that this applies to the first half
of the Tribulation because the Antichrist is the one who does all the
shouting in the second half!

*The end of the first half is marked by the martyrdom of these two
witnesses; the end of the second half is marked by the return of Christ
to set up his millennial kingdom on earth.*

The purpose of their calling

These two rugged individuals are empowered by the Lord for their
special ministry in the last days; they are uniquely equipped by the
Lord for the job he has for them to do; they are enabled by the Lord
to fulfil the role for which he has chosen them. They face a daunting
task. It is an uphill struggle. It is a lot for any man to handle. It is an
enormous challenge but, with the help of God, they will be able to
do it. Their confidence is rooted in God and there is no way he will
let them down!

They have a message of prophecy. The ministry they exercise is
one which has a distinctive prophetic flavour to it. They are there to
proclaim the good news of the kingdom; they are there in the midst
of chaos and crisis to point men to Jesus the King. That is what
gives a sharp edge to all they have to say.

It is obvious they have a measure of success in the early days for
it would seem that the 144,000 Jewish evangelists will respond to

their preaching and, in turn, they will go to the ends of the earth proclaiming kingdom truth.

They have a message of repentance. We read, they are clothed in sackcloth. None of your designer label, flashy, tailor made expensive suits here! This is the kind of cloth you pick up in the local flea market, not in Savile Row. We are talking about burlap, a type of coarse canvas which was often made from jute; this was the traditional garb of the Old Testament prophet when he was sent to warn of impending judgment; they could not wear anything better, this is most appropriate for these latter-day prophets are men who are preaching the need to mourn and lament over sin and to get right with God!

They have a message of truth. They are also there as a kind of check and balance; they are there to tell the truth; they are there to strip away the delusions, the lies and the satanic propaganda which the Antichrist is promoting. There was nothing attractive about them and there was nothing glamorous about them. You see, the men did not matter. It is the message that deserved top billing. Joe Public was not meant to look at them, he was supposed to listen to what they had to say.

The significance of their symbols

In verse 4, John describes these two agents in a rather unusual way. He says, *'These are the two olive trees and the two lampstands that stand before the Lord of the earth.'* If you know anything about the prophet Zechariah, you will recognise these twin symbols straightaway. You find them in chapter 4 of his book where he writes of two olive trees that drip their oil into a golden lampstand, as a witness to Israel in his day. John's reference here is an allusion to Joshua and Zerubbabel in the vision of Zechariah.

Joshua and Zerubbabel were the dual leaders of the local community; one of them had civic responsibilities and the other one specialised in religious affairs. They are the ones who would take the people back to Israel from exile and inspire them to rebuild the fallen ruins of the temple. Zerubbabel would lay the foundation of the temple and also finish it (Zechariah 4:9). When the final stone was set in place, we read there would be shouts of 'God bless it, God bless it!' as if to emphasise that God's Spirit enabled them to achieve this tremendous goal.

It seems to me, this historical incident points to a future day when the temple will be rebuilt. Just as Joshua and Zerubbabel were used by the Lord to challenge the people to rebuild the house of the Lord, I think it is extremely likely that the two delegates from heaven will have a similar impact on the hearts of the Jewish people in the Tribulation period. We can take it a step further when we realise that the olive oil is a beautiful symbol of the Holy Spirit. The light of their testimony is shining brightly because they have the Spirit of God flowing through them. It can be said of them, they are full of life and full of light! They have the anointing of God upon their lives and ministry! This anointing is not only pertinent to them, it is equally relevant to your life and mine!

> The mention of olive trees and lampstands in verse 4 is suggestive of the Holy Spirit sustaining these two men and also shining through them. What difference, if any, does it make to your attitude to witnessing knowing that the Holy Spirit works in the same way through you?

The identity of the witnesses

Can we identify them? Can we put a name to a face? The answer is, not really but we can have a go, we can try! It is good to remind ourselves that these two proxies are real people, they are real men, they are flesh and blood. They are so real you can hear their voices, you can shake their hands, you can show your feelings towards them.

Over the years, these two witnesses have been equated with the two testaments of Scripture, one as the Old and one as the New. Others have said, they represent the law and the gospel. Others say, they depict Israel and the church, or Israel and the word of God, as the two principal instruments of witness in the world.

Personally, I do not think these views hold too much water. I feel a fairly strong case can be made for Moses and Elijah, with one representing the law and the other, the prophets. Why?

Malachi the prophet predicted that Elijah would come to prepare the way for the Messiah (Malachi 3:1-3; 4:5,6). Elijah never experienced death, therefore, he could return and die, just as the witnesses do. The witnesses have the same sign that was given to Elijah in regard to rain (verse 6). Elijah was one of the two who appeared at the transfiguration of Jesus in Matthew 17:3 when the death of Jesus was the topic under debate.

Moses also appeared at the transfiguration of Jesus on snow-capped Mount Hermon. Peter was also there as an eye-witness of the majesty of Christ and, when he writes about this event in his epistle, he links it in with the second advent of Jesus; he sees it as a shadow of things to come (2 Peter 1:16-18). Moses also turned the waters into blood just as the two witnesses will do (Exodus 7:19, 20). Another contributory factor is that the body of Moses was preserved by God and only he is aware of its exact location. There is no grave for Moses anywhere in today's world. It is strange but in Jude 9 we see that even the devil wanted to know where it was.

Another name has often been thrown into the ring and it is the name of Enoch. He is the man who walked closely with God in a pagan secular society. In some ways, he is on a similar footing to the prophet Elijah for like him he never died. For both of them, it was instant glory without ever tasting death. One minute they were here and the next minute they were gone to glory! *For them, there was no dark tunnel of death; it was the golden bridge of translation.*

Actually, in some of the earliest Christian writings, there are references where Enoch and Elijah are named as the two witnesses of chapter 11. Having said that, it seems to me that the balance of probability weighs heavily in favour of Moses and Elijah. As someone has said, 'Moses and Elijah, mighty men of old and mighty men of the future!'

The provision for their witness

They know the Lord's protection. We see in verse 5 that the two witnesses are not the least bit concerned about their personal security.

They are immune and they are invincible until their work for God is finished. No-one can touch them, no-one can harm them, no-one can lay a finger on them! John says, *'If anyone tries to harm them, fire comes from their mouths and devours their enemies. This is how anyone who wants to harm them must die.'* God looks after them! God watches over them! They have supernatural protection. If anyone gets too close and attempts to rough them up, they will wish they had not bothered for their end will be swift. Justice will be meted out instantly.

They know the Lord's power. A closer analysis of verse 6 reveals they have three supernatural weapons at their disposal. They are armed with **drought** for we read, *'These men have power to shut up the sky so that it will not rain during the time they are prophesying.'* It is back to the days of Elijah when the absence of rain lasted for three and a half years. If they wish, it could happen again. At least the weather forecasters cannot get it wrong for every day it will be dry and hot with not a cloud in the sky.

They are armed also with **death** for we read, *'and they have power to turn the waters into blood.'* This has got to be Moses Mark II. It happened the first time in Exodus 7 as one of the ten plagues visited on the land of Egypt and there is nothing to say it cannot be repeated. Even though the magicians of Egypt were able to mimic that particular miracle, they were not able to reverse it.

The two witnesses are also armed with **disease** for we read they have power *'to strike the earth with every kind of plague as often as they want.'* In his day, Moses called for an infectious disease to be spread among the cattle and he also called for man to experience all sorts of weird medical conditions brought about by one virus or another. When you think of what is happening in our world, it is not too far fetched to believe that this kind of thing cannot happen again.

By any stretch of the imagination, these men are powerful individuals. They have the Lord on their side and they have a triple assault capability stashed away in their kit bag! For three and a half years, these men are untouchable, they are unbeatable, they are unstoppable.

The ending of their witness

John underlines this fact with his opening comment in verse 7, when he says, *'Now when they have finished their testimony.'* I happen to believe and we see it illustrated here, that a man of God living in the centre of the will of God is immortal until his work for God is finished. Nothing can happen to these men, unless God gives the word. Satan could not silence them and the old devil could not slay them!

Moses did not die until the tabernacle was finished building. Jesus did not die on the cross of Calvary until he cried with a loud voice, 'It is finished.' Paul did not die until he penned the words to young Timothy, 'I have finished the race.'

But now their time has come. Their mission is complete, their job is done, their task is finished! And so we read, *'the beast that comes up from the Abyss will attack them, and overpower and kill them.'* This is the first of 36 references to the Beast in the book of Revelation. It is a clear reference to the coming world ruler we call the Antichrist. He is Satan's puppet on a string. He is the devil incarnate. At his first real opportunity, the Antichrist goes for the jugular and kills them. They have been an irritant in his side.

It appears this is the first great act he will use to gain a wider following. The frenzied mob baying for blood will cheer the public executions. Remember, these two men are still in the centre of the purpose of God for their lives and on this occasion it spells martyrdom for them just as it has for many of God's dear people down through the years.

The sin of the great city

John provides us with a few more details concerning their death when he writes in verse 8: *'Their bodies will lie in the street of the great city, which is figuratively called Sodom and Egypt, where also their Lord was crucified.'* They are not even given the dignity of a decent burial; they are left lying in the same spot where they fell to the ground. They are there for all to see! What a macabre sight! What a grotesque spectacle!

The *'great city'* is a reference to Jerusalem. We know that because of the connection John makes with the death of the Lord Jesus. It is obviously a place of incredible violence. He also says, it is like Sodom and Egypt. He is not handing out bouquets here! There is no prize for guessing what those places represented!

Sodom is a picture of unbelievable wickedness and immorality and would focus on the vice of the city of Jerusalem. Egypt, on the other hand, is a symbol of oppression and slavery as well as being the capital of materialism. It depicts Jerusalem as a city renowned for its vanity.

It is a sad fact, by the middle of the Tribulation, Jerusalem has become a centre of corruption and persecution. It is no longer the holy city, it is more like a city from hell. John is razor sharp in his honesty for he tells it like it is!

A public exhibition

Verse 9 really throws the cat among the pigeons for we read, *'For three and a half days men from every people, tribe, language and nation will gaze on their bodies and refuse them burial.'* No matter where you are coming from, that is a staggering prediction for any man to make! In John's day this was an impossible feat, it just could not happen; but you know as well as I do, it can happen today with no problem. We have live TV pictures beamed into our homes from every continent and every time zone as major news stories are breaking. We can sit in the comfort and privacy of our lounge and watch events and dramas unfolding on the other side of the world as they take place.

Cameras will be despatched from every major news organisation for a special assignment in Jerusalem, and in homes and hotel rooms and on cinema screens in all the major centres of population and to the farthest corners of the earth, this event will be the top item of every news bulletin. I believe that is the day when God will use the mass media, the television, the satellite networks, the internet, to further his own ends. It seems to me, in that day, he will use modern technology to ultimately prove a point to a gloating population.

For years the critics have laughed at this prophecy, but now with the advances in science and technology from which we have all benefited, no-one can scoff any longer! At the end of the day, God is the one who will have the last laugh. He knew about it all along; he was not taken by surprise; he was not caught napping! For him, the future is now!

When you realise that the bodies were left on display for three and a half days, it defies logic. Customary practice is for people to be buried within twenty-four hours. That is the norm in that part of the world! The attitude of people from the top down to this torrid affair smacks of sheer contempt. It just goes to show how far man's moral decency has spun recklessly out of control. It is serious when man has degenerated to such an extent that his sense of respect for his fellow man is virtually nil. He is on a downward spiral.

A public celebration

What is even more incredible is that the people reckon it is time to have a party! And that is exactly what they do. We read in verse 10 that *'the inhabitants of the earth will gloat over them and will celebrate by sending each other gifts, because these two prophets had tormented those who live on earth.'*

Well, can you believe it, Christmas has come early! It is a satanic Christmas, it is an Antichrist-mas! It is a sham, it is a mockery, it is a counterfeit. It is geared to a pagan mindset for they turn these deaths into a public holiday, a time for fun and festivity. I am reminded of a saying that was common among ancient Roman generals, 'The corpse of an enemy always smells sweet!' And so the people rejoice in the demise of these so-called tormenting preachers. They are glad to see the end of them! It is worth noting that the Lord calls their witness a 'testimony' but the world sees it as a 'torment.'

It serves to underline the point that God has his agenda and it runs contrary to the ideas of the devil and his henchmen; heaven and hell are on a collision course. You can see this right here in this global carnival. The world is no friend to God. The world is no friend to the servants of God. The world is no friend to the gospel of redeeming love and grace.

> The hostility of the world to the people of God is highlighted in verses 9 and 10. Jesus said he had 'overcome the world' (John 16:33). Think of some occasions in your life when you have experienced the opposition of the world. How does the victory of Jesus make a noticeable difference to the way you respond to such aggro?

A public demonstration

Do you see what happens next? The greatest party on earth grinds to an unscheduled halt! The jubilation ceases, the drink stops flowing, the singing is interrupted, the laughter dies down, there is nothing happening on the dance floor, a fun-loving party community is at a standstill! There is an eerie, stunned silence all around the world. People are frozen with fear. They are riveted to the spot! Their dream turns into a nightmare for we read in verse 11 that, 'After the three and a half days a breath of life from God entered them, and they stood on their feet and terror struck those who saw them.'

Sometimes truth is stranger than fiction. The fact is, this is real. This is no joke. This is no figment of their fertile imagination run riot. Oh yes, dead men live! Sure, for eighty-four hours you have two dead men lying on the concrete; one second later and you have the same two men standing on their own two feet! Two decaying corpses have been renewed! The bits and pieces are put back together again, the vital organs are reactivated and they are alive and kicking! This is nothing short of a miracle! It is a demonstration of the kind of thing only God can do.

A triumphant resurrection

But that is not all, we read in verse 12, 'Then they heard a loud voice from heaven saying to them, "Come up here." And they went up to *heaven in a cloud, while their enemies looked on.'* The vast crowds milling around the cordoned-off scene in downtown Jerusalem did not only see what was happening to these two men, they also heard a loud voice from heaven saying, *'Come up here!'* These fellas have a triumphant rapture! They are here one minute and gone the next. They are bound for glory!

The people are struck with panic for they have never seen anything quite like this before. Oh yes, their man, the Antichrist, can do many signs and wonders but he cannot do this, he cannot duplicate this! You can visualise the scene: as these two men are ascending into heaven, the people are left standing - they are shell-shocked, they are confused, the most they can do is watch and wonder. They certainly cannot explain what they have just seen and they cannot explain it away either!

It is worth noting, when our Lord ascended into heaven, he was watched by a handful of close friends, we find that in Acts 1. When these men are translated into glory, they are watched by their enemies. In that sense, God has the last laugh; he leaves them standing with their eyes gawking and their mouths open wide! It is a classic case of divine retribution.

Isn't it great to realise that not even death can destroy the servants of God! No matter how we die, no matter where we die, there is a new day coming when we will be ushered into the immediate presence of Jesus. I think of the words of the apostle Paul when he said, 'we shall rise also.'

> The ultimate goal of our lives is not death, but resurrection and eternal life. Spend some time in praise and thanks to the Lord for such a great hope.

A terrifying conclusion

The story is gathering pace with every event that takes place; the momentum is picking up as the seconds tick by on the prophetic clock. We read the grim news in verse 13 of yet another disaster when John informs us, *'At that very hour there was a severe earthquake and a tenth of the city collapsed. Seven thousand people were killed in the earthquake and the survivors were terrified and gave glory to the God of heaven.'*

We have been down this road before but this time the impact of the earthquake, in terms of casualties and devastation, is much more localised. The earthmoving tremors and aftershock are focused on Jerusalem and its environs. At the same time, it must be stressed, this convulsion was no minor landslide; it was rated fairly high on the Richter scale for John classified it as *'severe.'*

Seven thousand deaths and 10% of the infrastructure destroyed may not seem that significant, but in a city like Jerusalem, it is quite considerable. When you add this tragedy on top of the spine-chilling horror which they have just seen with the ascension of the two witnesses, these poor folk do not know whether they are coming or going, they are reeling from one blow after another, they are staggering around like drunken men, they are living on their nerves. Emotionally distraught and terrified, they are gripped with an unbelievable fever of fear.

The little phrase at the end of the verse which says, *'they gave glory to the God of heaven'* would appear to indicate that this event drove some of them to their knees to call on the Lord and seek his face in repentance. I am inclined to feel that what we have here is a remnant of Jewish people in Jerusalem who believe in the Lord and worship him. They recognise that he is the God of heaven and that he has the whole world in his hands. They realise that he is the one who is running the show and that it is better to be on his side!

This is another splendid example of a God of glory and a God of grace giving man an opportunity to find forgiveness in his Son. There is no depth to which he will not stoop, no height to which he will not ascend, no lengths to which he will not go to save the lost from his own wrath for their sin. Because our God who is just is also merciful!

So far as the rest of them go, their hearts are pounding with fear and they cry to God to get them out of the mess they find themselves in; but there is a world of difference between calling on the Lord in terror and calling on the Lord in faith and repentance. It is one thing to be backed into a corner where you feel a sense of desperate hopelessness; it is quite a different matter for your heart to be breaking under conviction of sin.

And then in matter-of-fact language, John brings this act in the drama to a finale when he says in verse 14, *'The second woe has passed; the third woe is coming soon.'* Two down, one to go!

11:15-19

The seventh angel sounds his trumpet

The extent of the Lord's majesty

The final few verses of chapter 11 introduce us to angel number seven and the momentous role he plays in the unfolding drama of God's eternal purpose. This is a significant milestone in the book of Revelation for we read in verse 15 that, *'When he sounded his trumpet there were loud voices in heaven which said, "The kingdom of the world has become the kingdom of our Lord and of his Christ, and he will reign for ever and ever."'*

What a fantastic message! It is a timely reminder that God rules on high! The Lord reigns! Our God is Sovereign! Jesus is King! We are bowled over when we focus on the majesty of God and his plan for the world.

What a breathtaking statement to usher in the second half of the period of Tribulation. This is the remaining three and a half years of what we often call Daniel's seventieth week. It is a statement of intent and it announces that God is taking over! This was the moment the Old Testament prophets anticipated. I cannot help but think of the stirring messages which came from the likes of Daniel and Zechariah, and many more.

The *'loud voices'* which John refers to were probably the massed choirs of heaven; the whole place was resonating with the news that recognised and rejoiced that the Lord is King! It is a message that resounds from pole to pole; it reverberates to the ends of the earth.

It is true to say that Christ does not claim his royal rights until he returns but the victory has been won already! This is the inheritance the Father promised the Son away back in the second Psalm. It is one he earned the exclusive right to claim because of his conquest over sin at the place called Calvary. The apostle Paul gives an interesting slant on this transaction when he focuses attention in 1 Corinthians 15:24 on a time, as he put it, 'when Christ hands over the kingdom to God the Father.' Paul says it will happen at that climactic moment when Jesus has 'destroyed all dominion, authority and power.'

It is equally correct to say that today he rules over a spiritual kingdom and that your redeemed heart and mine is his royal throne. We often sing the worship song, 'Reign in me, sovereign Lord, reign in me.' You see, in your life and mine, we need to give him proper place; we need to understand the implication of his rule in our lives for his kingdom is within us. It is a spiritual kingdom, it is a personal kingdom. In that day, it will be global, it will be literal, it will be one thousand years of Jesus rule. Is it any wonder the cry goes out from the hearts of those who follow great David's, greater Son, 'Bring back the King!'

> Until the rule and reign of Christ is realised on planet earth, what can you do today to make his kingdom a reality where you are?

The exaltation of the Lord's majesty

When the tremendous news is heard that Jesus will reign for ever and ever, there is an immediate response from the twenty-four elders in heaven. One minute, they are sitting on their thrones before God and, the next minute, they are down on their faces worshipping the God of glory. The response was ecstatic, it was spontaneous, it was the right thing to do and there was no better time to do it. It was an acclamation of pure praise. Never devalue the currency of praise!

The fact that they got up from their thrones and fell down before him is a powerful example to the rest of us; this is what real worship is all about. It is a recognition of the greatness of God and, at the same time, that is reflected best in our humility before him. They knew their place before the Lord was one of obedience, worship and submission. It is also a thrill for us to realise that the throne of God in heaven is occupied!

The initial thoughts of the prostrate elders are conveyed in words of sincere gratitude and thanks for who God is. John fills us in with the details in the opening phrase in verse 17, when he says, *'We give thanks to you, Lord God Almighty, the one who is and who was.'* The God we are introduced to here is one who marshals the angelic host of heaven; he is one who was present in all our yesterdays for he is timeless in that he is eternal. He is one who is with us today for he is the God of the here and now!

They praise him because God's power is being proclaimed. In the closing sentence of verse 17 we read, *'You have taken your great power and have begun to reign.'*

They praise him because God's plan is being accomplished. This is inferred from verse 18, where we read, *'The nations were angry and your wrath has come.'* The veiled reference here is to the rebellion of the nations of the earth during the days of Tribulation. Did you notice their remarkable change in attitude? Their arrogance and joy, which we read about further up the chapter, has subsided; it did not last very long. Now the people are consumed with anger; there is an attitude of belligerence creeping into the minds of those who are living in these dreadful times. In fact, they are so volcanic in their outlook, the situation could erupt at any moment. One thing always leads to another and this is the final straw that breaks the camel's back as they prepare for Armageddon. They want to go their own way, they want to do their own thing and that is why they are angry!

This verse also draws attention to the wrath of God for the Lamb is also the Lion as we saw in chapter 5. There are two Greek words for anger: *thumos* which means 'rage, passionate anger' and *orge,* which is the word used here, which means 'indignation, a settled attitude of wrath.' Warren Wiersbe make the valid point that, 'God's anger is not an outburst of temper; it is holy indignation against sin. God's anger is not dispassionate for he hates sin and loves righteousness and justice; but neither is it temperamental and unpredictable.'

They praise him because God's promise is being fulfilled. In the same verse, we are told that *'the time has come for judging the dead and for rewarding your servants the prophets and your saints and those who reverence your name, both small and great.'* The emphasis here is very much on the fact that God's promise is being fulfilled. John anticipates a day when the people of God will be rewarded.

> **The New Testament says quite a lot about receiving rewards. Is this something you look forward to and how does this prospect influence the way you live from day to day?**

They praise him because God's punishment is being declared. In the closing phrase of verse 18, John hits a much more sombre note when he talks about the Lord *'destroying those who destroy the earth.'* Here God's punishment is being declared in unequivocal language. The bottom line is, the wicked do not get off scot-free, no-one gets away with anything; sooner or later, God will catch up with them and they will get their just desserts. One day, they will find themselves in the dock when they stand before the great white throne. I find it ironic that these people who live for earth and its pleasures are at the same time destroying the very earth that they profess to worship. Man exploits what God has entrusted to him. We are inclined to forget that man is a steward of creation, not the owner!

The expression of the Lord's majesty

John has another breathtaking vision for he writes, *'Then God's temple in heaven was opened and within his temple was seen the ark of the covenant. And there came flashes of lightning, rumblings, peals of thunder, an earthquake and a great hailstorm.'* Isn't it fascinating to observe that this chapter opened with a temple on planet earth and it ends with the temple of God in heaven! Here we have a visual reminder of God's sovereignty and faithfulness. The ark of God was the symbol of God's presence with his people. It stood behind the veil in the holy of holies.

God's glory rested on the ark and God's Law was inside the ark ... that, in itself, is a beautiful illustration that the two must never be separated.

God is a holy God who must deal righteously with sin but he is also a faithful God who keeps his many promises to his people. The vision of the ark would greatly encourage God's suffering people. It would be like a spiritual tonic and an uplift to them. It would remind them that God will fulfil his promises. John was saying to them, 'Look, God will reveal his glory ... give him time and trust him until he does!'

> What significance is there in the fact that the ark of the covenant, which speaks of God's presence, also contained a copy of the Ten Commandments, his basic guidelines for living?

No sooner has John given them words of assurance than he reminds the rebels on earth that worse is to follow. But God's people need not fear the storms for their God is in total control. The ark reminds them of his continued presence and loyalty to them.

At this juncture of the story, it is fairly obvious that the stage is being set for the dramatic appearance of the beast, the one who is Satan's masterpiece, the false Christ who will control the world for a short time. (More about him further along!) It seems to me that Revelation 11 has been a crucial chapter. We are now halfway through the book and we are also midway through the period of Tribulation.

12

War in heaven!

Act 4 ~ Scene 14.

The setting is William Shakespeare's *Antony and Cleopatra*. The comment made is an insightful one for it is the moment when Antony says, 'Sometimes we see a cloud that's dragonish.'

That rings true when I flick through the pages of Revelation and zoom in on chapter 12. Here we have a dark cloud which looms over human history. It is an ominous thunder cloud, it is a cloud that anticipates war on a scale beyond our human comprehension. It is not merely a war fought on some remote battlefield on planet earth between two opposing armies! It is a war in heaven itself. It is an unseen conflict being waged in the heavenlies. It is Dragon against Angel.

In the war of the universe, it is where good and evil vie for supremacy. It is the age-old struggle between the forces of darkness and light. But there is more, for shining brightly against the black backcloth like a lone star in a night sky is a poignant symbol of virtue and vulnerability. Here we have a mother and her new-born child.

And so, in chapter 12, we are spectators who watch the war between God and Satan and their heavenly armies. We also meet some leading characters in this great global conflict. At the end of the day, this really is a tremendous chapter; it is a chapter which is rich in symbolism and if we can crack the code, we are well on our way to putting the pieces of the jigsaw together. Some of them are reasonably straightforward; others are not so easy to ascertain. Having said that, we will take our time and pick our steps carefully; by the end of the study, I think you will have a fairly clear picture in your own mind as to the identity of these images flashing before us on the screen of Scripture.

Seven 'wondrous signs' of the Apocalypse:

Chapter 12	A woman
	A dragon
Chapter 13	A beast out of the sea
	A beast out of the earth
Chapter 15	Seven angels
Chapter 16	Three evil spirits
Chapter 19	The rider on a white horse

Four 'great things' in chapter 12:

A great sign (verse 1)
A great red dragon (verse 9)
A great eagle (verse 14)
A great wrath (verse 12 in *KJV*)

The four women of Revelation:

'That woman Jezebel' who depicts paganism (2:20)
'The great prostitute' who illustrates the apostate church (17:1)
'The bride' of the Lamb who represents the true Church (19:7)
'The sun clothed woman' who represents Israel (12:1)

12:1,2,4b-6

Wonder woman

We read in verse 1, that *'A great and wondrous sign appeared in heaven.'* That is quite an introduction to what comes next! The sign is a woman who is described in verses 1 and 2 as being *'clothed with the sun, with the moon under her feet and a crown of twelve stars on her head. She was pregnant and cried out in pain as she was about to give birth.'* Further down the chapter in verse 5, we read, *'She gave birth to a son, a male child, who will rule all the nations with an iron sceptre. And her child was snatched up to God and to his throne.'*

You are probably well on your way to unravelling the identity of this wonder woman, but some folk see her as being someone other than who she really is.

Who she isn't!

Mary Baker Eddy had no hesitation in equating this person with herself. The male child she bore was seen as the Christian Science Movement which came into being in the year 1879. She goes on to describe the dragon as the mortal mind which is ready to devour the teaching set forth in their publication, *Science and Health.* This particular view is a bit like the proverbial sieve, it holds no water so far as biblical truth is concerned.

Mary, the mother of Jesus. This is a very popular view, especially within the framework of the Roman Catholic Church who see Mary as the Queen of Heaven. A Spanish artist named Murillo painted some famous pictures to prove that Mary was this woman. One of the paintings showed her great with child and portrayed her assumption into heaven.

I can see where they are coming from and what they base their thinking on, but there is a trio of major hiccups with this interpretation. Number one, Mary did not have an assumption into heaven. Number two, why would she be shown pregnant in heaven after Jesus had already been born, resurrected and himself ascended into heaven? Number three, try as hard as you will but you cannot fit Mary into verse 6, which we will look at later.

The Church. It seems fairly obvious that the woman in chapter 12 does not represent a single individual but rather a community of people. So, other bright-eyed, well-intentioned folk come along, they jump on the bandwagon and they see the woman as representing the church. That is an intriguing view but when you analyse it you realise it is a non-starter. It has an insurmountable hurdle to overcome.

I think it is preposterous for the woman to represent the church because she is depicted as giving birth to Jesus. The historical fact is, Christ was never the child of the church, Christ is the founder of the church. The church did not produce the Lord Jesus; he is the one who produced the church! The church was born, as it were, out of the wounded side of Jesus.

Who she is!

I think she represents the nation of Israel. The bulk of the evidence points in that direction. It is overwhelming. The clues are significant. We read about the sun, the moon and the twelve stars in verse 1. There is only one other place in the Bible where you find all these symbols joined together in one place and that is in the well-known story of Joseph the dreamer in Genesis 37:9-11. In his famous dream, Joseph saw the sun, moon and eleven stars bowing down before him in an act of submission.

The sun represented his father, Jacob.
The moon represented his mother, Rachel.
The 11 stars represented his brothers.

We all know that Joseph's dream came true and from this graphic representation we can deduce that the woman was Israel and the twelve stars the founding fathers of her race. I am quite excited and assured when I realise that Joseph's dream was a token from God that Israel would be preserved through him.

When you carry this forward into chapter 12, you catch a glimpse of the glorious dignity which clothes the nation of Israel so far as God is concerned. Down through the years, she has failed repeatedly, she has failed miserably, but that does not diminish the fact that she belongs to God. He has not written off the nation, he has not eliminated her from his prophetic agenda. Her glory is the glory of the heavens and that explains why Abraham's seed is likened to the stars in Genesis 15:5. It is no wonder the old devil hates this nation for she is a powerful reminder to him of all that once was his and of the dizzy heights from which he fell.

She gives birth!

We also read in verse 5 that this woman gave birth to a son, she has a male child. Her cries of agony as intimated in verse 2 are an accurate portrayal of life in Israel around the time of the birth of Jesus. The nation was under the iron heel of Rome and the people had suffered intensely under the cruel oppression of Roman rule. The reference to pain in verse 2 is an indicator of the unthinkable and unbearable travail of the nation. They were going through an incredibly tough time. I suppose it can be said in this context, the Messiah is the child of the nation of Israel as well as the child of Mary.

The use of the word 'man' is a pointer to his humanity.
The use of the word 'child' is a pointer to his humility.

It seems to me, therefore, that the identification of this male child could not be clearer. Paul informs us in Romans 1 and Romans 9 that it was through Israel that Jesus Christ came into the world. We have an allusion to this event in Isaiah 66:7 and even further back in Genesis 3:15 we find he is spoken of there as well. Yes, away back in the book of beginnings, this was the first promise and prophecy of Scripture that one day the seed of the woman would crush the serpent's head.

Jesus was born, he died at Calvary, he rose from the dead, he ascended on high, he sat down at the Father's right hand, today he is exalted far above all. He is hailed as a prince and a Saviour and when he comes again, he will rule the nations with a rod of iron. John is talking here about the proposed millennial reign of Christ. It is a golden age, spanning one thousand years of Jesus rule; it is a time of unprecedented prosperity on a global scale and an era of unparalleled blessing reaching out to the ends of the earth.

Here is another piece of vital information for you. This is one of four references in the book of Revelation to the second Psalm. Someone has said, 'It would be a valid analogy to compare Revelation to an oak tree that grows and expands out of the acorn of Psalm 2.' I like that! It is just so succinct!

We will momentarily skip over verse 3 and the opening part of verse 4; do not worry, we will come back to them for they are of considerable importance!

> **Revelation has been described as 'God's glorious picture book' - with that in mind, is there a place for using visual arts and symbols to convey Christian truth?**

The menace of her enemy

Let us look at the gripping comment at the end of verse 4 where it says, *'The dragon stood in front of the woman who was about to give birth, so that he might devour her child the moment it was born.'* It is a kind of tableau; it is a scene from Madame Tussaud's. You walk into a wax museum where you have all these life size, three dimensional figures frozen in place at the climactic moment of some dramatic event. It is a playback on God's tape of global affairs. It is a slow motion action replay.

Satan, the great red dragon, is crouched with his fangs bared and his eyes smouldering. He is watching Israel as she prepares to give birth to her long promised Son. She is pregnant and crying out in her labour pains. The dragon's avowed intention is absolutely clear; he seeks to devour Jesus as soon as he emerges from the womb of Israel and makes his appearance on the earth. He is determined to sideline the Redeemer. It is a road he has been down many times before. From day one, when he heard God in the Garden of Eden spell out his ultimate fate, he has been bent on destroying the promised Seed.

He motivated Cain to kill Abel, but he had not bargained on the fact that God would raise up Seth to carry the royal seed ... he caused such evil in the world that God destroyed the earth by means of a flood, but God saved righteous Noah and his immediate family, and once again the godly line was secured ... he influenced Esau in a bold and brazen attempt to kill Jacob, but God preserved Jacob ... it looked like his big break was going to come with the slaying of Isaac, Abraham's son, through whom the covenant promises were to be fulfilled, but we know the happy outcome of that episode ... he moved Pharaoh to destroy all the male Hebrew children, but God saved Moses ... then, instead of being wiped out in Egypt, the people of God were delivered by God's mighty hand and outstretched arm ... at other times in Israel's history, he tried to short-circuit the purpose of God by killing all the Jews so the Messiah could not be born ... at one critical point, the royal line was limited to one little boy (2 Kings 11:1-3).

Needless to say, Satan did not succeed!

> **Despite all that Satan can do, and however fearsome he might be, the purposes of God are fulfilled. Is there someone you could encourage this week by sharing with them this wonderful truth? Why not do it?**

The message from history

The key question emanating from chapter 12 is, what is the historical reality represented by this grim and symbol laden tableau? It is relatively easy to see the events of that time woven into the tapestry of 12:1-4.

It takes us back to the birth of Jesus Christ, to that special moment in the history of the world when God became man; it takes us back to the Roman Empire and its crushing subjugation of the nation of Israel; it takes us back to the time of King Herod the Great when he was the puppet king of Rome and it shows us the malice and enmity that filled his heart when he learned of the birth of the Saviour of the world.

Herod, in his early days, was a reasonable kind of bloke; that does not lessen the fact that he was a despot, but at least he was a forward looking, progressive and benevolent one! By the time Jesus was born, he was renowned for his notoriously cruel streak. You did not argue with Herod! You did not step out of line or look at him the wrong way. His murderous paranoia was there for all to see. One day, in a fit of pique, he murdered his favourite among his eight wives as well as several of her family members. Later on, he brutally killed his own firstborn son, Antipas.

So his attempt to flush out the newborn Son of God by slaughtering the infants of Bethlehem was par for the course and the kind of action you would expect from such a man. Like a dragon, he lay in wait for the child to be born, then he pounced. So far as he was concerned, these children were surplus to requirements. They were no better than disposable items. He had no scruples about ordering their liquidation. Thank God, we know the sequel to the story ... the Lord Jesus was spared, taken by Joseph and Mary to the land of Egypt, to a place of comparative safety.

One more time, one more incident, to add to a very long list; one more occasion when the old devil was defeated and the purpose of God had not been thwarted! Yes, that is the glorious message of the book of Revelation: God is victorious! From cover to cover, it is all about the triumph of Jesus. God always wins! He never loses! The devil can do so much and no more. He can go so far and no further.

Satan could not harm Jesus, for he is the one who came, verse 4.
Satan could not halt Jesus, for he is the one who has conquered,
verse 5.
Satan could not hinder Jesus, for he is the one who controls,
verse 6.

Protection in Petra?

The spotlight reverts back to the woman and the main beam is shining on her as we read in verse 6, '*The woman fled into the desert to a place prepared for her by God, where she might be taken care of for 1,260 days.*' I think it is important for us to realise that the fleeing woman represents not the Jewish people as a whole for many Jews will be deceived and deluded by the Antichrist, but she refers specifically to a believing remnant among the nation of Israel.

This specific time allocation of 1,260 days is the period we often refer to as the Great Tribulation. It lasts for three and a half years, it is the second half of Daniel's seventieth week which we read about at the end of Daniel 9. The first half of this awful period is generally spoken of as 'the beginning of birth pains.' You find that colourful description in the Olivet Discourse of Matthew 24:8.

By the time you come to the second half, the tempo has moved up quite a few beats. It is a time when Satan will do his worst. He is not in the mood or frame of mind to drag his heels. He is on the warpath, he is pulling out all the stops, he is in overdrive. But, I am glad to tell you, all his plans will be foiled. The old fool never learns. He still has not grasped the fact that he is no match for the Lord. God has prepared a place already where the fleeing Jews will be safe and secure.

A lot of Bible commentators feel the place referred to here is the ancient city of Petra which is just across the Israeli border in the land of Jordan. The main gorge by which this rock-hewn city is approached looks down on a rivulet that threads its way along its entire length. Its rocky steeps are red and brown, purple and yellow. Its valley with its branching tributaries is about 4,500 feet long and is flanked on all sides by beetling sandstone cliffs. It is an awesome sight! An invading army would have to creep down that narrow, precipitous canyon, twisting and turning through the mountains, before ever the main citadel itself could be seen. Petra is a possibility, I suppose ... it may be, it may not be, we are only speculating. What matters is that God knows what he has in mind and, wherever it is, it is a place divinely chosen and appointed.

The delightful phrase, *'prepared by God,'* appears only one other time in the Bible. You find it in John 14:3 when Jesus turned and said to his forlorn disciples in the upper room, 'I go to prepare a place for you.' In that instance, it is a reference to the rooms in our Father's house, the mansions in the sky, we often sing about. It is all about heaven and the eternal home of the redeemed.

The abiding truth is that God's loving care for the nation of Israel is unmistakable. To this day they continue to be seen as the apple of his eye. They have an intrinsic role to play in the fulfilment of his prophetic schedule. They remain an integral part of his eternal purpose. The great news is, he has a location pinpointed on the map exclusively for them that will prove to be a place of gracious protection and generous provision. In the dark days of Tribulation, the Lord will look after them! And when you stop and think about it, he does the same for you and me, right now!

> **God makes provision in verse 6 like a caring, protective father. List a dozen or so things that God does for us or gives to us that reveal his fatherly nature and use these as a basis for prayer.**

12:3,4a,7-12

An enormous red dragon

It is because of the dark and dreadful days which are just around the corner that we need to preach the gospel with a real sense of urgency and passion to our contemporaries. Our ministry needs to have a sharp cutting evangelistic edge to it. The fact of the matter is this:

The death of sinners before the rapture of the church propels them into the unthinkable torment of hell. The survival of sinners after the church is translated to glory propels them into the unrelenting torment of the Tribulation.

Either way, they do not win, they cannot win. Sooner or later, they come face to face with the devil. And that does not take into account what will happen when they meet their Maker! The picture is not a pleasant one!

The dragon's disposition

That is what the apostle John is referring to when he says in verse 3, *'Then another sign appeared in heaven: an enormous red dragon*

with seven heads and ten horns and seven crowns on his heads.'
Ah! now we know where people get the idea that Satan dresses in
red and sports a long tail and horns!

What we have depicted here is not a photograph of how the devil
looks; rather, it is a symbolic representation of his cruel and vile
nature. His colour is red for his path has always been covered with
blood and death. From day one he has been vehemently opposed to
anything which even smacks of the name of Jesus. We know from
the insightful comments of Jesus in John 8:44 that Satan is a
murderer! History confirms that!

I read recently, 'When Satan saw the resurrection of Jesus, he
didn't have an Easter celebration!' We all know how he reacted for
he turned his fury on the church of Jesus Christ. He had those who
preached the gospel crucified; some of them had the ultimate
ignominy heaped on them for they were left hanging upside down.
He had others sawn in pieces and hacked to bits. He had an
uncountable number of them thrown to the wild beasts in the arena.
The devil saw it all as one big joke and at the same time it was a bit
of fun and entertainment for the Roman generals and politicians.
You can read the documented evidence of this in the closing verses
of Hebrews 11.

In the early days of church history, no time was wasted until
edicts were sent from Rome to destroy the Christians from the face
of the earth. That is what occupied young Saul of Tarsus. It kept
him extremely busy. You will remember he was on a mission to kill
when he was miraculously converted on the Damascus Road. So
far as the devil was concerned, the only good Christian was a dead
one! As the years rolled by, it is conservatively estimated that
upwards of 50 million Christians have paid the supreme sacrifice in
fire and blood. Whether we realise it or not, this is the wrath of the
dragon against the people of God!

That he is called a dragon does not do him any favours. It is a
word which appears a number of times in the second half of
Revelation. It shows him up for what he really is, it shows him in
his true colours. He is a cruel and ruthless persecutor of the people
of God.

The dragon's description

This dragon is *a seven headed monster*: the number seven in Bible arithmetic signifies totality and the 'head' conveys the idea of intelligence. The implication is, he has an IQ that goes off the chart. He is a star, he is not a rising star, he is a fallen star! He is a shrewd operator. He can effectively pull the wool over people's eyes and blind them to the truth. He lulls them into a false sense of security. That is what Paul tells us in 2 Corinthians 4:4 where we read, 'The god of this world has blinded the minds of unbelievers so that they cannot see the light of the gospel of the glory of Christ, who is the image of God.' Oh yes, the devil has a plan for your life; it is to keep you in the dark and to keep you from trusting Jesus Christ as your Lord and Saviour. It suits him perfectly to have you on his side! The statistics make grim reading for they clearly indicate he is winning with a lot of people. At this moment they are happy and content to dance in the dark with the devil, they prefer that to walking in the light with the Lord!

The fact that *he has seven heads and ten horns* links him with the Antichrist whom we read about in verse 1 of the next chapter. It shows his implicit involvement in the nations and governments of this world. (We will have more to say about this aspect of his role in global affairs when we study chapter 13.)

There is a similar allusion to this in Daniel 10 where we read about the conflict raging between the prince of the kingdom of Persia and the heavenly angel. It is an invisible war between the unseen forces of good and evil. A territorial spirit is maybe not the best way to describe it but Daniel certainly gives the clear impression that there are localised angels who have a special interest in a given situation.

The crowns which adorn his seven heads signify his power and authority over the major empires of the world. And again we will go into this in a fuller way when we come to it later.

> The dragon is described as super-intelligent with tremendous power and authority. However, James tells us to resist him and he will flee from us! What does this say about our position in Christ noting especially the context in which James 4:7 appears?

The dragon's downfall

In verse 4, we have a breathtaking statement when John takes us away back in time to the dim and distant past when it says of the devil that, *'His tail swept a third of the stars out of the sky and flung them to the earth.'* The theologians generally refer to this as the fall of Satan and, obviously, when he was removed and expelled from heaven, he did not go quietly! He caused a bit of a stir! He took one in three of the angelic host with him and today they are referred to as fallen angels, demons or evil spirits. Basically, they are the emissaries of hell, they are the devil's secret agents, they are the ones who help him run the show. Satan's mafia is extremely well organised.

They are competent, they are superbly skilled in administration, they are highly intelligent, they are unusually gifted, they are fired with enthusiasm, they are dedicated, they passionately believe in what they are doing, they are totally committed to the cause, they have the innate ability to orchestrate events for their own ends, they have the know-how to pull the strings and influence decisions among the movers and shakers in this world, they have enough clout to operate successfully in the big time, they have what it takes to control the world behind the scenes!

Influence in heaven. The fact that the devil was able to successfully prejudice so many angels to join forces with him is indicative of the incredible power and influence which he wields. We have no idea how many angels this involved in terms of actual numbers, no figures are revealed; we are given only a percentage here in verse 4. Suffice to say, it was highly significant and it left a big gaping hole in the ranks of the holy and elect angels. It is true to say, he made his mark and he left his mark!

I came across an interesting story involving the British preacher Leonard Ravenhill, the author of the excellent best-selling book *Why Revival Tarries.* Apparently he was in a prayer meeting on one occasion and he prayed something like this, 'Lord, we read where one-third of the angels fell from heaven and, praise God, that means two-thirds didn't fall! It means there are two angels for every demon. Thank you, Lord, for helping us look on the bright side!' That is good, isn't it!

War in heaven. Let us jump over verses 5 and 6 (we looked at them earlier) and go to verse 7. Here we are confronted with some foreboding sounding words in the opening sentence, it is a matter-of-fact kind of statement: *'And there was war in heaven.'*

John then proceeds in verses 7 to 9 to fill in some of the missing details when he advises that, *'Michael and his angels fought against the dragon, and the dragon and his angels fought back. But he was not strong enough and they lost their place in heaven. The great dragon was hurled down - that ancient serpent called the devil or Satan, who leads the whole world astray. He was hurled to the earth and his angels with him.'* Strong words! The fact that there is war in heaven is nothing new; having said that, it is not the kind of thing you expect to find there.

The conflict we are talking about here has been raging from time immemorial for the old devil has never given up thinking that his was the sole right to rule and reign. From the first day until now, he has been much too big for his boots and he has always had his beady green eyes on the throne of God. Even when he was unceremoniously thrown out of the presence of God the first time, he has never given up hope that one day his dream might just be realised.

He finds it impossibly hard to give up and give in. There is not even a remote chance that he will throw the towel into the ring, there is no way he will wave the white flag and surrender; on the face of it, he does not know when he is beaten. You can read about it in Isaiah 14 and Ezekiel 28.

Kicked out of heaven. Up until now the devil has been recognised as the prince of the power of the air. He has had reasonable, albeit limited, access into the presence of God to accuse the people of God, but here, in this section, we see him falling even further for he is confined to planet earth, he is restricted to this old world!

God has had enough of his antics. He has put up with him long enough so the devil and his angels are banished forever from access into his presence. It is a highly efficient operation for the devil and his henchmen are flung from the sky in one clean sweep. To borrow a famous statement from Israel's persecuted past, not a hoof will be left behind!

The role of the warrior angel Michael

In this scene we bump into Michael for the first time in the book of Revelation. He is an interesting character. His name means, 'One who is like unto God.' It would appear that he is number one in the angelic pecking order and he has a special ministry in relation to the nation of Israel. We read about him elsewhere in Scripture on a few occasions.

In the book of Jude we meet him embroiled in a raging controversy with the devil over the precise location of the body of Moses. Needless to say, he gives the devil short shrift. We also come across him in the book of the historian-cum-prophet, Daniel. In chapter 10, he is involved in the realm of conflict for he deals with the problem of unanswered prayer for Daniel ... the abiding lesson there is that God's delays are not God's denials. There was a battle raging in outer space between the forces of God and the powers of darkness. The crisis was solved only when Michael stepped down and personally intervened in the situation. And in the last chapter of Daniel, we meet him again; here he is seen as the 'great prince who protects' the people of Israel during some of the most frightening days of the Tribulation.

You are maybe wondering, when does all this happen? We touched on it briefly in chapter 9, but let us just remind ourselves. I think Satan's ouster from heaven takes place at the halfway stage of the Tribulation. I want to say right here that the devil takes it on the chin but he does not walk away subdued into retirement and oblivion. Far from it! He is no gentleman! He never has been and he never will be. He does not accept defeat graciously. You will not find him cowering in a dark corner licking his unhealable wounds, you will not find him sulking on his own.

So far as the devil is concerned, events now move fairly rapidly for him. The next development for him is the bottomless pit and the final move is confinement to the lake of fire. I tell you, he is on the way down and, in the providence of God, it will not be long until he is down and out!

> How does knowing there is a spiritual battle going on in which we are heavily involved help you to persevere in your Christian walk? Do you believe, in the light of your personal experience, that God's delays are not necessarily God's denials?

The dragon's designation

The archenemy of the people of God is identified in verse 9 by four different names:

The dragon	This speaks of his abject cruelty.
The ancient serpent	This reminds us of his cunning and crafty ways dating back as far as Adam and Eve in the beautiful and idyllic Garden of Eden. He is the great deceiver.
The devil	This portrays him as the accuser and slanderer of the Lord's people. He is only happy when he is pointing the finger at God's children.
Satan	This describes him in his proactive role as the adversary and opposer of all that is right. He is a highly motivated activist.

John's parting shot about him is succinct. He says, *'He leads the whole world astray.'* The devil deserves no credit for doing that; it just shows you how hugely successful he has been.

The dragon's defeat

Verses 10-12 are thrilling for they give us the secret of victory over the devil! These are wonderful words of triumph! John says, *'Then I heard a loud voice in heaven say, "Now have come the salvation and the power and the kingdom of our God, and the authority of his Christ. For the accuser of our brothers, who accuses them before our God day and night, has been hurled down. They overcame him by the blood of the Lamb and by the word of their testimony; they did not love their lives so much as to shrink from death. Therefore rejoice, you heavens and you who dwell in them!"'*

There is unsurpassed joy and sheer delight in heaven! There is impromptu praise and glorious worship in the presence of God! There is a proclamation reverberating around the throne of the Most High that the great day has come! It seems to me that this note of victory is based on the prospect of the soon coming of the messianic kingdom. The saints populating heaven realise that it will not be too much longer until Jesus is seen ruling and reigning in his millennial kingdom.

I think the sense of total relief and spontaneous rejoicing which sweeps across the vast spaces of heaven is both real and understandable. For many a long year the devil has pointed his accusing finger at the people of God. That cannot happen any more! It can never occur again for he has been ousted, he has gone, there is no way in for him, the door has been barred and bolted; it is shut tight for God has slammed it in his face!

Oh yes, we have all let the Lord down at one time or another. We have not always lived in a manner which pleases him. There have been many times when we have made it easy for the devil to tell tales but, from now on, the only thing heard in the presence of the Lord will be the victories of the people of God! Up until now, the case for the prosecution has collapsed every time ... we had acting on our behalf the best advocate, the very best defence, in the Lord Jesus Christ, and he has never been defeated, he has never lost a single case! John tells us more about that in his first epistle, chapter two.

The documentation of the saints

Do you see what is happening in heaven?

They are telling each other of *the cleansing of the saints*, how they overcame the devil by the power of the Lamb. There is tremendous power in the blood of Jesus!

They tell of *the confession of the saints*, how they overcame Satan by the word of their testimony. That shows us how vitally important it is to walk intimately with the Lord even though the environment is not user-friendly.

They tell of *the courage of the saints*, how they loved not their lives unto death. That shows us the desirability of living a life which is entirely surrendered and consecrated to Jesus. It is no wonder there is praise in heaven! If you cannot praise God for his salvation and deliverance, what can you praise him for?

> **Despite the powerful and ferocious opposition they faced, the believers overcame (verse 11). How did they do so and how can you achieve a similar result in your own life?**

The desecration of the earth

There may be deafening shouts of exuberant joy in heaven but it is an altogether different emotion which is felt on planet earth. We read in verse 12, the spine-chilling words: *'Woe to the earth and the sea, because the devil has gone down to you! He is filled with fury, because he knows that his time is short.'*

This is a stark warning to the inhabitants of the earth that the devil is now on the same level as they are! He is angry, he is furious, he is full of wrath, he is bent on causing enormous trouble in what amounts to his final fling. It appears he will explode in a volcanic eruption of unbridled fury in the last half of the Tribulation. Those who are followers of the Lamb will suffer intense persecution; they will suffer greatly and many of them will experience martyrdom.

The old devil wants to maximise his closing hours. He wants to go out with a bang, not a whimper. He is no fool, he is not stupid; he is an intelligent angel who knows his days are numbered. He adopts an air of realism for he is very much aware of the fact that time is rapidly running out. He is battling against all the divine odds which are heavily stacked against him. He is fighting back against the clock which is ticking away on God's wrist for time is short.

You see, even though all hell is let loose, the truth of the matter is this: God is still in control!

God is sovereign!

12:13-17

The persecution of the Jews

Anti-Semitism has been around for a very long time. It is not just a phenomenon which emerged in the middle of the 20th century with the horrors of the Holocaust. From day one, Satan has been the driving force behind it. He is the promoter of it, he is the prime suspect, he is the instigator of it.

It seems to me that verse 13 introduces us to what is probably the last wave of anti-Semitism that will roll over the world. The devil who is portrayed here as the dragon is bent on destroying the nation of Israel and, from his perspective, it cannot happen quick enough! So far as he is concerned, the sooner the better!

We should not really be surprised or taken aback by his fiendish attitude for it is a logical outworking of the prediction outlined in Genesis 3:15. It is an integral part of the constant enmity and hostility between the devil and the seed of the woman. He has ill blood flowing through his veins for his animosity and antagonism beggars description. That is why John makes it clear and plain: *'When the dragon saw that he had been hurled to the earth, he pursued the woman who had given birth to the male child.'*

We have seen that *'the woman'* who is mentioned here can be easily identified as the nation of Israel. You see, Satan cannot stand the sons and daughters of father Abraham. He has no time for them. He has always detested them because they are God's chosen people, they are the vehicle through which salvation came into the world. They gave us the Bible, they gave us the Lord Jesus Christ.

That surely explains the reference to the *'male child'* in verse 13. That is why they are top of his hit list! That is why they are sure to receive his hate mail. He wants to obliterate them, he wants to exterminate them, he wants to eradicate them. And he is spurred on with fresh impetus for he knows the time is drawing near for the Messiah to return to earth to set up his millennial kingdom.

Let us not fool ourselves, let us not kid one another, the devil knows the Bible. The chances are he knows it better than most other folk, and he knows a Jewish remnant must be ready to receive the coming King and form the nucleus for his promised earthly kingdom. If you want to dig deeper and find out more for yourself, this exciting truth is developed further in the closing three chapters of the book of Zechariah.

On eagles wings

Persecution is only one side of the coin. In verses 14-16, we also read about protection! John says, *'The woman was given the two wings of a great eagle so that she might fly to the place prepared for her in the desert, where she would be taken care of for a time, times and half a time, out of the serpent's reach. Then from his mouth the serpent spewed water like a river, to overtake the woman and sweep her away with the torrent. But the earth helped the woman by opening its mouth and swallowing the river that the dragon had spewed out of his mouth.'*

One commentator has said about these amazing verses that they show how Israel 'will be hated and hidden and hunted and helped during the coming trial.' The glorious truth woven into the fabric of them clearly intimates that the Lord will look after his people, he will care for them, he will watch over them, he will protect them. He will prepare a special place where the Jewish remnant can find a haven of rest and security. It is a place of welcome relief and respite.

I find it quite interesting that her escape is likened to a flying eagle for this is an oft-repeated image in the Old Testament with reference to Israel. Remember, God delivered Israel from Egypt 'on eagles wings' (Exodus 19:4). He cared for the people in the wilderness as an eagle would tenderly and faithfully provide for her young (Deuteronomy 32:11,12). We also read that their return from captivity in the land of Babylon was like 'mounting up with wings like eagles' (Isaiah 40:31).

> **What is it about eagles wings that makes this picture so appealing and so incredibly appropriate for the people of God?**

God looks after his people

It is impossible for us to say with hand on heart that we know the location of this safe place. The Bible describes it as *'a place prepared for her in the desert.'* The Lord knows where it is and that is what really matters. They will find out time enough! Having said that, some scholars have speculated on it being connected with the region of ancient Edom, Moab and Ammon. This is based on the words of Daniel 11:41 where the indication is that these three areas will be immune from the invading forces of the enemy. They will remain untouched and unscathed. Well, maybe that is the answer, but maybe it is not!

Other folk, as I indicated earlier, have narrowed it down to Petra which is a natural ancient fortress in the southern desert of Jordan. What matters most is that God will protect them in a specially designated area where they are beyond the strike capability of the enemy, they are well beyond the reach of the serpent.

And the God of their fathers will do it for a period of three and a half years (that is the meaning of the phrase, *'time, times and half a time').* The same period of time is mentioned further up the chapter in verse 6 where it specifically refers to 1,260 days.

The phrase, *'water like a river,'* which is mentioned in verse 15 is highly unusual. It is not explained but I think we can find a parallel to it in Psalm 124. The flood is possibly an outpouring of hatred and anti-Semitic propaganda. On the other hand, it may symbolise armies that invade Israel and seek to defeat the remnant. If that is the meaning, then the earth opening up could well be an earthquake that God sends to destroy the invaders and seriously frustrate their plans.

> **The Jews have a special place on God's heart and in God's purpose. How does that colour your attitude to that particular people group and to what happens in the cauldron of the Middle East?**

The devil does not like it

Yet again, with a single master stroke, God thwarts the enemy. The old devil is not too happy for we read in verse 17 that, *'The dragon was enraged at the woman and went off to make war against the rest of her offspring - those who obey God's commandments and hold to the testimony of Jesus.'*

True to form, the devil mounts a massive counteroffensive. He is infuriated to such an extent that he unleashes one of his bloodiest attacks on remaining believers. He is acting like a wild cat; the more he is backed into a corner, the more deadly and ferocious he becomes. These are the ones who were not carried to the hidden place of safety, they are fairly easy meat for him.

The term could refer to both Jewish and Gentile believers. Jews are part of her offspring by birth; Gentiles are part of her offspring by faith. The devil will go well for a wee while and he will appear to gain the upper hand, but it is only lent to him. His doom is certain, his defeat is guaranteed. You find that hinted at in 13:7. The bottom line is, there is nothing much the devil can do to gain the upper hand with the people of God.

If he locks them up in prison, they convert their warders! If he tortures them, they become partakers of the sufferings of Christ and heirs to a great reward! If he kills them, they become instant heroes in heaven! If he turns them loose, they evangelise the world!

And so the pace of events in Revelation is quickening. God's plan in human history is like a graph that has gone off the top of the page. It is moving toward its climax and culmination.

13

The devil's deadly duo

Revelation 13 is a very important chapter for it introduces us to two men who will have a global impact in the final months of the last days. They are the Antichrist and his right-hand man, the false prophet. John was not in the business of handing out compliments to these roguish individuals, he was not giving away any floral bouquets. Our initial introduction to them indicates they have one thing in common: he portrays them as beasts!

His identity

In verses 1 to 3a, John says, '*And I saw a beast coming out of the sea. He had ten horns and seven heads, with ten crowns on his horns, and on each head a blasphemous name. The beast I saw resembled a leopard, but had feet like those of a bear and a mouth like that of a lion. The dragon gave the beast his power and his throne and great authority. One of the heads of the beast seemed to have had a fatal wound, but the fatal wound had been healed.*'

When we think of the Antichrist, we are thinking of the second person in this satanic trinity:

The Devil:	*he is the one who imitates God the Father.*
The Antichrist:	*he is the one who imitates our Lord and Saviour.*
The False Prophet:	*he is the one who imitates the Holy Spirit.*

> **In what ways does the Antichrist imitate the Lord Jesus Christ?**

The Antichrist is also known as the 'man of sin' and the 'son of perdition.' He is called 'the mystery of iniquity' and he is sometimes labelled as 'the lie.' What a glaring contrast to Jesus! In him we see 'the mystery of godliness' and, at the same time, he is truth personified! The Antichrist is the visible expression of the invisible devil.

This is Satan's superman. He is the devil's Messiah, the devil incarnate, Satan manifest in flesh. Here is someone whose power base initially is Europe. He heads up a consortium which resembles a revived Roman Empire; he is the supremo of a United States of Europe, a ten nation confederacy. He is the one who, in the second half of the Tribulation, becomes the president of the planet, the world's last dictator.

This is what the people in today's world are looking for; they are looking for someone to lead them, they are looking for someone up front, someone with imagination and flair, someone with personality, someone who is a colourful and charismatic figurehead. They are looking for a man with a sense of mission, a man with a sense of destiny, a man with a sense of purpose, a man who knows where he is going, a man who knows what he wants.

Well, the Antichrist is the one who will make all their dreams come true! The flip side, the downside, is that some of those same dreams quickly turn into nightmares!

13:1-3a

His association

We read, he comes *'out of the sea.'* That is an interesting turn of phrase. When you fast forward to 17:15, we come across the same term. It refers to the sea of humanity, it speaks of the peoples of the world. Some Bible teachers feel this gives a measure of credibility to the notion that the Antichrist is of Gentile origin rather than someone who comes from Jewish descent. Actually, I think the locale can be narrowed down even further. When you turn back to Daniel 7, there is a parallel passage where the sea referred to is the Mediterranean. So it makes a lot of sense when you put all the pieces together to suggest that this person is of European extraction.

His ancestry

He is called a beast. God does not see him as a man made in the divine image; he sees him as a wild animal under the control of Satan. He is the kind of person you feel you have come across before, there is something familiar about him. It is the classic case of, once seen, never forgotten. And the way John describes him says as much. If you look at 12:3, and read what John says about the devil, you can see the link straightaway. Oh yes, there is a family likeness alright. Like father, like son! Both of them have seven heads and ten horns! The only areas in which they differ are in the number and position of crowns they have: the dragon has seven and they are on his head, the Antichrist has ten and they are on his horns!

The seven heads represent seven mountains (17:9) and, since Rome was built on seven hills, I think this must be a veiled reference to that powerful city. We need to remember that back in John's day this would be a most meaningful allusion. The ten horns represent ten kingdoms. We have come across that before in Daniel 2 and Daniel 7 and again in 17:12. It is a reference to a United States of Europe, the kind of scenario we see foreshadowed today in the European Union.

His appearance

Verse 2 reveals similarities to what we read in Daniel 7. John saw these animals or kingdoms in reverse order since he was looking back, while Daniel was looking ahead.

The leopard was symbolic of the Grecian Empire.
The bear represented the kingdom of the Medes and Persians.
The lion portrayed Babylon as the first great world power.

The Antichrist picks up the best and the worst of every world. He is the heir of the ages. He has all the speed of the leopard as he conquers all in sight. It is a spotted animal. God has his spotless Lamb in the person of Jesus! What a contrast! He has the feet of the Persian empire; he is strong, he is well organised, he is apparently fairly stable. He boasted of great things like Babylon, the lion. The Antichrist is a man who will communicate arrogantly, he will control extensively and he will conquer swiftly. He is the last person to claim the throne of the world prior to the second advent of Jesus.

His authority

Here is a man who is controlled by the devil. He is the one who calls the tune, he is the one who pulls the strings; Satan is the paymaster.

Satan gives him his power and that implies he energises him.
Satan gives him his throne and that means he enthrones him.
Satan gives him great authority and that suggests he empowers him.

There is a fascinating cross reference in Daniel 8:24 where we are told that 'his power shall be mighty, but not by his own power.' In other words, the devil is behind the emergence of this powerful and prestigious individual; he will have power to do everything he wishes and he will have power to do anything he wants.

The third verse is really quite incredible for sometimes truth is stranger than fiction. He has some kind of accident. The implication is that there will come a day when he will appear to be assassinated, fatally wounded, and then in a remarkable turnaround, his wound is healed. He is brought back from the edge, he is the comeback kid! What we have here is an imitation of the death and resurrection of the Lord Jesus Christ. That proves the point I have already made that Satan is the greatest con-man ever!

13:3b-10

His influence

The net result is recorded for us at the end of verse 3, where we read, *'The whole world was astonished and followed the beast.'* The impact is instant and it is quite incredible. The story is beamed all around the world, he has them eating out of his hand, he has successfully pulled the wool over their eyes. He has done it his way and people have fallen head over heels for it. This is his trump card and he played it at just the right time. Joe Public is spellbound, the punters are captivated by his personality. Men and women go delirious with delight at the sudden and unexpected change in his fortunes.

His adoration

This man is hailed as a hero, he is seen as a superman, he is a genius, he is a prince charming. Ordinary people from every corner of the planet will idolise him and will see him as some kind of cult figure. He is adored by millions, he sways the masses. His rise to international fame and stardom is meteoric; one day he is just another face on the stage of world affairs, the next day he has leap-frogged over everyone else and he is seen as the man everybody who is anybody wants to know. His leadership will be established without question. Men will feel he is incomparable for they reckon there is no-one else like him. They believe he is invincible for he has a proven track record.

They do not worship only the Antichrist as a man, they also worship his backer, the devil himself! John tells us in verse 4, *'Men worshipped the dragon because he had given authority to the beast, and they also worshipped the beast and asked, "Who is like the beast? Who can make war against him?"'*

That is the recognition the devil has always wanted. It is the acclaim he has always longed for. It is the adulation he has craved from day one. He wants to be worshipped. You find echoes of this in Matthew 4:8-10 where we read of his encounter with the Lord Jesus. Well, right here, he gets want he wants and he receives it through the beast, the Antichrist! They worship him, not only because of who he is, but because of what he has done. He has won the hearts and minds of the people.

The fact of the matter is, when men start to put the devil as number one in their lives, they are embarking on a journey of no hope, and it is also one which leads to a place of total despair for eternity. They have only themselves to blame. They rejected the truth as it is in Jesus and now they are happy to toe the party line of the dragon. What they fail to realise is that God sends them a powerful delusion and that is the reason why they are the way they are! There is no other explanation for it. If you tango with the Antichrist, you may as well dance in the dark with the devil. He will make the world believe that evil is good, that black is white, that up is down!

> **What do you think makes 'the beast' such a compelling political leader?**

His arrogance

The Antichrist will be given power to control the world but he is like a dog on a leash and the one holding the lead is God himself. The unassailable fact is that he can go so far and no further, he can do so much and no more. He can operate only within the parameters God sets down for him; he has to stay within the remit of his own orbit. This important truth emerges a few times in verses 5, 7 and 8 where it is made perfectly clear that he is delegated certain abilities. For example, we read he was given a mouth, he was given power to make war, and he was given authority over the peoples of the world.

When you read about his mouth in verses 5 and 6, it is obvious by any standards that his is a big one, spewing out torrents of vulgar blasphemy! It flows like sulphurous lava from his lips. John tells us, *'The beast was given a mouth to utter proud words and blasphemies and to exercise his authority for forty-two months. He opened his mouth to blaspheme God, and to slander his name and his dwelling place and those who live in heaven.'*

He is the epitome of downright brazen arrogance. He cannot lay a single finger on God, nor on the heavenly sanctuary, nor on the glorified saints, but he does the only thing he can do, and he does it well; he resorts to reviling them with his filthy tongue. So far as the person of God is concerned, so far as the position of God is concerned, and so far as the glorified people of God are concerned, he is impotent. He is helpless. He is on a hiding to nothing. His strike capability is rendered useless. All he can do is call them names!

Blasphemy, in this context, is an echo of Paul's words about the Antichrist in 2 Thessalonians 2:4 where we read, 'He will oppose and exalt himself over everything that is called God or is worshipped, so that he sets himself up in God's temple, proclaiming himself to be God.' That means he will deify himself. He will set up a statue of himself in God's temple proclaiming himself to be God. Like Nebuchadnezzar before him and many a cult leader since then, he will not be content until he has the swooning masses falling prostrate before him in worship.

His anger

In verse 7, John gives us a few more insights into what makes this man tick. He says, *'He was given power to make war against the saints and to conquer them. And he was given authority over every tribe, people, language and nation.'* His aim is not only to defy the God of heaven, he is committed to destroying the saints of God.

He cannot harm the deified saints in heaven but he can harm the believers on earth. These are the ones who have not been specially sealed against him; that makes them vulnerable, it means they are easy targets. Many of these dear believers will be martyred for their solid allegiance to Jesus Christ. They will lay down their lives in an act of supreme sacrifice; they will do it with praise on their lips and love overflowing from their hearts.

There is a time limit of forty-two months. Three and a half years, it is the second half of the period of Tribulation. It is long enough if you are the one going through the mill; it is long enough if you are the one who is on the receiving end but, thank God, at least it has a cut-off point. There is a light at the end of the long dark tunnel.

His insatiable thirst for power is hinted at in the closing comments made by John in verse 7. To start off, his power base will be restricted to Europe, but that is not big enough! He wants more. He has the whole world in his sights. He wants to dominate the nations of the world, north and south, east and west. He wants all people groups to acknowledge him as their leader, he wants every ethnic region to yield obedience to him. His influence will reach to the ends of the earth. It is the old story; he will sneeze in Europe and they will catch a cold in America. I suppose what we have here is a nudge in the direction of some kind of one world government, and he is the big chief. It will not last long, that is true, but for a season, he will have universal acclaim.

> What light is thrown on the devil's tactics in this chapter by what Paul tells us about him in 2 Corinthians 11:14,15?

His aim

This John sums up in verse 8, where he says, '*All inhabitants of the earth will worship the beast - all whose names have not been written in the book of life belonging to the Lamb that was slain from the creation of the world.*' His long term goal is to delude the masses of mankind and he will not be disappointed. He is guaranteed success from the word 'go.' The fact is, there are two types of people living in the world: there are those who are followers of the Lamb and there are those who are followers of the Antichrist; there are those who follow Jesus and there are those who follow the devil.

It has always been like that and, there is no reason to suggest, it will be no different then. You are either one or the other. You cannot have the best of both worlds, you cannot have a foot in both camps. Every individual born on the face of the earth has his name recorded in the book of life but it is only those who have trusted Jesus as Lord and Saviour who have their names penned in the Lamb's book of life.

The first one is a record of our natural birth.

The second one is an eternal record of our spiritual birth!

Thank God, once our name is recorded in the Lamb's book, it can never be erased! It can never be removed! It can never be deleted! It is permanent!

There is a beautiful reminder here of the redemptive work of Jesus on the cross at Calvary. His saving work is seen as something which is eternal in its value, it is also seen as something which was scheduled on heaven's agenda even before the world was made. So far as God was concerned, Calvary was on his mind and in his heart prior to anything which happened on planet earth. There is a timeless dimension to the cross of Christ.

Even though the crucifixion happened on a given day at a specific place, in one sense, it transcends both space and time. It is the summit of God's eternal programme. It seems to me, the cross casts its shadow over all of creation.

> **Contrast the ways of the Antichrist with 'the Lamb that was slain' as mentioned in Isaiah 53:7. What does this teach us about the way to victory?**

A word of caution

The next verse, verse 9, is only a couple of phrases, but they sound quite familiar. We have come across them before in our studies in the early chapters of Revelation: *'He who has an ear, let him hear.'* John is more or less saying: 'Sit up, listen carefully! There is a vitally important message coming! Do not miss it!'

And we have the message right here in verse 10, where John tells us, *'If anyone is to go into captivity, into captivity he will go. If anyone is to be killed with the sword, with the sword he will be killed. This calls for patient endurance and faithfulness on the part of the saints.'*

You could be forgiven for thinking that sounds rather strange, it is a wee bit obscure, it is a little unusual. What on earth is dear old John talking about? Well, when you stop and think about it, these words have a sharp cutting edge of meaning to them. They are words of great encouragement to the saints of the last days.

All over the world, faithful people are suffering for their faith in Jesus Christ and God does not want them to be discouraged or disheartened. He does not want them to cave in under the sustained pressure they are facing. He does not want them to wilt under the unrelenting sun of all kinds of trial and trouble.

The whole saga of suffering seems to be never ending. The Lord is saying to his battle weary soldiers, 'Look, judgment is coming soon and, do not forget, those who have persecuted you will receive the consequences of their sin. They will not get away with it. They will get their comeuppance. Do not let the seeming injustice and wholesale slaughter of these harrowing days hinder your faith. Hang in there! Hold on tight! Endure it for my sake! Keep the faith!'

The fact is, the devil will have his say for a season, he will have his way for a time, he will have his day, but God says what he says in verse 10 as a challenge to each of us today. It speaks loud and clear of divine retribution and divine revenge. Sin will be paid for, no-one gets off scot-free. A judgment day is coming! God sees all things, he knows all things, he has a good memory, he has a long arm. One day the culprits will be picked out from the crowd. You see, God always has the last word!

Personal qualities like 'patient endurance and faithfulness' are emphasised throughout Revelation; the sad fact is, they are not so popular in today's church. Why do you think this is the case and what can we do to restore such values?

13:11-18

Meet the spin doctor for the world's political leader

Now we are introduced to the third member of this satanic trinity. It is the *'beast coming out of the earth.'* He is the world's religious leader, he is the one who is often referred to as the false prophet. If you like, he is the right-hand man of the Antichrist, he is his personal *aide-de-camp*. He is a top PR man by profession; in modern parlance, he is a spin doctor. He is the propaganda chief or the spokesman for the man of sin. He is a man who knows how to handle the media and he is someone who knows how to milk every situation for its maximum potential.

There is every chance that this person may be a Jew. We read that he comes up *'out of the earth'* and that is often a symbol in the Bible for the Hebrew nation and for God's earthly people. At the end of the day, his main function is to glorify the Antichrist. Nowhere does he put the spotlight on himself. He always turns the attention of the people towards the Antichrist. He gives credibility and respectability to him. His key role in the Antichrist's administration is to keep his boss centre stage, he is there to make sure the main beam is always shining on him.

A helpful comparison can be made here between his particular role in relation to the Antichrist and the unique ministry undertaken by the Holy Spirit in relation to the Lord Jesus Christ. The implication is that the second beast is a counterfeit of the Holy Spirit of God. Now that he has arrived on the scene, the unholy trinity from hell is complete.

13:11,12

His description

John briefly describes him in verse 11, where he says, *'He had two horns like a lamb, but he spoke like a dragon.'* That says it all, doesn't it! The first beast, the Antichrist, had ten horns, this one has two horns. The image of the horns suggests that this fella has authority, but the absence of a crown indicates that his authority is not political. We have discovered that the ten horns speak of territory and that has to do with political clout and influence; the two horns are different in that they speak of testimony. And when we think about this guy, his is a false testimony.

Oh yes, he looks like a lamb, but you cannot judge a book by its cover, you cannot judge a man by his mantle. He is not the kind of individual you can afford to take at face value, the stakes are much too high. You could not trust him as far as you could throw him. So far as he is concerned, what you see is not necessarily what you get!

I have never yet met anyone who is afraid of a lamb; it is a gentle creature, it is as innocent as they come, it is a fairly harmless animal. And, I suppose, when he first appears a few feet away from the Antichrist, he will be seen to be all of these things. The danger is, he will be seriously underrated by man but that is all part of Satan's diversionary tactics. It is a strategy ploy to lull men into a false sense of security, the devil wants the general public to feel relaxed and comfortable with him around.

The great giveaway is when he opens his mouth for he *'speaks like a dragon.'* The minute he talks, he lets the cat out of the bag. It is the voice of Satan! He is the mouthpiece of the devil via the Antichrist!

John throws a lot more light on his deception when he informs us in verse 12 that, *'He exercised all the authority of the first beast on his behalf, and made the earth and its inhabitants worship the first beast, whose fatal wound had been healed.'* That is what I have just said: the two of them work hand in glove, they are in it together, both of them are marching to the beat of the same drum, they are holding hands under one umbrella! We can look at it like this:

The false prophet works as the chief executive officer of the new regime with the Antichrist free to operate in a presidential capacity. He is the organiser and propagator of the new religion which is focused on the Antichrist. It is the mindset which says, he deserves to be revered and acclaimed for he is like one who has come back from the dead!

He elevates the Antichrist. It is a role in which the false prophet is eminently successful. All credit goes to him for ensuring the Antichrist features as the main story on the top of every news bulletin! His antics are splashed on the front page of every newspaper and magazine around the world. It is almost like a syndicated news release. This guy is exceptionally good at his job.

He promotes religion. There is something else worth noting. It is not in the least surprising that he uses religion as a means of unifying the peoples of the earth. Something similar has happened down the years, it has been the pattern adopted throughout history by the good and the great. He will use all types of religious props and gimmicks to pull the wool over people's eyes. When it comes to truth, he bends it, he twists it, he distorts it, he is economical with it. He has no personal inhibitions as he plays on people's emotions; he takes advantage of man's basic need for some kind of religious experience.

You see, he makes it all look so plausible, it feels good, it sounds right, it makes a lot of sense to the unsuspecting man on the street. The fact remains, it does not go away, it is a religion without Jesus. It is the classic case of the blind leading the blind.

> Why is religion such a powerful tool which the devil can use to his advantage?

13:13-15

His deception

A miracle worker!

In verse 13, we read that, *'He performed great and miraculous signs, even causing fire to come down from heaven to earth in full view of man.'* This guy is a miracle worker. There will be all kinds of healings taking place, there will be many inexplicable happenings, there will be a wide range of significant events occurring; he can even bring fire down from heaven. If Elijah can do it, so can he! He sets the sky ablaze! This is no hocus-pocus of a well-paid magician, this is no mere sleight of hand. It is for real. He will blind mankind with his bag of spiritual tricks, there will be signs from heaven and signs from hell; he will pull them like rabbits out of a hat.

> What safeguards can we build into our lives so that we will not be deceived by such public displays and demonstrations of miraculous happenings? (Deuteronomy 13:1-3 and 2 Thessalonians 2:9-12 should help)

You see, God is not the only one who can perform miracles, the old devil can do them as well. And that is why, even today, we need to be ultra-cautious when we attribute a miracle to someone. It may be the real thing; on the other hand, it may be a counterfeit spun in the deceptive web of Satan's thinking. He has men eating out of his hand, men are bowled over with his incredible feats. The ordinary folk are impressed, they believe everything he tells them and shows them. They are taking it all on board.

13:16-18

His demands

To worship his idol

John's assessment of the situation is alarming for he informs us in verse 14, *'Because of the signs he was given power to do on behalf of the first beast, he deceived the inhabitants of the earth.'* In fact, so skilful has he been, so successful has he been, that John goes on to say, *'He ordered them to set up an image in honour of the beast who was wounded by the sword and yet lived.'*

That is bad enough but even that is not the end of the story. John continues in verse 15, *'He was given power to give breath to the image of the first beast, so that it could speak and cause all who refused to worship the image to be killed.'*

This is what Jesus spoke about in his major Olivet Discourse recorded for us in Matthew 24. It is what Daniel referred to in the closing verses of chapter 9 in his book. It is what is often called, 'the abomination of desolation.' It does not bear thinking about.

What we have here is a lookalike statue of the Antichrist erected in the newly constructed temple in Jerusalem. It is not there just to make him feel good and to appeal to his seriously inflated ego, it is there as a focal point of his desire to promote himself as a god who is worthy to be worshipped. He craves the affection and adulation of an adoring public and this is one way he is sure to get it.

Should there be any lingering doubts in the minds of the more sceptical inhabitants of the earth, believe it or not, the wily old devil is one step ahead. He breathes power into the statue and it begins to speak! It is a talking monument! In some ways, this is the crowning act of rebellion perpetrated by this less-than-illustrious duo. This is the height of all blasphemy.

Since Satan could not command worship in heaven, he goes to the next best place, the Jewish temple in the Holy City. It is a shambolic mixture of politics and religion. We need to realise that if men fail to toe the party line, if they refuse to bow down to the image of the Antichrist, they will incur the wrath of the beast. They are dicing with death, they will pay an awful price for they will be immediately executed.

To bear his mark

John gives us another chilling reminder of what life will be like when the Antichrist is in power. We read in verses 16 and 17, *'He also forced everyone, small and great, rich and poor, free and slave, to receive a mark on his right hand or on his forehead, so that no-one could buy or sell unless he had the mark, which is the name of the beast or the number of his name.'* The pressure is piling on! It is his way and his way alone.

The political agenda of his government is to introduce a common faith policy, a common foreign policy, and a common financial policy.

Every member of society from the highest to the lowest will be required to receive the mark of the beast. There will be no exceptions to the rule, none will be exempt, it is all inclusive. It is a global decision. If you have it, all will be well; if you do not have it, you will face massive and insurmountable problems. If you go with it, life will go on as before; if you rebel against it and oppose it, you will be economically sidelined. It is a case of: no seal, no sale.

That policy decision applies to the big time industrialist trying to close a billion dollar investment package as well as to the kids at the bottom of the street wanting to buy a packet of sweets in the corner shop. The boycott is total. The mark of the beast is a token of allegiance, it is a show of solidarity, it is a mark of loyalty and identification. It is a passport to the future.

The only choice given to Joe Public is where he receives the brand of the beast. The alternatives are spelled out: it is either on the right hand or on the forehead. Surely this is a strong allusion to the Caesar worship in the Roman Empire but, let us not forget, this same policy has been used by political leaders throughout history. Solomon is right when he tells us, 'There is nothing new under the sun.'

The technology to accomplish this is already in place. It is called a credit card. A person's entire credit profile can be encoded on that little magnetic strip on the back of the card. Thanks to the credit card, we are rapidly becoming a cashless society. Whether we like it or not, we have become a plastic society.

The next step is an obvious one, it is a logical one; you can put whatever information you want on the card or on some other miniature device like a computer microchip which could then be implanted on a person's skin. It is happening today in the animal and bird world where a number of conservation agencies are employing this particular strategy. They are even doing it in Europe for an aptly named 'pets passport.'

It seems to me, what we have here in chapter 13 is not in the least absurd, it is not far fetched, it is not John living in a fantasy world, he is not in cloud-cuckoo land, far from it! We need to realise this whole process could be implemented tomorrow if the powers that be wanted to go down that particular road.

> **What do you understand by the boycott envisaged in verses 16 and 17 and how could the people of God cope with it?**

It is no wonder John begins the final verse in the chapter with the statement, *'This calls for wisdom.'* He goes on to say, *'If anyone has insight, let him calculate the number of the beast, for it is man's number. His number is 666.'* That is a number we are all familiar with, we hear it bandied about all over the place. It is the kind of catch question you expect to be asked on an evening of trivial pursuits, a hyped-up religious guessing game.

Gallons of ink have been spilled as men have tried to crack the code; ream after ream of paper has been churned out by well-meaning writers trying to decipher its meaning. People have read all sorts of things into it. They have even come up with some potential candidates to fit the bill. Some of the names which have been proposed have ranged from the sublime to the ridiculous. The list is as long as your arm.

The theory goes that if you substitute numbers for letters you can arrive at a numerical value that will add up to 666 and that will give you the name of the Antichrist. They base this on the fact that many ancient languages used letters for numbers; the Romans did it and the Greeks went along with it as well. The obvious fallacy so many seem to ignore is that they are trying to solve this riddle using the English alphabet! To me, it makes as much sense as a first-century Greek trying to do the crossword in today's edition of *The Times*.

Some of the people who have been blacklisted include the likes of Caligula, who was the mad despot of Rome; he was quickly followed by the ruthless Nero, and after him, with a little manipulation, the name of Domitian was added. Oliver Cromwell, John Knox and Martin Luther have all been included. A varied assortment of Roman Catholic popes made the list. In the 20th century, the infamous list has included such names as diverse as Adolf Hitler, John F Kennedy, Henry Kissinger, Pope John Paul II, and Mikhail Gorbachev.

By fair means or foul, the name of each of these individuals was somehow calculated to equal 666. It is fairly obvious, they cannot all be the Antichrist!

We need to take on board what John says in verse 18 that *'this calls for wisdom.'* We are talking here about insight and perception; it says nothing about pocket calculators and an alphanumerical dictionary. One writer makes a wise comment when he says, 'On this subject we seem to have a shortage of insight but no shortage of imagination.'

When you go back to the Bible, you find the number 6 used on different occasions. Let me show you what I mean: Goliath, the giant from Gath, was 6 cubits in height, his spear's head weighed 6 shekels and he had 6 pieces of armour; Nebuchadnezzar's image was 60 cubits tall and 6 cubits wide; man was created on the 6th day and is expected to work 6 days out of 7; a Hebrew slave could not be a slave for more than 6 years; the fields of the Jews could not be sown for more than 6 years running.

It seems to me that the most logical explanation for the mark is that the number 6 in the Bible is the number assigned to man. And that is precisely what John is at pains to emphasise when he tells us it is *'man's number.'* The Antichrist represents the ultimate in human ingenuity and cleverness. He is no fool!

The children of the great composer, Bach, found the easiest way to rouse their father from a siesta was to play a few lines of music and leave off the last note. Apparently, Bach would get up immediately, make a beeline for the piano, and strike the final chord. A similar story is told of the great preacher, Donald Grey Barnhouse. He awoke one morning during the Christmas season, went straight to the piano and played 'Silent Night,' purposely stopping before striking the last note! He then walked into the hallway of his home and listened to the sounds coming from the children's rooms upstairs. His eight-year-old son was trying to find the final note on his harmonica. Another of the children was singing the last note with great volume and enthusiasm. His wife called, 'Donald, did you do that on purpose?' Wives seem to have that intuition!

You see, the lesson is, human nature demands the completion of the last note! The number 666 powerfully reminds us that something is definitely missing. That missing 'something' is Someone! He is a 7 and that, as we know from earlier chapters, is the complete number, it is the number of perfection.

God has given his seven-headed Lamb as the second person
of the Trinity.
He has the seven Spirits of God as the third member of the Trinity.
He has his people singing a sevenfold doxology.
Satan has his 6 ... but God is 7!

The devil comes up as the triple six. The fact is, he works hard, he tries hard, but he always comes up short. The old masquerader will never be able to fool all of the people all of the time, he will only fool some of them some of the time.

The message of chapter 13 is one that is gaining new urgency and new relevance with every passing day. We are crazy if we adopt the ostrich mentality and bury our head in the sand. We need to be living on red alert, a people who are vigilant and wide awake! The pace of world events is picking up speed and many of us feel we are rapidly approaching the great cataract of human history.

14

Something special

As the world moves into the second half of the Tribulation, heaven is not silent. The voice of God is heard for what we have here is a preview of coming attractions on the movie screen of history. In verse 1, John says, *'Then I looked, and there before me was the Lamb, standing on Mount Zion, and with him 144,000 who had his name and his Father's name written on their foreheads.'*

We have met these good folk before; the last time was back in chapter 7. These are the 144,000 endtime Jewish missionaries, the 12,000 from each of the twelve tribes who are the sealed servants of God. The last time we saw them they were down here on planet earth, here they find themselves in heaven. Previously they were anticipating the Great Tribulation, now they are looking forward with bated breath to the glorious triumph of Jesus the King.

14:1-5

Look at the special company

They are exalted!

The presence of the Lamb. This is truly marvellous when you appreciate all that is entailed in the compass of this single verse. The focus here is very much on the protection of God. God looks after his people! We are confronted with the stunning truth surrounding the presence of the Lamb. He is seen to be with them. That statement should not surprise us. He said he would in Matthew 28:20 and we have the same promise reiterated in Hebrews 13:5. How reassuring that must have been for them and for you and me as well!

The place where they are standing. Did you see where they are? They are on Mount Zion! The key question is, which one? Is it the heavenly one or is it the earthly one? I think it is probably a reference to the heavenly one.

We have here a thrilling scene that anticipates the coronation of Christ and the establishment of his kingdom when he returns to earth. You find this referred to in many other places but Zechariah 14:4 is a classic reference to it. We discover from Psalm 2:6 that Christ is presently enthroned in the heavenly Zion and, according to the apostle Paul in Ephesians 2:6, we are seated alongside him. We have grandstand seats in heaven. The thought encapsulated here is one of glowing assurance to God's people that he cares for us and that finally he will take us home to glory. All his plans will be achieved; all his purposes and promises will be fulfilled.

The print of God's name. It involves the print of God's name on their foreheads. This seal is a reminder that they belong to God and to the Lamb. It is in sharp contrast to the 'mark of the beast' we read about in chapter 13. The challenge facing each of us is this: what marks our lives? Is it the brand of a secular society? Or is it the imprint of the kingdom of God? Do we embrace the present world system or do we honour his great name?

> **How firmly is the Lamb's name attached to you by what you do and say?**

They are euphoric!

John sets the scene for us in a way that captivates the imagination. He says, *'And I heard a sound from heaven like the roar of rushing waters and like a loud peal of thunder. The sound I heard was like that of harpists playing their harps. And they sang a new song before the throne and before the four living creatures and the elders.'*

This is colourful language, it is quite expressive; but what a beautiful sound it must have been when the harpists were strumming away and how sweet the harmony to the ear when they began to sing their brand new song. It is strong, it is majestic, it is sensitive, as it is performed with idyllic tones of tenderness.

It is *'new'* because their experiences in the Tribulation are unique to them. Let us face it, not many have walked through the flood and the flame as God's untouchables! We come across a select handful in Hebrews 11. Some of them are childhood heroes, like the Daniel's of this world who lived to tell the tale when God gave the lions lockjaw; like the trio of Hebrew teenagers, Shadrach, Meshach and Abednego, who would not bend or burn when thrown into the fiery furnace ... such characters are few because good folk are always scarce. They are deliriously happy in their worship, they are ecstatic with praise. It is always good to remember that one day in God's time, all our sorrows will be transformed into songs! It is amazing, the minute you bring the Lamb into the picture, you hear the people singing!

> **In what ways do the rewards of the hereafter compensate for the problems of the here and now?**

They are exclusive!

John informs us, *'no-one could learn the song except the 144,000 who had been redeemed from the earth'* (14:3b). It is a praise item that no other group can share, it is exclusive to them. The Lord has saved them, he has delivered them, he has given them the victory, he has brought them through ... redemption is theirs, it is no wonder

302 Worthy is the Lamb!

they break forth into song! It would be strange if they did not! This is God's choir in the sky. They celebrate their victory with a freshly composed medley before the throne of God in heaven.

They are exemplary!

John fills us in with all the details when he says, *'These are those who did not defile themselves with women, for they kept themselves pure. They follow the Lamb wherever he goes. They were purchased from among men and offered as firstfruits to God and the Lamb. No lie was found in their mouths; they are blameless'* (14:4,5).

Their conduct. These men are morally pure. The phrase which John uses here implies they remained celibate, they never married. These men are not chauvinists; it just so happens marriage was not on God's agenda for their lives. Their time, their energy, their life, is totally wrapped up in serving the Lord. There is nothing to sidetrack them, there is no-one to distract them, they are God focused and Christ centred.

Their consecration. These men will go wherever the Lord wants them to go, theirs is a no-strings-attached commitment. They will go anywhere, they will do anything. Their dedication to Christ and his cause is total, it is 100% surrender for their all is on the altar. I suppose we could say they are latter-day Caleb's. It is a fitting comparison for it was said three times of Caleb in Joshua 14 that he 'wholly followed the Lord.' The same spirit is found in the hearts of these gentle giants.

Their calling. John pays eloquent tribute to the work of God's grace in their lives when he freely acknowledges that they were purchased from among men. He goes on to say that they were offered as *'firstfruits'* to the Lord. This means, they were a token of the harvest which was yet to come, they represented the whole harvest.

The feast of firstfruits was one of the seven feasts in the Jewish calendar. It always falls on a Sunday and follows the week in which the Passover occurs. What happened was this: the farmer went into his field of swiftly ripening grain and cut out one sheaf to be presented to the Lord, it was given to the priest who waved it before the Lord as a sign that the entire harvest belonged to him. You find that documented in Leviticus 23. You have a similar analogy in the well-known resurrection chapter of 1 Corinthians 15.

Their conversation. John mentions their conversation in verse 5 as something of special significance. These men were individuals without any trace of guile in their lips. There was nothing false in them. When they opened their mouths, they spoke the truth, the whole truth, and nothing but the truth.

Their character. Allied to this tremendous virtue is the fact that they are exemplary in their character for John says they are blameless. They are without blemish. No-one could point a finger at them, no-one could stand up and accuse them. Their lives were above and beyond reproach. They were glass-house believers, you could see right through them. They had no hidden agenda, there were no skeletons hiding in the cupboard. These men were genuine through and through, they were transparent.

We have here a grand company of men who are saved, men who are sealed, men who are separated, men who are sanctified, and men who are spotless. What a wonderful group of people ... men who will do anything for Jesus, men who are sold out to Christ! It is a mouth-watering picture of the redeemed of the Lord. The stirring challenge facing you and me in the third millennium is an obvious one, can the same be said of us?

> The 144,000 give us a checklist for self-assessment: they had purity, devotion and integrity. How does the church at large measure up in these three areas? If change is needed, what should be done to bring this about?

14:6-13

Listen to the special commission

A favourite song of mine has as its first line, 'Great is the gospel of our glorious God.' It was written by a Welshman who is the minister of a flourishing church in the capital city of Cardiff. The lyrics are so full of meaning, they are pregnant with truth. He makes every word count! The same can be said of John's breathtaking insights in chapter 14.

The proclamation of the gospel

John shares his uplifting experience with us when he says, *'Then I saw another angel flying in mid-air, and he had the eternal gospel to proclaim to those who live on the earth - to every nation, tribe, language and people. He said in a loud voice, "Fear God and give him glory, because the hour of his judgment has come. Worship him who made the heavens, the earth, the sea and the springs of water."'* What can we learn about this gospel?

It is an everlasting gospel. Here is a message which is eternal in its significance. It is timeless. It does not have a sell-by date stamped on the outside of it. It is truth unchanged, truth unchanging. It is consistently relevant. The gospel has always been an integral part of God's eternal plan. There is nothing new outlined in this verse. It is the old, old story of redeeming love, it is the same glad tidings but we are coming at it from a different perspective, it is the evangel with an added dimension.

> **Does the angel's message of verse 7 guide us in what we should include in our evangelism?**

Apart from anything else, the general thrust of the message is the creative power and love of God. We read many times in the Bible that the universe itself is a potent witness to the presence of God. David, in Psalm 19:1, tells us that, 'The heavens declare the glory of God, the skies proclaim the work of his hands.' Paul goes down a similar track when he says in Romans 1:20, 'For since the creation of the world God's invisible qualities - his eternal power and divine nature - have been clearly seen, being understood from what has been made, so that men are without excuse.'

Those are only a couple of examples but they provide an eloquent testimony to the skilful work of his hands. The praises of God's people in heaven reflect the same combination of his work in creation and his work in redemption (the same twin truths are echoed in chapters 4 and 5.)

It is proclaimed by an angel. This is most unusual for in this present age angels are not privileged to preach the good news. That solemn responsibility rests on your shoulders and mine. We are his witnesses, but in the closing days of the Tribulation, this heavenly messenger will be sounding out the message of God's salvation.

It reaches all nations. In that day the great commission of Matthew 28:19,20 will be fulfilled. Here we have a communiqué which is universal in its scope, it is global in its appeal. It is reaching out to the ends of the earth, the whole world is his parish. A similar thought is expressed by the Lord himself in Matthew 24:14, where we read, 'And this gospel of the kingdom will be preached in the whole world as a testimony to all nations, and then the end will come.'

It results in salvation. The direct result of the dissemination of this powerful message is that it brings men into a dynamic relationship with God. This is a point I want to highlight; this is the gospel as it really is, it is a life changing message, it is a life transforming message!

The Antichrist with his synthetic gospel is saying, 'Fear me, glorify me, worship me!' The true gospel of sovereign grace declares, 'Fear God, glorify God, worship God!'

It involves conviction. This is the gospel as it always has been: it brings men in from the cold into the warmth of the love of God. In a nutshell, it is a healthy fear of the Lord. The gospel of Christ sorts out the agenda of our lives like nothing else can; it enables us to get our priorities right when we are down on bended knee before the cross of Jesus. When we fear God, it puts the terror of the Lord in a heart that is strangely awakened.

It involves conversion. Conviction is the first step down the road which leads to conversion. This is the first time the word *'judgment'* is used in Revelation; this is not merely a coming day of judgment at some distant date marked in God's calendar, it is actually narrowed down so that John refers to the *'hour'* of judgment. The sinner denies God the glory which is due to his holy name, while the Christian gives God the glory which is rightfully his. Surely that is God's great goal as expressed on the morn of creation, that is also his all-consuming passion in securing our redemption, to bring glory to himself. A gospel that falls short of bringing men to God to give him glory is insufficient, it is only a watered-down version; it is so diluted it is not the authentic gospel of Christ.

It involves consecration. Conviction and conversion are followed by consecration. Worship is the ultimate experience we can have this side of heaven. It is the overflow of a life filled with wonder, love and praise. It is the natural outcome when we are enraptured by the beauty of Christ. It is inevitable when our hearts are beating in sync with his. Intelligent worship is when we pour out our lives as a drink offering to the Lord; it is when we lay our all upon the altar in an act of complete surrender. It is your life and mine responding to the overtures of his love and grace.

> **Throughout the Bible, God tells us to give him glory. Why is it right for God to seek his own glory in this way and why is it right for us to give it? In reality, what does it mean to give God glory?**

Babylon ... the writing is on the wall!

The mood changes in verse 8 with the arrival of the second angel. His message is conclusive, it is a fait accompli. He says, *'Fallen! Fallen is Babylon the Great, which made all the nations drink the maddening wine of her adulteries.'*

If the first proclamation was good news, this prediction is great news! This is the first mention of Babylon in the Apocalypse and it is by no means the last. What we have here in verse 8 is a single brief statement that is later expanded on with considerable flair in chapters 17 and 18. In those two chapters, John has an eye for detail; here we have it in anticipation.

Various views are held concerning Babylon's role during the Tribulation. Some believe that Babylon refers to a literal city, yet to be rebuilt in Iraq. Others believe it refers to the city of Rome. I think it is forward to the day when the political and economic and religious system of the Antichrist will suffer total collapse, it anticipates the day when the whole organisation will crash around his feet.

The angel stressed the seriousness of the situation when he repeated the word *'fallen'* twice. It is a double exclamation, it is a double whammy. The evangelical prophet Isaiah was on the same wavelength when he reported in 21:9 that, 'Babylon has fallen, has fallen! All the images of its gods lie shattered on the ground.' The message is crystal clear, there is no beating about the bush, Babylon is doomed!

The reason for her spectacular downfall is elucidated with precision in the same verse and the point is underlined in bold capital letters in 17:2,5. John pulls no punches when he reveals that political leaders throughout history have committed fornication with this woman; they have done a tango with this false and corrupt religious system and the people of planet earth have accepted it willy-nilly.

The second angel throws the spanner in the works with his declaration that judgment will come. In fact, from his vantage point, it is as good as done. The future is ominous, it is bleak. Judgment cannot be avoided, judgment cannot be averted. The obituary of Babylon has already been written, her demise is guaranteed. For the second time, the writing is on the wall. To all intents and purposes, she has gone past the point of no return.

Beast worshippers ... your time is up!

The next three verses are startling words, a spine chilling reminder of the awful and dreadful fate of those who choose to say 'no' to Jesus Christ. John leaves us in no doubt when he says, *'A third angel followed them and said in a loud voice, "If anyone worships the beast and his image and receives his mark on the forehead or on the hand, he, too, will drink of the wine of God's fury, which has been poured full strength into the cup of his wrath. He will be tormented with burning sulphur in the presence of the holy angels and of the Lamb. And the smoke of their torment rises for ever and ever. There is no rest day or night for those who worship the beast and his image, or for anyone who receives the mark of his name"'* (14:9-11).

The evidence. I think it is clear for all to see: if you worship the Antichrist and his image you are showing allegiance and loyalty to him. To receive his mark is a matter of economic survival, we came across that in chapter 13. The implication here is that the state will be god in that day, it will wield total and absolute control over the lives of its citizens. The message is therefore one which is urgent. It is short, it is blunt, it is plain.

The explanation. He also gives us a reasonable explanation for their self-inflicted agony. They have brought it on themselves because they chose to reject God's way. They have only themselves to blame.

The Antichrist cries out, 'Worship me ... or be doomed!'
The Lamb cries out, 'Worship me ... or be damned!'

That is it in a nutshell. It is a straightforward choice facing the inhabitants of planet earth. If you worship the devil's messiah, you will drink the wine of God's fury. The cup out of which they drink is described as the wrath of God himself and it is full strength!

The extent. It is spelt out in the clearest of terms. Here you have all the horrors of hell depicted in the most vivid language. It is eternal retribution, it is undiluted torment, it is never ending, it just goes on and on and on! There is no reprieve, there is no escape. How frightening! How terrifying! How awesome a thing it is to fall into the hands of the living God! There is no rest afforded to them. Their days become one long horror tale of anguish; their nights become black nightmares of unthinkable dread.

> **What answer would you give to those who say that the punishment meted out to the wicked in verse 11 is too severe, perhaps even cruel?**

The patience of the saints

In one sense, there is a feeling of enormous relief when John changes gear in verse 12 and addresses the subject of the patience of the saints. The contrast is patently obvious, it is an abrupt transition. He says, *'This calls for patient endurance on the part of the saints who obey God's commandments and remain faithful to Jesus.'* It is a clarion call for patience; it is an incentive for the people to show remarkable perseverance.

Their characteristics. The wonderful characteristics of these good folk are outlined for us. Basically, they are happy to obey God's word and they are intensely loyal to God's Son. The Antichrist says to them, *'I'll make you suffer!'* They reply, *'You'll make us saints!'* The Antichrist threatens them, *'I'll persecute you to the grave!'* They reply, *'You'll promote us to glory!'* The Antichrist tightens the screw, *'I'll blast you!'* They reply, *'God will bless us!'* The Antichrist may roar and rage. He may blow a lot of hot air and let off a fair bit of steam. It will all be in vain; he will fail at the end of the day.

Their condition. In verse 13, John speaks with a tender touch as regards their condition. He says, *'Write: Blessed are the dead who die in the Lord from now on.'* *'Yes,'* says the Spirit, *'they will rest from their labour, for their deeds will follow them.'*

They are *'blessed who die in the Lord.'* This is the second of seven beatitudes mentioned in the book of Revelation. In other words, they will be ushered into the near presence of the Lord, they will see the King in all his impeccable beauty. Their rest is gloriously eternal; there are no more struggles, there is no more pain or suffering, there is no more exhaustion, it is rest forever. These folk will be recompensed for nothing anyone has done for the Lord is ever overlooked. Everything done in his name and for his glory will be amply rewarded. Paul says as much in 1 Corinthians 15:58 when he encourages us to recognise that 'our labour in the Lord is not in vain.'

> **Rest and reward await the saints (verse 13). Commit to memory the verse quoted above ... 1 Corinthians 15:58.**

14:14-20

Learn from the special command

The final section of chapter 14 is a most intriguing one.

A word of introduction

John says, *'I looked, and there before me was a white cloud, and seated on the cloud was one "like a son of man" with a crown of gold on his head and a sharp sickle in his hand.'* We are introduced initially to the one who is the reaper of the harvest. There is no doubt as to his identity, the one who was the sower in the parable of Matthew 13 is now the reaper in Revelation 14. There are four things about him worth considering.

His human personality. He is called *'the Son of man.'* This was the title he used for himself; it reminds us that he is one who knows what we are like. This is the last time we read of him using this particular name. The first time was in Matthew 8:20, where we are told, 'The foxes have holes, the birds of the air have nests, but the Son of Man has nowhere to lay his head.' That familiar reference had to do with his first advent, this one refers to his second coming. Then his poverty was in view; now it is his power which is in sight.

His moral purity. He is seated on a white cloud and the cloud, as we have seen elsewhere, is a symbol of the presence of God. The white underlines the righteousness of God.

His great power. The golden crown is the mark of a king who is also a conqueror. If you fast forward to 19:12, you will notice he has many crowns adorning his brow. In the next breath, he is hailed as, *'King of kings and Lord of lords.'*

His awesome purpose. He has a sharp sickle in his hand. That can only speak of a harvest being reaped. Here we see the Lord acting in judgment. There is an allusion to this in Matthew 13:37-43.

> The 'white cloud' and the designation 'son of man' speak of deity and humanity respectively. How does this qualify this individual to act as the 'reaper'?

A word of instruction

'Then another angel came out of the temple and called in a loud voice to him who was sitting on the cloud, "Take your sickle and reap, because the time to reap has come, for the harvest of the earth is ripe." So he who was seated on the cloud swung his sickle over the earth, and the earth was harvested. Another angel came out of the temple in heaven, and he too had a sharp sickle. Still another

angel, who had charge of the fire, came from the altar and called in a loud voice to him who had the sharp sickle, "Take your sharp sickle and gather the clusters of grapes from the earth's vine, because its grapes are ripe"' (14:15-18).

It is fairly clear from John's comments that the judgment of God will come according to his time schedule. Some people wonder why God has not acted sooner. They question why God does not stop all the trouble in today's world. Well, he will act when the time is right. The fact it has not happened yet does not mean it is on the back burner, far from it! The day will soon dawn when judgment will be felt to the uttermost ends of the earth. It will all be brought to a grand climax.

Ripe and rotten. The picture here is of a harvest that is ripe. The Greek word suggests it is 'ripe to the point of being rotten or withered.' So, when God does move in judgment, it will be long overdue but it will not be a minute too soon. Not even the extreme cynic can accuse God of acting on the spur of the moment. When his hand is lifted in such a manner, it will not be in haste for this is no rash decision of an ill-tempered God.

His judgment is a reflection of his justice. And the apparent delay says more about the patience and long-suffering of God than anything else.

> **What are some of the reasons why God delays the final judgment?**

You have another picture of it unfolding in Joel 3:12-16. The Old Testament prophet draws back the curtain and shows us what will transpire when God acts in judgment on the nations who have come against Jerusalem and the people of Israel. They will meet their Waterloo in the environs of the Holy City; it is there that their blood will flow like a fast flowing stream. For them, it is the valley of decision.

Grain and grapes. John talks about grain in verses 14-16 and then he changes the metaphor in verses 17-20 to talk about grapes. The picture may change but the event remains the same; it is the judgment of the nations which is brought into sharp focus. If you want to find out more about it, you can read the appropriate section in Matthew 25.

Timely and terrible. That is what this vision of Armageddon is, timely and terrible. The closing couple of verses are graphic as John reminds us of the incredible impact of this hour of judgment.

A word on its impact

John says, '*The angel swung his sickle on the earth, gathered its grapes and threw them into the great winepress of God's wrath. They were trampled in the winepress outside the city, and blood flowed out of the press, rising as high as the horses' bridles for a distance of 1,600 stadia*' (14:19,20).

A winepress in ancient Israel was hewn out of solid stone. Grapes were cast into the press and crushed under foot until all the juice was squeezed out of them. That is the analogy John gives us when he says they are like grapes trampled under foot, they are like mulch in a winepress, they have been walked over! What an appalling scene!

The distance from Dan to Beersheba is about 200 miles and that is how long the river of blood will be! The carnage will reach up to the horses' bridles and that is a height of four or five feet! It does not bear thinking about.

It is a solemn picture as God walks all over his enemies ... they do not stand a chance, he will sweep them aside. It is a day of wholesale slaughter, unprecedented so far as this world is concerned. The like of it has never been witnessed before. The abiding message of this passage is that it is better to trust in Jesus as Saviour now, rather than run the risk of being alive in the Tribulation and facing him as your Judge!

15

A sign ~ a song ~ a scene

Length is not everything! Brevity means nothing! This is the shortest chapter in the book but, I can assure you, that is no reflection of its significance and importance. Compacted into an octet of verses is a little chapter with a lot to say.

15:1,2

The sign

It is interesting to note that the sign depicted in the opening verse as *'great and marvellous'* and the first few words of the song recorded for us in verse 3 are exactly the same. There is nothing tenuous about such a link; there is nothing coincidental about it either. The connection is a valid one because they both relate to the God of glory, the awe-inspiring God. He is the focus of attention. He is centre stage. The spotlight is shining solely on him. So what can we learn about him?

A final nightmare for earth

We read all about the sign in verse 1, where John says, *'I saw in heaven another great and marvellous sign: seven angels with the seven last plagues - last, because with them God's wrath is completed.'*

This third sign is of mega importance and it is one which we dare not underestimate. It is called *'another'* sign meaning it is like the others that have preceded it, namely the sign of the woman and the sign of the dragon. Here we are introduced to phase three on the agenda of God's judgment programme.

These seven bowls are poised to tip over, they are ready to spill out a torrent of white-hot wrath upon a fallen humanity. We have already come across the seven seals in phase one and the seven trumpets in phase two. Now we have seven bowls or vials which are scheduled to be poured out on planet earth.

There is no Plan B

If you like, here is the final judgment of God. When these bowls are emptied, then the wrath of God on this old world will be complete. This final set of judgments is the turning point. It is the historical pivot upon which God's plan now turns. God is exceedingly angry with a world that is increasingly rebellious. It is helpful to remind ourselves that God's wrath will not continue forever; once he has exercised the divine prerogative and done what he has said he will do, then that is it. There is no plague number eight, there is no plan B. We glean that much from Psalm 103:9 where David says, the Lord 'will not always accuse, nor will he harbour his anger for ever.'

The word *'complete'* speaks of a plan being carried out, it refers to a goal being fully accomplished. It is inextricably linked to the phrase at the end of 16:17 where the voice from the throne says, *'It is done'* or *'It is finished.'* It is quite ironic. Do you see what happens? When all this drama is unfolding on planet earth, at precisely the same time something extraordinary is happening in heaven!

Harps and heroes in heaven!

John fills us in with the details when he tells us in verse 2, *'And I saw what looked like a sea of glass mixed with fire and, standing beside the sea, those who had been victorious over the beast and his image and over the number of his name. They held harps given them by God.'*

The apostle sees an incredible number of people in his vision standing beside the sea of glass. That is a phrase we first came across in 4:6 where we noted it functioned like a mirror reflecting God's glory and majesty. The sea is also symbolic of God's purity, his holiness and his separation from creation. The significant difference is that here it is *'mixed with fire'* typifying the divine judgment that is about to be manifested from a holy God.

I was intrigued with another interpretation of this particular picture which John paints for us so vividly in verse 2. It favours the view that the sea of glass represents the word of God. So when you think of the sea of glass, do not picture an ocean or a lake; think of a laver or a basin similar to what was found in the tabernacle in the wilderness and later in the temple in Jerusalem. It stood adjacent to the holy place and those who ministered in the things of the Lord would first of all wash in the laver before entering the sanctuary.

The implication is, there is cleansing from our sin when we allow the word of God to purify our hearts and that God is looking for clean vessels to engage in his service. Paul said as much in his moving letter to the believers in Ephesus and Jesus hinted at something similar in John 15:3 when he said, 'You are already clean because of the word I have spoken to you.' It is fascinating that the *'sea'* John describes here in verse 2 has no-one washing in it. Instead, they are standing on it! The fact is, there is no further need for them to wash, they are in heaven! They have been promoted to glory!

It seems the 'sea' of verse 2 is linked with the cleansing effect of the word of God. In what way is this connected with the place of unique service to God which they exercised in verses 3 and 4? How can you apply this principle to your own experience?

Some through the fire ...

The *'sea'* John writes of is *'mixed with fire'* and this particular view supports the idea that this speaks of the troubles the saints have experienced. But they have come through the fire and, because of that, their troubles are beneath their feet. They have overcome! Fear no longer grips their heart and panic no longer dogs their every step for they are standing four-square on the word of God. You see, there is a stability in the word of God. That is just another way of looking at it from a slightly different angle.

The question remains, can we identify these people? Who are they? I think the answer is a relatively simple one: they are the martyrs of the Tribulation. These are the ones who laid down their lives for the sake of Jesus, they paid the supreme sacrifice. These are the brave folk who refused to worship the Antichrist. They gallantly swam against the tide of anarchy and lawlessness, they defiantly stood their ground and would not participate in any semblance of Satan inspired religion.

They have been victorious in the day of severe trial. They have not succumbed to the fierce onslaught from the enemy when the battle was raging all around them. In the hour of conquest, they did not cave in under enormous pressure. They said a firm 'no' to being branded with the mark of the beast and, there they are, standing with their heads held high in heaven itself. They have been well rewarded. They may have died on earth but they are very much alive in heaven where they are treated and honoured as heroes.

I think that offers immense encouragement to all of us, and even more so, when we realise the Lord has designated a special ministry just for them. They form a marvellous orchestra with their harps. There is the sweet sound of beautiful music permeating the atmosphere. There is inspired singing and worshipful praise emanating from their cultured voices. It is a delightful symphony and these folk are intimately involved in every part of the proceedings. You can see it for yourself. They rejoice in the ultimate victory of God.

15:3,4

The song

John tells us in verses 3 and 4, they *'sang the song of Moses the servant of God and the song of the Lamb: "Great and marvellous are your deeds, Lord God Almighty. Just and true are your ways, King of the ages. Who will not fear you, O Lord, and bring glory to your name? For you alone are holy. All nations will come and worship before you, for your righteous acts have been revealed."'*

What a wonderful song of praise to our God!

The martyr's song

We can learn a lot from these words. It is the music of heaven itself. It is sung by those who have tasted deeply of the grace of God. They have known his forgiveness and cleansing (we saw that in 7:14); they also know what it is to suffer and to give their lives for the Lord (you find that when you fast forward to 20:4). This is a song of martyrs!

The title of the song is most informative in that it is referred to as the *'Song of Moses'* and the *'Song of the Lamb.'* We are presently exploring Revelation 15 and you can find out more about the song of Moses in Exodus 15. Let me give you some remarkable comparisons between the two of them:

The song of Moses was sung at the Red Sea, the song of the Lamb is sung at the crystal sea; the song of Moses was one of triumph over Egypt, the song of the Lamb is one of triumph over Babylon; the song of Moses told how God brought his people out, the song of the Lamb tells how God brings his people in; the song of Moses was the first song in scripture, the song of the Lamb is the last one recorded on the sacred page; the song of Moses had a triple commemoration, the song of the Lamb deals with the same three themes - the execution of the foe, the expectation of the saints, the exaltation of the Lord; the song of Moses was sung by a redeemed people, the song of the Lamb is sung by a raptured people.

Basically, it is a song which is broken down into two parts. The first part tells us what the ransomed will sing. It is a threefold stanza for it says, 'How great thou art! how good thou art! how glorious thou art!' The second part tells us why the remnant will sing and you find that alluded to in verse 4. It is because of the majestic virtue of God; it is because of the magnificent victory of God; and it is because of the manifest vengeance of God.

This stunning song in chapter 15 is pure, unadulterated praise! It is praise at its finest and best. It is praise as God intended it should be. The more you look into it, the more you listen to the words being sung, the more you recognise the sheer quality of each carefully chosen word and the more you appreciate and value the harmony of heaven.

They are praising the marvellous works of God ... they emphasise his power

These varied judgments demonstrate the mighty power of God; he is omnipotent. They tell us what he can do. You find an echo of this in Psalm 145:10-13, where we read, 'All you have made will praise you, O Lord; your saints will extol you. They will tell of the glory of your kingdom and speak of your might, so that all men may know of your mighty acts and the glorious splendour of your kingdom. Your kingdom is an everlasting kingdom, and your dominion endures through all generations. The Lord is faithful to all his promises and loving towards all he has made.'

> List a dozen 'great and marvellous' deeds done by the Lord throughout biblical history as well as global history!

They are praising the mysterious ways of God ... they emphasise his plan

The psalmist picks up the same thread when he reminds us that the Lord is right and just in all that he does. You find that in Psalm 145:17, where we read, 'The Lord is righteous in all his ways and loving towards all he has made.' He is faithful to all his promises. Here is a God who is totally reliable. We may not always understand the plan of God especially as it relates to justice and the future, but we can be assured, there is a plan and the plan is correct and it is on schedule. We can affirm with a high degree of confidence, there is no panic in heaven over events on earth.

> God is described as 'just and true' in verse 3 and the same could be said of Jesus in his earthly life. In practical terms, what does it mean to be just and true and, from the example of Jesus, how could we get nearer to this godly example?

They are praising the manifold worth of God ... they emphasise his perfection

Here is one who is holy, one who is transcendent. Our God is one who is completely separate from all that he has created, that is a distinction unique to him. Only he deserves the glory and praise. It is something quite exclusive.

They are praising the majestic worship of God ... they emphasise his purpose

God's ultimate purpose is for all nations to praise him. His eventual goal is for all creation to praise him. You find that outlined in Psalm 66:4, where we read, 'All the earth bows down to you, they sing praise to you, they sing praise to your name.'

We have a similar note in Psalm 72:11, where Solomon says, 'All kings will bow down to him and all nations will serve him.' And when we take a look at Isaiah 66:23, we see an amazing prophecy which anticipates a day when 'from one New Moon to another and from one Sabbath to another, all mankind will come and bow down before me.' Paul declared in Philippians 2:10,11 that one day all men will bow the knee before him and every tongue will confess that Jesus Christ is Lord! Yes, all nations, all of creation, will worship him!

Based on verse 4, what does it mean to fear the Lord? The
picture of all nations worshipping before God is reflected in
Philippians 2:9-11 where even his enemies bow the knee before
him; why is this universal acknowledgment that God is God
revealed as an appropriate part of the final judgment?

15:5-8

The scene

John shares a profound experience with us in verses 5-8 by informing
us, 'After this I looked and in heaven the temple, that is, the tabernacle
of the Testimony, was opened. Out of the temple came the seven
angels with the seven plagues. They were dressed in clean, shining
linen and wore golden sashes round their chests. Then one of the
four living creatures gave to the seven angels seven bowls filled
with the wrath of God, who lives for ever and ever. And the temple
was filled with smoke from the glory of God and from his power, and
no-one could enter the temple until the seven plagues of the seven
angels were completed.'

We are taken into the holy of holies in heaven, and what do we
notice? We have the appearance of the seven angels. These are the
same ones you read about elsewhere in the Apocalypse. They are
specifically chosen by God to execute his purposes upon the world
and that teaches us a couple of important lessons:

Their coming out of the temple reminds us of the faithfulness of God

The temple is called 'the tabernacle of the Testimony' and the
'Testimony' refers to the Law of God. These were the ten
commandments that were written on two tablets of stone and placed
within the ark of the covenant. It reminds us that God's covenant
with his people will be kept; it has never been annulled, it has never
been set aside. God will honour his high and holy standards for it is
his name which is at stake. His severe judgment will fall upon those

who reject him and his principles. In other words, God will be rigidly faithful to what he has said.

Their clothing reminds us of the righteousness and majesty of God

What they will do in pouring out God's wrath upon the inhabitants of the earth is a powerful demonstration of God's holiness and righteousness. What they do is terrible, but at the same time, it is right! They also have *'golden sashes round their chests'* and that could be seen as symbolic of the priests who ministered in the temple but, more than likely, it is a picture of the majesty and greatness of our kingly God. You can compare their clothing with that which is worn by our exalted Lord in 1:13, and when you do that, it is apparent that this is the apparel of a sovereign ruler.

Their assignment is spelled out clearly in verse 7 when one of the worship leaders gives the seven golden bowls to the seven angels. Each of these vessels is filled to the brim with the undiluted anger of God. This means that God's anger is at boiling point as the seven last plagues are emptied out upon this world in a most comprehensive manner. We see him as the eternal one and that in itself is a token reminder of the nature of his punishment.

The atmosphere in the temple is easily detected in verse 8. What an awesome display of God's presence and power! Two facets of this noble attribute are emphasised in this verse:

the intensity of God's power ... when the evangelical prophet Isaiah had his spectacular vision of the Lord of hosts, we read in 6:4 that 'at the sound of their voices the door posts and thresholds shook and the temple was filled with smoke.' Remember the incident detailed in Exodus 40:34 where again we observe that God's presence was often pictured by a cloud or smoke. There we read, 'Then the cloud covered the Tent of Meeting and the glory of the Lord filled the tabernacle.'

the importance of God's plan ... God's wrath is part of his unerring plan and it will be completed. His mission will not be aborted. Until it is effectively and efficiently carried out, no-one can enter the temple in heaven. That is quite dramatic but it reminds us of the importance of these seven last plagues in the ripening of the eternal purpose of God. It seems to me that the Tribulation is a demonstration of the wrath of an angry God against all those who flatly refuse to trust in the Lord Jesus. And so far as the sinner is concerned, the worst is yet to come!

At the end of the chapter, God is seen as a consuming fire of blazing glory. 'Who among us,' asks Isaiah, 'can dwell with everlasting burning?' Can you honestly answer that question?

16

Armageddon ... the coming world conflict

Revelation 16 is one of those chapters in the Bible that makes the hair stand on the back of your neck. You can feel the shivers going down your spine. It makes your legs turn to jelly and the old butterflies work overtime in your tummy. It is a chapter where you can almost feel a tremor in each line as the scale of the disaster facing the world becomes increasingly apparent. One respected Bible commentator describes this chilling chapter as the 'Saturday evening of the age.'

Judgment and justice

The storm is about to break. What follows is undoubtedly the darkest chapter in the history of mankind. John informs us, *'Then I heard a loud voice from the temple saying to the seven angels, "Go, pour out the seven bowls of God's wrath on the earth."'* There is no mistaking that message! It is precise, it is straight to the point, it is God going for the jugular. As we shall see, the consequences do not make for pleasant reading.

You see, the world has been ruined by the Fall; the world has flatly rejected the Lord Jesus Christ; the world has been ruled by Satan; now, in an hour of swift and decisive judgment, God initiates a rescue mission. You know, and I know, that the ways of God are strange. They are often shrouded in an air of mystery. There is a certain mystique about the mind of God but, in the midst of all the chaos and confusion, we must never forget the final chapter; so far as God is concerned, those closing lines have already been penned.

Today, we see a world in a total mess; tomorrow, we see a world where the glory of the Lord is manifest. Today, we see wrath and anger; tomorrow, it will be worship and adoration.

That is the supreme goal our God is tirelessly working towards. But before it can be fully achieved, man must be taught a salient lesson on the unchanging character of God: God is holy, God is angry, God is sovereign, and God is a God of justice!

> This chapter well illustrates the words of Daniel where he says in 4:17 that 'the Most High is sovereign over the kingdoms of men.' How can this fact influence your prayers for nations and political events?

And so, one after another, the seven angels empty their bowls and, as they pour out the wrath of the Lord, indescribable things begin to happen. Much of what is recorded here is reminiscent of the plagues called down by Moses on the land of Egypt.

16:2

Plague number one!

In verse 2, John says, *'The first angel went and poured out his bowl on the land and ugly and painful sores broke out on the people who had the mark of the beast and worshipped his image.'*

The target

The principal target of this plague are the committed followers of the Antichrist. These are the people who have the mark of the beast on their right hand or on their forehead; these are the ones who are happy to worship the image of the beast which was set up in the rebuilt temple in Jerusalem. Their past catches up with them with breathtaking speed. Their crazy decision to opt for the easy alternative and go with the crowd returns to haunt them. Remember that the Antichrist is the one who thinks he is God Mark 2. By this time he is well established as a world leader; he is highly respected as a major player on the stage of global affairs. Here is the final government credited to modern man, these are the last of the last days. When the Antichrist is at his peak, God strikes ... and he does it with impunity!

The affliction

God's strategy is to attack the health of men and women. He hits them where it hurts most and it is not a pretty sight. We are told that *'ugly and painful sores'* break out on their bodies. The thought here is of ulcerous, contagious, putrefying sores which infect the body like a malignant cancer. It is some kind of skin disease which is incurable. If you have ever experienced an outbreak of boils on your body, you will know they are extremely painful, they are inflamed, they are pus filled; that gives you a tiny inkling of what it will be like in a coming day, only then it will be so much worse.

The ramifications

What an awful affliction that must be and it is made a million times worse because these folk are used to pampering themselves. How much worse it is when it is inflicted on a people who are obsessed with their personal appearance! Pain affects a person's disposition, they are hard to live with, they find it difficult to get along with other people. Emotionally, it will be a radical upheaval; psychologically, it will be a disaster!

16:3

Plague number two!

Plague number two is outlined for us in considerable detail in verse 3, where we read, *'The second angel poured out his bowl on the sea, and it turned into blood like that of a dead man, and every living thing in the sea died.'*

The target

That is grim, it really is. It does not bear thinking about. Away back in the days of Moses it was the River Nile that was turned to blood ... here it is the sea itself.

The affliction

What an incredible sight for the naked eye! The sea becomes an ocean which is foul, offensive and poisonous. It turns into a thick coagulated mass of fluid which stinks like a badly decomposed corpse. What a disgusting smell for an aroma conscious generation to inhale! The reek is stifling and oppressive.

The ramifications

Every living creature in the sea dies and that is nothing short of a major catastrophe for it hits the food supply of the world, it affects the global economy adversely. It will be as though the bruised world is lying in its own gore. Everything to do with the sea grinds to a sudden halt, it comes to a standstill with a jerk. What a tremendously awesome display of the power of a God who can do anything! Man is left reeling from the impact of this lethal blow of the wrath of God. Can you even begin to imagine the fetid stench that will rise from such terribly polluted waters?

I do not know if John means the sea will literally turn to blood for he says it will be *'like that of a dead man.'* There is a condition known as the 'red tide.' This is caused by minute organisms that multiply incredibly fast and cause everything in one area to die. Scientists cannot put their finger on the reasons behind this condition, they do not know what causes it but they presume it is due to cobalt from nuclear waste. This may be what happens or it may not be; either way, the seas will be contaminated.

16:4-7

Plague number three!

John continues in verses 4-7 to provide us with vital information which is relevant to plague number three.

The target

He says, *'The third angel poured out his bowl on the rivers and springs of water, and they became blood. Then I heard the angel in charge of the waters say: "You are just in these judgments, you who are and who were, the Holy One, because you have so judged; for they have shed the blood of your saints and prophets, and you have given them blood to drink as they deserve." And I heard the altar respond: "Yes, Lord God Almighty, true and just are your judgments."'* The sheer magnitude of this is unimaginable, it is inconceivable!

The affliction

The Lord's first miracle in Cana of Galilee was to turn water into wine; now he turns water into blood. All of the world's springs and rivers are now affected. That means the drinking water supply is polluted and corrupted to such an extent that global panic is unavoidable. If the world is so bloodthirsty, God will give it to them - fountains of blood, springs of blood, rivers of blood, oceans of blood!

The ramifications

That which is essential for the maintenance of life is now rendered useless. You cannot quench your thirst if you cannot drink the water! There is a limit to the stockpiles of bottled mineral water and canned soft drinks. There will be the inevitable health problems as a direct result of what has happened and this will serve to increase the agony of daily life.

All the comforts and necessities of life are being taken away gradually, bit by bit, and then finally! I think it will slowly dawn on the minds of people that the end of the world is just around the corner. The fact is, this is not man messing around with the environment. This is supernatural, this is divine, this is God! Down through history, we discover an age old principle which dictates that the punishment fits the crime.

Pharaoh tried to drown the Jewish male babies, but it was his own army that eventually drowned in the warm sparkling waters of the Red Sea. Haman planned to hang Mordecai on the gallows and exterminate the Jews, but the tables were turned when he himself perished and his family was wiped out entirely. Saul refused to obey the Lord and slay the Amalekites; his foolish scheme tragically backfired when he was slain by one of them.

The response of the angels to this incredible intervention by God in the affairs of man indicates a recognition of the righteousness of God; they also make much of the holiness of God and they are happy to elucidate so clearly the eternal nature of God. Here we have volumes of praise dedicated to one who acts. It is an eloquent tribute to a God who is unafraid to move when he senses the time is right. The God we meet here is one who sets the record straight. This incident reminds us that God answers the prayers of those martyred saints which are recorded for us in 6:9-11. They asked, *'How long?'* God says, 'Their time has come, their number is up!'

> **The angel took delight in God's ability to fit the punishment to the crime. How do you think you will react to seeing perfect justice meted out?**

16:8,9

Plague number four!

In verses 8 and 9, we are introduced to plague number four.

The target

The verse begins in the same way as all the others have, when John says, *'The fourth angel poured out his bowl on the sun, and the sun was given power to scorch people with fire. They were seared by the intense heat and they cursed the name of God, who had control over these plagues, but they refused to repent and glorify him.'*

The affliction

The light from the sun is not reduced but its capacity to bring heat to the earth is massively increased. It will get hotter and hotter. What is normally seen as a blessing to man, quickly becomes a curse, as men are scorched by the sun's burning rays.

The ramifications

Anyone who has been exposed to the sun for any length of time knows it can be a merciless foe rather than a warm friend. Ask anyone who has suffered sunstroke for their opinion and I think you will discover it is not something they would like to experience again. This plague strikes right at the heart of man's personal security and quest for survival. This is no Indian summer, this is no freak heat wave. The earth will be scorched and the heat will be so intense it will have a searing effect upon man. The extreme heat will boil the oceans dry and melt the polar ice caps as well as affect the people. One commentator puts it succinctly when he says, 'The earth turning on its axis begins to resemble a pig roasting on a spit.'

Such a situation begs the question, what is man's initial response to this crisis in his personal life? Well, they cursed the name of God; that is fairly typical, isn't it! It is par for the course! To put it mildly, they blame God! They blaspheme the precious name of the Lord of heaven. You can detect something of the dogged determination of ordinary people when they dig in their heels and actively pursue their wilful rebellion against God. They refuse to repent. Their granite hearts are so hardened that they cannot even be melted by the torch of a solar flare. Oh yes, they are as stupid and as stubborn as that.

You know, that is what sin does for you, that is what sin does to you. Like the sun, it blinds you and, at the same time, it leaves you in the dark, sweating it out!

16:10,11

Plague number five!

The target

Plague number five is spoken about in verses 10 and 11, where John tells us, *'The fifth angel poured out his bowl on the throne of the beast, and his kingdom was plunged into darkness. Men gnawed their tongues in agony and cursed the God of heaven because of their pains and their sores, but they refused to repent of what they had done.'*

The affliction

So far the Antichrist has been immune but now his throne is shaken and, like Pharaoh of old, he is powerless to defend himself. His kingdom is plunged into darkness. We are not talking here about a dark night; it is not the kind of night when you say, 'It's pitch black out there!' No, it is not like that at all! It is not when the clouds cover the moon and the stars cannot be seen. It is worse! It is when it is so inky black that men cannot see each other even when they pass each other on the Main Street. This means no-one dares move! It is a veritable blackout! In some ways, this darkness is a preview of hell itself. Jesus described that as a place of 'outer darkness' where men will 'weep and gnash their teeth.'

The ramifications

Do you see what is happening here? The darkness is so intense and the pain is so bad that people express their anguish by gnawing their tongues. It appears that the darkness makes their pain unbearable. Things always get worse at night time! There is no ease, there is no let up, there is no relief. And what happens? Well, man just goes on cursing the God of heaven, refusing to get right with God. Even though it is tough, they want to continue with their sinful lifestyle. This crescendo of hurt brings in its wake a crescendo of hate.

It is amazing, that even when men experience all the fury of God and their circumstances are so appallingly awful, they still go on heedless and careless. They are happy to live their lives without the Lord. In their darkest hour, they want to maintain the status quo so far as their relationship with God is concerned. They have a victim's mentality!

> The men of verses 10 and 11 suffered immense hurt and the immediate effect was to harden their hearts. What habits can we build into our lives to prevent our hearts becoming hard?

16:12-16

Plague number six!

The next paragraph in chapter 16 leads us to consider plague number six. It is the penultimate one and it is probably the one which most people are familiar with for it is all about the Armageddon campaign.

The target

The details are spelled out with remarkable insight in verses 12 to 16, where John tells us, *'The sixth angel poured out his bowl on the great river Euphrates, and its water was dried up to prepare the way for the kings from the East. Then I saw three evil spirits that looked like frogs; they came out of the mouth of the dragon, out of the mouth of the beast and out of the mouth of the false prophet. They are spirits of demons performing miraculous signs, and they go out to the kings of the whole world, to gather them for the battle on the great day of God Almighty. "Behold, I come like a thief! Blessed is he who stays awake and keeps his clothes with him, so that he may not go naked and be shamefully exposed." Then they gathered the kings together to the place that in Hebrew is called Armageddon.'*

The affliction

This is mind-blowing stuff! It is fascinating! This great river Euphrates, one of the great rivers of the world, dries up! The river is called *'great'* because of its significant location. It is the longest river in western Asia, flowing almost 1,800 miles from Syria to Babylon before emptying into the Persian Gulf. It forms a natural and formidable eastern boundary for the Roman Empire.

The ramifications

John informs us it dries up to prepare the way for the kings from the east. If that were to happen, it would make it possible for armies to come across from the Orient into the Middle East. The winding depths of the dry cracked river bed will be the pavement for the march to the final battle field. In that day, the yellow peril will become a reality!

What is envisaged here is the gathering of the armies from the lands of the rising sun to participate in the bloodbath at Armageddon. It is all about a coming invasion and John leaves no stone unturned when he says they will all be present at the final conflict of the ages. Many folk refer to it as World War III. I have often heard people quoting the famous line from Rudyard Kipling which says, 'East is east and west is west and never the twain shall meet.' Well, you know, that is not strictly true, for one day they will meet, right here at Armageddon.

The name Armageddon comes from two Hebrew words, *har Megiddo*, which means, 'the hill of Megiddo.' The word 'Megiddo' means, 'the place of troops' or 'the place of slaughter.' It is also called in today's map-speak the Plain of Esdraelon and the Valley of Jezreel. The area is about fourteen miles wide and twenty miles long and forms what Napoleon called, 'the most natural battlefield of the whole earth.' You can stand on Mount Carmel (and I have done it) and you can see for yourself exactly what Bonaparte meant when he said what he did.

> *It was here that Deborah and Barak defeated the armies of Canaan (Judges 5).*
> *It was on this plain that Gideon met the Midianites (Judges 7).*
> *It was here that David defeated the giant Goliath of Gath (1 Samuel 17).*
> *It was here that King Saul lost his life in a tragic manner (1 Samuel 31).*
> *It was here that an Egyptian king killed Josiah (2 Kings 23).*
> *Titus and the Roman army used this natural corridor, as did the Crusaders.*
> *The British General, Allenby, used it when he defeated the Turkish army in 1917.*

On 2 September 1945, when General Douglas MacArthur supervised the signing of the peace treaty with Japan, this is what he said, 'We have had our last chance. If we will not devise something greater and more equitable than war, Armageddon will be at our door.' Those words have come back to haunt us, they are prophetic in the best sense of that word. He was absolutely right!

Today, planet earth is like a powder keg. The fuse is lit and very soon the explosion will be heard. U Thant, a former secretary to the United Nations said, 'I'm afraid that what we are witnessing today is the setting of the stage for World War III.' The prophet Amos said the nations are like 'a basket of summer fruit.' If that is the case, it means planet earth is rotting, it smells, it is ripe and ready for judgment. I can tell you, Armageddon is no figment of the imagination. One day, it will be a reality ... and the morning after, it will be history.

The strategy deployed at Armageddon. John draws attention to three evil spirits that looked like frogs coming out of the mouths of this trinity of evil. Basically, they are there to wage a concerted propaganda campaign. It is an exercise in PR, as they rally people together in a racist spirit of anti-Semitism. They are there to sow seeds of hate, they are there to inflame the passions of men, they are there to stir things up, they are there to ensure Armageddon becomes a reality *'on the great day of God Almighty.'*

Already there are evil men causing all sorts of trouble in the Middle East, but when these demons go to work there will be a final push to unite the Arab world against Israel. Satan, the author of death, looks forward with a measure of glee to the harvest of souls he will reap at Armageddon. Great hordes of people will march in gathering for the final battle. You can read some of the grim and gory statistics in the closing verses of chapter 19.

It is interesting to note that these demons are extremely capable of *'performing miraculous signs'* and wonders. In some ways, this will be the final delusion before the millennial reign of Jesus Christ. Men and women are hoodwinked as they are led further down a dark alley of spiritual blindness. They will lull men into a false sense of security, they will incite them to war; men will believe what they see with their own two eyes. Their single devil inspired objective will be realised when all hell breaks loose on the plains of Megiddo.

These hyperactive demons are pulling the strings, they are manipulating world leaders, they are setting up situations, they are manoeuvring nations from behind the scenes. The ultimate goal is the same throughout: their evil mission will not be accomplished until the final war of human history is launched.

Isn't it amazing, but in the middle of all this, in verse 15, we have the Lord reminding his people of his coming. He says, he is coming 'like a thief' and that suggests the idea of surprise. Those who are passing through times of severe suffering in the dark days of the Tribulation can hold on a little while longer for they know his advent is no longer imminent, it is immediate! There is the promise of blessing to those who remain on red alert and who avoid contamination from the world around them. It is a challenge for them to walk with their heads held high for they know the Lord is returning for them, and for them alone. They have something to look forward to when the pressure may seem unbearable. This truth keeps them going!

One of the key purposes of the Lord's coming is to strip off the garments of hypocrisy with which the human race has clothed itself. And that is explicitly stated at the end of verse 15 where Jesus coined a rather unusual phrase. You see, it is always God's work to remove the facades, to expose the shams, to strip away any highly polished veneer, to tear off the mask; that is his job. He cannot tolerate anything which smacks of a cover-up; he detests that which is not authentic and real, and he does it to bring the truth out into the open.

> **If the Lord returned unexpectedly right now, how well dressed would you be?**

Armageddon may be a lot closer than people care to think, the drums of war can be heard in the distance. You might remember that World War I was given the optimistic title of 'the war to end all wars.' It is a name that could not stick, it was not earthed to reality. But the war effort that takes place on the vast plain of Esdraelon in the beautiful and fertile valley of Jezreel will undoubtedly be 'the war to end all wars.' There is no disputing that fact! The man who argues with this assessment is not living in the real world, he is living in cloud-cuckoo land. His pie-in-the-sky views do not tally with the teaching of the Bible.

It seems to me that Armageddon will precipitate the final bowl of judgment. It will ring down the final curtain on the human drama. It will signal the end.

> What is particularly frightening about these punishments is
> their sheer finality. No-one repents. The day of grace has passed.
> In what ways does this stark reality influence you to 'make the
> most of every opportunity' as Paul encourages us to do in
> Colossians 4:5?

16:17-21

Plague number seven!

The target

John continues to inform us of what is destined to happen to earth
when he says that, *'The seventh angel poured out his bowl into the
air, and out of the temple came a loud voice from the throne, saying,
"It is done!" Then there came flashes of lightning, rumblings, peals
of thunder and a severe earthquake. No earthquake like it has ever
occurred since man has been on earth, so tremendous was the quake.
The great city split into three parts, and the cities of the nations
collapsed. God remembered Babylon the Great and gave her the
cup filled with the wine of the fury of his wrath. Every island fled
away and the mountains could not be found. From the sky huge
hailstones of about a hundred pounds each fell upon men. And they
cursed God on account of the plague of hail, because the plague
was so terrible.'*

This is the last of the seven bowls of judgment and it will finish
God's wrath upon the earth. It will be the most terrible and awful
judgment to hit this world, and hit it, it certainly will.

The affliction

It comes hard on the heels of Armageddon and it probably describes
the effects of nuclear warfare which would release vast clouds of
poisonous radiation upon the earth. The disastrous nuclear accident
at Chernobyl gives us some idea of what would happen to the air we
breathe in the event of a nuclear fallout. So it may well be, as one
commentator remarks, that, 'The final bowl of God's judgment is

tipped by the finger of man himself - a finger that is even at this moment poised over the nuclear button. In our hi-speed, hi-tech, ballistic age, humankind is never more than a few minutes away from potential doom.'

God's answer to the pollution of the atmosphere is to shake the earth with the greatest quake the world has ever known. There has never before been anything like this recorded on the Richter scale. This is the 'big' one the punters often talk about.

The ramifications

The earthquake causes phenomenal damage to property and it also causes an enormous loss of life. The lives of ordinary people are shattered, countless millions of hearts are broken, there is blind panic on a massive scale as the magnitude of the earthquake finally sinks in. Men are scared stiff. They are frozen with fear. Every tremor causes them to tremble in their shoes.

This convulsion is unprecedented in terms of world history! It brings, in its wake, a tale of incredible destruction to the major cities of the world. The impact is such that the infra-structure is reduced to rubble, it is a state of total collapse. All the metropolitan centres of population are razed to the ground, important capital cities are virtually wiped out, the world is rocked in a global disaster of mega-proportion. (The *'great city'* which John mentions in verse 19 is probably a reference to Jerusalem.)

There is not only chaos and confusion so far as the cities of the world are concerned, the after shocks reach out to the mountains and islands. You could not see them, you cannot find them. This implies there will be considerable changes in the topography of the planet. Nothing will ever be the same again. The once easily recognised features of planet earth will be radically altered.

John also talks about huge hailstones falling at random from the sky. They will pepper the earth at great velocity. Man will be bombarded and blitzed with solid missiles of ice hurtling down on him. These are estimated to weigh about one hundred pounds each and that is nothing to laugh at! That is heavy! Can you imagine it?

Great chunks of ice falling from the sky, landing all around you with indiscriminate force. It is quite unthinkable! It is horrific!

Just as Pharaoh and the Egyptian leaders did not repent, so the earth dwellers will not repent. It is the last thing on their mind. Actually, if the truth be told, it is not on their mind at all! In fact, they curse God! They blaspheme his great and holy name. When you stop and think about it, it is no wonder the hail comes for blasphemers are supposed to be stoned to death; you find that in Leviticus 24:16. These folk are getting their just desserts. They have brought it on themselves.

> **Based on verses 17-21, in what ways is God seen to be Almighty?**

When you go back up the chapter to verse 17, it is good to remind ourselves of the message coming from the throne of God. It is short, it is sweet, it is straight to the point. It indicates that God's work of judgment is complete. He says, *'It is done!'* A similar cry echoed from the lips of the Lord Jesus when he was crucified on the cross at Calvary. He shouted in a loud voice in John 19:30, 'It is finished!' That was a declaration of victory, it was a note resounding with glorious triumph, it was a celebration of his conquest over sin and Satan. On that first Good Friday, he bore the punishment for our sin. In a day soon to dawn, men will bear the judgment of God for their sin. They will pay an awful price for rejecting the Lord Jesus Christ. They will do it in time and they will do it in eternity.

17

The last world empire

In Revelation 17 and 18, the spotlight is on the classic tale of two Babylon's: one is mystical, the other is material; one is religious, the other is economic. One grows out of the other: the Antichrist controls the first and he creates the second; the religious system paves the way for the political system. In the early days, the religious system supports the political system but, as time marches on and things begin to change, the political system supplants the religious one. The religious system is represented in chapter 17 as the Babylonian mother, the political system is graphically portrayed as the Babylonian monster.

Babylon is mentioned more times in the Bible than any other city with the notable exception of Jerusalem. It brings to mind a host of incredible images of a nefarious city-state which is enmeshed in an abominable religious system. The tentacles of this highly organised and well-blended mixture of religion and politics reach out to the far flung corners of the earth. True to form, it will corrupt and taint everything it touches! This is the kingdom of the beast, the

Antichrist, the Man of Sin. It is the last world empire where man is centre stage.

John draws back the curtain in these two chapters and gives us an extensive insight into the far-reaching implications of God's statement of intent in 16:19 where we read, *'God remembered Babylon the Great and gave her the cup filled with the wine of the fury of his wrath.'* This duo of chapters fills in the blanks. We are left in absolutely no doubt as to what God thinks of this final kingdom of man. It is the worst kept secret in the entire book of Revelation! God is not in the least impressed nor is he amused with all her antics either! In the laser-like eye of God, Babylon does herself no lasting favours with all her shenanigans. These two eventful chapters spell desolation and destruction! When you examine it from God's perspective, it is as good as done. You will remember the words of the high flying angel in 14:8 where he called out, *'Fallen! Fallen is Babylon the Great!'*

These two chapters are, therefore, a running commentary on the couple of verses just referred to. And that is good. It makes life a lot easier for all of us. You may recognise the name of A W Pink, a highly respected and much loved Bible commentator who passed away in 1952. As he lay dying at his home in Stornoway on the Isle of Lewis in the Outer Hebrides, some of his last recorded words were, 'The Scriptures explain themselves.' He could not have said a truer word. That is certainly the case with chapters 17 and 18.

17:1-6

The scarlet woman

The Bible says, *'One of the seven angels who had the seven bowls came and said to me, "Come, I will show you the punishment of the great prostitute, who sits on many waters."'* The scene outlined here is one of high drama. The seven bowls have been poured out on planet earth resulting in unimaginable pandemonium and havoc. The world is littered with the scars of an invasion from another platform, the dust and debris of a devastated world is everywhere.

And then, out of the blue, one of the seven angels comes over to John and has a word in his ear. He explains the ins and outs of all that has happened. He exposes the power structure of the empire of the Antichrist. He shows it up for what it is, we see it in its true colours. When the angel invites John to see this great harlot or prostitute, he is told quite candidly that he will be viewing her punishment.

Her apostasy

We all know what a prostitute is! It is someone who engages in a promiscuous sexual relationship, it is someone who offers a momentary thrill of sexual gratification at a price, it all comes with no commitment or love attached. The analogy is clear! The woman depicted here is guilty of a serious breach of faithfulness to God. She is two-timing the God of glory. She says one thing and does the exact opposite.

Her ability

She is also heralded as something which is *'great.'* That underlines her all-pervasive influence throughout history and it also highlights the seriousness of that seduction in the eyes of God. It is not to be taken lightly. It cannot be glossed over and it certainly cannot be swept under the carpet. The sequel to this forecast of doom and gloom is found in 19:2 where we read, *'He has condemned the great prostitute who corrupted the earth by her adulteries. He has avenged on her the blood of his servants.'*

Her address

We are told she *'sits on many waters.'* This phrase is explained for us further down the chapter in verse 15 where John says, *'The waters you saw, where the prostitute sits, are peoples, multitudes, nations and languages.'* In other words, people all over the world are swayed by her to one degree or another. She has a fair bit of clout and as far as public opinion goes she can muster an incredibly high level of support. Her influence is widespread. She has reached out to the ends of the earth, she has successfully permeated every people group and infiltrated every ethnic minority. She has embraced all the nations of the world with her ideology.

Her associations

John goes on to make some incisive remarks about her when he says in verse 2, *'With her the kings of the earth committed adultery and the inhabitants of the earth were intoxicated with the wine of her adulteries.'*

We all know what adultery is, it is sexual immorality. The thought encapsulated here is that she has used sex and alcohol to entice and seduce world leaders; she has pursued the same course of action with the rest of the population as well. I think you will agree this is rather graphic and vivid language which John is employing here. It is a picture of unrestrained deception; it is a picture of wholesale manipulation. That is her way of doing things and she has been eminently effective. From day one she has sought to influence the governments of this world and history confirms how competent she has been. She has flirted with world leaders. By fair means or foul, she has been happy to further her own interests by jumping into bed with anyone.

Call it what you will, it boils down to illicit intercourse with the political systems of the world. People are intoxicated with her. They think she is wonderful. The fact is, people can be so gullible. They can be easily led astray, they can be easily fooled. She has dulled their powers of perception, she has deadened their critical faculties. She has all but removed their ability to assess situations correctly. She has tampered with the truth. She will do everything in her power to make people happy; she will do everything possible within her remit to bring a false sense of elation to men and women. She knows how vitally important the 'feel good' factor is to the man in the street. That is what John says quite categorically in verse 2. All that he says here fits perfectly into the jigsaw of the end times. Having said that, the prostitute will have her day of prominence but her downfall is guaranteed. We must never forget that God is on the throne. He knows what is going on!

Her ascendancy

Before John continues with a fairly comprehensive picture of what is happening, he throws in a single sentence which says more than we possibly realise. The apostle refers to his transit experience by saying, *'Then the angel carried me away in the Spirit into a desert.'* This is where John sees her, the one who has been labelled the great whore, and he is taken there by the Spirit of God. She is in a desert, a place of desolation and waste and barrenness. It powerfully reminds us that death, not life, is the environment in which she thrives best.

There is more than just a touch of irony here. Genesis 2 speaks of a pure bride in a lovely garden in the idyllic setting of Eden; but, by the time you come to the end of the Bible, civilisation has degenerated to such an extent that the picture changes to an impure harlot stuck in a wilderness. That is what sin does to the world!

When John reaches his destination in the desert he is confronted with a most unusual sight. He tells us in verse 3 what he saw with his own two eyes: *'There I saw a woman sitting on a scarlet beast that was covered with blasphemous names and had seven heads and ten horns.'* The fact that the woman is sitting on the beast indicates that she is in control of it. She is asserting authority over the beast; she is directing the movements of the beast. At this point in time, she is the dominant one in that relationship.

We have come across the beast before in 13:1 where John was speaking at great length about the Antichrist; to me, it is a classic case of, once seen, never forgotten! The two descriptions are exactly the same, they match each other in every important detail so there is no possibility of mistaken identity. The one we are talking about here is the leader of the western bloc of world powers. He is the president of the United States of Europe, he is the top dog in a federation of states which resembles a revived Roman empire. (We will talk about the seven heads and ten horns when we progress down the chapter.)

Her alliance

Her shameless depravity is seen in her unholy alliance with such a despicable political leader. It is almost a case of church and state being wedded together as the woman rides the beast. The fact is, she will milk the system for as long as she can, and she will do everything she can to achieve her goals. She has her own agenda.

At this point the religious system will have the upper hand over the political system, but that will not last. It will all change as we will discover later on. You see, politics and religion commit themselves to each other but it is only for a relatively short time. It is like many other marriages of convenience; one member of the team wants to buy out the other and sometimes push can give way to shove in such a fragile partnership. She is on a precarious perch but she seems oblivious to that fact.

Her apparel

The stunning appearance of the woman in verse 4 leads many folk to equate her with the religious system we know as Roman Catholicism. That was certainly the opinion of the Reformers and it was also the solid conviction of many of the early church fathers. That may be the case but I do not think we can narrow it down to just one religion. I think we can widen the net for what we have here is a mixed bag, a pot pourri of many cults and ism's. It is a worldwide ecumenical movement.

I am inclined to agree with the commentator who said, 'The scarlet woman represents an apostate religious system that will combine weak Protestantism with Catholicism, spiritualism, humanism and the occult into one great satanic connection.' It is a bag of religious allsorts! I often refer to it as Satan's superchurch. At the end of the day, it is a false religious grouping which is acutely riddled with apostasy.

> **The woman's ideology is a bag of religious allsorts! What evidence is there that our society is moving towards such a mixture in its belief system?**

She is seen as a harlot which is in stark contrast to the true church for she is portrayed as the bride of Christ. The apparel of this woman catches John's eye for he says, *'she was dressed in purple and scarlet.'* The fabric which she wears was the most expensive cloth available in the ancient world and it typifies one who enjoys the glamour of ecclesiastical pomp and pageantry. The simplicity of a godly lifestyle as outlined in 1 Timothy 2:9,10 is far removed from the up-market style we have promoted here. These are the garments of royalty and prosperity and they are often seen as the colours associated with the papacy.

Her adornment

We read in verse 4, *'she was glittering with gold, precious stones and pearls.'* It is a look of ostentatious extravagance. Think of the phenomenal wealth that has been accumulated by organised religion. The staggering riches acquired in the name of religion throughout human history are awesome indeed. Their coffers are bulging. The cynics are right when they tell us that religion is big business!

Her abominations

At the end of verse 4, we are given an inkling of her abominations. John says, *'She held a golden cup in her hand, filled with abominable things and the filth of her adulteries.'* A golden cup in anyone's hand is an item of beauty. It is an object to be admired, it is pleasing to the eye.

Gold in the Bible is a symbol of divine activity, so this golden cup gives every appearance of being a utensil used in the service of God. That is fine, until you look inside, and then we are horrified to find it is filled to the brim with her unholy passions. Her idolatry, her spiritual adultery, her immoral liaisons, her flirtatious behaviour with all and sundry, all of these are in the cup! Yes, it looks attractive on the outside, but when you look inside, it is repulsively vile and nauseating. Her cup is full and the reference in Jeremiah 51:7 to this analogy spells it out with precise clarity that her days are numbered. We need to remind ourselves that God looks on false religion as an abomination - he detests it, he cannot tolerate it.

Her appellations

In verse 5, we discover she has a name or a title written on her
forehead. This is what God calls her, this is how God refers to her.
Just before I tell you what they are, it is interesting to note that the
common prostitute in John's day wore her name on a headband upon
her brow; in a similar way, the great whore of chapter 17 is recognised
by the names on her forehead. John advises us in bold capital letters
that her title is, *'Mystery, Babylon the great, the mother of prostitutes
and of the abominations of the earth.'* There are two things which
are perfectly clear from this appellation.

She is a mystery. This would seem to suggest that neither ancient
Babylon nor its site is intended. It teaches us to look a little deeper.
We need to explore beneath the surface. We are to see her as
representing something in a figurative manner rather than taking it
in a literal sense. A mystery is not something mysterious but
something previously hidden that has now been revealed to those
given understanding. It is something that only the spiritually initiated
can decipher. To grasp one of God's mysteries requires a combination
of spiritual intelligence and discernment.

She is a mother. She represents that which began with Babylon
and has continued throughout history. She is the mother of prostitutes
which means she is not alone in her adulteries. She has spiritual
offspring who also practice her idolatries and spread her false
teachings. She has been instrumental in seducing multitudes and
using other harlots to accomplish her objectives. It seems to me that
the Babylonian system has, in one way or another, given birth to all
false religions. The finger of blame points in her direction, it is
aimed at her and her alone!

Babylon means different things to different people. It is a word
which appears over 250 times in the Bible. So when we talk about
it, it helps if we know what we mean when we speak of it. When
Babylon is mentioned in the context of chapter 17, there are generally
three main positions which have been embraced by conservative
Bible teachers:

Number one, the word 'Babylon' represents an ecclesiastical and political organisation. Ecclesiastical Babylon refers to apostate Christendom with its headquarters in Rome, it speaks of a one world church. You find that in verses 1-6. On the other hand, political Babylon is a revival of the old Roman empire. It is the last form of Gentile world domination and it will be headed by the Antichrist. You find that in verses 7-18.

Number two, the word 'Babylon' refers to the religious and political systems which I have just mentioned and then it goes on to say that it also anticipates a rebuilt city of Babylon located near the Euphrates river.

Number three, it refers to the rebuilt city of Babylon whose end time existence and subsequent annihilation were predicted by Isaiah, Jeremiah and Ezekiel. According to this interpretation, Babylon is a literal city of religious and political significance yet to be constructed. Proponents of this theory base their argument on the teaching enshrined in verse 18.

To me, it seems fairly clear from this chapter that *'mystery Babylon'* is linked to Rome in two ways. Firstly, in a religious sense and, secondly, in a political sense. At the same time, it would appear from reading between the lines in chapter 18 that Babylon may be rebuilt!

When we speak about Babylon as a religious entity, it is good to look back in the annals of history and trace her roots. They stretch right away back to the early chapters of the book of Genesis where we come across a man called Nimrod. He is the man credited with the establishment of the city of Babel in Genesis 10:8-10 and he is also recognised as the world's first dictator. It was through him that a false and diabolical religious system was born on the plains of Shinar in ancient Babylon.

In an act of total defiance of God and because the people wanted to make a name for themselves, he built a huge tower that would reach to the heavens. It was known as a *ziggurat* and it was made of sun dried bricks. It was like a pyramid except that the successive levels were recessed so that you could walk to the top on steps. At the top was a special shrine dedicated to a god or goddess. In building this imposing edifice the people were not trying to climb up to heaven to dethrone God; rather, they hoped that the god or goddess they worshipped would come down from heaven to meet them.

The structure and the city were called Babel which means 'the gate of the gods' (Genesis 11:4). The tower was recognised as a temple or rallying point and it stood as a pugnacious symbol of man's pride and open rebellion against God. It was not long before other nations jumped on the bandwagon and constructed similar towers in honour of their heathen deities. This infamous tower of Babel was also used for studying the stars and it established the basis and foundation for astrology. So from the very beginning, Babylon was linked with sorcery and a wide range of extra-terrestrial activities.

You will recall from Genesis 11 that this was more than God was prepared to take, so he poured out his judgment on the people by scattering them across the face of the earth. At the same time, they were thrown into a state of total disarray for seeds of confusion were sown in their language. Before their dispersal, they were one people and one language; now, they are all over the place and they cannot communicate with one another.

That did not mean the demise of the Babylonian religious system. The bell may have tolled but it was not the death knell. History records that Nimrod's wife, Semiramis, became the first high priestess of a system of secret religious rites known as the Babylonian Mysteries. This was user friendly idolatry and it was easily accessible to the ordinary people.

According to legend, she had a son by the name of Tammuz. The story goes that he was miraculously conceived by a sunbeam. He was presented to the people as a saviour in fulfilment of the promise made to Eve concerning her seed in Genesis 3:15. Tradition says that Tammuz was killed by a wild boar but, after the people fasted for forty days, he was resurrected from the dead on the feast of Ishtar. Part of the celebration of Ishtar was the exchanging of Ishtar eggs, symbolising new life. Believe it or not, the term Easter is derived from Ishtar!

It was in this story of Semiramis and Tammuz that the cultic worship of 'mother and child' began to spread to the four corners of the earth. Such folklore was rapidly absorbed into many religious practices and it developed to such an extent that it was headed by a priesthood that promoted salvation by means of sprinkling holy water, ceremonial cleansing, and purgatorial cleansing after death. Semiramis went on to establish an order of virgins dedicated exclusively to religious prostitution. The liturgy of worship was clearly defined as the mother was identified as the 'queen of heaven' which we read about in Jeremiah 44:15-19.

On one occasion, the prophet Ezekiel was called by the Lord to go to the temple and see this cultic practice in process. The old prophet watched the women of Israel observing the forty days of Lent for the slaying of the pagan, Tammuz. The Lord called this an abomination in Ezekiel 8:13,14. Jeremiah condemned Judah for offering cakes and burning incense to the 'queen of heaven' in 7:18 and 44:17-19,25. It is interesting to note that after the Medo Persian empire took over Babylon, the city and temples were eventually destroyed. You can read all about that transfer of power when Daniel prophesied concerning it in his interpretation of Nebuchadnezzar's dream in Daniel 2.

Having said that, the Babylonian cult survived and found a new home in Pergamum of Asia Minor. We came across that in an earlier study in chapter 2. Apparently, it was repackaged and it thrived under the new name of Etruscan Mysteries and, eventually, it was based in Rome. The chief priests wore mitres shaped like the head of a fish in honour of Dagon, the fish god, the lord of life; this was another form of the Tammuz mystery.

In Rome, the chief priest assumed the title of Pontifex Maximus, which means, the greatest high priest. When Julius Caesar became head of the Roman Empire, he had no personal inhibitions so he took this name for himself. And from that day down to Constantine, the title was held by all of the Roman emperors. You will remember that Constantine was head of both church and state; he is the man who mixed religion with politics; he is the man who made Christianity popular when he adopted it as a state religion.

The title of Pontifex Maximus was later adopted by the Bishop of Rome and, today, this person is recognised as the Pope. It is a well documented fact that over an extended period of time the church in Rome took on board many of the Babylonian practices and idolatrous teachings, the obvious one is the worship and elevation of the Virgin Mary. The fact is, there is no such thing in the Bible as the worship of a female deity and Mary was never presented as anyone other than a humble servant of God who was chosen as the vessel to bear the Lord Jesus Christ.

'All roads lead to Rome' is what the familiar proverb tells us, but I have news for you, they began in Babylon. In the last days, Rome as a religious system is inextricably linked with Babylon, and vice-versa, Babylon is intertwined with Rome. I believe the link between the past and the present so far as global religion is concerned is more than just a coincidence, it is much more than a casual acquaintance, it is a lot more than a nod and a wink. In fact, part of the problem we have discovered already, is that this false religion, this counterfeit religion, is amazingly like the true Christian faith in so many facets.

You see, evangelical unity which has a high view of Scripture and which is based on the doctrines of grace is one thing; an ecclesiastical unity which is all things to all men is quite a different matter. And the picture we have emerging here in chapter 17 is a cameo of the latter. It is highly likely that readers in John's day would have no problem identifying the harlot with the Roman empire. The chances are that readers in the Middle Ages would identify her as Roman Catholicism. Many of us, in our day and generation, are happy to see a close link between the harlot and the Babylonian system in an apostate world church; that is a church where doctrinal truth is minimised, it is a church where the authority of the word of God is rejected, it is a church where attempts are made to unite professing believers on some other basis than faith in Jesus Christ. In a nutshell, it is Satan's superchurch!

And so this superchurch rises as the consummate manifestation of religion without reality. It is a religion, as John says in verse 6, which is *'drunk with the blood of the saints, the blood of those who bore testimony to Jesus.'* You can see John's reaction to all that he saw and heard ... he was dumbfounded. We read that he *'was greatly astonished.'* He could not quite work out all that was happening, a lot of it did not make sense. He could understand why pagan Rome would torture and kill believers because he had seen this with his own eyes, he had witnessed it himself.

> A false church is usually a mixture of good and bad, both in its creeds and its congregations. How should we relate to such a church, affirming the good while at the same time not compromising on essentials?

Her atrocities

You see, at the time John recorded his vision, the church in Rome was the church of the catacombs. It was a persecuted and suffering church which had no earthly power and no worldly influence. But John was mesmerised to think that religious Rome could be so malevolent. That really took the wind out of his sails, it left him shocked and surprised. When we look at the 'benevolent' church of Rome today, we find it hard to believe that it could ever be classified in this way.

However, if we study the annals of history, it all fits together like pieces in a jigsaw puzzle. It is a well-documented fact that, down through the years, apostate Christianity has always persecuted true Christianity. In the name of religious zeal and with a spirit of unbridled fanaticism, many people have been butchered and cruelly slaughtered. The atrocities wreaked upon God's people by Rome fill whole volumes of church history. In the Middle Ages, she ravaged like a tiger for we have all the horrors of the infamous Inquisition. It was the main agency in the papacy's effort to crush the Reformation. For example, it is stated that in the thirty years between 1540 and 1570, almost one million Protestants were put to death. Untold numbers have been burned at the stake, more have gone missing and never been found, millions have spent days in the gruelling confines of a torture chamber. We are told that when the massacre of Saint Bartholomew took place and Christians throughout France were murdered, Rome appointed services of thanksgiving and the church bells pealed out in victory. Sir Robert Anderson estimates that she is guilty of the death of 50 million Christians.

> Based on the above historical survey, can you pick out some of the tactics Satan uses to deceive the nations?

Her activity

The harlot is depicted here in verse 6 as one who is *'drunk'* and that would appear to indicate that it is continual carnage which is envisaged here. It is not just a 'one off' moment in history when believers were martyred. I do not know about you but I find the imagery here quite repulsive. We have a woman who becomes intoxicated, and euphorically so, by drinking the blood of the righteous! The bottom line is, it has happened before, it will happen again. During the Tribulation, the proponents of this false church will hunt down and kill anyone who makes a brave and bold decision to follow Jesus Christ.

John talks here about *'saints'* and *'those who bore testimony to Jesus.'* It is an interesting dual description for it may be referring to the same group of people; on the other hand, it may apply to those before the time of Jesus and those after the time of Jesus. If that were the case, it means this woman would then picture a religious system both before and after the time of Christ.

17:7-14

The angel's explanation

When we move to verse 7, we find the angel's immediate response to John's stunned reaction to the vision of verses 1-6. John is obviously out of his depth, he is lost for words, he is struggling to cope with what has just been revealed to him. So the angel says to him, *'I will explain to you the mystery of the woman and of the beast she rides, which has the seven heads and ten horns.'* That must have come as an enormous relief to John. At least someone was going to explain the entire picture to him and that made him feel immeasurably better.

The angel elaborates a little more in verse 8 when he says, *'The beast, which you saw, once was, now is not, and will come up out of the Abyss and go to his destruction. The inhabitants of the earth whose names have not been written in the book of life from the creation of the world will be astonished when they see the beast, because he once was, now is not, and yet will come.'*

The resurrection of the beast

This is a rather strange verse, to say the least. I think if we are going to understand it, we need to remember that the emphasis is not so much on the beast as an empire but on the beast as an emperor. In some ways, it is his personal history that is chronicled for us. It is true to say that the Roman empire will be revived, there is no question about that, but the language employed here goes far beyond that! An empire cannot emerge out of the abyss and later be consigned into perdition. It seems to me, the terms and phrases used here best describe the history of an individual, not that of a nation. This individual comes up out of the abyss for the narrative concentrates specifically on that part of his chequered history which is plainly supernatural.

It begins with a satanic miracle of the highest calibre for the beast is seen to be a resurrected man. It appears that Satan will duplicate as far as possible the miracle of Christ's resurrection. You can imagine the global sensation caused by such a high-powered miracle. We have thought about the impact of that already in our study which focused on chapter 13.

At first, the beast will be a fairly normal human being. He will be a world figure in his own right by virtue of his charismatic personality, his genius and his political acumen. He will appear to be assassinated and then before the eyes of the world he will come back to life. After that incredible feat, his authority on planet earth will be absolute, at least for a short time. Now we know where he is coming from. I have no hesitation in describing him as Satan's man and it seems that his second coming will take the world by storm.

The reason for his appearance

He is coming to deceive the Christ rejecting masses of mankind. It is inevitable, when you read verse 8 in conjunction with Paul's insightful comments in 2 Thessalonians 2, that when a person deliberately turns his back on the truth, he automatically embraces a lie.

You see, in his superhuman appearing, the beast emerging triumphant from the abyss, still bearing in his body the marks of his deadly wound, will fire the imagination of men and lead them captive at his will. Ordinary people will be eating out of his hand, they will hail him as the greatest thing since sliced bread. They will worship him with incredible doses of adoration and devotion. They will be spellbound by his magical charm and they will be won over with his big hearted liberal generosity. They will stand in awe of him. The sad fact is, their names are not written in the book of life, and they are ready for the lie of all lies. They will follow their leader, all the way to hell itself!

The angel's caution

Verse 9 begins with the words, *'This calls for a mind with wisdom.'* In one sense, the angel is putting all his cards on the table and he is reminding us of the need for spiritual insight if we are going to unravel successfully the mysteries of this section. We need to prayerfully think it through, we need to look to the Lord for clarity of mind and openness of heart as we approach it together. We need illumination from above. Having said that, such a principle holds true for any portion of Scripture which we seek to interpret. It is just that sometimes we need more wisdom than others!

Seven heads

You will remember we discovered the beast has seven heads and ten horns. Here in verse 9, we note the seven heads represent seven hills, and in verse 10, they symbolise seven kings or kingdoms. That means they can be interpreted in one of two ways: first, they can be viewed geographically as the seven hills of Rome or, second, they can be seen in their historical context as seven kingdoms.

We read in verses 9-11 that, *'The seven heads are seven hills on which the woman sits. They are also seven kings. Five have fallen, one is, the other has not yet come; but when he does come, he must remain for a little while. The beast who once was, and now is not, is an eighth king. He belongs to the seven and is going to his destruction.'*

The seven hills of Rome are the Aventine, the Caelian, the Capitoline, the Esquiline, the Palatine, the Quirinal, and the Viminal. Having named the hills, we cannot ignore the clear implication of verse 10 that they typify seven kings. The seven kings represent political empires or kingdoms as well as individual rulers. We are told that five of these kings or kingdoms have passed off the scene, one was present in John's day, and one was yet to come.

If you prefer the view that these are referring to kings, the five which are past are, Julius Caesar, Tiberias, Caligula, Claudius and Nero; the present one, in John's day, is Domitian; and the Antichrist is the one yet to come. If you feel happier in adopting the other position, it means the five kingdoms are Egypt, Assyria, Babylon, Medo Persia, and Greece. The present kingdom, so far as John is concerned, is Rome; and the future kingdom anticipated is that of a revived Roman empire (we can describe it as a federation of ten European states in and around the Mediterranean seaboard). Out of this seventh empire of ten nations will arise a world leader, who we can identify with no problem as the Antichrist, who will in himself become the eighth empire of the world. You find that alluded to in verse 11.

Ten horns

If we want to appreciate in a fuller measure the teaching enshrined in verses 10 and 11, we must consider them in the light of what John reveals to us in verses 12 and 13. There we read, *'The ten horns you saw are ten kings who have not yet received a kingdom but who, for one hour will receive authority as kings along with the beast. They have one purpose and will give their power and authority to the beast.'*

The beast not only has seven heads, he also has ten horns which represent ten kings. These are very special kings, these are the ones who enable the beast to rise to a place of ultimate power. They are even willing to relinquish their own authority and hand it all over on a plate to him. If you want a fuller discussion on these kings, flick back in your Bible to the book of Daniel and zoom in on chapter 7.

You can probably remember when we looked at chapter 6, that was when the first of the seven seals was opened, that was when the Antichrist began his peaceful conquest of the nations. He organised a United States of Europe, he brought a measure of peace and calm to the cauldron of the Middle East, he appeared to be the great leader a troubled world was seeking, he was the answer to every man's prayers. Then, in the middle of the seven year period of Tribulation, he broke his covenant with the nation of Israel and he began to ruthlessly persecute the people of God as well as the nation of Israel. Then in chapter 13, we noted he was energised by Satan, he was ably assisted by his right hand man, the False Prophet and, at the end of the day, he became the world's dictator and its god. In that sense, the beast was both one of the seven kings or kingdoms but he was also the eighth. You see, his kingdom is nothing but a revival of the Roman Empire; that is, it was designated as one of the seven but, at the same time, it was a new kingdom, hence it was labelled number eight! It is the final form of Gentile world rule.

His personal destiny is destruction, you find that in verse 11. His global enterprise will be obliterated by Christ at his second advent in power and great glory ... you find that later in the book in chapter 19. His crowning achievement rises with him, it also falls with him!

He does not have a particularly bright future! The same can also be said for his partners, even though their time spent in his service will be relatively brief. It appears their role will be to head up the kingdom of the Antichrist. It will be divided up into ten administrative districts and each one will be managed by one of these ten officials. It is worth noting, there is no way these kings can be literally or symbolically applied to any nation in the past because they will not receive a kingdom until Daniel's 70th week. They will not reign successively but they will govern simultaneously during the period of Tribulation. Their power will be allocated to them by the Antichrist and their allegiance to him will be total.

The influence of the kings will extend to the end of the Tribulation for we read in verse 14 that, '*They will make war against the Lamb, but the Lamb will overcome them because he is Lord of lords and*

King of kings - and with him will be his called, chosen and faithful followers.' They will do everything in their power to defy the Lamb, they will harness all their resources, they will pull out all the stops, they will leave no stone unturned. The truth of the matter is, they are fighting a battle they cannot possibly win, they are on a hiding to nothing, they are losers all the way.

The Lamb is victorious! The Lamb is triumphant! The King of kings is coming and nothing will impede or hinder his progress! The Lord of lords is on the march and no-one will stand in his way!

The Lord is accompanied by a vast company of those who are devoted to him and dedicated to his cause. These godly believers who are *'called and chosen and faithful'* will share in Christ's victorious conquest, they will share with him in his moment of glory. What a thrilling statement of intent for the people of God! We are on the winning team! And by the same token, what a glaring contrast between the bride of Christ and the harlot of world religion! The same truth is echoed in the words of Psalm 2 and it pays eloquent testimony to the ability of God to turn every situation around for his praise and glory.

> The Lamb's followers are commended as those who are 'called and chosen and faithful'. Can you spot the difference between the first two and the last, and how does being called and chosen help us also to be faithful?

17:15-18

The shoe is on the other foot!

The final paragraph of chapter 17 is one which is breathtaking in its scope; it is a powerful reminder that the tables can turn very quickly! We read in verses 15-18, *'Then the angel said to me, "The waters you saw, where the prostitute sits, are peoples, multitudes, nations and languages. The beast and the ten horns you saw will hate the prostitute. They will bring her to ruin and leave her naked; they will eat her flesh and burn her with fire. For God has put it into their hearts to accomplish his purpose by agreeing to give the beast their power to rule, until God's words are fulfilled. The woman you saw is the great city that rules over the kings of the earth."'*

These words are unbelievable! They predict a day when the Antichrist and his European empire will do an about turn. Up to this point, which is halfway through the Tribulation, they have been going along with every whim of the scarlet woman who represents the global false church of the last days. She has been riding the beast and he tolerates it!

Now the tables turn, the shoe is on the other foot, and the Antichrist assumes control. It all ends in bitter tears with recriminations against one another. The whole saga ends in divorce! Her charm and seduction will have lost their lure and their openly professed love for all things religious will turn to hate and contempt. The harlot will be made desolate by the very system that carried her.

I think it is vitally important for us to note that *the beast carries the harlot.* The fact is, Satan and the Antichrist will use the apostate religious system to accomplish his own ends and that for him means attaining world power. When he has arrived at the pinnacle of his career, he will do away with the harlot and establish his own religious system and all of that fulfils the word of God as detailed for us by John in verse 17. The emphasis here weighs very heavily in favour of the truth of the sovereignty of God in the affairs of man. They do not know it but they are pawns in the divine game of chess! How true it is, God is behind the scenes directing the scenes which he is behind!

Since the beast sets up his image in the temple in Jerusalem about the middle of the Tribulation, we can safely assume that the harlot and the beast work together during the first three and a half years. You find a hint of that in verse 16 for the ten kings who initiate and bring about her downfall are the same ones who set him up in power. There is nothing strange about that; political systems have often used religion as a tool to further their own ends, to advance their own cause, and when they have achieved their goal, they ditch them! The entire incident can be summarised like this:

At first, the harlot will team up with the Antichrist; at the end, she will be torn apart by the Antichrist.

> The nature of unbridled political power is seen in this chapter
> as blasphemous (verse 3) and unprincipled (verse 16), even
> destroying the ideology that first gave it a measure of
> respectability. What does this tell us about the true nature
> of those who seek to rule without reference to the Lord?

This is the great reversal. It is poetic justice! It is God making the wrath of man to praise him! We read, she is detested by them for there is no love lost between them. She is put out of business by them for they are determined to bring her to her knees. She will be divested of all the extraordinary wealth she has amassed over the years, her goods will be confiscated, her properties will be seized. She is disgraced by them for they will not rest until they have stripped her of every vestige of respectability. She will be seen for what she really is and her corruption will be exposed for all to see. She is devoured by them for they will consume her like a pack of wild dogs; and finally, she is destroyed by them for she will be left smouldering in a pile of ashes.

> The action of verse 16 is seen in verse 17 as the fulfilling of
> God's words. What does this tell us about the power of his
> words and does this influence our attitude to his other words
> i.e. the Scriptures?

To all intents and purposes, there will be nothing left of her, she will be totally eliminated and wiped out ... she will be yesterday's church! She will be the has-been religious movement of the end times.

If you believe that all roads lead to Rome and you are happy to be a member of the church that Satan builds, your future is bleak! And even worse, your destiny is guaranteed.

18

The two Babylon's

A quick glance at chapter 18 reveals that we are still talking about Babylon, but it is Babylon from a different angle, it is Babylon from a new perspective. The Babylon presented here is effectively portrayed by John as a political and economic force. Here we have represented the world system of the Antichrist.

Do you recall the story of Nebuchadnezzar when he was at his peak? In a moment of arrogant pride he looked out over the magnificent city of Babylon with its massive walls, its hanging gardens, its broad boulevards, its stunning beauty, its unequalled strength, and he cried, 'Is not this great Babylon which I have built?' In a coming day the last of the great Gentile rulers will boast over a rebuilt Babylon. It seems in Bible prophecy that Babylon should rise again from the dust in order to meet its final doom. It was foretold of Babylon that:

It would be a place of perpetual desolations (Isaiah 13:9,12); it would be a place where no man would dwell anymore (Jeremiah 50:1-4,40-46); it would be a place where the Arabian would be afraid to pitch his tent, it would be the abode of dragons, it would be empty and without inhabitants, it would be a place whose destruction would be exceptionally violent (Isaiah 13, 25, 50, 51).

None of these prophecies have been completely fulfilled as yet. The key word is, *yet!* One day in God's perfect timing they will come to pass.

Babylon founded by a man called Nimrod became the first centre of population we read of in the Bible which was ruled by violence; she was once the capital of the then known world; in a day soon to dawn she will again rise to prominence and become the central city of the world. She will again be known as the home of idolatry, she will be seen as a place where the occult is encouraged, she will be a city renowned for its interest in demonism, and she will be recognised as a centre of false religion.

I feel the clear indications are that Babylon will be rebuilt with a commercial system that will function on a worldwide scale. We are not told precisely what the actual relationship will be between Babylon and Rome; obviously it will be centred there at first but when the scarlet woman is crushed by the kings of the earth, it will be expedient and prudent to find a better capital. What better site than ancient Babylon on the banks of a river that dominates both east and west!

The book of Revelation is virtually silent on how and when it will be built; it is concerned primarily with her fall! Having said that, there is a lot happening in the region at present and it is a well established fact that Saddam Hussein of Iraq is committed to rebuilding the city to the specifications of Nebuchadnezzar. He is pouring millions of petro-chemical dollars into the project and an incredible amount of manpower and resources are being channelled in that direction. Apparently, rumour has it, he is even using some of the stones from old Babylon.

It must be said, there are other Bible commentators who say that the Babylon of chapter 18 is to be equated with Rome, particularly since the harlot and the beast cooperate so well during the first half of the Tribulation. Perhaps Peter was using 'Babylon' as a code name when he wrote his first letter (1 Peter 5:13). They feel that John's readers would automatically think of the Roman Empire as they read these words about Babylon. For them, there is too much of a similarity for it to be anything else but a cryptic reference to Rome. And so, the choice is yours, with regard to the rebuilding of Babylon. You can make up your own mind with the help of two simple questions: will it or won't it?

18:1-3

The prediction ... a voice of condemnation

John introduces the subject of Babylon when he addresses the matter surrounding her fall. We read in verse 1, *'After this I saw another angel coming down from heaven. He had great authority, and the earth was illuminated by his splendour.'*

John is very impressed with what he sees in verse 1. The angel is described as one who is *'great'* and that is an obvious reference to his authority. At the same time, John is startled and amazed at his sudden appearance and the immediate impact it has when he lights up the earth with his resplendent glory. It is the kind of thing which happens when you walk into a darkened room and switch on the light! When all is said and done, this angelic being is one of God's shining ones, and that explains why his presence caused such a stir in John's heart and mind. The identity of the angel is not revealed but the chances are he is the *'mighty angel'* mentioned back in chapter 10.

> There is much about the ministry of angels in Revelation. What part do they have in your understanding of how God works in the world?

It is against this backdrop of glory that the double-barrelled message is heard resounding throughout the earth. This is a moment of high drama. The angelic shout is a sign of cataclysmic destruction. He said in the opening phrase in verse 2, *'Fallen! Fallen is Babylon the Great!'* It is a double exclamation. In other words, if you did not get the message first time, you would be sure to get it second time around. It is clear and unmistakable.

*The repetition of the word 'fallen' adds considerable fuel to the
fire for it suggests a dual judgment. We can look at it like this: we
have one fall, but it happens in two separate stages. We have phase
one which zooms in on the downfall of ecclesiastical Babylon who
was depicted as the prostitute in chapter 17; and we have phase two
which anticipates the demise of political and economic Babylon
which is demonstrated here in chapter 18.*

A double whammy!

I think this line of argument is amplified in verse 6 when God
announces that Babylon will receive *'double'* for her many sins.
Without question, this is a momentous event, it is a significant
milestone in the ripening of the eternal purposes of God. You see,
from God's vantage point, Babylon is as good as gone! So far as
God is concerned, she has fallen already! Her destruction is
earmarked for a future date but from God's perspective it is a classic
case of mission accomplished! I suppose this confirms that prophecy
is history written in advance. The reasons for her eventual
extermination are spelled out very clearly in verses 2 and 3. We
read, *'She has become a home for demons and a haunt for every evil
spirit, a haunt for every unclean and detestable bird. For all the
nations have drunk the maddening wine of her adulteries. The kings
of the earth committed adultery with her, and the merchants of the
earth grew rich from her excessive luxuries.'*

> **Do you agree with the comment that prophecy is history
> written in advance? If you do, can you substantiate it
> with documentary evidence?**

Why is Babylon snuffed out?

Because of the sheer magnitude of her sins. Her character is
despicable. It is a city given over to demonism and depravity on a
massive scale. It is the home of demons and the headquarters of
depravity. The thought is that of imprisoned evil spirits hovering
over the entire area like scavenger birds over their prey. It is a

repugnant description of the occultist system of the president of the planet, the Antichrist; it speaks of the foul spirits that will control the minds of men. It refers to Satanism, witchcraft and astrology.

Because of her evil and decadent relationship with other nations and people groups. She is the centre of social, political, cultural, and commercial life on this planet. And because of her privileged position, she has seized the initiative, she has taken advantage of the prevailing situation, she has polluted the whole world, her influence has reached out to the ends of the earth. The tentacles of her pernicious ways have spanned the universe. Her impact is global.

Because she used her powers of seduction to ensnare others in her tangled web of deceit. The fundamental sin which has driven her every action is that of wooing in order to win. The system intoxicated the people of the world with all the riches and pleasures it had to offer and, human nature being what it is, they were very glad to be on the receiving end. When you stop and analyse the situation from an unbiased perspective, it all boils down to greed; the bottom line is money, everyone wants to line their own pockets, everyone is in it for what they can get out of it, everyone wants to milk the system for their own ulterior motives.

It is ironic but the trap set by this system will lead to its eventual downfall. The Bible warns about rich oppressors, you can read it for yourself in James 5:1-5. The chances are if you dig a hole big enough, you will fall into it yourself one day! And that is what happens right here!

> There has been a mushrooming of interest in the occult in recent years. How would you respond to someone involved in such things?

18:4-8

The plea ... a voice of separation

In verses 4 and 5 we have an impassioned plea to the people of God. It was transmitted by another voice from heaven which said, *'Come out of her, my people, so that you will not share in her sins, so that you will not receive any of her plagues; for her sins are piled up to heaven, and God has remembered her crimes.'* This is a clarion call to biblical separation. It is a challenge to God's people to adopt a position of holiness.

It is worth pointing out that this serious admonition parallels the stern warnings we have in Jeremiah 50 and 51. God says in rather terse and brusque language, *'Come out of her.'* That simply means, have nothing to do with her! Do not touch her with a disinfected barge pole! You cannot run with the foxes and at the same time expect to hunt with the hounds. You cannot two-time the Lord. There is to be a disassociation from this diabolical system and from the purveyors of such appalling evil who are operating within the system. There is nothing unusual about such a call. This is not the first time it has happened:

When God called Abraham, he ordered him to get out of his country; God separated the Jewish nation from Egypt and warned them not to go back; even the church is commanded to steer well clear from that which is ungodly and from that which could seriously damage our testimony or impede our service for the Lord (Romans 16:17,18; 2 Corinthians 6:14-7:1).

From day one the Lord has been looking for a purified people, a people who will walk only with him and a people who will be 'in the world' but not 'of the world.'

It is fairly clear from the text that God has two vitally important matters written on his agenda. Number one, he wants to protect his people; number two, he wants to punish Babylon where it will hurt most for her trade and traffic is accursed by God. The message is that believers are to withdraw from her embrace. Every enticement and allurement offered to them should be resisted at all times and at any cost. The assumption is that some true believers will be caught within her web otherwise the appeal would not be necessary.

Separation from apostate Christendom is something which God demands. It is a clear-cut injunction. There are no bargaining chips on the table when this matter is handled in Scripture. It is one of those major issues which are non-negotiable. The man is a fool who thinks he can do a tango in the dark with the devil. The people of God need to come clean, they need to stand clear. He says, do not become tainted by her in any way; do not give in to her enticing ways and words.

> What does a call for separation like that issued in verse 4 mean in our day-to-day lives?

The charge levelled against Babylon is that she has filled her cup of sin to the brim. Or to change the metaphor to the one which John has employed in verse 5, *'her sins are piled up to heaven and God has remembered her crimes.'* Remember Genesis 11 and the infamous tower of Babel? That is the analogy we have here for her sins are stacked one on top of another like bricks in the old tower; it is a situation where each stone is an indictment about its sick condition. God says, you are at it again! You are up to your old tricks!

We can put it like this, God sees, God knows, and when the time is right, God will deal with her effectively and efficiently. That is the way it was in the days of Noah, that is why he sent the flood. It was true of the twin cities of Sodom and Gomorrah, they were blitzed from above and within an hour, they were reduced to a pile of rubble. It was equally true of the city of Nineveh after God intimated in Nahum 1:5 that he was standing against her.

There comes a time when the repugnant stench from the sins of a city or a nation reaches up to heaven and cries aloud for God to act. Heaven may seem to be silent but God is not indifferent to such corruption and crime. He does not turn a blind eye to what is going on down here; he never turns a deaf ear to all that is happening on planet earth. One day, in his sovereignty, he will act in judgment and when he does it will be swift and decisive.

18:6-8

The payment ... a voice of justice

That is why verses 6-8 send a quiver down the spine, you feel a chill when you read them. They are an awesome reminder that no-one

368 Worthy is the Lamb!

gets off scot-free, no-one gets away with anything; it is payday, someday!

Sooner or later, God catches up with man. When he does, his vengeance will be revealed. At the same time he will always vindicate his people.

The baseline is, you cannot sidestep the Lord, you cannot hide from the Lord, you cannot outwit the Lord. That is what makes the extent of her payment all the more pertinent for we read in verse 6, *'Give back to her as she has given; pay her back double for what she has done. Mix her a double portion from her own cup.'*

There is a timeless principle woven into the fabric of this verse: what we sow, we reap. God would treat her just as she treated his people. The Babylonians visited upon Jerusalem all the awful and unthinkable horrors of war; the sons and daughters of father Abraham experienced her unbelievable cruelty, they encountered her violent lusts as she ravaged the people and the community and they came face to face with her horrendous and horrible excesses. The Jewish people cried out, 'Lord, pay her back in kind!'

You see, the law of Moses demanded an eye for an eye and a tooth for a tooth, and it was a just and righteous law. Many a Jewish mother picked up the broken lifeless form of her little one and called out to heaven, 'A life for a life, O God of our fathers; a life for a life!' You find tender echoes of that sad prayer in Psalm 137.

For this new Babylon, the heir of the sins of Nimrod's Babylon and Nebuchadnezzar's Babylon, it is not justice which is decreed, it is vengeance which is demanded!

It is the law of retribution which is applied in this particular context and it is fitting and proper that it should be. It is not just an eye for an eye or a tooth for a tooth, it is double! Three times in one short verse it is written; for all the hard times inflicted on others, double! I think it is doubled to emphasise the colossal enormity of her sin. No mercy will be shown, no grace will be extended. She is handed down a double portion of the undiluted anger of God and, with more than a hint of irony, she drinks it from her own cup! That is a cue to what we saw earlier in 14:10. God will get her, and for her, there will be no hiding place.

It is like many unbelievers today; this woman firmly believes she will never experience sorrow or torment for her lifestyle and luxurious living. She reckons she is immune, she does not feel threatened, she feels she is beyond the reach of God's hand and outstretched arm. The fact is, she aint!

We read in verse 7, *'Give her as much torture and grief as the glory and luxury she gave herself. In her heart she boasts, "I sit as a queen; I am not a widow, and I will never mourn."'*

The fact is, she is not living in the real world, she is living in cloud-cuckoo land. She is downright naive! She reasons that the kings of the earth are her lovers; the truth is, she is a widow in that God has forsaken her. These words are gleaned from Isaiah 47:8-11 and even though they applied in the first instance to the fall of ancient Babylon, they are surely a shadow of things to come. There are two prominent traits in her character: she glorifies self and she indulges in a sensuous lifestyle.

And so when the day of judgment comes, it is not unexpected, it is not undeserved; she gets her comeuppance. She has brought it on herself because of her rampant infidelity. She has only herself to blame! *You can't sin and win!*

> The self-satisfied complacency of verse 7b is a common reaction from those we witness to. What approach can we best use to get behind this barrier?

We read some sober words in verse 8 where the angel declares in a very matter-of-fact kind of way, *'Therefore in one day her plagues will overtake her: death, mourning and famine. She will be consumed by fire, for mighty is the Lord God who judges her.'* When judgment eventually comes to Babylon, it will be swift, it will be sudden, it will be sure. In a single day she will be gone. Actually, verse 10 intimates it will all be over within 60 minutes! It is as quick as that! It has happened before.

You will remember the scenario at the end of Daniel 5 where the writing was on the wall and poor old Belshazzar was so petrified, he was riveted to the spot in a state of blind panic. Before the dawn broke on a new day, he was a dead man and the kingdom of Babylon had fallen to the Medes and Persians. The head of gold had given way to the chest and arms of silver as predicted in Nebuchadnezzar's metallic statue vision of Daniel 2.

There is no pussy-footing when God strikes in judgment. There is no messing around when God moves to execute justice. He makes no idle threats; he means what he says, he says what he means. If he makes a promise, he will carry it out. He does not back off, he never backs down! A combination of divine anger and divine aggression ensures that the entire operation is carried out smoothly and without a hitch. Such divine intervention pays eloquent tribute to a God who is mighty and a God who is sovereign. Her total collapse is such that only God could be responsible for it!

It was the last thing on Babylon's mind. She exudes confidence, she is the epitome of defiance, she never even entertained the thought that judgment was a possibility. She lulled herself into a false sense of security and found herself living in a fool's false paradise. But come it will. God will bring Babylon to the dust in ruin beyond repair. The much vaunted global economic system will plummet to such a degree that it makes any fall on Wall Street look like a temporary blip on a computer screen. In fact, this will be the greatest economic crash in the history of the world's financial markets.

Sometimes God's judgments work silently like a moth eating away at a garment hanging in a closet; but other times they are compared to a lion and spring suddenly. Whatever angle you choose to view it from, there is no escape route. You find those helpful and fascinating allusions which have been culled from the world of nature in Hosea 5:12,14.

From a prophetic standpoint, all is going according to the divine schedule, all is on track for God never goes off the rails. It is apparent in every sphere of life that the principle enshrined in the law of cause and effect comes into force. That is most definitely the case when it comes to the spectacular fall of Babylon. The repercussions from her downfall are staggering, the ripples emanating from the disaster are felt in many different areas. I think the reactions to her collapse are quite understandable and they fall broadly into two camps.

On one side, there are those who are genuinely grieved; on the other side, there are those who are jumping up and down for joy!

18:9-19

The people ... a voice of lamentation

The long tale of woe told by all kinds of people and the grief shared by many individuals makes most impressive reading in this section. It is worth noting that, not only do the merchants lament the fall of Babylon, the kings of the earth go down the same road. Business and government are so intertwined that what affects one seriously impinges on the other. It is a solemn lament. It is a situation where the air is heavy, where the atmosphere is sullen and people are brooding in the pits of abject depression. It seems the very bottom has fallen out of their lives and, in one sense, it has! They have every reason to mourn.

The effect on government

The response of the high and mighty, the movers and shakers, the royalty of this world, is outlined for us in verses 9 and 10 where we read, *'When the kings of the earth who committed adultery with her and shared her luxury see the smoke of her burning, they will weep and mourn over her. Terrified at her torment, they will stand far off and cry, "Woe! Woe, O great city, O Babylon, city of power! In one hour your doom has come!"'*

These folk have shared her bed, as it were, and because of the intimacy and closeness of their relationship, they enjoyed tremendous prosperity. There was a high level of stability in the markets, a downturn seemed light years away. And so when the unthinkable happened, theirs is a profound sense of loss, there is a depth to their personal feelings of anguish and bereavement, there is a fearful apprehension surrounding the future. They are terrified, they are scared stiff. Maintaining a stiff upper lip is out of the question. They are really struggling to come to terms with all that has happened.

They are finding it immensely difficult to cope with the massive losses they have sustained. Their gilt edged security has nosedived into tarnished oblivion.

It seems that the alarm bells are ringing in their ears. They are becoming increasingly edgy and their nerves are frayed. They are living on tenterhooks. They probably sense that their own days are numbered and that for them time is rapidly running out. They are sitting on a potential time bomb. It is a scenario which is not that uncommon but it is one which they can well do without. It is what the political pundits often refer to as the years of boom and bust! The fact is, it is a high risk policy when you put all your eggs in one basket. That is what they have discovered. The problem is it is too late to do anything about it; they will never recoup their losses!

The effect on commerce

There is more to it than meets the eye for we read in verse 11 that those who are involved in the commercial sector are seriously affected. The voice from heaven says, *'The merchants of the earth will weep and mourn over her because no one buys their cargoes any more.'* These folk are in a bit of a quandary because they have lost their customers. And if you have no customers you have no source of regular income. It is as simple as that! The net result is their standard of living will fall. It means luxury items will be hard to come by, unless you want to pay an inflated price on the black market.

Babylon's collapse has come as a bolt from the blue, it has left the business community reeling. It is something they did not plan for, it is something they never seriously anticipated, it is something they never made provision for. To make matters a million times worse, it all happened so quickly, there was little or nothing they could do about it.

John gives us an inventory of some of the commodities that brought enormous wealth to the traders of Babylon. The list is amazing! We can do a stock take ourselves in verses 12 and 13 and this is what we find: *'cargoes of gold, silver, precious stones and pearls; fine linen, purple, silk and scarlet cloth; every sort of citron wood, and articles of every kind made of ivory, costly wood, bronze, iron and marble; cargoes of cinnamon and spice, of incense, myrrh and frankincense, of wine and olive oil, of fine flour and wheat; cattle and sheep; horses and carriages; and bodies and souls of men.'*

It is nothing but the best for anything less is not good enough! You name it, you can have it; you want it, you can get it! It does not matter what the item is, anything from a needle to an anchor, if you are willing to pay the price, it is yours! Such was the opulent lifestyle of Babylon!

However, when the system went down and took everything along with it, it was a classic case of your best dream turning overnight into your worst nightmare. It is a level playing field for everyone and the environment is one of rust and dust! There is no point in them praying to the secular god of materialism in that day, for he has gone. The profit motive, the 'get all you can as quick as you can' syndrome, the self-help rags-to-riches philosophy, all of these are fine in a textbook on business management, but in the real world in which these folk now find themselves, it is cold comfort!

The last entry on the list and I think probably the one which is the most disturbing is the mention of the *'bodies and souls of men.'* Human life will be cheap and people will be exploited by ruthless and unscrupulous individuals. They will be treated as if they were merchandise sitting on a shelf.

I cannot help but wonder, is John making a veiled comment here on the way people are handled by senior management in the workplace? An employee's freedom is gradually eroded to such an extent that he feels he has no option but to cave in to the pressures of those in the board room. It is either toe the party line and do what is demanded of you or you are out of a job!

On the other hand, it could be a reference to pornography and prostitution where men and women barter their bodies for some insignificant trifle. One thing is absolutely clear, the world system championed by the Antichrist will dehumanise mankind as any system without God will do.

> What does it mean to dehumanise someone? What examples are there of this happening in our present day society?

The effect on the people

When we turn to verses 14 and 15, we are reminded that Babylon deceived the people of the world about wealth. The Bible says, *'They will say, "The fruit you longed for is gone from you. All your riches and splendour have vanished, never to be recovered." The merchants who sold these things and gained their wealth from her will stand far off, terrified at her torment. They will weep and mourn and cry out.'*

It is sad to say but religion has been guilty of materialistic goals. It has often conned people into believing that prosperity was a token sign of God's approval and blessing. In many instances it has created a hunger for wealth so that people are never satisfied with what they have, they are always wanting more! This is borne out very clearly in verses 16 and 17a when we hear the cry of broken hearts and shattered dreams.

The devastated people say, *'Woe! Woe, O great city, dressed in fine linen, purple and scarlet, and glittering with gold, precious stones and pearls! In one hour such great wealth has been brought to ruin!'* It is the old story, riches are temporal, they do not last. These folk may have been born into the lap of luxury with a golden spoon in their mouth; the truth is, they brought nothing into this world and they will discover before long that there are no pockets in a shroud! All that they worked for, all that they accumulated, all that they made by fair means or foul, it has all gone up in a plume of smoke. One minute they had it and they were not afraid to flaunt it; the next minute, all their stocks and shares and everything else they had in their personal portfolio had slipped through their buttery fingers and they have nothing to show for it. It was reduced to heaps of rubble and they were reduced to tears!

> How well are you keeping the biblical balance between having and using money, and not loving it (cf. 1 Timothy 6:17)?

The effect at sea

The spin-offs of this awful calamity do not affect only the monarchy, the merchants and the masses, they also encroach on the livelihood of those in the maritime industry. We read in the second half of verse 17 through to the end of verse 19, *'Every sea captain, and all who travel by ship, the sailors, and all who earn their living from the sea, will stand far off. When they see the smoke of her burning, they will exclaim, "Was there ever a city like this great city?" They will throw dust on their heads, and with weeping and mourning cry out: "Woe! Woe, O great city, where all who had ships on the sea became rich through her wealth! In one hour she has been brought to ruin!"'*

Mariners will be seriously affected by the consequences of Babylon's fall. It is interesting to note that the prophet Ezekiel spoke graphically of God's coming judgment on the seaport city of Tyre in chapter 27 of his prophecy. His pronouncement of doom focuses on the reaction of the shipping magnates to the fall of ancient Tyre and it is remarkably similar to John's description of the fall of Babylon in chapter 18.

What will happen is this: the need for freight to be transported on the busy sea lanes of this world will grind to a halt, the fishing industry will suffer astronomical losses, the luxury cruise liner holiday market will experience a massive downturn in profits. This undoubtedly means that a lot of ordinary people will be out of a job. They will have to depend on handouts from relatives and friends and whatever social security they can muster from the government of the Antichrist.

When you sit down and piece the entire jigsaw together, you can see the complete picture; my gut feeling tells me, it makes the teaching in chapter 13 on the mark of the beast easy to believe. It makes a lot of sense. The response of these folk as they bemoan their fate is to reminisce of better times. They are thinking about the good old days when order books were full and bank accounts were in the black. Their sore lament is peppered with meaningful reflections on the halcyon days.

No matter which of these groups you look at, they have a trio of common features: they all extol the wonderful virtues of Babylon as a city for they acknowledge something of her greatness; their doleful lament on the once great city begins with a double woe; and they all draw attention to the incredible speed with which she fell - the most decadent metropolis the world has ever known was reduced to ashes in sixty minutes and that has left all of them gasping for breath.

18:20-24

Praise and pronouncement ... a voice of celebration

The reaction in verse 20 to the fall of Babylon is markedly different from anything we have witnessed so far. The people of God see the whole episode from a loftier perspective. We read, *'Rejoice over her, O heaven! Rejoice, saints and apostles and prophets! God has judged her for the way she treated you.'*

Vindication!

Heaven rejoices! Heaven resounds with praise! You see, heaven is vitally interested in what happens on planet earth. All those who wrote about it, all those who foretold it, all those who preached it, they will all know it has happened. They are called upon to look down on the world they left behind and they see that the vile figure of Babylon has come to her final doom ... and they know she will never recover! She has been counted out cold on the canvas! For her, there is no way back.

The prayers of God's people have been answered. They are thrilled with what God has done. They cannot contain their excitement so they break forth into spontaneous praise and in a song of unison and rapturous worship they shout, 'Glory!' For them, it is a good enough reason to throw a party. It is a cause for joyous celebration. They give to their God a round of applause and they hail him as one who always vindicates his people. And, as I have said again and again, he does it in his own good time.

God is patient with his enemies but when he does begin to work he acts suddenly and thoroughly. He is decisive!

Violence and vengeance!

The narrative continues in verse 21 where an angel informs us that her fall is a violent one. We read, *'Then a mighty angel picked up a boulder the size of a large millstone and threw it into the sea, and said: "With such violence the great city of Babylon will be thrown down, never to be found again."'* Grim words. That is fighting talk!

The analogy speaks for itself and it underlines the indisputable fact that for Babylon there is no way back. Like the boulder in the ocean, she has gone down and under, she will never reappear in any shape or form. That is it! She is finished! End of story! The full stop has been placed at the end of the sentence and nothing more will be written about her. She has come and she has gone!

The curtain falls!

The vastness of her fall is indicated in verses 22 and 23 where the word *'never'* is repeated like a haunting note from a funeral march. We read, *'The music of harpists and musicians, flute players and trumpeters, will never be heard in you again. No workman of any trade will ever be found in you again. The sound of a millstone will never be heard in you again. The light of a lamp will never shine in you again. The voice of a bridegroom and bride will never be heard in you again. Your merchants were the world's great men.'*

There is an awesome finality to what has happened; there is an eerie stillness which permeates the atmosphere. The curtain falls.

There is no music for the orchestra has played the last waltz.
There is no marriage for romance and love will be a thing of the past.
There is no manufacturing for the bottom has fallen out of the economy.

Darkness envelops the streets. God flicks the switch and puts out for good the lights of Babylon. The language used in these verses is similar to that used in a legal document as though God were covering the pronouncement from every possible angle so as to leave no loophole. Pardon the pun, but in the light of verse 21, he leaves no stone unturned.

God makes no apology!

Justification! The final thoughts on the fall of Babylon are left to the angel who is convinced of the rightness of what has happened. We read, *'By your magic spell all the nations were led astray. In her was found the blood of prophets and of the saints, and of all who have been killed on the earth.'*

God never has to justify his actions; he does what he does because he is who he is! God offers no apology for his attitude in relation to Babylon. Her pride, her presumption, her perversity, her persecution of God's people - all of these sins, and scores more that have not been catalogued, contributed to her ultimate downfall. What happened to her is perfectly valid.

In one sense, she brought it on herself; on the other hand, she had it coming to her. It was an event waiting to happen. And happen, it certainly did! She went out with a bang, but do not forget, it was God who lit the fuse!

19

The King is coming!

On the 23rd of March 1743, *The Messiah* was performed for the first time in London. In attendance was King George II of England. He was deeply moved as the Hallelujah Chorus was sung and at the words, 'For the Lord God omnipotent reigneth,' the king rose to his feet and stood until the end of the premiere performance of this major cantata. From that time to this, people all around the world have stood when the Hallelujah Chorus is performed. When Handel composed *The Messiah* he was so immersed in what he was doing for the twenty-three days he took to write it that he hardly ate or slept. At times he would run to the harpsichord, waving his arms and singing, 'Hallelujah! Hallelujah!' Handel apparently said, 'I think, I did see all heaven before me, and the great God himself.'

19:1-6

The praise of God is proclaimed

In these opening verses the apostle John did not see the Lord but he recorded a strangely similar experience. We read his moving testimony in verse 1, *'After this I heard what sounded like the roar of a great multitude in heaven shouting: "Hallelujah! Salvation and glory and power belong to our God."'* The phrase *'after this'* refers back to the dark and ominous scenes we have recorded for us in chapters 17 and 18. It is all about the demise and ultimate doom of Babylon as an apostate religious system operating alongside and in cahoots with the Satan inspired economic/political system.

The scene then shifts with dramatic emphasis from earth to heaven. The inky blackness has gone ... now the sun is shining brightly! John's description of the scene flashing before him is incredibly vivid and graphic. It is so real you would know he is writing firsthand from his own personal experience. The sound he hears is compared to the roar of a great multitude in heaven shouting. Louder than a thousand football stadiums! That is powerful stuff. It is loud and clear. There is nothing muffled about the noise: it is thunderous, it is deafening! For an old man, there is nothing defective with John's hearing. He missed nothing. He heard every word.

This vast innumerable company are extolling the virtues of the one who is seated upon the throne. The voices of this heavenly congregation are blending together in harmony as they praise the Lord for battles fought and victories won. The question is, can we identify those who make up God's celebration choir? I think we can:

> *It is the church triumphant!*
> *It is those redeemed by precious blood!*
> *It is the saints at home with the Lord!*

And the chances are it also includes those who have been martyred in the killing fields of the Tribulation. There they are, beholding the King in all his impeccable beauty! There they are, gazing on the lovely face of Jesus! There they are, worshipping the glorified Lord in his unrivalled holiness! And what do they do? They break forth into song, they rise to their feet in a standing ovation of praise.

Hallelujah!

This is the only time you find the word mentioned in the entire New Testament. However, it is an expression that is used frequently in the Old Testament, where it is a transliteration of the Hebrew, 'praise the Lord.'

They are praising the Lord for all he has done. They are praising the Lord for who he is: he is the one who inhabits eternity, he is God blessed forever. They are praising the Lord for where he is: he is the Lamb exalted on high, he is the King seated upon the throne.

Redemption ... he is the Saviour!

Their paean of praise is a recognition of the salvation of God in their lives. The one who plucked them as brands from the burning, the one who kept them daily by his power, he has now taken them home to Immanuel's land! They have been called, justified and glorified, and together they acclaim the marvellous truth that salvation is of the Lord.

They are quick to point out the intrinsic wonders of his glory. Here is the *shekinah* of God, the brightness of his person, the excellence of his wonderful name. Here is glory personified in one who is all glorious within! They make much of his strength for they readily acknowledge his power. Here is one who is omnipotent, a God who can do anything, a God who is abundantly able, a God who is limitless in his might ... for with him, all things can become a reality.

Retribution ... he is the Judge!

The second stanza in the hallelujah chorus puts the main beam on the severity of God. Paul makes mention in one of his epistles of the 'goodness and severity' of God. That is what we have here in cameo.

In the first verse of the chorus, we saw the goodness of God; now we fix our eyes on the other side of God's nature, his ability to act in judgment. The scene so vividly portrayed for us in verses 2 and 3 is one of total destruction and complete devastation. We read, *'"True and just are his judgments. He has condemned the great prostitute who corrupted the earth by her adulteries. He has avenged on her the blood of his servants." And again they shouted: "Hallelujah! The smoke from her goes up for ever and ever."'*

Satan's superchurch has been erased. From day one it was obvious the devil was the captain of a sinking ship. This global ecumenical shrine of the last days lies smouldering in the dust of the earth. This great harlot and mother of harlots has met her doom; she has been wiped out in one fell swoop. The one who corrupted the minds and hearts of men with her spiritual fornication is now in ruins. The empire of evil has at last been eclipsed by the inrushing kingdom of love and light. And the singing has begun! The Bible bluntly states that her smoke goes up for ever and ever. In other words, there is an undercurrent of permanence with what has happened. It is irreversible! It is over!

When I read a statement like this, I cannot help but recall the words of the prophet Malachi when he reminds us, 'Vengeance is mine. I will repay, says the Lord.' God has the final say; the last word is exclusively his!

The emphasis here is not primarily focused on the titanic struggle between God and Satan, epic and momentous as that undoubtedly is; it is centred on the fact that God is true and righteous. You see, the proper way to honour him is not only to rejoice at the greatness of Babylon's fall as if this were the be-all and end-all, the best way to magnify him is to elevate his attributes to a high place in our praise and worship. We discovered in chapter 8 that God's throne and his altar are always related to his judgments. Because God is who he is, that is why he does what he does. There is never a contradiction between his attributes and the wide range of his activities; they actually complement one another.

> The 'shout' of verses 1 and 2 starts with God's salvation and ends with his vengeance. Together with Romans 11:22, what picture does this give us of his nature?

Realisation ... he is the Greatest!

The third praise item is found in verses 4 and 5 where the focus is on the sovereignty of God as they affirm his greatness. John informs us, *'The twenty-four elders and the four living creatures fell down and worshipped God, who was seated on the throne. And they cried: "Amen, Hallelujah!" Then a voice came from the throne, saying: "Praise our God, all you his servants, you who fear him, both small and great!"'*

Believe it nor not, this is the last time the elders and living creatures are mentioned in the book of Revelation. They appear first when the throne of God is introduced and they appear now at the climax of all things to say a hearty *'amen'* as a ringing endorsement of the purpose and plan of God. They are prostrate before the throne of God in heaven for they realise the stunning magnitude of the greatness of God. As my friend Woodrow Kroll says: 'God is not just filled with some awe; he is awesome!'

The fact that they bow before him is a meaningful tribute to the sovereignty of the one who is King of kings and Lord of lords. Every being in the universe is encouraged to give praise to the Lord as an act of solidarity with the one who has been guiding events on planet earth. It does not matter who they are or where they see themselves on the ladder, the invitation is an open one to the small and the great; the only criteria stipulated is the need to fear him. Each one is exhorted to bless the name of Jesus in a tidal wave of enthusiastic and ecstatic celebration.

> **From verse 5, what are the qualifications for being a worshipper?**

Ruling and reigning ... he is the King!

All the host of the redeemed shout a final hallelujah in verse 6 which emphasises the supremacy of our God. John gives us a remarkable insight into what happens when he says, *'Then I heard what sounded like a great multitude, like the roar of rushing waters and like loud peals of thunder, shouting: "Hallelujah! For our Lord God Almighty reigns."'*

What a tremendous finale to the hallelujah chorus! It is a rousing crescendo of praise; it is an unambiguous acknowledgment that our God reigns. It is marvellous for it echoes throughout the hills of heaven; it is majestic for it resounds around the valleys of earth.

The comparisons John makes are quite stunning in their own right. The voices of this choir will sound like a waterfall cascading down the side of a mountain and the booming of thunder reverberating throughout the sky. This magnificent burst of praise is an echo of Psalm 97:1 where we read, 'The Lord reigns, let the earth be glad; let the distant shores rejoice.' The literal translation is, 'The Lord God Almighty has begun to reign.' This does not suggest that heaven's throne has been empty or inactive, far from it! You know as well as I do that the omnipotent God has been accomplishing his purposes on planet earth, all day, every day, from the very first day!

I suppose we can look at it like this: in his sovereignty he has permitted evil men and fallen angels to do their worst; but now, in his providence, the time has come for God's will to be done on earth as it is in heaven. And nothing, absolutely nothing, will circumvent the plan of God! It will not be hijacked, he will not be sidelined!

19:7-8

The preparation of the bride is announced

The great hallelujah chorus is an introduction to the most magnificent wedding festivities of the ages. There is a word of instruction to all in verse 7 where the words, *'Let us rejoice and be glad and give him glory!'* are really an encouragement to keep on praising the Lord. We are urged to get enthused and excited about the marriage of the Lamb and his bride. There is a celebration and it is all a prelude to the ceremony.

Today, in most western cultures, when we think of a wedding, all eyes are on the bride. Even before the special day, we have bridal showers, she can visit bridal shops, and there is a host of other events which the bride can attend so that her big day can be suitably enhanced. Oh yes, she is the centre of attention, and rightly so. It is ironic, you have all of this and so much more, and the man standing beside her, who is not even called the 'best man' is dressed in a hired suit!

This elegant wedding in chapter 19 is significantly different. It is unique. This is the wedding of time and eternity and the focus here is on the bridegroom, he is the one who makes the difference, he alone is the centre of attention. The marriage of the Lamb is patterned after the Jewish marriage custom of Bible times. I think if we look at this it will clarify the distinctive teaching we have in these wonderful verses and we will be in a position to better understand what John is saying to us.

The arrangement

After the fathers of the bride and groom negotiated a marriage contract, the bride's father was given the 'bride price' as a dowry. *The bride price for God the Father was the blood of his Son (Ephesians 5:25).* This usually happened when the couple were quite young but the question of age depended more on local custom. The engagement was binding and could be broken only by a form of divorce. Any unfaithfulness during the engagement was considered adultery. To all intents and purposes, the couple were legally married but they were not allowed to have sexual relations during this particular period.

The betrothal

Phase two is generally spoken of as 'the preparation' or 'betrothal.' It normally lasted for a year or sometimes longer and during this time the bride was closely observed to display her purity. During the year the bridegroom would work long hours to prepare a home for his bride; more often than not, this was attached to his father's house. *In like manner, Christ is in heaven preparing a place for his bride, the church (John 14:1-3).*

On the wedding day, the groom would leave his father's home to claim his bride. After taking her from her home, the groom would then lead the bridal procession back to his own home. *This typifies the rapture of the church which Paul talks about in 1 Thessalonians 4:13-18.*

The marriage ceremony

Before the marriage, there was the writing of a legal wedding document called the *Ketubah,* it was signed by two witnesses who were not related to the wedding couple. This important document was a marriage covenant, a willing agreement between the bride and groom that included specific obligations in relation to the husband and it also outlined many of the rights of the wife.

On this occasion the bride was beautifully dressed, she looked like a queen. She had precious jewels plaited in her hair and clothing and a long veil covering her face. In Bible times the ceremony was conducted at the home of the groom. It was attended by the immediate family, two witnesses and a few close friends. Today, the ritual and customs vary from country to country, a lot depends on local tradition.

The ceremony is normally held under a *huppah* which is a kind of marriage canopy. It begins with the benediction of betrothal, recited over a cup of wine, which is taken by both the groom and his bride. A ring is placed on the bride's finger, the *Ketubah* is read and Seven Blessings are recited by a rabbi over a second cup of wine. The ceremony concludes with the groom breaking a glass in memory of the destruction of the temple.

Back in Bible times it was the done thing for the couple to leave their guests at an appropriate point to actually consummate the marriage. *This is a wonderful picture of the church as the bride of Christ consummating the marriage of the Lamb.*

The marriage feast

The fourth and final phase is known as the marriage feast. The friends of the bride and groom were invited to this so they could share in the joys of this happy occasion. It was a good excuse for a long party. Sometimes it lasted a few days, other times it went on for a week; it depended how rich the host was! After the feast, the couple would settle into their new home and get on with the rest of their lives together.

> **With the data available, what does the picture of a bride tell us about the nature of the church?**

The bride's apparel

The second half of verse 7, into verse 8, serves to remind us of the importance of the bride's apparel. We read, *'"For the wedding of the Lamb has come and his bride has made herself ready. Fine linen, bright and clean, was given her to wear." (Fine linen stands for the righteous acts of the saints.)'*

The status of this is seen from the parables of our Lord. One classic example you can read about is in Matthew 22:1-4. There the kingdom of heaven is likened to a marriage supper which a certain king gave for his son. Those who did not have a wedding garment were cast out into an eternity of loss and separation from God. The implication is, if you have not got a wedding garment, you cannot get into the wedding banquet.

You will notice in these two verses that the bride is ready and she is robed. I have been to many weddings in my day and I have performed quite a number as well and I cannot remember a single occasion where the bride was not beautiful! She has planned and prepared for this moment and she comes out looking her best.

Her clothing, which is really her wedding dress, is described for us in detail and a fascinating explanation is appended to it as well. We know from reading elsewhere in Scripture that we are clothed from head to toe in the garment of his righteousness. That is an imputed and an imparted righteousness, it is one which is given to us at the moment of our salvation; it is a gift of sovereign grace. But the garment we read about here in verse 8 is a different one. The only similarity is that it is also one which is given to us.

The *'fine linen'* represents the righteous deeds of godliness and goodness produced in us and through us by the Holy Spirit. These are the 'good works' Paul refers to in Ephesians 2:10 which bear witness to our personal relationship with Jesus Christ.

> In what sense has the bride 'made herself ready' and what does it mean that 'fine linen' has been 'given her to wear' (verses 7 and 8)?

The timing of the event

The key event addressed here in chapter 19 will be immediately after the judgment seat of Christ which Paul writes about at length in 1 Corinthians 3 and 2 Corinthians 5. It is payday for the people of God, it is our moment of evaluation and appraisal, it is the place of accountability for each of us as the servants of God. All our foibles and mistakes will burn up before our eyes for they are symbolised as wood, hay and straw; the gold and silver and costly stones of our service and devotion will stand the test of his scrutiny and he will amply reward us for these. That is why I think the reference here points us in the direction of the Bema; it speaks of our ability to magnify him and the greater our reward, the greater will be our capacity to glorify Jesus.

When the church arrives in heaven for her hour of grand review, she is not the most attractive or beautiful ... in fact, she is covered in spots, wrinkles and blemishes, according to Paul in Ephesians 5:27! But now! What a difference! She is radiant in her glory! How true it is, we weave on earth what we wear in heaven. Sometimes the reality of that has not sunk in, that how we use the gifts God gave us on earth will determine the way we are presented to the bridegroom when he comes. I just wonder, will we be dressed shabbily or lavishly? That is a challenging thought. It reminds me of the familiar lines, 'Only one life, it will soon be past; only what's done, for Christ will last.'

19:9-10

The marriage feast

Have you ever done something on the spur of the moment and lived to regret it? Have you ever responded in an emotion charged atmosphere only to discover minutes later that you got it all wrong? If we are honest, most of us would have to answer 'yes' to each of these questions! John certainly would. Right here in chapter 19, as a mature old man, and as a well-seasoned observer of all things spiritual, he got it disastrously wrong. It all happened after the praise party in heaven to celebrate the intervention of God in the affairs of men; it came about after the rousing angelic invitation to the wedding feast of the Lamb which we read about in verse 9. *'Then the angel said to me, "Write: 'Blessed are those who are invited to the wedding supper of the Lamb!'" And he added, "These are the true words of God."'*

> What are the conditions of each of the seven blessings as set out in the book of Revelation?

It was after this that John made a serious error of judgment; mind you, it was a rare gaffe on John's part ... it shows he is just as human as the rest of us, and that is good! We will have more to say about John's blunder in a moment but let us backtrack and open the envelope which has heaven's postmark stamped on it. It would be good if we examined this unique invitation in a bit more detail.

Who is on the guest list?

It is an extremely positive invitation! It indicates quite clearly that all those whose names appear on the guest list are truly blessed. This is the fourth of the seven beatitudes found in the book.

Who receives an invitation to this legendary banquet? Well, it is not the church for the bride is never invited to her own wedding! She is there already for you cannot have a wedding without a bride!

I believe the invitation is extended to all those who fit into the category of Old Testament saints, to those saints who have been martyred during the Tribulation, and to those believers who have emerged from the seven years of Satan's rule and reign of terror.

The time and the place!

Is it on earth? During the eternal state, no distinctions will be made among the people of God but, in the kingdom age, in the millennium, differences will exist as the church reigns with Christ and as Israel enjoys the promised messianic blessings. I have no doubts in my mind that this wedding banquet will take place on earth and I would be inclined to suggest that it could even take place during the forty-five days mentioned in Daniel 12:11,12. That means, it could happen during the interregnum between the end of the period of Tribulation and the beginning of the millennial kingdom of Christ. In that sense, the kingdom would then be seen as a one thousand year honeymoon to be enjoyed by the church as she shares in the glorious rule and reign of Jesus as King.

Since not everyone holds my view on this particular issue, it is only fair that I should lay before you what others feel on the matter.

Is it in heaven? The other major position adopted by Bible scholars suggests that the marriage supper will be held in heaven while the seven years of Tribulation are taking place on earth. The proponents of this view give four main reasons for their argument.

One, they say the marriage supper mentioned here is related to Jewish marriage customs in the Bible; *two,* they say the marriage did not take place in the bride's home but in the bridegroom's home after he brought her to that prepared place; *three,* they say it was customary for the marriage supper, given by the groom's father, to be held at the bridegroom's home on the same night as the marriage ceremony; and, *four,* they say the Old Testament teaches that there will be another marriage supper at the beginning of the millennium, associated with a second marriage of God the Father and the nation of Israel which is implied in Isaiah 25:6. Thus, they say, the future marriage of God the Father and the marriage of the Lamb have two different brides - the bride at the marriage of God the Father is the nation of Israel and the bride at the marriage of the Lamb is the church. According to this view, the marriage supper of the Lamb will take place in heaven after the rapture of the church and it will include the church along with Old Testament saints and martyred Tribulation saints as specially invited guests.

The choice is yours! Whether the venue is down here or over there, one fact is constant: his banner over us will be one of love, and the whole experience will be a feast for the eyes for we will see the Lord; it will be feast for the ears for we will hear his voice; it will be a feast for the heart for we will be enthralled with him. He says, 'Come and dine!' and I imagine most of us will be happy to do just that!

The host

And then in a bold attempt to allay all our fears as to the source of the invitation, the angel appended to it the cast-iron assurance that it came direct from the Father himself. It is genuine! It is authentic! It bears his signature, it is in the handwriting of God! This is no fairy tale, this is for real!

A breach of etiquette!

John's immediate response to all of this is what I was referring to above. It is a serious breach of etiquette! Poor John, he got it badly wrong! The problem was he did not only do it once, he slipped up a second time; you see that faux pas mentioned in 22:8,9.

We read about the initial incident in verse 10: *'At this I fell at his feet to worship him. But he said to me, "Do not do it! I am a fellow-servant with you and with your brothers who hold to the testimony of Jesus. Worship God! For the testimony of Jesus is the spirit of prophecy."'*

In all fairness to John, he is big enough to admit his mistake and it is there for the rest of us to learn from! He was so carried away by the wonder of all that he saw and heard that he instinctively fell down and worshipped the angel. The angel was having none of it; he rebuked John and told him in no uncertain terms that God is the only one who deserves to be worshipped! The angel had no airs or graces for he saw himself as a bondslave; there was nothing pretentious about him for he was only a servant; this was no ambience of false humility. He and John were standing on a level playing field.

When it comes to worship, both men and angels have no alternative but to direct it to the one who sits upon the throne.

> **When are we tempted to put men in the place of God? What is the basic difference between admiration and adulation? Do you always point people away from yourself to the Lord?**

Prophecy is a person!

Another fascinating thought in this verse surrounds the explanation given to the phrase, *'the testimony of Jesus.'* We are told it is *'the spirit of prophecy.'* That means prophecy is not a fortune teller who reads the palm of your hand or the leaves in a tea cup; prophecy is not an astrologer who consults the stars; prophecy is not someone who is a good guesser or a date fixer; prophecy is a person! And that person is Jesus!

Some folk think that the purpose of prophecy is to open a window on the future. Nothing could be further from the truth. The pure essence of prophecy is to bear witness to Jesus. He is the central figure of all Scripture. He is the central person of history. Our focus is the Lord for all prophecy is wrapped up in him.

On one hand, he is the revealer; on the other hand, he is the revelation!

That is what the Apocalypse is all about ... it is a full-blown revelation of Jesus Christ!

19:11-14

The rider on the white horse

We are moving now into the second half of chapter 19. In many ways, this is the climax of Bible prophecy, it is the hour when the

King will come! We are talking here about the second advent of Jesus Christ in power and great glory. This has to be the most extraordinary event in history. It is certainly the most dramatic moment in prophecy. This is a major doctrine woven into the fabric of Scripture.

Did you know that ... one-fifth of the Bible is prophecy? one-third of those prophecies relate to the second coming of Christ? there are at least 333 prophecies concerning Christ in the Old Testament? only 109 of these were fulfilled at his first advent, that leaves 224 (more than twice as many) to be fulfilled at his second appearing!

Did you know that ... of the 46 Old Testament prophets, fewer than ten speak of events related to Christ's first coming, while 36 speak of events linked with his second coming? there are 7,959 verses in the New Testament, 330 of which refer directly to the second coming of Christ? the Lord Jesus speaks about his return to earth no fewer than 25 times? throughout the New Testament there are more than 50 exhortations for people to be ready for the coming of Christ?

I believe those are interesting facts, but they are a lot more than fodder for an enthusiastic statistician ... they drive home the truth that Jesus is coming again! That was the message in 1:7 where we read, *'Look, he is coming with the clouds, and every eye will see him.'* Here it is at long last! The day has finally dawned!

He is reliable!

John informs us in verse 11, *'I saw heaven standing open and there before me was a white horse, whose rider is called Faithful and True. With justice he judges and makes war.'* It is a helpful exercise to make a comparison of John's experience on this occasion with what happened to him earlier in chapter 4. On that instance he saw only a door open in heaven, but here he sees all of heaven open. This is a grander and fuller view than he had before. This is the great unveiling. The scene is awe-inspiring. John sees a rider on a

white horse. This one is called *'Faithful and True'* in direct contrast
to the pseudo ruler of the world we met in chapter 6.

> **Look up some other examples of 'heaven standing open' and
> try to analyse what sort of occasions these were and why
> this experience was granted!**

His first advent. Christ rode into the city of Jerusalem on the
back of a donkey; he was given no throne, only a cross; his crown
was one of thorns, his sceptre a reed.

His second advent. The Lord of heaven is seated on a white
stallion, ready to depart heaven as a warrior king; he is poised for
battle! When he comes, he will deal effectively and adeptly with his
enemies.

That he is returning on a white horse is highly significant. In
Bible times, Roman generals always returned from victorious
campaigns riding white horses. They, and their legions, would parade
up the Via Sacra, the main street of Rome, that led from the Forum
to the Temple of Jupiter on the Capitoline Hill. They would be hailed
as heroes, the cheers of a jubilant people would greet them all along
the route. So the white horse is a symbol of triumph!

The rider is called *'Faithful and True'* and that emphasises the
reliability of his name. Back in 1:5 he is described as *'the faithful
witness'* and then in 3:14 he is seen as *'the faithful and true witness.'*
This name is, therefore, a fitting description of his character and it is
also a pointer to a couple of his attributes for he is a God of
faithfulness and a God of truth. It means he is trustworthy; he is
someone who can always be relied upon; he is dependable and he is
one who always keeps his promises.

To say he is true is to affirm that he is genuine; he is real. He is
not a counterfeit. There is nothing fake or false about him. He is
authentic. Because he is eternally faithful and true, it means many
wonderful blessings are ours to enjoy right now. For example, he
makes good on his promises (Deuteronomy 7:9; Hebrews 10:23),
he helps us in our temptations (1 Corinthians 10:13), he protects us
from Satan (2 Thessalonians 3:3), he will never forsake us (2 Timothy
2:13), and he will forgive our sin (1 John 1:9).

He said he would bring peace and social and political justice to mankind, and he will; he will deliver the goods in his own good time.

The rider on the same colour of a horse in 6:2 is the exact opposite. He is dangerously deceptive and dishonest. There is all the difference in the world between the Antichrist and the Lord Jesus Christ.

> **What titles and descriptions lead us to identify this figure as the Lord Jesus Christ?**

He is right!

This verse makes it abundantly clear that what he does, when he comes again, is done justly. There will be no charge of injustice levelled against him when he makes war. In heaven's cabinet, he is the minister for war. The nations have been depicted already as an overripe harvest; they are rotting and smelling like a basket of summer fruit and when he touches down on planet earth, his will be a swift execution of justice. He is the grim reaper. Here is the one who, through the millennia, made peace through the blood of the cross; now he makes war over that blood. Human sin has reached the highwater mark; global rebellion has gone over the top. It must be put down once and for all, and when it is, it will all be over in a flash!

> **The Lord makes war and brings judgment against evil on a cosmic scale. In what sense are we called, if at all, to 'make war' against evil and to help others face their personal judgment (the Greek word is *krisis*)?**

He relates!

John does not stop there. He tells us more in verse 12 for we read, *'His eyes are like blazing fire, and on his head are many crowns. He has a name written on him that no-one knows but he himself.'*

The reference to the eyes of Christ indicate a penetrating gaze that flash with intelligence and righteousness. It is the look of divine wrath upon sinful man. It is a look that sees right through you. His eyes can pierce through every human shield. His is an all-searching eye, an eye that discerns, an eye that roves, an eye that scans. Nothing can be hidden from his all-seeing eye, no-one can hide from his sight. In that day all will be exposed, all will come under his scrutiny. All will be laid bare before him. The coming King is one who sees all and one who knows all!

He rules!

The many crowns or diadems speak of his magnificent rule and sovereignty; so here is one who is omnipotent, one who is all-powerful. It draws attention to his royalty and his majesty and it is a token reminder of the title given to him in the Psalms where we often read, 'The Lord is King!'

It would seem that John was able to see the name written on him but, for some reason, it was incomprehensible to him; it is a name shrouded in mystery. There is so much about our Lord we simply do not know, but he knows! It is a secret name; maybe it is the same as the *'new name'* we read about in 3:12.

The knowledge of the Lord is described in the same way in Psalm 139:1-6 where David honestly concludes, 'Such knowledge is too wonderful for me, too lofty for me to attain.' We read elsewhere in Psalm 145 that 'his greatness is such that no-one can fathom it.' That is what makes eternity an exciting enterprise, it will be an educational experience for in heaven we will learn new things about the Lord Jesus!

He routs!

John continues in verse 13 by sharing with us, *'He is dressed in a robe dipped in blood, and his name is the Word of God.'* At a quick glance, it seems a strange comment for John to make, but the question is, where did the blood come from? One thing we do know for sure, it was not his own blood shed on the cross at Calvary for the work of redemption is complete, that event has long since passed. Rather it is the blood of his enemies and we glean that truth from

Isaiah 63:1-3. The evangelical prophet gives us a breathtaking description of the approach of a great warrior with crimson stained garments. It is a prophecy about the coming of the Lord and his robes are stained with the blood of those he has destroyed. This is the same bloodbath we have described in vivid detail in 14:20. He is a God of vengeance, a God of anger!

He reveals!

He is called *'the Word of God.'* That sounds familiar, doesn't it? The same ascription is given to him back in John 1:1,14. It is the same person in view for he is the embodiment of God's truth, he is God on display. He is the Father's revelation of himself. When you look at him, you see God. When you listen to what he says, you hear the voice of God. Anne Graham Lotz makes this comment, 'The Bible that people even today deny, distort, dilute, defy, doubt, and disobey is the same as his name!'

He is royalty!

And then we read in verse 14, *'The armies of heaven were following him, riding on white horses and dressed in fine linen, white and clean.'* This is tremendous! It is a powerful reminder that when our Lord returns he will not be alone for the armies of heaven accompany him; they follow in his train. Now you are wondering, who is he talking about here? Well, first of all, I think the angels have a vital role to play in this military style operation. We know from the Olivet Discourse, in Matthew 25:31, that they will be present and Paul says as much in 2 Thessalonians 1:7. But we also know from 1 Thessalonians 3:13 and 2 Thessalonians 1:10 that the saints will also participate in this venture. You and I! We will be there as part of his entourage. After all, it is a royal visit and we just happen to be the wife of the Lamb! Jude is batting from the same crease when he alludes to it in verses 14 and 15 of his book, as is the prophet Zechariah in 13:5. The 'holy ones' in both cases have a dual meaning in that they can refer to believers and angels. We are there beside him; we are there behind him.

It seems to me, this is the moment Paul talks about in 2 Thessalonians 1:10 when he says, 'He comes to be glorified in his holy people and to be marvelled at among all those who have believed.' We are not there to fight, ours is purely a supportive role, for Christ himself will defeat the enemy through a trio of great victories.

It is an awesome display of glory! It is a regal demonstration of splendour! It is a stunning sight of unbelievable grandeur. It is a magic moment for this is the hour when every eye will see him and every knee will bend before him and every tongue will confess that Jesus Christ is Lord!

> *All hail the Lamb enthroned on high,*
> *His praise shall be our battle cry!*
> *He reigns victorious, forever glorious,*
> *His name is Jesus! He is the Lord!*

19:15-21

The Lamb wins!

In verse 15 John tells us, *'Out of his mouth comes a sharp sword with which to strike down the nations. "He will rule them with an iron sceptre." He treads the winepress of the fury of the wrath of God Almighty.'* This is an amazing verse. It is action packed.

> Try to imagine a world with Jesus totally in control. What do you think it would be like?

He strikes the nations

The sharp sword refers to the long and heavy sword commonly used by the Thracians. Having said that, it can also describe a sword long enough and light enough to throw as a spear or a javelin. We are all aware of the fact that the word of God is represented by a sword in Ephesians 6 even though the phrase used there refers to the two-edged hand weapon popularised by the Romans.

What matters is this: it is his word that strikes the nations. He merely speaks the word and his judgments are executed swiftly. This lethal blow is outlined for us in Psalm 2:9 and Isaiah 11:4. Not a shot will be fired! The last battle, the conflict of the ages, will be won by the word of God! The opposition will crumble before him; the enemy will bite the bullet and melt in the sunlight of his glorious appearing. Christ will be victorious! One word, and that is that!

> How is it possible for Jesus to subdue his enemies and establish his authority simply by speaking a word as in verse 15?

He shepherds the nations

That is the thought behind ruling them with an iron sceptre or, as some translations put it, a rod of iron. Either way, it employs the Greek word for 'shepherd.' The shepherd's rod is frequently used for correction. Paul hints at this in 1 Corinthians 4:21 when he poses the question, 'Shall I come to you with a rod, or in love and a spirit of gentleness?' The Lord Jesus is called the great shepherd of the sheep in Hebrews 13; he is seen as the good shepherd in John 10; and he is spoken of as the chief shepherd in 1 Peter 5. All of these express warm encouragement to the people of God. Because of the unique relationship we have with him, even the shepherd's rod can be a measure of comfort to the believer (Psalm 23:4).

However, the rod or sceptre the shepherd of the nations will use is made of iron. This is not to be taken lightly. It is a rod that will bring order and justice to a world that is riddled with chaos and confusion and corruption. The nations will be shepherded with sovereign and kingly authority. This is no softly-softly approach to global government. This is Jesus Christ putting his foot down; he is exercising his right to universal domination. He and his followers will rule the nations of the world when his kingdom is established on planet earth, it will be one thousand years of Jesus rule. Men will have no option but to conform to the righteous standards of God. They will have no say in the matter, there is no alternative, there is no other way! As someone has said, 'A chicken won't peep, a rooster won't crow, and a man won't move without his permission.'

The word 'rule' is 'shepherd' - what light does this throw on the nature of Jesus' kingship, bearing in mind that he is called the great, the good and the chief shepherd in Scripture?

He stomps the nations

This is echoed in the last phrase of verse 15 where it describes the trampling of the peoples of the world in the winepress of God's wrath. This imagery portrays grapes being trampled under foot until all the juice is squeezed out of them. The chilling fact is, it is blood, not grape juice, that will spurt from the winepress of God's anger!

This is the great and terrible Day of the Lord; it is the day of vengeance of our God; it is the awful day of his wrath; it is a day when his unbridled fury is poured out upon the unbelieving nations.

These same truths are reiterated by the prophets in Isaiah 63 and Joel 3. No matter where you look, all of these drive us to the sad conclusion that, in the day of judgment, it is too late for men to expect mercy from God. There is nothing more inflexible and intransigent than divine judgment where the grace of God has been spurned.

His identity

His title

In verse 16, John says, *'On his robe and on his thigh he has this name written: King of kings and Lord of lords.'* What a splendid title that is! King of kings and Lord of lords. Daniel throws in another one for good measure when he says, he is the Prince of princes!

Truly the Lord is sovereign, he is exalted, he is enthroned on high. He is unique for he is the unrivalled Son of God. He is peerless for he is the incomparable Christ!

I venture to suggest that this is Christ's most important name. It brings to mind such glowing references as Daniel 2:47 and Deuteronomy 10:17 where his transcendence is underlined. Paul jumped on the bandwagon when he used the same title for our Lord in 1 Timothy 6:15. So far as Paul was concerned, it did not matter one iota what Caesar was on the throne, Jesus Christ was his Lord and King. *The bottom line is, he is God and before him, all else must bow the knee!*

His robe and thigh

The thigh on which this title is emblazoned is symbolic of power; the robe on which this title is emblazoned has to do with his position. You find those truths beautifully illustrated in the lives of Jacob and Joseph.

The impact of his return

The closing verses of the chapter remind us of the terrible destruction that will come. Armageddon has arrived; that feared day when the final war of humanity takes place is now before us. Human history, as we know it, will come to a close. God's day, when old scores will be settled, will explode upon the world scene in a spectacular display of his power and glory. The whole world will know that Jesus Christ is King of kings and Lord of lords!

We see Satan's rickety empire collapsing like a pack of cards when the Lord appears from heaven. The essential information is provided by John in verses 17 and 18 where we read, *'And I saw an angel standing in the sun, who cried in a loud voice to all the birds flying in mid-air, "Come, gather together for the great supper of God, so that you may eat the flesh of kings, generals, and mighty men, of horses and their riders, and the flesh of all people, free and slave, small and great."'*

The angel

The unusual position of the angel is a moment of high drama. He is *'standing in the sun.'* Some folk have taken this to be a one-off phenomenon but the most natural explanation is that the angel is standing in the light of the sun which means he is shining with even greater brilliance than he normally does.

The image is one of incandescent light speaking of the glory of God. The prophet Joel intimates that the sun will be turned into darkness. Perhaps the position of the angel initiates that process by which people on earth will know that the judgment day has arrived.

His voice. The sound of a loud voice is an activity we have come across six times previously in the book. It always introduces some event of mega importance relative to the vengeance and victory of God.

His message. The omens are dreadful. The message directed explicitly to the birds is akin to what we have in the Olivet discourse of Matthew 24:27,28. It is a parallel passage to this one where both speak of carnage at the coming of Christ.

The 'carcass' depicts the nations of the world who have gathered against the Lord and his people in the Armageddon campaign. *The 'vultures'* represent all the birds of heaven who will literally feed on the flesh of those armies destroyed by the advent of the King. A vulture is a voracious eater. It descends swiftly upon carrion and devours it in minutes. In that hour, they will have a field day, millions of men from every strata of society will be consumed within a 200 mile radius of Jerusalem. It will be a terrifying spectacle, beyond human imagination.

It is ironic that the great supper of God anticipated here in verse 17 is in direct contrast to the supper envisaged at the marriage of the Lamb in verse 9. I can tell you which one I would rather be at!

The beast and his army

John reflects in a solemn mood in verse 19 when he testifies: *'Then I saw the beast and the kings of the earth and their armies gathered together to make war against the rider on the horse and his army.'*

You can see what is happening: the world is mobilised, they have come from every corner of the earth and have converged on Armageddon. They are there for World War III. For a while they fight one another in the conflict of the ages; the killing is mindless, it is senseless, it is relentless. And then, suddenly, something happens. There is a change in their attitude, old animosities are quickly forgotten, past grudges are rapidly buried, they are united by the challenge from on high.

They join hearts and hands in their rebellion against the coming King. The beast and the kings of the earth marshal the armies of the world, they line up their tanks, they aim their missiles, they poise their nuclear warheads, they position their battleships, all to make war against the one who is Lord! Against the one who is their Creator!

It is the same old story. The nations stood shoulder to shoulder against the Lord Jesus at his first coming and it is not in the least surprising, history will repeat itself at his second advent; and the man leading his troops from the front is none other than the Antichrist. It is the final cataclysmic punch-up between good and evil.

The outcome

It is an ill-fated assault on the advancing army of the King of kings. It is doomed from the moment they get out of the trenches! They are on a collision course with the Lord of the universe and we know who comes off the worst! John says as much in verses 20 and 21, *'But the beast was captured, and with him the false prophet who had performed the miraculous signs on his behalf. With these signs he had deluded those who had received the mark of the beast and worshipped his image. The two of them were thrown alive into the fiery lake of burning sulphur. The rest of them were killed with the sword that came out of the mouth of the rider on the horse, and all the birds gorged themselves on their flesh.'*

Hyped up though Armageddon was, at the end of the day it boiled down to a rather one-sided contest. The assembled armies with all their hi-tech weapons of war do not present any real threat to the Lord Jesus Christ. He is invincible! He speaks a word and it is all over! He has done it before.

Once, he spoke a word to a fig tree, and it withered away. Once, he spoke a word to the wind and the waves, and all was peace and calm. Once, he spoke a word to a legion of demons, and instantly they fled. Now, he speaks a word, and the war is over!

The loud mouthed Antichrist is riveted to the spot. He is captured and taken away by the scruff of his brazen neck. The miracle working false prophet who is a PR windbag from the pit is punctured and he suffers a similar fate to his supremo. The pair of them are rounded up and unceremoniously bundled into hell. Their time is up. They have had their say, they have had their way, they have had their day. Now they get their just desserts. They have the rare honour, if you want to call it that, of being the first two who are cast into hell ... even the devil is not there yet!

The Antichrist who is probably the greatest intellectual, the greatest politician, the greatest statesman, the greatest economist, who ever lived, becomes the greatest fool when he tries to mastermind a quick one over the Lord Jesus Christ.

Another word and the massed troops from all around the world fall down dead. Not one person escapes. It all happens so quickly, no-one can jump ship or change sides; there is no time to hoist the white flag of surrender. The sombre fact is no-one is left standing. It is a total wipe-out! The birds of prey can hardly believe their luck.

It is a blanket victory for the King of kings and Lord of lords.

20

The great judgment morning

Revelation 20 is one of the great chapters of Scripture. It is a chapter that shows what happens immediately after the second coming of Jesus Christ. We have a clear indication of this because one phrase is repeated no fewer than six times in the first seven verses ... it talks about *'a thousand years.'* That is what we generally refer to as the millennium. It comes from two Latin words, *mille* and *annum*, meaning a thousand years. It is fair to say that theologians differ on their views of the millennium and, for many believers, the whole subject has been rated so highly controversial that honest, open discussion has frequently generated more heat than light!

Approaches to the millennium

Amillennialists believe there will be no earthly reign of Christ before or after his second coming. The kingdom, from their perspective, is not something which is political or visible; it is something which is principally spiritual in nature.

Postmillennialists believe the world will continue to get better as Christians spread the gospel and this will be the age of the millennium. They see the advent of Christ taking place after the millennium.

Premillennialists believe that Christ will return before the millennium to reign on the earth for a literal one thousand years.

On a personal level, I will be interpreting this passage from a premillennial standpoint. From that angle, the teaching of John makes a lot of sense. You see, the ultimate overriding purpose of human history is the glory of God. God was not created for man; man was created for God. We are brought into the family of God so that God's glory will shine through us throughout the endless ages.

God's glory was manifested in creation. God's glory was manifested in redemptive history. God's glory was manifested in the tabernacle and in the temple. God's glory was manifested at Calvary in the death of Jesus. God's glory was manifested in the church. God's glory was manifested, above all else, in the person of the Son of God. And, in an amazing way, God's glory is manifested through the nation of Israel.

If men want to see and know what God is like, they should watch how he deals with Israel! When Jacob was about to leave the land of promise, God spoke to him in Genesis 28:15. He told him, 'I am with you and will watch over you wherever you go, and I will bring you back to this land. I will not leave you until I have done what I have promised you.' In those five promises the entire history of the nation of Israel was kaleidoscoped.

If God does not keep his word to Israel, then he is not true. If God does not have power to fulfil his purposes, then he is not omnipotent. If God does not know certain things are going to occur, and gets caught off guard, then he is not omniscient. If God has wearied of Israel, then he is not longsuffering. If God has changed his mind, then he is not immutable. And in this we must be absolutely clear ... if God has changed his mind in relation to his purpose for Israel, perhaps he will change his mind concerning his purposes for the church.

A reflection of God's character

In the first instance, the millennial issue is not prophetical, it is theological. It is not so much a consideration of what will happen tomorrow, it deals with what God's character is like today and he is a faithful God!

He will keep his promises to Israel ... that requires a literal kingdom on earth over which Jesus Christ will preside.

He will keep his promises to the believer ... that requires a home in glory in his presence forever.

When you draw all the strands together and, at the risk of sounding simplistic, it seems to me that is where amillennialism infringes on God's glory by calling into question his attributes when they say, there will be no literal kingdom.

Postmillennialism detracts from God's glory by attributing to the church a purpose God never intended. It was never God's idea, it was never written on his agenda, that man through the proclamation of the gospel will bring in the kingdom.

Premillennialism acknowledges God's glory by taking God at his word; this is implicit in the recognition that Jesus will rule on the earth for one thousand years. To me, it is a special time when the kingdom of God is here upon planet earth; these are days of peace and prosperity, days of untold spiritual blessing. In the words of Isaac Watts' old hymn, 'Blessing abounds where e'er he reigns.'

These are days when he will be king over all the earth, days when he will sit on the throne of his father David in the city of the great king, days when the kingdoms of this world will become the kingdom of his dear Son, days when the glory of the Lord will cover the earth as the waters cover the sea, days of heaven on earth, these will be times of refreshing because Jehovah Shammah will be in the midst.

It is a golden age! Above all, these are days when Satan is under the feet of Jesus and that is what we have outlined here in the opening verses of chapter 20.

20:1-3

The devil on death row!

We are advised in verses 1 and 2 of the period when Satan is bound; in the first half of verse 3, we are informed of the place where Satan is bound; and in the second half of the same verse, we are shown the purpose for which Satan is bound. It is to keep him from deceiving the nations any more! John says in these verses, *'And I saw an angel coming down out of heaven, having the key to the Abyss and holding in his hand a great chain. He seized the dragon, that ancient serpent, who is the devil, or Satan, and bound him for a thousand years. He threw him into the Abyss, and locked and sealed it over him, to keep him from deceiving the nations any more until the thousand years were ended. After that, he must be set free for a short time.'*

Satan is under detention and there is no escape. He finds himself on death row! God has sidelined the devil for a very long time. His influence is nil, his power is zero, he has been completely disarmed. So long as he is in the pit, he is a spent force.

In 12:9 he was cast out of heaven ... now he is cast out of the earth!

He is out of the way and, because he is under lock and key, life on planet earth is a million times better. Come to think of it, it is always like that when Jesus is in control!

> **What does it say about the relative place of Christ and Satan that Christ does not act in person to bind him but delegates it to an angel?**

20:4-6

Spotlight on the saints!

John tells us, *'I saw thrones on which were seated those who had been given authority to judge. And I saw the souls of those who had been beheaded because of their testimony for Jesus and because of* the word of God. They had not worshipped the beast or his image and had not received his mark on their foreheads or their hands. They came to life and reigned with Christ for a thousand years. (The rest of the dead did not come to life until the thousand years were ended.) This is the first resurrection. Blessed and holy are those who have part in the first resurrection. The second death has no power over them, but they will be priests of God and of Christ and will reign with him for a thousand years.'

This is great stuff! This is wonderful news! The devil is well out of harm's way, he is confined for ten centuries in the abyss, he is chained, he is under lock and key, he is going nowhere during the millennium. That explains why in these few verses John gives us a further trio of reasons to justify his incarceration. Do you remember what Paul promised the Christians in Rome? He said in Romans 16:20 that, 'The God of heaven will soon crush Satan under your feet.' Well, this is it! Here it is!

They are crowned!

Those on the thrones are the people of God in the church and the saints who have walked close with the Lord down through the ages. John sees those who are loyal to the Lord during the dark days of the Tribulation and who gave their lives in an act of supreme sacrifice. It is fascinating to read elsewhere in 1 Peter 2:9 that we are 'a royal priesthood' and away back in 1:6 that we are kings and priests unto God. The kingly aspect of it comes out in our role with him during the millennial kingdom. What a tremendous privilege to be ruling and reigning with him!

> How do you view the prospect of being given authority to judge and rule over others? In what ways has your Christian experience equipped you for such a task?

He makes it very clear that this is all part of the first resurrection. The questions are, if this is the first one, and it is for those who are saved, what happens at the second one and when is it? It happens at

410 Worthy is the Lamb!

the end of the millennium and it is for the sinner, it is for those who are lost, but more about that when we reach verses 11-15.

Try as you might, you will be hard pushed to find a reference in the Bible to sustain the argument for a so-called 'general' resurrection. In fact, the opposite is the case. The reality is, there are two resurrections, one before the millennium and one at the end of the millennium.

The first resurrection is in three distinct stages and what makes the whole subject much more interesting is the way it is compared to a harvest.

Stage one is when Christ arose on that first Easter Sunday morning as the firstfruits. You find that alluded to in 1 Corinthians 15:20. When they had a harvest in the Old Testament, the high priest would go out into the field, take a handful of grain and bring it into the temple as a sacrifice to the Lord. It was a guarantee of that which was yet to come. That is what happened when Jesus rose from the grave. He is the firstfruits of the promises of God. It is the assurance that what happened to him will one day happen to us!

Stage two is what Paul refers to in 1 Thessalonians 4:13-18 when, at the rapture, when the trumpet sounds, the saints of God are gathered into the immediate presence of Jesus. If you like, this is the harvest proper. All of us who are in the Lord will meet him in the air, that will be the greatest harvest of souls ever; this is the fruit of his death at Calvary.

Stage three is at the end of the Tribulation when the Old Testament saints along with the Tribulation saints will rise to new heights of glory. These are the gleanings, the leftovers, which are picked up after the main harvest has been gathered home.

We can put it like this: it is one resurrection in three different phases; sometimes it is called the 'resurrection unto life' as in Daniel 12:2. The key phrase if we want to understand the resurrection aright is found at the end of verse 4 where John says, *'they came to life.'* It actually means 'to stand up!' Apparently the Dutch have a word for it in their vocabulary; they call it 'oopstanding!' That is what the resurrection does for us, it enables us to stand up!

The story is told of the famous American evangelist, D L Moody, who one day was addressing a company of people. 'One of these fine mornings,' he is reported as saying, 'you will read in your newspaper that D L Moody is dead. Don't you believe it! On that day, I'll be more alive than I've ever been!' That is the resurrection spirit!

Their character

Again, at the beginning of verse 6 we have one of those familiar beatitudes (this is number five; the last two, numbers six and seven, are in 22:7,14.)

Our state. We are what we are because we are active participants in the first resurrection. To be blessed is to be happy. It hints at joy and satisfaction.

Our standing is one of holiness. We cannot be anything else for we are in the presence of the Lord. How true it is, happiness and holiness always go hand in hand.

Their confidence

At the end of verse 6 we discover that the saints have confidence because the second death has no power over them. The old saying is true, to be born once is to die twice, but to be born twice is to die only once! And because we have taken part in this great resurrection programme, we are not only kings who will share in his rule, we are also confirmed as priests. That means we will enjoy unlimited access into the presence of the Lord and we will benefit from unbroken intimate fellowship with our God and Father.

Ministry will take on a whole new meaning in that day. It will have an added dimension to it. We are exalted in Christ, we are entrusted with diverse roles in the kingdom of God, there is great dignity and responsibility attached to all that we are doing. Our pride and pleasure in that day will be found in our association with Jesus Christ as his vice-regents on planet earth. It will last for one thousand years, and then ... something incredible happens!

> Many followers of other religions seek to be free from the body to experience salvation but the Christian looks forward to being given a new body. What does this tell us about what it really means to be spiritual and how God values the physical world?

20:7-10

The devil plays Russian roulette!

We read in verses 7-10, '*When the thousand years are over, Satan will be released from his prison and will go out to deceive the nations in the four corners of the earth - Gog and Magog - to gather them for battle. In number they are like the sand on the seashore. They marched across the breadth of the earth and surrounded the camp of God's people, the city he loves. But fire came down from heaven and devoured them. And the devil, who deceived them, was thrown into the lake of burning sulphur, where the beast and the false prophet had been thrown. They will be tormented day and night for ever and ever.*'

At the end of the millennium the devil will be released from prison for a short season. It is his final fling for the clock is ticking away. You know as well as I do, you cannot teach an old dog new tricks ... so what does the devil do? True to form, he is at it again! He has lost none of his cunning. He does not know anything else; he does not know any better. Deception is the name of the game! He has had a thousand years to plot his revenge.

After his dramatic reappearance, after his re-entry into the real world, he makes a dynamic appeal to man. He gathers the dissidents from around the world, he rounds up all the rebels from the four corners of the earth and together they launch a concerted attack on the city of Jerusalem. He is hyped up, the adrenaline is flowing, it is high risk. He is playing a dangerous game of Russian roulette. It is an insurrection but the devil meets his Waterloo. They perish to a man, zapped by a tornado of fire from heaven. It is mass cremation. The only evidence that something has happened are the ashes on the ground. At the same time, the devil is thrown into the lake of fire forever. He will not be alone for the first people he meets are the

Antichrist and the false prophet. This is not annihilation. This is felt, this is real! This torment is something they actually experience. They know all about it and it never ends, it just goes on and on and on.

> **The sentence handed down in verse 10 is severe, unrelenting and endless. Why would anything less than this not be just?**

We can summarise it like this:

In verse 8, we have the deception of the nations.
In verse 9, we note the destruction of the rebellious nations.
In verse 10, we see the final destiny of Satan.

It is worthwhile pointing out that the reference to Gog and Magog in verse 8 has nothing to do with the major battle referred to in Ezekiel 38 and 39. These are the same names which are used but this battle is different in time and details.

The Ezekiel battle will take place during the first half of the Tribulation. The Revelation battle will take place after the millennium. In Ezekiel 38 and 39, the nations will not come from the four quarters of the earth as they will in Revelation 20. After the Ezekiel battle, the dead will be buried; in Revelation, they will be devoured from heaven. Satan will lead the army mentioned in Revelation 20 but he is conspicuous by his absence in the Ezekiel battle.

The term is used here symbolically for the unsaved people who will rally to Satan's cause in a foiled attempt to overthrow the Lord's rule on earth. It is amazing but these folk will have spent their days in an ideal environment, in near perfect living conditions, in an era when the Sermon on the Mount is the norm, and still they want to go their own way and do their own thing. It says a lot about the heart of man!

> **Following one thousand years of perfect and benevolent rule by Christ, the people of earth still take the opportunity to destroy his people when given the chance. What does this say about human nature?**

20:11-15

Sinners in the dock!

Before God wraps up human history, one great event remains - it is the day when sinners are in the dock. This is the greatest trial in history, this is the great judgment morning, this is the moment when men will meet their Maker and they will wish they could turn back the clock and rewrite their personal history! The language employed in these closing verses of chapter 20 is legal so I want to couch my comments to you in similar terms.

John says, *'Then I saw a great white throne and him who was seated on it. Earth and sky fled from his presence, and there was no place for them. And I saw the dead, great and small, standing before the throne, and books were opened. Another book was opened, which is the book of life. The dead were judged according to what they had done as recorded in the books. The sea gave up the dead that were in it, and death and Hades gave up the dead that were in them, and each person was judged according to what he had done. Then death and Hades were thrown into the lake of fire. The lake of fire is the second death. If anyone's name was not found written in the book of life, he was thrown into the lake of fire.'*

These are solemn words indeed! I have preached on this passage many times over the years and every time I come to it, my heart aches for those who do not know Jesus as Lord and Saviour. When I think of their awful fate when they stand before God, the tears flow and my heart melts with compassion on their behalf. The problem is, by now it is too late! They are beyond the help of man; they are beyond the reach of prayer.

The bar

It is great. This is true because of its unique position. It is not in heaven and it is not on earth; it is somewhere suspended in space. That makes it quite exceptional. Its greatness is also reflected in the millions of people who will stand before it. You can probably think of the many famous trials which have been conducted in court rooms all around the world, all pale into insignificance in the light of this one. All eyes are turned upon it, all paths converge there.

The maximum penalty which is handed down each time pays a silent tribute to the momentous nature of this occasion. This is no petty sessions, this is no high court, this is no supreme court, this is no European court; this is the only court which is convened by one whose jurisdiction is universal! It is great because of the majesty and mystery which surround it. This is the greatest assize every held. Try to envisage the sheer vastness of the scene.

It is white. In Bible-speak this is the symbol of purity and justice and holiness. After all, the one who is sitting there is the righteous Judge; those in the dock receive their due rewards, they get exactly what they deserve. Men will stand there in the terrible ugliness of their sin and against the white backdrop everything will be shown up in bold contrast.

In Isaiah 6, the throne has an altar of sacrifice beside it; the throne in the holy of holies had blood sprinkled on it; the throne in chapter 4 had a rainbow encircling it, reminding us of the covenant promises of God; but here in chapter 20, there is no blood, there is no sacrifice, there is no rainbow!

It is a throne. In Hebrews 4:14 we read about the throne of grace, a place of supplication for the saints; in Hebrews 12:1,2 we read about the throne of God, a place of exaltation for the Saviour; in Matthew 25:31 we read about the throne of glory, a place of glorification for the Sovereign Lord; and in 20:11 we read about a throne of gloom, a place of condemnation for the sinner!

> **What are the major differences between the great white throne and the throne outlined for us in Hebrews 4:15,16?**

The Judge

We read in the gospels that all judgment has been committed unto him (John 5:22). Richard Bewes writes: 'How amazed Jesus' listeners must have been! Before them was a man in working clothes - the son of a carpenter. Was he really to be the judge of all humanity? Only a few at that time recognised in him the pivotal figure of all history, the focal point when the balances are weighed at the last.'

On the cross of Calvary, it was God in Christ reconciling a lost world unto himself; at the great white throne, it is God in Christ judging a world which rejected his offer of love and mercy in the gospel.

We read that before his face the heavens and earth flee away, they dissolve, they melt with fervent heat; as it were, they are loosed from their moorings, they undergo a massive change. It is renovation time for the old gives way to the new. The same truth is outlined in greater detail in 2 Peter 3:12.

The prisoners

These are men and women of all shapes and sizes, people of all classes and colour, ordinary folk from every corner of the world, and they find themselves in the dock! They are fetched here on the morning of their trial from the prisons of death and Hades. As someone has said, 'Those who were buried at sea or on land, those who were eaten by cannibals or who died peacefully in their sleep, those who were burned on some fiery pyre or embalmed in some Egyptian tomb, those who were laid to rest in satin-lined caskets or in primitive pine boxes, those who were buried in vaults, surrounded by treasure, and those whose bodies were left for the vultures - all will be raised to stand before the Judge! God knows every speck of human dust, and he calls it forth from deserts, caves, jungles, seas, tombs, ghettos, and palaces.'

Death is that which holds their bodies.
Hades is that which holds their souls.
The two are united and marshalled before the Judge.

The prisoners are standing before the throne. They are not kneeling for this is not the time to pray nor is it the time to plead for clemency. The day of opportunity has long since flown. Those who are present on this final day of reckoning are labelled as the *'great and small.'* It does not matter how insignificant these people may be; in that day they will have nothing to hide behind and no-one to hide behind. They may be great intellectually, and financially, and politically, and religiously, but that holds no water. All will be there, irrespective of who they are, or what they are, or where they are from.

The books

Augustine of old explained these books as symbolic of what he called the 'divine memory'. These are the records of your life which are available to the Judge - the deeds, the words, the thoughts and the motives that are packed into our lives have not gone unrecorded. All is noted in God's book, absolutely nothing is missing!

Think of all the wrongs that have been perpetrated during our human story! All the egotistical designs that came off; every evil coup that succeeded; the tricks, lies, conspiracies and take-overs that have passed into history. Many of them have stayed undiscovered and to this day remain a secret. But not for ever! You see, he knows all there is to know about you! And you cannot fool him! Because of the evidence which is available to him, each person is guaranteed a fair trial.

> What are the different purposes between the book of life and the book of deeds? Does this passage teach there will be variations in the punishment people receive? Will there be a similar flexibility in the degree of blessedness enjoyed by the saints in glory?

The sentence

The proceedings reach a climax when the triple impact sentence is handed down:

It is a death sentence, eternal death, as mentioned in verse 14. It is the maximum penalty; it means to be separated from God eternally. What would it be like to never know the voice of God, to never feel the touch of God, to never feel the love of God, to never receive any blessing from God at all - to be totally without God for ever and ever and ever!

It is a life sentence for this will go on forever, it will never end, it just keeps on going, it is everlasting.

It is a fire sentence as John indicates in verse 15. The pain and the hurt do not bear thinking about. It is excruciating agony in a place of total darkness.

The agony and the feeling of being abandoned will play havoc with the mind and what makes matters infinitely worse is that the sinner is conscious throughout these aeons of eternal punishment. You see, hell is a place of no security for it is depicted as a bottomless pit. To be placed into a bottomless pit is to have the sensation of falling, falling, with nothing to cling to, nothing to catch yourself on, nothing to break your fall!

There will be no parole, there is no possibility of an early release, there are no special privileges granted for good behaviour, there is no escape, there is no higher court of appeal, there is no advocate to represent you at the bar of God!
The harsh reality is: you are on your own!

Here is a judge with no jury, a prosecutor with no defence, a sentence with no appeal!
The nagging question in my mind is: will you be there? You do not have to be! You can trust in Jesus today and know the joy and peace of sins forgiven! If you know him and love him as Saviour, you will never have to face him as Judge. That makes a lot of very good sense!

21

All things new!

We have spent a lot of quality time together as we have travelled with John on a prophetic time machine. We have met a lot of people, we have seen a lot of faces, we have been to many places. After all the devastation and destruction of previous chapters, here we are taken forward into a fabulous future where we can enjoy the presence of God in the midst of his people.

John gives us a breathtaking and exhilarating preview of eternity in the future; he speaks of a day when a new heaven and a new earth will be created. It is immensely difficult for you and me to imagine what it is going to be like; it is genuinely hard for us to comprehend what lies before us. We need a lot of creative thinking to try to visualise in our mind's eye what awaits us on the other side of death.

It seems to me, in God's eternal day, the crowning jewel will be the Holy City, the new Jerusalem. This is what it is all about; this is what contributes to make our salvation by grace eminently worthwhile. I like the way Warren Wiersbe puts it, 'Human history begins in a garden and ends in a city that is like a garden paradise.'

It is a fair comment to make for we have gone full circle! We could say, here is paradise regained for what began in Genesis is brought to completion in Revelation.

There is something new anticipated here. We read about a *'new heaven'* and a *'new earth'* and a *'new Jerusalem.'* In verse 5 we hear a voice declaring, *'I am making everything new!'* Isn't that thrilling? It will not only look fresh and new, it will feel fresh and new!

Here is a God who is timeless, a God who is unchanging, but this God is one who delights in doing new things. That is what I love about the Lord. He is not stereotyped in any way; he is not typecast; you never find him in a self-imposed straitjacket. So come with me on the last stage of our voyage of discovery into a bright new world!

21:1-8

A new creation

It is distinctive!

The opening verse in chapter 21 intimates that what God has in mind for us is planned as a new creation. John says, *'Then I saw a new heaven and a new earth, for the first heaven and the first earth had passed away, and there was no longer any sea.'* This should not surprise us for this is what God has consistently promised to his people.

We read along similar lines in Isaiah 65:17 where God says, 'Behold, I will create new heavens and a new earth.' The bottom line is, the old creation must make way for the new creation if God is to be glorified. The world as we know it today will be phased out in God's time and a new world will come into being.

It will disappear!

Our present physical environment will pass away. Jesus called this great event, 'the renewal of all things' (Matthew 19:28). It was part of his answer to an earlier question posed by the disciples which showed they were not a little confused about his mission and message.

The picture portrayed by Christ in his response is that of rejuvenation. Peter explained it in much more detail when he envisaged it as a cleansing and regeneration by fire (2 Peter 3:10).

Someone has said, 'Our world has a core of molten fire and one day God will light the fuse that will explode this seething mass. Every stain of sin and every evidence of evil will be taken away, and we will have a new heaven and a new earth that will abide forever.'

There is no thought of the world being totally annihilated. That would be a serious misreading of the text if we took that idea on board; the thought is, they will be remade or rebirthed in a sovereign act of cosmic renewal. The word *'new'* actually means 'freshness' or 'renovation.' It is like taking an old building and remodeling it, refashioning it, redesigning it. In that sense, it is new in character!

It is different!

Our future environment will be radically different. The Bible is essentially silent concerning the earth's atmosphere as well as the structure of planets in the universe. All it does say in verse 23 is that there is no need for the sun or the moon. Very little is said on the new earth's form, colour or vegetation, so we have only been told what God feels is best for us to know at this point in time! We are in for a pleasant surprise when we get there and I am sure we will not be disappointed.

Having said that, John does share with us a fascinating insight when he comments on the absence of any sea. This does not mean, there will be no more water for we read about the river of life in the next chapter! I think it simply indicates that the new earth will have a different arrangement so far as water is concerned. Three quarters of the globe today is under water but things will be fundamentally different in the eternal state. The earth will take on a very different look. In John's day, the sea threw up all sorts of unpleasant images in the minds of the people ... it meant danger, storms and separation. The chances are, John is giving us more than just a geography lesson in this phrase!

Why is there no sea on the new earth?

A new city

We are told several wonderful things in verse 2 where John is thrilled with the provision of a new capital city. He says, *'I saw the Holy City, the new Jerusalem, coming down out of heaven from God, prepared as a bride beautifully dressed for her husband.'*

People friendly!

Its intrinsic character is the first factor which grips John's understanding. It is a city that is cleaned up! There is no more sin, no more crime, no more pollution, and it is a place where not a single sinner will be found walking the streets. It is a holy city, in the best sense of that word.

Out of this world!

John also makes a meritorious contrast for the new Jerusalem is unlike the earthly one. In 11:8, the earthly city where our Lord was crucified and rose again was referred to as Sodom and Egypt; I can assure you, those were less than complimentary terms! But this one is significantly different!

An architect's dream!

He was quite impressed with its coming down from heaven and this reminds us that the source of it is divine. God is the designer, the builder and the maker; this glorious city is the place the patriarch Abraham was looking forward to with bated breath and itchy feet!

A 'big day' experience!

The apostle makes an absorbing comparison when he likens it to a bride on her wedding day. I think the thought encapsulated here is that this city will be one renowned for its unsurpassed loveliness. It will be a special place of incredible charm and idyllic splendour. The God who painted the butterfly, the God who sculpted the rose, the God who designed the sunset, is the brains behind this eternal city. It is the kind of place that will make your head turn with a sense of awe at its stunning beauty. It is a knockout! It is a winner! It is a gem!

> **Many people today are glad not to live in a city. What is so different about the new Jerusalem that makes it a des res?**

A new community!

Perhaps the most important thing about the city is that God dwells there with his people as the heavenly Emmanuel. We read in verses 3 and 4 that it is a place specially prepared for a new community. John tells us, *'And I heard a loud voice from the throne saying, "Now the dwelling of God is with men, and he will live with them. They will be his people, and God himself will be with them and be their God. He will wipe every tear from their eyes. There will be no more death or mourning or crying or pain, for the old order of things has passed away."'* This is terrifically good news for the people of God! This is the last of twenty-one times that *'a great voice'* or *'a loud voice'* is mentioned in the book of Revelation. The fact that the voice is loud implies that the subsequent information is important and authoritative. And so it is!

There are two main points here: in verse 3, the purpose of God will be fulfilled, his eternal dream will become a reality; and in verse 4, the past will be erased for John tells us what God will do with a string of *'no mores.'* The inhabitants of this fine city are blessed with the presence of God among them. Because the Lord is with them they will experience a fulness of joy and a sense of boundless delight.

Faith will be replaced by sight! Emblems will give way to substance!

Remember the Garden of Eden before the Fall when God came and walked with Adam in the cool of the day? In eternity, God will stay with men forever and they will delight in his nearness and close company. We will be taken up with him and we will be taken in with him. We will be captivated by him to such an extent that our affections will be drawn out after him with every passing moment. Thank God, we will be there, and best of all, he will be there!

> Seeing the beauty of this present world, spoilt as it is by sin,
> imagine the stunning wonder and beauty of the new world.
> Structure a time of praise around these thoughts!
> If you had the power to create a new earth, how would it be
> different from today's world?

Thank God, some things will not be there! The past is firmly put behind us; it will vanish and according to the prophet Isaiah it will be blotted out from our memory. You know, these missing elements have been deliberately omitted. They are all familiar aspects of earthly life that each of us can readily identify with. Death will be a thing of the past, there will be no more funerals, no more open graves, no more fond farewells, no more hospitals or medical centres, no more broken homes, no more arguments, no more hurt feelings, no more injured egos, no more shattered dreams, no more fractured relationships, no more pain, no more tears! What a day of rejoicing that will be! This is really sublime. This is ineffable blessedness, this is uninterrupted bliss.

> What light is thrown on the value God places on us by the fact
> that he is going to come and live with us for ever and personally
> 'wipe every tear from our eyes?'

In the first century these words must have been a source of tremendous uplift and encouragement to a suffering church. In our day the hope of heaven retains its huge appeal. It has lost none of its built-in power to keep us going even when the going is incredibly tough! John more or less tells us to hang in there, the future is bright, the best is yet to be!

A new constitution!

Verse 5 is one that has richly blessed the hearts of God's people down the years. It puts into sharp focus the truth that the one who is seated on the throne is not just an interested spectator standing on the terraces of heaven! He is down there on the field of play, he is actively engaged in a transforming ministry so that all he creates will ultimately radiate the rich diversity of his attributes.

He is able to do it because of what he is!

John says, *'He who was seated on the throne said, "I am making everything new!" Then he said, "Write this down, for these words are trustworthy and true."'* This simply confirms our growing awareness that the promises of God will all be realised. The one who is able to bring the whole package together is none other than the Creator God. His ability is beyond question. After all, he made the heavens and the earth in the beginning so it should not be too much of a problem for him to change it all and get it into better shape for eternity. He knows what he is doing.

He is able to do it because of what he says!

He reinforces his argument by affirming to John the authentic nature of his word. It is something we can rely on. Everything he proposes rests upon the veracity of God himself. It is a million times more than a mere verbal promise, it is a written guarantee, it is a divine undertaking. If you like, it is God signing his name on the dotted line! He writes the cheque and it will not bounce! It can be trusted and so can he!

He is able to do it because of who he is!

The entire concept is taken a major step further in verses 6 and 7 when John reveals a little more of the conversation the Father had with him. He says, *'He said to me: "It is done. I am the Alpha and the Omega, the Beginning and the End. To him who is thirsty I will give to drink without cost from the spring of the water of life. He who overcomes will inherit all this, and I will be his God and he will be my son."'*

It all happens in an instant. It is as quick as that! He snaps his finger and it comes to pass. You see, the God who is the First and the Last does not need any lapse of time for this whole project to come together. There is nothing revolutionary about it, neither is it a long drawn-out exercise.

The God who begins is the same God who ends; the God who initiates is the same God who consummates.

That was true of his finished work of redemption at Calvary. It is equally appropriate that we apply the same criteria to his provision of an eternal home for us in glory. It is complete! It is done! Has there ever been anything which he has commenced and failed to finish? The answer from all of us is a resounding 'no!' Here is a God who controls everything in such a way that all his counsel is accomplished, all his designs are fulfilled, all his promises are performed, and all his ends are reached. The God who inspired Paul to pen Philippians 1:6 is the same God who can bring it to fruition.

A great place to live ... because of what is there!

It is a satisfying place to put down your roots. The resources are infinite. The saints in glory who thirst after God will be refreshed in him and by him. Our souls will be totally satisfied in eternity for the springs of living water never dry up. We also receive a special inheritance when we enter into the good of the Lord's last will and testament. It will be a privilege and a responsibility for us to administer that to the glory of God. We are acclaimed as *'overcomers!'*

> **How can you use the promises of verse 7 to strengthen your resolve to be an overcomer in the fight of faith?**

A glorious place to live ... because of who is there!

Probably one of the most rewarding aspects of eternity is the relationships we will enjoy. How wonderful is our God! In the compass of a few words, John transferred to the glorified saints the messianic formula of intimate relationship which God the Father has with Christ. Look at it like this:

He gave us his Son, as in John 3:16.
Then he gave us his Holy Spirit, as in Luke 11:13.
And finally, he gives us himself!

A grand place to live ... because of what is not there!

John makes it abundantly clear in verse 8 that it will be an extremely safe place to live for certain categories of people will not be present among the population. We have a long list of those who are barred and banned from God's new world. Their eternal destiny is the lake of fire. There is for them only the grim prospect and harsh reality of the second death staring them in the eye. They face a life of separation from God. Such is the fate of those who do not know Jesus.

I wonder, in your mind's eye, can you visualise a holy city?

It would be a community where no one lied, no shady business deals would ever be discussed, no unclean movies or pictures would be seen. The sole reason why these influences are eliminated is because, as we read in verse 8, *'But the cowardly, the unbelieving, the vile, the murderers, the sexually immoral, those who practise magic arts, the idolaters and all liars - their place will be in the fiery lake of burning sulphur.'*

In all honesty, you would not expect these folk to be present in God's heaven. They had their chance to turn to God and they blew it. They messed around with their own lives and with other people's lives. The sin that has ruined this present world will not be allowed to ruin the world to come. The new earth will be pure and the people in it will be pure. Nothing and no-one will be allowed to jeopardise the perfect environment of God's eternal abode. It is immune from any and every outside influence; they will never gatecrash into glory!

21:9-27

The character of the holy city

John places an important emphasis on the character of the Holy City, the new Jerusalem. He begins that theme at this point and it remains the main thread of his argument through to 22:5.

It is exclusive

What a place it is! This is what sells houses in our day and generation. Any estate agent worth his salt will tell you, there are three factors which go a long way to boosting the sale of a property: location, location, location. Well, you cannot get a better location than this. It is a new city in a brand new world and it is all for the people of God! It is the exclusive residence of those who know Jesus as Lord and Saviour.

Its mystique

In verses 9 and 10 John says, *'One of the seven angels who had the seven bowls full of the seven last plagues came and said to me, "Come, I will show you the bride, the wife of the Lamb." And he carried me away in the Spirit to a mountain great and high, and showed me the Holy City, Jerusalem, coming down out of heaven from God.'*

This is truly amazing for the city is identified with the bride. There is nothing unusual about that! You will remember that Babylon was set forth in a dual way, both as a woman and as a city. The same is true of the Holy City, the new Jerusalem. In other words, the city and its inhabitants are closely linked.

The eternal city is not only the home of the bride, it is the bride!

> Christ 'loved ... and gave himself up for' his bride, the church.
> What is your response, as part of the bride, to such a husband?

Its sanctity

A city is not buildings, a city is people. The city John saw in his vision was breathtakingly beautiful, it was holy and heavenly, it descended to earth from heaven where it was prepared. It seems to me that vital piece of information is an echo of the promise of Jesus in John 14:3. This means it is a sanctified city.

Its beauty

The vista John saw staggers the imagination even accepting the fact that a great deal of symbolism is involved. His first impressions are mouth-watering. John saw it and he wrote about it in terms that were meaningful to him. That in no way detracts from the fact that this is a real place for real people.

We read in verse 11, *'It shone with the glory of God, and its brilliance was like that of a very precious jewel, like a jasper, clear as crystal.'* It is lofty and dignified; there was something regal and majestic about it. At the same time, it felt strange for it gleams with a light all its own. It has an inherent lustre and this has to be unique. It shines with the resplendent glory of God. It is not unlike the *shekinah* glory that filled the tabernacle in the wilderness and the temple in Jerusalem because of God's divine presence. It will be illuminated also by the light of Jesus as we read further down in verse 23.

The jasper stone is like transparent crystal, it is opaque. This city is very similar to a diamond as it sparkles in the sky, and its facets scintillate with every colour found in the rainbow. It is a stone which is brilliant in its brightness and surely that is a poignant reminder that the city reflects all that God is. It is a spectacle which glistens with his renown and his eminence. The place glows with the dazzling glory of God. It is incandescent with his splendour.

Its security

We read in verses 12 and 13 that, *'It had a great, high wall with twelve gates, and with twelve angels at the gates. On the gates were written the names of the twelve tribes of Israel. There were three gates on the east, three on the north, three on the south and three on the west.'*

This is tremendously impressive. And what is even more remarkable is that God has deployed a highly reputable security firm to look after the place! His angels are on patrol at each of the points of entry. So much for all the jokes we hear about Peter standing at the pearly gates! A sentinel from heaven's security service is always on guard duty at the four points of the compass. There will be no intruders, no-one can break in and no-one can break through. Security is top priority and it is guaranteed.

These walls are a highly visible reminder of God's protection of his people. The many gates symbolise freedom to enter the city from all sides. The implication is that the citizens of eternity will be able to travel elsewhere on the new earth and possibly also in the new heaven. I wonder is this an echo of John 10:9 where we read, 'He will come in and go out and find pasture.' And the gates are all open because the cross of Jesus has unlocked them.

We are not told the precise order in which the names of the twelve tribes will be placed on the gates but the chances are they will correspond to the pattern presented in the millennial Jerusalem which we read about in Ezekiel 48. If that is the case:

on the north side, going east to west, will be Levi, Judah and Reuben;

on the east side, going north to south, will be Joseph, Benjamin and Dan;

on the west side, going north to south, will be Naphtali, Asher and Gad;

on the south side, going east to west, will be Simeon, Isaachar and Zebulun.

This is what father Abraham looked forward to all his days

according to Hebrews 11:10, and the fascinating truth is, the city will have the names of his descendants engraved on its gates to show Israel's direct role in God's programme in eternity.

Its strength

John also informs us in verse 14, that *'The wall of the city had twelve foundations, and on them were the names of the twelve apostles of the Lamb.'* This suggests that the walls are firmly embedded in twelve foundations and the names of the apostles are inscribed there. In other words, when you think of Paul's comments in his letter to the church at Ephesus, the city is rooted and grounded in truth. You find that illustration in Ephesians 2:20-22.

> **What point is being made by having the apostles' names on the foundation stones?**

Its permanence

It also conveys the idea of permanence in contrast to the tents in which pilgrims and strangers lived, you find that allusion in Hebrews 11:8-10. Although the twelve apostles came out of Israel, the mention of one of the twelve apostles on each foundation links the church to a major role in the new Jerusalem. Even though Israel and the church are brought together in the new Jerusalem they will continue to retain their distinctive identities in eternity and they should not be lumped together in one group. Saints of the old covenant and saints of the new covenant are united in a way that pays a moving tribute to the grace of God.

Its dimensions

John provides us with some incredible detail on the finer points of the city plan and at the same time he gives us a vast amount of information relative to the whole city of God. He starts the ball rolling by focusing on the dimensions of the place and these are outlined in verses 15 and 16: *'The angel who talked with me had a measuring rod of gold to measure the city, its gates and its walls. The city was laid out like a square, as long as it was wide. He measured the city with the rod and found it to be 12,000 stadia in length, and as wide and high as it is long.'*

There are no cutbacks in the architectural department of God's government, there are no half measures employed here. It is a golden rod which the angel has in his hand and which he uses to measure the place. The result is truly staggering. A reed of measurement was generally assumed to be about ten feet long but sometimes it could be longer. The city is a perfect cube in its shape. It is about 1,500 miles square and high. It is hard to comprehend the size of this city but, it seems to me, all the cities in the world are mere villages compared to the new Jerusalem.

Where big is beautiful!

One engineer calculated the total base area of the city would be 2.25 million square miles and this is not counting the height which reaches far above the atmosphere into the regions of space! It is amazing! It is immense! It is colossal! One writer says, 'To grasp something of the enormity of the city, consider that this figure is 40 times the area of England, 20 times that of New Zealand, and 10 times that of Germany or France. The ground floor alone would provide enough living space for far more people than have ever lived in the history of the world. And this is just the first floor ... there are around 1,500 miles of additional floors above it.'

You have a similar analogy in the Old Testament when you think of the shape of the holy of holies in the tabernacle and later on in the temple. This one, however, is 240,000 times as big! And what is even more exciting, this time there are no partitions, there are no curtains, there are no walls, there are no restrictions barring the people of God from enjoying moments of intimacy with the Almighty.

Design and build!

It has often been referred to as 'the city foursquare' and I think that indicates something of the perfection of God's eternal city. Nothing is out of shape, nothing is out of balance. It is known for its symmetry. It is a place where everything is in harmony and in proportion. This golden city of God will be perfect in its measurements, perfect in its materials, and perfect in its majesty. It is really quite ridiculous to suggest it could be anything else for God himself combines a dual role: he is both the architect and the builder.

It is awesome

John talks about the wall and he describes it for us with superb imagery in verses 17 and 18 where he says, *'He measured its wall and it was 144 cubits thick, by man's measurement, which the angel was using. The wall was made of jasper, and the city of pure gold, as pure as glass.'*

What we see here is a wall approaching 216 feet in height (based on a cubit being eighteen inches in length). It is made of jasper, the clear, unblemished crystal mentioned earlier. No city has ever had such a magnificent enclosure! This will be one of the many wonders of the new world! To add to the glistening impact of the jasper, the city itself is comprised of pure gold. Its see-through effect makes it a joy to behold. The whole place resembles a huge holy of holies!

The rich and colourful language John is using here is used with powerful effect to enforce the idea that there will be no hindrance to the glory of God being transmitted from top to bottom, from the inside out; in other words, no matter where you are in the city, you will be consciously aware of the blaze of God's glory. The sheer effulgence of God's radiant glory will be manifest all over the place.

Its foundations

John says in verses 19 and 20, *'The foundations of the city walls were decorated with every kind of precious stone. The first foundation was jasper, the second sapphire, the third chalcedony, the fourth emerald, the fifth sardonyx, the sixth carnelian, the seventh chrysolite, the eighth beryl, the ninth topaz, the tenth chrysoprase, the eleventh jacinth, and the twelfth amethyst.'*

Twelve foundations, twelve precious stones! It is interesting to note that building foundations are generally underground, you cannot usually see them; but these foundation stones will not only be visible, but beautifully garnished with all kinds of precious gems. It is a reasonable assumption to say these stones represent the glory of God in a dozen different ways. Whatever angle you view it from, the lasting impression is one of unsurpassed wealth on a grand scale. It is so magnificent, it is well beyond anything ever seen on planet earth. It is, in essence, out of this world ... these are, without doubt, the palaces of God.

Think of all the colours blending beautifully together! You know, our God will lavish his beauty on the city he calls 'home' for his redeemed people! The colour palette of the stones is such that they may be classified into the four basic colours that every artist uses in variation on his palette. It is different this time for here we have the master designer who has drawn the blueprints and he has specified the most exquisite colours. He has chosen a fireworks of splendour! It is an inspiring sight!

The jasper stone is clear crystal and reflects all the colours of the spectrum in wondrous brilliance; the sapphire is blue in colour and possibly flecked with gold; the chalcedony is a translucent milky or greyish quartz with coloured stripes running through it; the emerald is a brilliant grass-green transparent variety of beryl; the sardonyx is an onyx stone with alternating brown and white bands running through it; the carnelian is a red translucent stone like a ruby; the chrysolite is gold in colour resembling a yellow beryl or a golden jasper stone; the beryl is a translucent bluish or sea-green coloured stone; the topaz is a translucent yellow or yellow-green stone; the chrysoprase is a translucent apple-green stone; the jacinth is a translucent bluish-smoke, violet-coloured stone; the amethyst is a brilliant purple or violet transparent stone.

I think you can begin to appreciate, the foundations of the city will be an extremely pretty sight. It simply underlines the point that our God is a God of beauty and in the words of Ecclesiastes 3:11, 'He has made everything beautiful in its time.'

It would not surprise me if the apostle Peter had the holy city in mind when he wrote about the 'manifold graces of God' in his first epistle (1 Peter 4:10). The word translated 'manifold' means 'many-coloured, variegated.' Paul goes down the same track in Ephesians 3:10 where he makes much of the 'manifold wisdom of God.'

Our God is a God of infinite variety, a God who is multi-coloured in the display of his attributes. There is nothing drab or boring about him!

Its gates

In the opening sentence of verse 21, John talks about the gates of the city. We read, *'The twelve gates were twelve pearls, each gate made of a single pearl.'* Isn't that wonderful! The old gospel songs says, 'He the pearly gates will open.' Back in John's day, the pearl was reckoned to be a royal gem.

A pearl is formed within the oyster, it speaks of beauty born out of pain. The oyster receives an irritation or a wound when a tiny grain of sand gets inside its shell and around the offending article that has penetrated and hurt it, the oyster builds a glowing pearl. That means the pearl is the answer of the oyster to that which injured it; we can say the glory land is God's answer in Christ to wicked men who crucified his beloved Son. And that means every time we look at the gates, we will remember we are only there because of Calvary!

Its street

The remainder of verse 21 introduces us to the street of the city where John informs us, *'The great street of the city was of pure gold, like transparent glass.'* You will notice that the word *'street'* is in the singular but I think that is intended to be a generic expression to refer to all the streets of the city.

It is hard for you and me to visualise what it will be like to walk on a street of gold in God's eternal city. It will be so clear, you can see right through it. All the walks and ways of that city will reflect the glory of God; every step we take will bring glory to Jesus!

What the city does not have

This city is some place, it is the city of the future. It is extra special, not only for the things that are there but also for the things that are not there. There are certain elements missing, for example:

No sanctuary. We read in verse 22, *'I did not see a temple in the city, because the Lord God Almighty and the Lamb are its temple.'* One is not needed! The entire city will be indwelt by the presence of God; people will be aware of him no matter where they are. This eliminates the dichotomy we often make down here between that which is secular and that which is sacred. Over there it will be impossible to distinguish between the two for whatever we do will be seen as an act of worship.

We need to remember that our God is not someone who is localised, he is not someone who is restricted to a few metres in the same sacred corner, he is not confined to one particular spot. He will be all and in all! That means we will not go to church, as it were, in the new Jerusalem; there will not be a special place or day set aside for times of worship. Buildings and structures will be redundant in that eternal day; prayer books and hymn books will be a thing of the past. We will not need them for the Lord will be with us. Our worship of him will be spontaneous and, thank God, it will be unaided by any emblem or liturgy for faith will have given way to sight.

> **Why was a temple needed in the old Jerusalem but not in the new? In what sense is the church already God's building (cf. 1 Corinthians 3:16; Ephesians 2:19-22; 1 Peter 2:4,5)?**

No substitutes. In verse 23 we read, *'The city does not need the sun or the moon to shine on it, for the glory of God gives it light, and the Lamb is its lamp.'* That means exactly what it says. There will be no need for the sun or the moon; the city will be well lit with the glory of God. There will be no created light ... the light which he diffuses throughout eternity is the unclouded, undimmed glory of his own holy presence. God's light will permeate every nook and cranny, his light will illuminate every corner of the new Jerusalem.

The Lamb of God will be its eternal lamp and over there we will walk in the light of his countenance. There will be no dark days, no cloudy days, there will be no night ... this is God's eternal day.

These are the most ideal conditions imaginable! It is a land of no shadows! Today, in this gospel dispensation, Jesus is seen as the light of the world; in a day to come, he will light up a whole new world for eternity and in a wonderful way he will brighten up all of our lives!

No secrets. We glean this from the information John shares with us in verses 24 to 26. He says, *'The nations will walk by its light, and the kings of the earth will bring their splendour into it. On no day will its gates ever be shut, for there will be no night there. The glory and honour of the nations will be brought into it.'*

The gates stand open all the time, there will never be a single moment of darkness, everything is out in the open, there is no hidden agenda. In other words, there will be no secrets. The mystery of God will be over and all things will be made plain. In that day the promise of Paul in Romans 8:18 will be a glorious reality; the ups and downs of this life will fade into oblivion in the light of the glory of God. This is the hour the old song refers to when it says about life's hassles and hurts, 'we'll understand it better bye and bye.' People will come and people will go, they will bring honour to the Lord and God will abundantly bless them and enrich them in return.

John appears to be saying that heaven and earth will be accessible to all the redeemed of the Lord. Freedom of movement is the name of the game and yet wherever we go we will still be conscious of the closeness of the Lord.

No sinners. The last thought on John's mind in this section is recorded for us in verse 27 where he reminds us, *'Nothing impure will ever enter it, nor will anyone who does what is shameful or deceitful, but only those whose names are written in the Lamb's book of life.'* Name a city, any city, in today's world, and what do you find? They are centres of sin! Why is that the case? It is because they are populated by sinners and where you have one you invariably have the other. That is probably stating the obvious but it needs to be said nonetheless. However, in the new Jerusalem, they will not be there, not one! This is an exclusive haunt for those whose names are recorded in the Lamb's book of life. It is only those who know the joy of sins forgiven who are eligible for entrance into God's eternal city.

The sad fact is, if your name is not there, you will not be there. It is as simple as that!

22

No loose ends in God's plan

We are in the final chapter now and, in many ways, it follows on very neatly from the previous one as John continues to place an important emphasis on the character of the Holy City, the new Jerusalem. When we consider the opening paragraph in this fascinating chapter, we move inside the city precincts and we find it is like walking into a beautiful garden. John gives us a guided tour. He takes us on a kind of walkabout. It is reminiscent of the idyllic garden in the east, apart from the fact that there were four rivers in Eden and there is only one river in the heavenly city (you find that comparison mentioned in Genesis 2:10).

22:1-5

The life of the city

In verse 1, John says, '*Then the angel showed me the river of the water of life, as clear as crystal, flowing from the throne of God and of the Lamb down the middle of the great street of the city.'* Every time I read this verse I cannot help but recall the words of the well-known song in Psalm 46:4 where we read, 'There is a river whose streams make glad the city of God, the holy place where the Most High dwells.'

Down by the riverside!

You probably realise that Jerusalem is one of the few major cities in the world which is not built on the banks of a river. Many of the great Egyptian cities were located on the banks of the Nile, Babylon was built on the Euphrates, Rome is built by the Tiber, London by the Thames, Glasgow by the Clyde, Edinburgh by the Forth, Belfast by the Lagan, Dublin by the Liffey, and so we could go on! It was not until Hezekiah dug his famous tunnel that Jerusalem had a water source within the city walls.

The psalmist says here that although Jerusalem is not situated beside a river, it has one! And it comes from the holy place, the throne of God, indicating that he is the fountain-head. A similar truth is echoed in John 7:37 where we are reminded that the rivers of living water, the rivers of joy, flow out from his presence.

In the Bible, water for washing is a picture of the word of God, but water for drinking is a picture of the Spirit of God. We may drink by faith from this heavenly stream and when we do we will have the joy, the refreshment and the empowerment of the Lord.

The river we are talking about here is a pure river, it is pollution free, it is clear, it is clean, and it flows from the throne of majesty. This river contains the very essence of life itself. And coming from where it does it reminds us of the blessings and benefits which are ours when we drink from him. There is pleasure and prosperity associated with this stretch of water. We find that alluded to in Psalm 1:3 and Psalm 36:8 where he says, 'You give them drink from your river of delights!' It seems to me, therefore, that life in God's city is renowned for purity, pleasure, and prosperity, and each of these rich qualities is inextricably linked to a right relationship with the throne of the Lamb.

> **What daily habits will help us to wash in the word and be refreshed in the Spirit? What qualities can you assume the river of verse 1 has, given its source?**

Fruit of the month!

This is the theme of verses 2 and 3 where John says, *'On each side of the river stood the tree of life, bearing twelve crops of fruit, yielding its fruit every month. And the leaves of the tree are for the healing of the nations. No longer will there be any curse. The throne of God and of the Lamb will be in the city, and his servants will serve him.'*

Here we have uninhibited access to the magnificent tree of life. It flourishes in glory, it graces the celestial city, it lines both sides of the bank of the river, it runs in splendour down the central boulevard. It is not there just to be admired for we can enjoy the fruit of the tree and the nations of earth benefit from the healing properties of its leaves. When you put all of this together we are reminded of the abundant life which is ours in such a beautiful and delightful environment. It is picturesque. It is paradise! The tree we are talking about here is quite different from anything we know of in today's world. It will produce an annual harvest of twelve different fruits. Someone has said with tongue in cheek, 'This is the ultimate fruit-of-the-month package!'

The thought behind the word *'healing'* conveys the idea that there is something therapeutic or health giving about its leaves. The fact remains, there will be no disease in the new Jerusalem for the curse will be removed and eradicated forever. That takes us back to Genesis 3:14-19 where the curse began but, thank God, it will be lifted! The leaves will probably be used in some way known only to the divine horticulturist to enhance the sheer joy of life in eternity. Someone has written, 'No longer will leaves fall, plants die, grass wither, flowers fade, and birds sing in minor key!'

The loyalty of the city

In verse 3 we are told we will *'serve him.'* We are not going to
heaven for a perpetual holiday, as it were; we are there to engage in
joyful service and true spiritual worship. We are not there to serve
one another, important as that is. We are not even there to serve
ourselves and look after number one; we are there to serve him.
There will be nothing to hinder us, there will be nothing to hamper
or frustrate our efforts; it will be the thing to do and we will simply
get on and do it! And, believe it or not, we will relish and enjoy
every minute of it! It is perfect service in a perfect environment.

The Lord of the city

In some ways, verse 4 is the climax of everything. It is all we have
ever dreamed of, it is the moment of supreme pleasure and
satisfaction, it is the icing on the proverbial cake. John says, *'They
will see his face, and his name will be on their foreheads.'* What a
blissful moment that promises to be! What a noble eternal occupation
that is, to gaze on the lovely face of Jesus!

> *To see him ... that will make all the hassles and hiccups of this
> life worthwhile!*
> *To see him ... that will put everything encountered down here
> into perspective!*
> *To see him ... that will be the crowning joy in our salvation
> experience!*
> *To see him ... that ushers in the dawn of God's eternal day!*

This is what Paul talks about in his great chapter on love in 1
Corinthians 13, this is the rapturous moment he anticipates when
we see him, 'face to face.' John tells us in his epistle, 1 John 3:1-3,
that when we see him, we will not see him as he was but we will see
him 'as he is.'

> *He is the Lamb, exalted far above all.*
> *He is the Lamb, enthroned on high.*
> *He is the Lord, crowned with glory.*
> *He is the Lord, clothed with honour.*

The more I think about it, the more excited I become! I can hardly wait to walk through the gates of heaven and get my first glimpse of Jesus!

The inscription of his name on our forehead indicates that we belong exclusively to him. He is the one who bought us with his precious blood at Calvary. Now, in eternity, he is the one who is claiming us for his own! We are his prized and purchased possession.

> **From 1 Corinthians 13:8-13, contrast seeing Jesus face to face in heaven with seeing a 'poor reflection' now. How should this affect our attitude now and our anticipation of 'then'?**

The light of the city

The final insight in this intriguing section is found in verse 5 where John homes in on the light of the city. He says, *'There will be no more night. They will not need the light of a lamp or the light of the sun, for the Lord God will give them light. And they will reign for ever and ever.'*

Heaven will be incredibly bright because of the light of the face of Jesus. He will shine eternally and we will shine as the stars of the morning reflecting his glory. The citizens of the Holy City will experience life in the illumination of God's *shekinah* glory.

We will also have the distinct honour of sharing in his rule and reign. You see, from God's vantage point, we are not only recognised as servants in heaven, we are also reckoned to be kings! That means we will gladly share in Christ's royalty and we will live like kings in the palaces of God! What a fantastic reward awaits us on the other side! What an inestimable privilege is ours!

We have no idea what this particular role and responsibility entails and there is no point in wasting our time on idle speculation. Suffice to say, when we get there, we will find out soon enough! There are so many questions in each of our minds which remain unanswered but, one day, we will come out of the dark into God's eternal light and then all the problems will be solved, all the mysteries will be revealed. 'We shall know as we are known.'

John closes his book by reminding us not to get waylaid into bypath meadow; he warns us of the serious danger of being sidetracked; he challenges us with the thought that we have solemn responsibilities today, because we are going to heaven! And, between here and there, between now and then, we need to get our act together!

Heaven is more than a destination, it is a motivation. Knowing that we will dwell there eternally should make a huge difference in our lives at this moment. The exhilarating prospect of the *there and then* should spur us on in the *here and now*; it should motivate us to live today in the light of tomorrow! It was the prospect of a brighter and better tomorrow that enabled the patriarchs to walk with God in an alien society. That explains why they served God to the best of their ability (Hebrews 11:10,13-16). The same can be said of the Lord Jesus Christ. The fact that heaven was just around the corner encouraged him as he faced the agonies of the cross (Hebrews 12:2).

So it makes all the difference in the world if we keep heaven to the front of our minds; it makes a world of difference to our mindset in relation to all that is happening around us.

22:6-10

The word of God

This final section is an epilogue to the entire book. It is John reminding us that what God starts, he always finishes! There are no loose ends in his plans for the planet.

It is most interesting to note that in the prologue, in chapter one, we were told that prophecy is from God. We also know that he sent an angel to bring this message to John. And when we read the message from cover to cover we are promised a blessing. We were also informed that the end is near. When you turn to the last chapter, the same promises are repeated in verses 6, 7 and 8! The vital lesson we learn is this: God does not change his mind partway through a manuscript and decide to end the story with a question mark. No, what he begins, he completes! So let us see what we can learn from these last words of God to his people.

Some folk have suggested that all we have in these closing verses is an untidy collection of random thoughts from an aged apostle. They feel, he has finished saying what he has had to say, but he just cannot get stopped! Nothing could be further from the truth.

In verses 6-10, for example, John has a lot to say about this. I cannot think of a better way to end a book than to affirm your convictions about the word of the Lord.

The Bible is accurate

In verse 6, he highlights the accuracy of Scripture when he says, *'The angel said to me, "These words are trustworthy and true. The Lord, the God of the spirits of the prophets, sent his angel to show his servants the things that must soon take place."'* Obviously the immediate reference here is to the great truths enshrined in the Apocalypse. Sooner or later they will come to pass! The same God who spoke through the prophets also spoke through John. But the statement is much wider than that ... there is no need to narrow it down to the Revelation; it embraces the whole Bible.

The truths it contains have been transmitted, recorded, arranged and preserved, exactly as God intended. In the original manuscript, every word, every letter, every jot and tittle, was God breathed. When we hold the word of God in our hands, we can say with heartfelt conviction that it is divinely inspired, it is inerrant, it is infallible. The Bible is the living word of the living God. Because of that, it is trustworthy and true. It is credible, it is dependable, it is reliable, it is something on which we can stake our life! There are no doubts about the veracity of God's Word, it is renowned for its integrity. In legal-speak, the word of God is the truth, the whole truth, and nothing but the truth! John addresses this subject in verses 7 to 9 and he has three things to say about it.

> In what ways does verse 6 confirm our trust in the Scriptures as the Lord's authoritative word for us? How should this affect how we respond to them and handle them?

The Bible has authority

In verse 7, he shows us how the truth is declared. We read, *'Behold, I am coming soon! Blessed is he who keeps the words of the prophecy in this book.'* In the previous verse, we heard the distinctive tones of the angel; in this verse we detect the voice of the Lord himself. What he had to say was far too good to be passed along merely by an angel! The Lord says, *'I am coming soon, I am coming quickly!'* That means his coming is personal for his word is his bond. And his coming is near; in fact, it has never been nearer than it is right now!

Then he throws in a stirring challenge for good measure when he says, *'Keep my word!'* In other words, the spur to holy living is the imminent appearing of the Lord from heaven and the steps to holy living are given in his word. A special blessing is guaranteed to the followers of Jesus, not only when they assimilate the truth of his word into their hearts and minds but when they live in the light of it day by day. It is not just a matter of taking his truth on board, it is a matter of working it out in the rough and tumble of everyday life. That is where the blessing is found! (By the way, this is the sixth beatitude we have come across in the book of Revelation.)

The driving force, the motivational influence, the get-up-and-go factor, is the realisation that the advent of Jesus is getting so much closer every passing hour. It seems to me, we need to keep the advent hope burning bright in our hearts. It is a positive experience!

> **Jesus is coming soon! What guidance does Paul give in 1 Thessalonians 5:1-11 for living in the light of his coming?**

In verse 8, John shares a word of personal testimony when he takes the lid off his response to the angel's message. It is a candid confession. He is open and honest about it. This is what he says, *'I, John, am the one who heard and saw these things. And when I had heard and seen them, I fell down to worship at the feet of the angel who had been showing them to me.'* John did not learn the lesson first time around, he makes the same mistake a second time. It happened before and now it happens again. He falls down in worship before the angelic messenger! John is so overwhelmed with the wonder of it all that he just keels over. One minute he is standing up and the next minute he is prostrate on the ground.

You know, this thrilling book is all about the exaltation of Jesus Christ, and yet, here is John, in the frailty of the flesh, attempting to worship an angel. The Lord has broken in with some fantastic earth moving news, and what does John do? He worships an angel! I think it reinforces the idea that we need to be ultra careful lest we fall into the same trap. It is so easy to be enthralled with the message and in a moment of madness to give all the credit to the messenger. You see, the best of men are only men at best. Oh yes, they should be appreciated and acknowledged but when it comes to homage and reverence it is God who deserves the glory. He alone, and no other, is the focal point of worship.

The angel did not beat about the bush in his immediate response to John. He did not mince his words; he told him, in no uncertain terms, in verse 9, *'Do not do it! I am a fellow-servant with you and with your brothers the prophets and of all who keep the words of this book. Worship God!'*

After the angel sternly rebuked John it is interesting to see with whom he aligns himself. He took his place with all those who govern their lives by the revealed word of God. He says in effect, all authority is in this book; it speaks of God, it brings you to his feet! This is really tremendous. It is excellent counsel and advice to pass on to anyone who hijacks the glory of God. The way the angel did it was to lead John back again to the authority of Scripture. He did it courteously, he did it conscientiously, and he did it completely. If you like, the word of God is our first and final court of appeal for all matters of faith and practice.

> Despite the greatness of the revelations he has received, and his position as an apostle, John is honest about his failings (verses 8 and 9). What guidance does this give about how we should regard ourselves, whatever our calling?

The Bible is accessible

John says in verse 10, *'Then he told me, "Do not seal up the words of the prophecy of this book, because the time is near."'* What an unusual message! Remember Daniel 12 where he was told to do the exact opposite? He was instructed to seal up the vision that God had given to him. Why was that? Well, another dispensation was to intervene before the vision would be fulfilled. But that is not the case with the great truths revealed in the Apocalypse. They are written in an open book for all to read. We have the word in our hearts and minds; we hold the word in our hands, it is accessible to each of us.

What we need to understand is that a lot of what is prophesied in Scripture is coming to pass before our eyes! The stage is set. It will not be long until the Lord returns and then the book of Revelation will come on line. The prophecies John wrote about will then be fulfilled, one by one. The challenge we all face in the light of the near return of Christ is to live with the values of eternity in view! The future is now!

22:11-16

The work of Christ

John writes a seemingly strange and enigmatic comment in verse 11 where he says, *'Let him who does wrong continue to do wrong; let him who is vile continue to be vile; let him who does right continue to do right; and let him who is holy continue to be holy.'*

This verse is best understood in the context of the entire chapter where the emphasis is on the suddenness of the advent of Jesus Christ. It is a fast moving event; in fact, it all happens so quickly that men will not have time to change their characters or adopt a different lifestyle. In effect, John is advocating the status quo for the believer and the non-believer. If the sinner does not respond positively to the message, then that is it! He may as well just keep on going the way he is going; he may as well just keep on doing what he is doing. The same rule of thumb applies to the Christian. The message should impact our lives to such a degree that we will be led into a more fruitful and meaningful relationship with Jesus Christ. Having heard the prophetic word of God we can never be the same again!

What we have here is an extremely solemn and sober warning that decision determines character and character determines destiny.

It settles what we are!

It all goes back to Calvary and how men have handled the finished work of Christ in their personal decision making process. The cross of Christ is the great divide; it is the watershed between the saved and the lost. Remember, on the cross the Lord Jesus separated two common criminals, two petty thieves. Times have not changed, he separates them still! One of them trusted in the dying Saviour and went on to paradise; the other turned his back on Jesus and rejected him and he is lost forever in hell. The Bible tells us that all men are born in sin and every one is shaped in iniquity. It is only through the atoning death of Jesus that they can be fashioned anew and fitted for glory.

The cross of Jesus stands between the sinner and the saint. It separates the one from the other in time and in eternity.

There is a line of demarcation between the two and at the second coming of Jesus you cannot jump from one side to the next. It is an either/or proposition and no-one can sit on the fence. Today's decision has eternal ramifications; the consequences will be felt for aeons to come! Charles H Spurgeon said at this point, 'There is no hope of change of character. Where death leaves us, judgment finds us, and eternity keeps us.'

Did you cast your vote for Jesus? Time will tell and so too will eternity!

It settles where we are!

In verses 12-15 we are introduced to a couple of groups of people. In verses 12-14 we meet those who will be with the Lord Jesus and in verse 15 we come across those who will be without him. It seems to me that those who are associated with Jesus Christ have two things in which to rejoice: there is the promise of his coming and there is the provision of his cross.

Those who will be with the Lord. The emphasis on this event is found in verses 12 and 13. Jesus Christ is returning and when he does he will reward his children. John passes on the message which the Lord spoke directly to him and this is what he said, *'Behold, I am coming soon! My reward is with me, and I will give to everyone according to what he has done. I am the Alpha and the Omega, the First and the Last, the Beginning and the End.'*

What a tremendous incentive to walk with Jesus today and in all our tomorrows! What a fine stimulus to serve the Lord now and to keep at it for the rest of our lives! The King is coming! That is wonderful news! The verb is in the present tense and that means even though it is futuristic, the action is impending! His reward is with him. Our God is ever mindful and aware of all our sufferings and our service and nothing we do down here will ever be done in vain if it is done for him and his glory! That is the ethos and heartbeat of 1 Corinthians 15:58. At the Judgment Seat of Christ, or the *Bema*, which it is sometimes called, believers will be fairly judged according to their works. Generous rewards will be given to those who have been loyal and faithful to him.

After telling us what he is going to do, the Lord now shows us the reason why he is able to do it. It is because of who he is! He identifies himself in three ways and this is enormously uplifting and encouraging to you and me. Basically it means, whatever he starts, he finishes! Each of the three double-barrelled titles refer to this aspect of his character.

Because he is the Alpha and the Omega, there is nothing before him or after him; because he is the First and the Last, he was before creation in eternity past and he will be present in eternity future ... he is the author and the finisher of all things; because he is the Beginning and the End, he is the one who created all things, he is the one who controls all things, and he is the one who will consummate all things.

Those are his impeccable credentials!

In verse 14, John harks back to his provision of the cross to sustain his people. We read, *'Blessed are those who wash their robes, that they may have the right to the tree of life and may go through the gates into the city.'*

It is clear from this verse that cleansing is found only in the blood of the Lamb of God. It is because the blood of Jesus has been effectively applied to our hearts that we have access into the heavenly city. We are there only because of God's amazing grace. And John tells us, we are *'blessed'* indeed because of the redemptive aspect of his work in our lives. (This is the last of the seven beatitudes in the book of Revelation and it is a really good one to finish with!)

Those who are without the Lord. The next verse in the chapter is quite disconcerting, and even the opening word sends a cold shiver down the spine. We read a long list of those who are denied access to the presence of the Lord. John spells out who they are in verse 15 where we read, *'Outside are the dogs, those who practise magic arts, the sexually immoral, the murderers, the idolaters and everyone who loves and practises falsehood.'*

They are outside! What a powerful phrase that is! It is bad enough for them to be lost throughout eternity but it will be even worse to know that they are on the outside with no prospect of ever coming inside. I believe in hell that such people will have full knowledge of all that might have been theirs in heaven, but it is lost forever to them. The agonies of the rich man in Luke 16 must have been greatly intensified by the sight of the bliss of Lazarus; the damned wealthy individual in the parable told by Jesus was not only conscious of where he was but he was very much aware of what he had missed!

It seems to me, those who are lost are in eternal exile and the shame and scandal of their sin will haunt them forever. They will be cut off and isolated from all that is good, and beautiful, and lovely. They will easily recall neglected opportunities, they will remember friends of old who were saved and who are now walking the golden streets of heaven. These folk are shut out to face the remorse, the awful despair, the misery and pain of a Christless eternity. The tragic fact is they brought it on themselves!

It settles whose we are!

Verse 16 says, *'I, Jesus, have sent my angel to give you this testimony for the churches. I am the Root and the Offspring of David, and the bright Morning Star.'* This is a mind-blowing verse for it provides us with a strong personal testimony from Jesus that leaves us in no doubt that he is the one who authored the book of Revelation. He attests to that fact and he says it is indisputable. He affirms and authenticates that the content of this book was inspired and revealed by him. Here is a title of Jesus to make the most pessimistic heart thud with expectation!

> *He is the Lover of the church!*
> *He is the Lord of the earth!*
> *He is the Light of creation!*
> *He is the Wonder of wonders!*
> *And we, belong to him!*

The titles Jesus assumes here when speaking about himself are most interesting and instructive. The *'root'* is buried in the ground where no-one can see it but the *'star'* is in the heavens where everyone can see it! In the *'root and offspring of David'* we have the Jewish national name of Jesus but in the *'bright morning star'* we have his universal name, a global name. One speaks of humility, the other of majesty and glory. As the *'root of David,'* Jesus Christ brought David into existence; as the *'offspring of David,'* Jesus came into this world born a Jew from David's line.

Both the deity and the humanity of Jesus are evident here. A suitable parallel is drawn for us in Matthew 22:41-46. The *'morning star'* announces the soon arrival of the dawn. It is the brightest star in the heavens prior to the new day breaking. Jesus Christ will come for his church as *'the morning star.'* But when he returns to judge it will be as the 'sun of righteousness' in burning fury (Malachi 4:1-3).

> **What different truths are revealed about the Lord by his titles in verses 12, 13 and 16?**

22:17-21

The witness of the Holy Spirit

It is fitting and appropriate that the sacred canon of Scripture should finish with a reference to the chief executive of the Godhead. After all, it was through his inspirational influence that the book was birthed. He is the omniscient genius behind this miracle which we call the Bible. He is the one who holds a fair bit of clout when it comes to the ripening of the purposes of God as outlined in the masterpiece of Revelation.

The last welcome

In verse 17, John says, *'The Spirit and the bride say, "Come!" And let him who hears say, "Come!" Whoever is thirsty, let him come; and whoever wishes, let him take the free gift of the water of life.'* Here we have the grandest word in the gospel, it is the four letter word, *come.* It was first heard in the days of Noah and down through the centuries it has often been heard. Now before closing the book for the last time we hear it again. It is a triple invitation, for the Holy Spirit says *come,* and the bride says *come,* and even those men who have responded to the message join in by saying, *come.*

We can understand the Holy Spirit extending an invitation to sinful men to come to faith in Christ, that is his unique role and specialist ministry. But the fact that the bride is also involved in a similar exercise is something which should challenge all of us. It is a clarion call for the people of God to be totally involved and heavily committed in a ministry of evangelism. We need to reach out to people where they are and offer to them an alternative in Jesus to their present lifestyle. We have an obligation to share our faith openly with others. We owe it to them to tell them of one who is mighty and strong to save. We have a solemn responsibility to the unconverted man down our street to tell him at least once that Jesus is a wonderful Saviour.

It is an open invitation to all who are thirsty, to those who are parched, to those whose lives are dry and arid, that they can come and drink freely from the water of life; their thirst can be fully quenched in the Lord Jesus. The classic example which springs to mind is the Samaritan woman of John 4.

> Although it would be easier for him to work alone, the Spirit chooses to work in partnership with the church (verse 17). Why is this and how is this an example to us to work in partnership with others?

The last warning

John challenges us in verses 18 and 19, *'I warn everyone who hears the words of the prophecy of this book: If anyone adds anything to them, God will add to him the plagues described in this book. And if anyone takes words away from this book of prophecy, God will take away from him his share in the tree of life and in the holy city, which are described in this book.'*

That is a fairly stern warning. It is straight-from-the-shoulder stuff. You cannot help but get the message. He says, do not tamper with the truth of the word of God by adding anything to it or taking anything away from it. Do not make it say anything other than God intended it should say! Do not twist the truth of Scripture! Failure to toe God's three-line whip on this one leads to the imposition of a severe penalty.

Either way, on both counts, it is a fait accompli. People cannot take what they want, the bits they like, the portions that do not squeeze their comfort zone, and leave the chunks they find unacceptable or unpalatable! It is all or nothing! We are not to add to God's word as though it is insufficient in itself and we are not to take one word away from it as though it is irrelevant or unreliable or unimportant or untrue!

There is nothing new! There is nothing less! There is nothing else but the word of God, as it is!

We need to remember that with the giving of this book the canon of Scripture is complete. All that God wants to say he has said to this generation. Anyone who claims to receive direct communication from God today in a personal revelation is deceiving himself. He is disobeying the clear teaching of the Bible. It just does not happen for God never contradicts himself. He never backtracks on his word. He never goes against anything he has said. The last word has been written. The full stop has been added. God has drawn a line at the bottom of the page and, from his perspective, that is it!

There will be no further disclosure from heaven; there will be no appendix to the word of God.

> **What parts of the Bible's message are you tempted to avoid and why? And, when are you tempted to go beyond what the Bible says?**

The last word

In the closing two verses of the Bible we read, *'He who testifies to these things says, "Yes, I am coming soon." Amen. Come, Lord Jesus! The grace of the Lord Jesus be with God's people. Amen.'* You know, this is the third time in this chapter we have heard him say, he is coming soon. The reason for the seemingly apparent delay in his return is explained well by Peter in 2 Peter 3:9 as an ideal opportunity for men to repent of their sin and enter into a dynamic personal relationship with Jesus Christ.

We all know that two thousand years have come and gone. The simple fact is we are nearer today than we were yesterday. We are a lot closer now at the beginning of the 21st century than they were in the 1st. At any moment now, he may choose to break through the clouds and touch down on planet earth. It is no wonder the people of God respond with a heartfelt and spontaneous cry, *'Even so, come, Lord Jesus!'*

This all-consuming passion for the advent of Jesus is the last prayer recorded in the word of God and it is one that we would all do well to pray on a daily basis. *Maranatha!* Perhaps today! That is what living with a sense of expectancy is all about. That is what it means to have a keen spirit of anticipation in your heart and mind. Our hearts should be beating faster, our pulse should be racing ahead, the excitement should reach fever pitch as time marches on.

It is interesting to note that the invitation we have in verse 17 and the invitation we have in verse 20 are two sides of the same coin. The first one is an invitation for the world to come back to Jesus

Christ, so we preach it. The other one is for Christ to come back to the world, so we make it a matter of urgent and fervent prayer.

> **Are these two invitations reflected in your life and in the life of your church?**

The benediction focuses exclusively on the grace of our God. Isn't that just like him to end the book in this way! John's closing comment is akin to one of Paul's salutations. Both pay compelling tribute to the grace of God in the lives of his people. From start to finish, it is all of grace!

Grace chose us.
Grace saved us.
Grace keeps us.
Grace will present us faultless in glory.

No more fitting conclusion can be given to this volume which puts the spotlight on the God of eternity who has a vested interest in the things of time. And that is only because he is a God who is oozing and overflowing with grace. Like John Newton, we join hands with the people of God down the ages, and together we celebrate the grace of God in our lives as that which is truly amazing!

> **Think about it: every blessing outlined in Revelation is totally undeserved, it is the Lord's love gift to his people. Praise him!**

It is grace abounding to sinful men. It is grace which is adequate and available for all the saints of God. Ah, there is a superb sufficiency to the grace of God. And you know:

When we've been there ten thousand years
bright shining as the sun,
we've no less days to sing God's praise
than when we've first begun!

And that song of praise is ...

'Worthy is the Lamb, who was slain, to receive power and wealth and wisdom and strength and honour and glory and praise!'